In this major new interpretation of the crisis of democracy in Italy after World War I, Douglas Forsyth uses unpublished documents in Italy's central state archives, as well as private papers, and diplomatic and bank archives in Italy, France, Britain and the United States, to analyze monetary and financial policy in Italy from the outbreak of war in August 1914 until the March on Rome in October 1922. Forsyth argues that the collapse of parliamentary government resulted from the failure of governments after 1918 to balance the conflicting claims of great power politics, social welfare, economic growth, and macroeconomic stability. Liberal reformers, such as Giovanni Giolitti, had performed a difficult balancing act between these goals under exceptionally favorable circumstances prior to World War I; after the war their room for maneuver was drastically reduced; and they chose stability, sacrificing the redistributive and social policies which would have been necessary to secure broad electoral support. Forsyth focuses on four aspects of Italy's political economy which shaped the post-war crisis: large budget deficits, and the inability of liberal governments to reform the tax system; the vulnerability of the Italian banking system to crises, which in turn threatened to undermine the basis of economic growth; persistent tensions between monetary and Treasury authorities in Rome on the one hand, and the leadership of the country's largest commercial banks in Milan on the other; and the collapse of the pre-war equilibrium in Italy's international balance of payments.

THE CRISIS OF LIBERAL ITALY

THE CRISIS
OF LIBERAL ITALY

MONETARY AND FINANCIAL
POLICY, 1914–1922

DOUGLAS J. FORSYTH

Associate Professor of History,
Massachusetts Institute of Technology

CAMBRIDGE
UNIVERSITY PRESS

Published by the Press Syndicate of the University of Cambridge
The Pitt Building, Trumpington Street, Cambridge CB2 1RP
40 West 20th Street, New York, NY 10011–4211, USA
10 Stamford Road, Oakleigh, Melbourne 3166, Australia

© Cambridge University Press 1993

First published 1993

Printed in Great Britain at the University Press, Cambridge

A catalogue record for this book is available from the British Library

Library of Congress cataloguing in publication data
Forsyth, Douglas J.
The crisis of liberal Italy: monetary and financial policy,
1914–1922/Douglas J. Forsyth.
p.   cm.
Includes bibliographical references and index.
ISBN 0 521 41682 5
1. Finance, Public–Italy–History.   2. Finance–Italy–History.
3. Monetary policy–Italy–History.   4. Italy–Politics and
government–1915–1922.   I. Title.
HJ1185.F67   1963
338.945′009′041–dc20   92–17789   CIP

ISBN 0 521 41682 5 hardback

CONTENTS

FIGURES

TABLES

ACKNOWLEDGMENTS

In the course of researching and writing this study I have incurred many obligations. This study began as a Ph.D. dissertation at Princeton University, and my primary debt is to my doctoral adviser, Arno J. Mayer, who is largely responsible for whatever elements of conceptual and stylistic clarity it has come to possess. I also learned a good deal from the comments and criticisms of the other three members of my Ph.D. committee: Harold James, Anthony Cardoza, and Marta Petrusewicz. Other readers and critics at Princeton from whose advice I benefited include David Abraham, Michael Bernstein, and my colleagues in the Graduate School: David Noble, Astrid Cubano, James Searing, Alice Conklin, and Greg Dowd.

In Italy my primary debt is to Professor Franco Bonelli of the University of Rome. My intellectual debt to Professor Bonelli will be evident to readers of this study on almost every page. In addition, Bonelli encouraged me to embark on a study of monetary and financial policy despite my professional formation as an historian rather than as an economist. He has discussed practical and conceptual problems with me repeatedly over the years, and also facilitated my access to Bonaldo Stringher's papers prior to their deposition at the archive of the Bank of Italy. In this regard, I would like to express my thanks also to the Stringher family. Professor Antonio Confalonieri, of the Catholic University of Milan and formerly President of the Cassa di Risparmio delle Provincie della Lombardia, discussed my dissertation with me, and put the historical archive of his institution at my disposal. The late Professor Rosario Romeo, of the University of Rome, Professor Adrian Lyttleton of the University of Pisa, Professor Gian Giacomo Migone of the University of Turin, Dr. Giuglio Sapelli of the Feltrinelli Institute, and Professor Peter Hertner of the European University in Fiesole have been patient in listening to me explain my dissertation project at various stages, and in giving me advice. Professor Leonardo Paggi of the University of Modena read most of my thesis manuscript and offered stimulating criticism. While working on my dissertation I benefited also from interchanges with several Italian scholars of my own generation, who have revived interest in the economic and diplomatic history of the World War I and post-war years, including Luciano Segreto, Anna Maria Falchero, Marta Petricioli, Marina Storace, Bruno Bezza, Duccio Bigazzi, Amilcare Montegazza, and Ferdinando Fasce.

While I was writing my dissertation in Ann Arbor, Michigan in 1985–86, I benefited from the criticism of Raymond Grew, and members of his graduate seminar on modern Italian history at the University of Michigan. Richard Bosworth, Victoria De Grazia, Richard Drake, Roland Sarti, and Alice Kelikian also offered me assistance, advice, and encouragement on various occasions. In Britain, Professor James Joll offered me useful advice.

Since coming to MIT as an assistant professor four years ago, I have incurred additional obligations, as I have reworked my dissertation into a book manuscript. Professor Charles S. Maier, of Harvard University made invaluable suggestions as a reader for Cambridge University Press. I also would like to thank Cambridge's second, anonymous reader, as well as my very supportive editor, Mr. Richard Fischer. Professor Alexander De Grand of North Carolina State University read a draft of my entire manuscript, asked challenging questions, and saved me from making several embarrassing errors. Professors Franco Modigliani, Peter Temin, Suzanne Berger, Charles Sabel, Carl Kaysen, and David Ralston of MIT, Ambassador Sergio Romano, Drs. Pierluigi Ciocca and Fabrizio Barca of the Bank of Italy, and Professor Marcello De Cecco of the University of Rome read and discussed all or part of my book manuscript or related work with me.

Professor Gianni Toniolo of the University of Venice, Vera Zamagni of the University of Casino, and Roberto Vivarelli of the Scuola Normale Superiore in Pisa have been highly critical of my work. Indeed, their criticism has been so fundamental that more than the usual disclaimers apply in their regard. But even though none of them would approve of the contents of these pages, they have forced me to review my arguments and re-examine my evidence, and I believe for my part that a better study has emerged as a result.

It would be impossible to recognize all of the people who have helped me with my research in libraries and archives. At the Bank of Italy I was accorded very gracious support by the director of the historical archive, Dr. Benedetto Valenti, along with his staff, among them Filomenilde Castaldo, Bruno Capozi, and Bernardino Mazzetta. Dr. Ann Maria Biscaini-Cotula of the Bank of Italy's Servizio Segretario Particolare put important documents at my disposition, which during the early 1980s had not yet been deposited in the bank's archive. Dr. Francesca Pino-Pagolini has done students of the economic history of modern Italy a great service by reorganizing the archive of the Banca Commerciale Italiana. She put her extensive knowledge of the Commerciale's papers at my disposition during my stay in Milan in January

1990, greatly facilitating my work. Dr. Ubaldo Sassone of the Credito Italiano was an equally accommodating host. At the Archivio Centrale dello Stato, Dr. Giovanna Archangeli helped me find my way through the Nitti and Schanzer archives, both in the process of being reordered. Dr. Gaetano Contini helped me gain an overview of material there of relevance to my study. The staff of the study room in the Archivio Storico del Ministero degli Affari Esteri greatly facilitated my research. Dr. R. De Longis of the Biblioteca di Storia Contemporanea helped me locate difficult to find publications, as did Dr. Maria Fraddosio of the Biblioteca della Camera dei Deputati. At the archive of the Fondazione Einaudi in Turin I was assisted by Dr. Dorrigo-Martinotti and Dr. Fadini; at Harvard University's Baker Library by my former student José Alvarez; at Amherst College by Ms. Daria D'Arienzo; at Princeton University's Mudd Library by Mrs. Holiday, and Mrs. Brester; and at the archive of the New York Federal Reserve Bank by Ms. Rosemary Lazenby and Mr. C.W. Backlund. I am also grateful to the staffs of the National Archives in Washington, the archive at Quai d'Orsay in Paris, the Public Record Office, and the Bank of England in London. The staffs of the Firestone graduate library at Princeton, the Hatcher graduate library at the University of Michigan, the Dewey and Hayden Memorial libraries at MIT, and Harvard University's Widner Library gave me invaluable help. I wish to acknowledge in particular the efforts of the inter-library loan departments at Princeton, Michigan, and MIT, for without their efforts this study could never have been written.

My dissertation research was assisted by a Fulbright Fellowship, a summer research grant from the Council for European Studies, and various grants from Princeton University. It is a particular pleasure to acknowledge the assistance of Dr. Cipriana Scelba and Mr. Luigi Fildoro of the Commission for Educational and Cultural Exchange Between Italy and the United States, who helped me in so many ways in Rome. Since defending my dissertation I have received travel grants for additional archival research from Princeton University and MIT. MIT reduced my teaching load during one semester so as to enable me to complete this project expeditiously. Naturally, the responsibility for any shortcomings or errors is my own.

MIT undergraduates, Kathryn Alexis Black, Furio Ciacci, Emil Dabora, Eugene Lin, and Sheetal Shah, aided my research under the auspices of the Undergraduate Research Opportunities Program.

Friends, Luisa Torchia, Armando Trio, Saro Lo Turco, Susan Taylor, Susanna and Massimo Cretara, and Ruggiero Vitrani in Rome, and Alan Deyermond in London, often made me feel more at home abroad than in the United States. Only Mercedes Vaquero knows how much this dissertation and its author owes to her.

INTRODUCTION

This study rests on the premise that a critical analysis of monetary and financial policy from the outbreak of World War I until the March on Rome can illuminate important, even crucial aspects of the crisis of liberal Italy. Monetary and financial policy is a particularly useful prism through which to view political conflict. What is at issue are the manifold forms of state intervention in the economy, including the role of government in accumulating and expending resources, and the role of the central bank as a macroeconomic stabilizer – some of the basic aspects of the state's interaction with society. In particular, this study focuses on real and perceived conflicts and often painful choices in monetary and financial policymaking between great power politics, economic growth, macroeconomic stabilization, and the preservation or strengthening of democratic consensus. The key issue it proposes to explore is why the post-war governments, although headed by prime ministers of the center-left, were unable to press ahead with the democratic reformism which characterized the "Giolittian era," 1901–14.

Rapid economic growth at the beginning of the century allowed political leaders in the pre-war years, most notably Giovanni Giolitti himself, to promote social reform and broaden the basis of political consensus in the liberal state, while at the same time pursuing an expansionist foreign policy designed to stake out a claim for Italy as a great power. Giolitti and his associates allowed trade unions organizational freedom, and instituted government neutrality in labor disputes, expanded workers' rights, created an embryonic welfare state, and promoted public works projects. On the eve of the Great War, universal male suffrage was introduced, and parliamentary elections were held with the newly expanded franchise. At the same time, Giolitti maintained the allegiance of the old political elites: the king, the military, the foreign policy establishment, and parliamentarians representing landowners, commercial farmers and business interests. After World War I, however, efforts to resume the cautious reformism of the early century failed, and by 1922 the parliamentary regime was superseded by Europe's first fascist dictatorship. This study

1

argues that Giolitti's reforms rested on rather fragile economic and
financial supports. Changes in the international environment and the
economic policy choices of Italy's leadership during the war seriously
eroded these supports, and reduced the margins for political and social
bargaining. Great power politics, monetary and financial stability, economic growth, and political and social reform proved less easily reconcil-
able in the post-war era. Particularly after the onset of economic recession
in 1920–21, when liberal leaders were confronted with choosing between
these objectives, they put stability ahead of reform, contributing in no
small measure to parliamentary paralysis and the collapse of the liberal
state.

This study focuses on four problems in monetary and financial policy
that contributed significantly to undermining the parliamentary regime in
the post-war years: (1) large budget deficits and the inability of liberal
governments to reform the tax system; (2) the vulnerability of the Italian
banking system to crises, which in turn threatened to undermine the basis
of economic growth; (3) persistent tensions between monetary and
Treasury authorities in Rome on the one hand, and the leadership of the
country's largest commercial banks in Milan on the other; and (4) the
collapse of the pre-war equilibrium in the international balance of payments, the emergence of Italian financial dependence, first on Great
Britain, and later on the United States, and the difficult process of
readjustment produced by the termination of US and British financial
assistance in 1919–20. In each of these areas, the options of policymakers
were constrained by the central dilemma of the political economy of
liberal Italy: the tension between the imperatives of a strategy of economic
growth based on tariffs and subsidies designed to encourage the development of strategic or armaments-related industries on the one hand, and
the imperatives of generating greater prosperity and wealth on the other.
In pre-war Italy, state policies promoting industrial development, to wit,
subsidies and tariffs for iron and steel manufacturing, shipbuilding, armaments, and non-competitive shipping lines, required the transfer of
resources from non-strategic economic sectors to the strategic sector.
Whether liberal Italy's strategic goals could have been reconciled with its
economic goals in a more satisfactory manner than actually occurred must
remain an open question; in any event, the industrial policies which were
adopted tended to constrict the private market for industrial goods, rather
than expand it, leading to what Bonelli aptly has called, "the equilibrium
of low consumption."[1] The promotion of strategic industries remained the

[1] Franco Bonelli, "Il capitalismo italiano. Linee generale d'interpretazione," in Ruggiero
Romano and Corrado Vivanti, eds., *Storia d'Italia*. Annali I: *Dal feudalismo al capitalismo*
(Turin: Einaudi, 1978), pp. 1195–255.

centerpiece of state economic policy from the beginning of industrialization in the mid-1880s until the demise of parliamentary government and
beyond. The need for Italy to assert itself as a great power, and to build a
strategic industrial base was never seriously questioned by left-liberal
reformers. The core institutions and ideology of the Italian state – the
monarchy, the military, and the primacy of foreign over domestic policy –
were bound up with great power politics. Both Giolitti and Francesco
Saverio Nitti, his would-be successor as leader of a reformist parliamentary majority, remained loyal to these conservative political institutions
and conceptions. Left-liberals promoted social and political reform and
favored rising living standards in order to bolster, rather than subvert the
conservative institutions and ideology of the Savoian monarchy; but as a
consequence of the war it became increasingly clear that an economic
policy predicated on military and strategic considerations undermined
reform and limited prosperity.

The budget deficit and tax reform

As the figures in Table 21 (Appendix, p. 326) indicate, on the eve of World
War I the Italian state spent more, and taxed its citizens more heavily, as a
percentage of gross national product than Britain, Germany, and France.
This was an inevitable consequence of liberal Italy's great power and
developmental aspirations, and the relatively slender economic base upon
which they rested.[2] Despite comparatively high taxes, large budget deficits
were the rule during most of the post-unification era. However, beginning
in 1899, Italy ran a series of budget surpluses. The extraordinarily favorable condition of public finances allowed Giolitti to refinance the state
debt between 1903 and 1906, replacing consols bearing 4% and 5% with
new securities bearing 3% and 3.5%. The soundness of public finances
was an important precondition for monetary stability and economic
growth, and left national savings available for financing industrial
development.

In the last years before the war, however, budget deficits reappeared;
largely due to the costs of rearmament and the Libyan War; but also due
to increased social spending, notably for public works, disability insurance,
and pensions. After the Libyan War, the Italian state was constrained to
issue 5-year treasury bonds at 4%, and the earlier debt conversion seemed
in danger of being undone. Long before the reappearance of budget

---

[2] Giorgio Brosio and Carla Marchese, *Il potere di spendere. Economia e storia della spesa pubblica
dall'unificazione ad oggi* (Bologna: Il Mulino, 1986), pp. 50–51 and passim; Antonio Confalonieri, *Banca e industria in Italia dalla crisi del 1907 all'agosto 1914* (Milan: Banca Commerciale Italiana, 1982), I, pp. 55–67.

deficits left-liberal political leaders had advocated shifting Italy's tax burden, notably by reducing indirect taxes on items of mass consumption, and introducing a progressive income tax. ~~However,~~ ALTHOUGH parliamentary resistance to tax reform had always proved insurmountable,[3] By August 1914 tax reform was high on the political agenda; it was no longer just an issue of social justice, but also of financial stability.

The enormous growth of state expenditures and budget deficits during World War I only made the problem worse. Unlike France and Germany, the Italian government could not claim to have been the innocent victim of foreign aggression, and could not pretend that Austria should be made to pay the costs of war. The Risorgimento tradition of making fiscal sacrifice for unification also tended to preclude such a policy. Consequently, the government raised existing direct and indirect taxes, at the same time that it imposed heavy taxes on war profits. Nominal Italian tax revenues rose to a level that inspired the admiration even of John Maynard Keynes, at the time a British Treasury official.[4]

But another set of policy goals first complicated and ultimately subverted the line of fiscal austerity. Political authorities sought to use the war to reinforce the financial base of domestic industry and even to promote industrial growth. The desire to favor industrial development made successive governments reluctant to control the prices charged by suppliers and restrict private investment. Italian tax policy was undermined by the lack of rigorous controls on prices paid by the state to private contractors for war-related purchases. High tax assessments were passed back to the state in the form of higher prices, a practice dubbed the *partita di giro* or "circle game" by contemporaries. It was widespread and simple, given that state spending accounted for more than half of gross domestic product by 1917–19. In effect, the policy of fiscal rigor, which was dictated by considerations of high politics, both domestic and international, was undermined by government solicitude for the strategic industrial sector.

War loans were also to a considerable degree fictitious. Anxious to secure large nominal subscriptions, the Treasury and the Bank of Italy applied pressure on large banking and manufacturing firms to make subscriptions to the war loans well in excess of the amount of capital they were willing to tie up in government securities. To regain their former liquidity

[3] Constantine McGuire, *Italy's International Economic Position* (New York: Macmillan, 1926); Epicarmo Corbino, *Annali dell'economia italiana*, V, *1901–1914* (Città di Castello: Leonardo da Vinci, 1938); Luigi Einaudi, *La guerra e il sistema tributario italiano* (Bari: Laterza, 1927); Benedetto Croce, *A History of Italy, 1871–1915* (New York: Russell and Russell, 1929), p. 230; Frank Coppa, *Planning, Protectionism and Politics in Liberal Italy: Economics and Politics in the Giolittian Age* (Washington DC: Catholic University of America Press, 1971).

[4] Keynes, internal Treasury memo, 18 November 1916, Public Record Office (PRO), London, Treasury files (T-files), T1/12033/5070/17.

positions, private firms subsequently dumped war bonds on the market, depressing their prices, or used them as collateral for bank loans. Rather than absorbing purchasing power and restraining inflation, the war loans, to a significant degree, stimulated the expansion of bank credit. At the same time, small savers who held on to their war bonds suffered capital losses when the market price of state securities declined, and when the expansion of bank credit produced inflation. Consequently, state borrowing was not only inflationary, but also damaged the interests of middle-class investors, who formed the state's most loyal clientele. Particularly in the post-war years, dissatisfaction with the government's inflationary financial policies proved an important factor in the estrangement of the middle classes from the political leadership and institutions of the liberal state.

The high tax rates imposed during the war only began to have a significant impact on taxpayers in late 1919 and early 1920, when war contracts dried up and the transition to a market economy began. During this period of transition, the incongruities and technical deficiencies of wartime fiscal legislation began to weigh on taxpayers. Two flaws in the tax system were of critical importance. First, assessments for direct taxes were highly inaccurate. In the pre-war period, Italian direct tax rates had been exceedingly high by contemporary European standards. They were in fact so high that the personnel of the Ministry of Finance had long since settled into a *modus vivendi* with taxpayers, whereby taxes were assessed on the basis of a mutually agreed upon figure far lower than the real income. Such arrangements were made on an *ad hoc* and personal basis, so that the true tax burden was distributed in an unsystematic and unequal manner. The second major difficulty with the Italian tax system was that direct taxes were not personal, but real, i.e. they were assessed not on the basis of total individual income, but on single income-earning activities. Such a system of direct taxation should have precluded the introduction of progressivity, because an individual with a given income derived from a single source would pay a higher tax than an individual with an equal income derived from a plurality of sources. And in fact, prior to the war direct taxes in Italy were not progressive. During the war, however, the Ministry of Finance introduced progressive rates on real taxes, creating another significant element of inequality in the direct tax system. In the immediate post-war years, the tax burden on individuals and firms with unfavorable assessments became quite heavy, producing a wave of fiscal bankruptcies.[5]

Tax reform was thus both financially and politically an urgent necessity in post-war Italy. Not surprisingly, however, the question of tax reform

[5] Einaudi, *La guerra e il sistema tributario.*

soon became linked to state spending. When the final liberal governments proposed draconian, even confiscatory tax measures, business interest groups and conservatives successfully mobilized opposition in parliament. It became increasingly clear during the Nitti and Giolitti ministries from June 1919 to June 1921 that the Italian upper and middle classes and their parliamentary representatives would only consent to fiscal reform on the condition that state spending be reduced and a government installed that would not be beholden to pressure for welfare-related expenditure on the part of socialists and Catholics. The final liberal governments progress-ively cut back budget deficits, but they did so at the cost of alienating their actual (Catholic) and potential (reformist socialist) mass political con-stituencies. A thoroughgoing tax reform was only implemented by Mus-solini's first Finance Minister, Alberto De Stefani, in 1922–25. Significantly, the fascists managed to reduce the size of government as a percentage of GNP to pre-war levels by the mid-1920s; in Britain and Weimar Germany in contrast, both government spending and revenue stabilized at appreciably higher levels, in part due to new commitments in social policy (see Table 21 Appendix, p. 326).[6]

The vulnerabilities of the Italian financial system

The German-inspired mixed or universal banks were the fulcrum of industrial finance in the Giolittian era. As Gerschenkron and others have demonstrated, the mixed banks, notably the Banca Commerciale Italiana (Comit) and the Credito Italiano (Credit), which were founded by Ger-man-led international banking syndicates in 1894 and 1895 respectively, played a leading role in promoting Italian economic growth. These two banks established their preeminence in finance and industry from 1898 to 1907, when the economy grew at 3.4% annually, and industrial output at 5.9%, the highest sustained rate of growth prior to the "economic miracle," 1958–63.[7] The mixed banks not only engaged in ordinary com-mercial operations, but also made long-term industrial investments. They actively participated in the formation of joint-stock companies by under-writing and purchasing securities. Bank directors commonly sat on the boards of companies with which the banks maintained close financial relations.[8] But the rapid process of growth predicated on mixed banking

---

[6] See also Brosio and Marchese, *Il potere di spendere*, pp. 61–63.

[7] Istituto centrale di statistica (ISTAT), *Sommario di statistiche storiche dell'Italia 1861–1955* (Rome: ISTAT, 1958), pp. 212–13; cited in, Gianni Toniolo, *Storia economica dell'Italia liberale, 1850–1918* (Bologna: Il Mulino, 1988), p. 163.

[8] Alexander Gerschenkron, "Economic Backwardness in Historial Perspective," and, "Notes on the Rate of Industrial Growth in Italy," in, *Economic Backwardness in Historical Perspective: A Book of Essays* (Cambridge MA: Harvard University Press, 1962), pp. 5–30, 72–89.

bore with it significant costs. The close relationship between banking and manufacturing firms left the former vulnerable to insolvency in periods of industrial recession. Banks made commercial loans against industrial securities deposited as collateral, making their loan portfolios vulnerable to fluctuations in stock prices. Further, nominally commercial loans were often used to finance fixed investments; in good times, manufacturing firms would repay such credits by issuing stock or bonds on the securities markets; in bad times, however, the banks' commercial portfolios tended to become illiquid. The vulnerability of the mixed banks to a decline in industrial activity meant that a recession in manufacturing would ripple rapidly through the banking system and the economy as a whole. Relatively minor shocks on the securities markets could produce crisis and stagnation for the entire economy. Such was the case in 1907, which saw the failure of a third mixed bank, the Società Bancaria Italiana (SBI), which had been modeled on the Comit and the Credit. The SBI's failure provoked a general collapse of industrial securities prices; thereafter the stock markets remained volatile and smaller savers turned to safer, but less productive forms of investment. As a consequence, Italian firms had great difficulty raising substantial sums of capital on the securities market. In the period 1907–13, industrial output grew at the more modest rate of 2.0%. In the years just prior to World War I, Italy appeared to face economic stagnation, in no small measure because of the decline in industrial investment.[9]

The role of the state in favoring investments in non-competitive heavy industries tended to exacerbate the problem. The mixed banks favored industries that enjoyed tariff protection, subsidies and state contracts. A significant proportion of the total share capital invested in Italian joint-stock companies was tied up in iron and steel, shipbuilding, armaments, and companies exploiting subsidized shipping lines. Such investments represented resources drained off from the consumer-oriented sectors of the economy, and the overall multiplier effect of strategic investments was probably modest.

For industry, the war served as a financial *deus ex machina*; old debts were paid off and huge war profits permitted new and sometimes daring investments. Between 1915 and 1918 Ansaldo began building the pharaonic iron and steel works and electricity generating facility at Cogne, in the mountains of the Val d'Aosta; Fiat built a steel-making plant and the mammoth Lingotto automobile factory in Turin, modeled after Henry Ford's facilities in Dearborn; Silvio Crespi rebuilt his cotton textile works in Upper Lombardy; and Franchi Gregorini, the Brescia based steel and

---

[9] Franco Bonelli, *La crisi del 1907. Una tappa dello sviluppo industriale in Italia* (Turin: Fondazione Luigi Einaudi, 1971).

armaments concern, embarked on an ambitious program of investments and expansion. The government actively encouraged new industrial investments during the war, even though private firms competed with the military for scarce raw materials and labor. Construction of new plant was undertaken with public encouragement, even when it was clear that new capacity would not come on line until well after the war was over, and that such investments would therefore detract from, rather than enhance the war effort.[10]

Meanwhile, large war profits allowed manufacturing firms to repay their debts to the commercial banks. The commercial banks, in turn, were able to redress their troubled liquidity positions and improve their relative position within the banking system at the expense of more conservative financial institutions, notably the savings banks. The banks were induced to recycle their profits and the liquid resources they accumulated through an influx of deposits in new industrial investments. This was particularly the case in 1919–20, after war-related state contracts dried up, and manufacturing firms once again looked for external financing, often to complete ambitious projects begun during the war.

The pell-mell industrial expansion of the war years caused the post-war recession to be far more severe in Italy than in the other victorious powers, and the peculiar relationship between industry and banking transformed the recession into a devastating financial crisis. Industrial expansion had taken place without reference to post-war markets, and much of the new capacity built up during and just after the war became idle. Not surprisingly, the iron and steel, armaments, shipbuilding, and shipping industries were hardest hit in the post-war recession. In 1921–22, the two largest heavy industry conglomerates in Italy, Ilva and Ansaldo, and two of the four largest private banks, the Banca Italiana di Sconto and the Banco di Roma, essentially failed and had to be restructured financially with state support. In effect, the enormous public contribution to industrial expansion during the war – through armaments contracts and the toleration of tax evasion – was continued after the war in the form of government-

[10] On Ansaldo: Richard Webster, "La tecnologia italiana e i sistemi industriali verticali: il caso dell'Ansaldo," *Storia contemporania* (1978), 2, pp. 205–39; Thomas Row, "Economic Nationalism in Italy: The Ansaldo Company, 1882–1921," Ph.D. dissertation, Johns Hopkins University (1988); on Fiat: Valerio Castronovo, *Giovanni Agnelli. La Fiat dal 1899 al 1945* (Turin: UTET, 1971); on Crespi: Roberto Romano, *I Crespi: Origini, fortuna e tramonto di una dinastia lombarda* (Milan: Angeli, 1985); on Franchi Gregorini: Alice A. Kelikian, *Town and Country under Fascism: The Transformation of Brescia, 1915–1926* (New York: Oxford University Press, 1986). See also, Alberto Caracciolo, "La crescita e la trasformazione della grande industria durante la prima guerra mondiale," in, Giorgio Fuà, ed., *Lo sviluppo economico in Italia*, 3rd ed., vol. III (Milan: Angeli, 1978), pp. 195–248; Luciano Segreto, "Armi e munizioni. Lo sforzo bellico tra speculazione e progresso tecnico," *Italia contemporania* (1982), nos. 146/7, pp. 35–66.

sponsored rescues of troubled banks and manufacturing firms. This policy has been described appropriately by Bonelli as, "the retroactive state financing of industry."[11]

The severity of the economic and financial crisis in post-war Italy tended to circumscribe the policy options of left-liberal political leaders. The tax base collapsed at a time when drastic tax increases were being considered. Public institutions, including the Bank of Italy, were constrained to rescue insolvent financial and industrial firms, thereby diminishing the resources available for other purposes, including public works. The panic engendered by the collapse of prominent banks increased pressures on the government to cut welfare-related expenditures and return to financially orthodox policies so as to restore international confidence, at a time when maintaining or increasing such expenditures would have been necessary in order to obtain broad political support for the liberal state. At the same time, high unemployment exacerbated social and political conflicts. The deflationary fiscal policies as well as the rescue of heavy industry and speculative mixed banks, contributed to the erosion of the parliamentary base of the last liberal governments, engendering growing hostility among the Catholics, and strengthening the radical element within the Socialist Party.

The Milan–Rome conflict and the "war between the banks"

The structural vulnerabilities of Italy's financial system were aggravated by a long-standing, bitter conflict between officials of the Treasury and the Bank of Italy in Rome and the leadership of the largest commercial banks in Milan. The conflict had its origins in the financial crisis of 1893. At that time, the two largest commercial banks in the peninsula, the Credito Mobiliare and the Banca Generale, along with an important Roman issue bank, the Banca Romana, failed. It was in the wake of this crisis that the Banca Commerciale and the Credito Italiano were founded by German-led international banking syndicates. Meanwhile, parliament enacted legislation consolidating three of the six issue banks which the Kingdom of Italy had inherited from the predecessor states to form the Bank of Italy. The Bank of Italy, which continued to share the privilege of issuing bank notes with two smaller southern banks, the Banco di Napoli and the Banco di Sicilia, was envisaged by the legislators as an instrument of stronger public regulation and intervention in the financial markets. However, the new issue bank was constrained to absorb the stricken Banca Romana, and emerged from the crisis with a portfolio of bad loans and

---

[11] Bonelli, "Il capitalismo italiano."

over-valued real estate assets, which it was obliged to liquidate over the following two decades. The Bank of Italy was thus in no condition to pursue an active monetary policy during the early years of sustained economic growth, when the Banca Commerciale and the Credito Italiano were consolidating their positions in Italian finance and industry. As the Bank of Italy became stronger after the turn of the century, it sought to play a more active role on the financial markets; however, the leading Milanese banks were unwilling to submit to its authority.[12]

Sharp conflicts developed between the leadership of Italy's largest private banks and the premier issue bank in two key areas: the Milanese institutions resisted the Bank of Italy's efforts to regulate interest rates and the volume of bank credit; and they refused to participate loyally in syndicates headed by the Bank of Italy to rescue other banks in distress. The central difficulty of the Italian banking system was that it was particularly vulnerable to liquidity crises, given the involvement of deposit-taking banks in industrial promotion, while at the same time tensions between the commercial banks and the Bank of Italy made it difficult for the latter to regulate the credit markets effectively and exercise its lender-of-last-resort function in the event of a crisis. This problem was manifest in the crisis of 1907, and it was particularly devastating in the financial crisis of 1921–22.

The largest Milanese commercial banks also often found themselves at odds with the Italian government over foreign policy. Before the war, they were frequently reluctant to participate in overseas investments urged by the government to reinforce Italy's colonial and imperial policy when such investments promised indifferent or uncertain economic returns. Although the foreign interest in the Banca Commerciale and the Credito Italiano declined to a modest proportion of share capital after the turn of the century, a substantial number of foreigners still sat on the boards of both banks, where they could oppose investments in Balkan and Mediterranean projects suggested by the Italian Foreign Ministry. In addition to foreign board members, many of the executive directors of the two banks were foreign-born, making the two institutions vulnerable to charges of lack of patriotism. Such charges seemed to be confirmed by the imperiousness with which the commercial bankers resisted the efforts of the Italian government and the Bank of Italy to regulate the credit markets, behavior reminiscent of European bankers in Latin America or other semi-colonial environments. But while the major commercial banks resisted pressures to further the Consulta's aims in foreign policy, they were at the same time deeply involved in financing firms in the strategic sector that enjoyed tariff

---

[12] Bonelli, *La crisi del 1907*; Antonio Confalonieri, *Banca e industria in Italia (1894–1906)*, 3 vols. (Milan: Banca Commerciale Italiana, 1977–80).

protection, subsidies and government contracts. The largest commercial banks thus found themselves in the contradictory position of being simultaneously financiers of rearmament at home, and opponents of adventurism abroad. In the process, the Milanese commercial bankers made important political enemies on the left and on the right: left-liberal reformers criticized the power of the banks, favoring more active government intervention in the economy, while conservatives accused the banks of undermining Italy's great power aspirations due to their association with foreign financial interests, and lack of enthusiasm for the imperial program of the Consulta.[13]

The tensions between the Milanese commercial banks and the government led the Bank of Italy and successive governments of both the left and the right to challenge the financial predominance of the Banca Commerciale and the Credito Italiano. Prior to the war, Bonaldo Stringher, the General Director of the Bank of Italy, sought to bring the two commercial banks to heel by favoring the growth of the Società Bancaria Italiana. Meanwhile, the Consulta cooperated with another commercial bank, the adventurist Banco di Roma, which established subsidiaries and financed enterprises in Libya, opening the way for the Italian invasion. However, neither the Società Bancaria nor the Banco di Roma were well managed: the SBI, as was noted, was badly hurt in the financial crisis of 1907, and only salvaged *in extremis* by the Bank of Italy; and the Roma was also on the verge of bankruptcy by 1914. Another contradictory aspect of the tensions between Milan and Rome, therefore, was that the public authorities were driven to cooperate with the more speculative and corrupt banks in their efforts to gain greater control over the financial markets, thereby further destabilizing the banking system.[14]

Tensions between public authorities and the major commercial banks were an essential element in the "war between the banks" that rocked the Italian financial system between 1918 and 1922. In 1915 a new commercial bank, the Banca Italiana di Sconto, was formed through mergers among several smaller banks, including the greatly diminished Società Bancaria. From the beginning the Bansconto, which made its headquarters in Rome, was envisaged as a nationalist Italian alternative to the allegedly foreign-dominated Milanese institutions. It established close relations with Ansaldo, the only firm engaged in iron and steel production and shipbuild-

---

[13] Bonelli, *La crisi del 1907*; Confalonieri, *Banca e industria (1894–1906)*; Confalonieri, *Banca e industria, 1907–1914*, 2 vols.; Richard A. Webster, *Industrial Imperialism in Italy, 1908–1915* (Berkeley: University of California Press, 1975); Brunello Vigezzi, "Otto Joel, il principe di Bülow e i problemi della neutralità," in *Da Giolitti a Salandra* (Florence: Vallecchi, 1969), pp. 203–62.

[14] Bonelli, *La crisi del 1907*; Luigi De Rosa, *Storia del Banco di Roma*, II (Rome: Banco di Roma, 1983, published privately, restricted distribution).

ing that was outside the orbit of the Commerciale. Armaments contracts allowed both the Bansconto and Ansaldo to expand rapidly during the war, enabling the new financial-industrial trust to challenge quickly the domination of the Milanese banks.

From the beginning, the *banca italianissima* enjoyed broad political support. The Ansaldo–Bansconto group maintained close relations with radical groups through its financial support for *Il Popolo d'Italia*, Mussolini's interventionist newspaper, and *L'Idea Nazionale*, the newspaper of the radical-rightist Italian Nationalist Association. But its intimate relationship with Francesco Saverio Nitti was of even greater importance. Nitti, a corporate lawyer, professor, and influential left-liberal deputy from Basilicata, had served as Minister of Agriculture, Industry, and Commerce in Giolitti's fourth government, 1911–14. Thereafter, in 1914–15, he acted as legal counsel to the interests that established the new bank. Nitti later exercised a dominant influence on government financial policy as Minister of the Treasury from November 1917 to January 1919 and Prime Minister from June 1919 to June 1920. The southern Italian political leader believed that continuing the reformist policies of the Giolittian era in the post-war period would require firmer government control over the banking system and the financial markets. In public, Nitti and the financial press close to him advocated "bank cooperation," or the suppression of bank rivalries and the submission of the commercial banks to the leadership of the Bank of Italy and the Treasury. During Nitti's tenure at the Treasury in 1918 and again during his tenure as Prime Minister in 1920, the Bansconto made two unsuccessful hostile take-over bids on the Banca Commerciale. Although historians sympathetic to Nitti have confirmed the southern politician's denial of complicity in the Bansconto's "escalades" of the Commerciale, Falchero has argued recently, more convincingly, in my view, that Nitti considered the Bansconto's actions as being in conformance with his program of bank cooperation.[15]

In any event, the rivalry between the Banca Italiana di Sconto on the one hand, and the Banca Commerciale and, to a lesser degree the Credito Italiano, on the other, added an additional element of turbulence to Italy's political economy in the World War I and post-war years. The severity of the post-war recession, and in particular the spectacular collapse of the Bansconto in January 1922, was a direct product of what Mori has called

[15] Alberto Monticone, *Nitti e la grande guerra (1914–1918)* (Milan: Giuffré, 1961); Francesco Barbagallo, *Nitti* (Turin: UTET, 1984); Anna Maria Falchero, "Banchieri e politica. Nitti e il gruppo Ansaldo–Banca di Sconto," *Italia contemporanea* (1982), nos. 146/7, pp. 62–92; Anna Maria Falchero, "Il gruppo Ansaldo–Banca Italiana di Sconto e le vicende bancarie nel primo dopoguerra," in Peter Hertner and Giorgio Mori, ed., *La transizione dall'economia di guerra all'economia di pace in Italia e in Germania dopo la prima guerra mondiale* (Bologna: Il Mulino, 1983), pp. 543–71.

the "parallel wars" between rival financial-industrial groups.[16] While the question of the degree of Nitti's complicity in the hostile take-over bids of 1918 and 1920 may not be resolvable on the basis of available documents, it is clear that the rise of the Bansconto owed much to the tensions existing between the major commercial banks and central bank authorities and political leaders.

Likewise, it is clear that the acrimony with which the major financial-industrial groups conducted their struggle for hegemony over the Italian economy had a lacerating effect on Italy's political elite. Flushed with war profits, the largest private business groups bought up most of the peninsula's newspapers and publishing houses during the war, acquiring unprecedented political influence. The battles on the stock exchanges spilled over to Montecitorio, and the final liberal governments were crippled by infighting between politicians beholden to rival business concerns.[17] According to his own testimony, Nitti's ministry was weakened and ultimately undone by the unbending opposition of the Banca Commerciale.[18]

The balance of payments deficit

The rapid economic growth of the Giolittian era rested on an unusually favorable situation in Italy's international balance of payments. Receipts from emigrant remittances and tourism allowed Italy to run an extraordinarily large merchandise trade deficit without incurring significant foreign debts. The size of invisible foreign exchange earnings at the beginning of the century was particularly crucial, as the strategy of industrial development favored by Italy's political leadership presupposed running a large trade deficit. As we have seen, industrialization in Italy was bound up from the beginning with the decision to acquire a heavy industrial base for strategic-military purposes. The non-competitive nature of Italian heavy industry compounded the strain which importing technology inevitably places on the balance of payments of newly industrializing countries. Thus state support for heavy industry exercised a depressive effect not only on popular consumption, but also on Italy's international balance of payments.

In the latter decades of the nineteenth century, Italy's structural trade deficit translated into financial dependence on creditor nations. In the

[16] Giorgio Mori, "Le guerre parallele. L'industria elettrica in Italia nel periodo della grande guerra (1914–1919)," in *Il capitalismo industriale in Italia* (Rome: Riuniti, 1971), pp. 141–215.

[17] On the press see, Valerio Castronovo, *La stampa italiana dall'Unità al fascismo* (Bari: Laterza, 1970).

[18] Francesco Saverio Nitti, *Rivelazioni. Dramatis personae* (Naples: Edizioni scientifiche italiane, 1948), pp. 49–51, 543–44.

1860s and 1870s Italy looked to France to finance the balance of payments deficit, which was aggravated in those years by military expenditure and railroad construction. After the diplomatic rupture with France in the 1880s, Italian leaders were forced to look to Germany for new loans. But from the last years of the nineteenth century, growing invisible exchange earnings loosened Italy's dependence on creditor nations, and facilitated a foreign policy of greater independence. In brief, the favorable balance of payments situation in the Giolittian era was both a precondition of economic growth, and the *sine qua non* of independence in Italian foreign policy.

After the outbreak of World War I, Italy's invisible exchange earnings rapidly diminished: tourists disappeared from the peninsula almost overnight, and emigrant remittances were reduced by the repatriation of Italian workers from Central Europe, and the reluctance of Italians in the Americas to change their savings into lire given the unsettled economic and monetary conditions at home. In order to even partially preserve the process of accumulation and economic development characteristic of the pre-war period, Italy once again was constrained to enter into a close relationship with creditor nations, to wit, Great Britain, beginning in 1915, and the United States, beginning in 1917. Although the evidence suggests that economic motives did not play a significant role in the decision of Antonio Salandra (a conservative who replaced Giolitti as Prime Minister in March 1914) and Sidney Sonnino (Foreign Minister beginning in November 1914) to intervene in World War I in the spring of 1915, it is nevertheless clear that had Italy remained neutral, a drastic retrenchment in imports, and economic recession would have resulted. Although imports of crucial raw materials, including cotton and coal, remained well below pre-war levels throughout the war, such imports presumably would have ceased practically altogether in the absence of Italian belligerency, and British and American credits.

The negative consequences of Italy's dependence on credits from the two English-speaking powers became evident in the latter half of 1919 and in the course of 1920, after Allied financial assistance was terminated. As Giolitti noted shortly after the armistice, accumulating large foreign debts has two inherent inconveniences: first, the need to repay them, which is the lesser of the two; and second, after a certain point the inability to borrow further, which is the greater.[19]

Italy faced greater difficulties in coping with the cessation of international lending and the readjustment of its international accounts than

---

[19] Conversation of Giolitti with Olindo Malagodi, 23 November 1918, Malagodi, *Conversazioni della guerra, 1914–1919*, ed. Brunello Vigezzi, II (Milan and Naples: Riccardi, 1960), pp. 455–58.

either France or Belgium, which also had become dependent on Anglo-American financial and material assistance during the war. The pre-war trade deficit of Italy had been considerably larger than those of Belgium and France, and the principal invisible items in Italy's international accounts, emigrant remittances and tourism, recovered slowly and incompletely. Moreover, relatively low living standards reduced Italy's margin to absorb politically and economically the shock of readjustment and recession.

The difficult process of readjustment in Italy's international balance of payments naturally accentuated post-war industrial and financial problems caused by the rapid and unbalanced growth of heavy industry during the war. Lack of means of payment kept Italy's imports of essential raw materials throughout 1919 and 1920 at levels considerably below those of the pre-war years, and only slightly higher than during the wartime trough. The dearth of raw materials prevented Italy from fully participating in the post-war boom that characterized the American and British economies in 1919 and early 1920. Imports of coal, cotton, and wool by volume only recovered to pre-war levels again after the March on Rome. But despite the decline in the volume of essential imports, Italy ran a very substantial balance of payments deficit from 1919 to 1922. In the absence of long or medium-term loans, this deficit was financed by short-term commercial credits and purchases by Italian importers in lire. Large (but unquantifiable) speculative lira balances accumulated in creditor nations, particularly the United States. Such lira balances contributed to the instability of exchange rates: foreigners who held lire in expectation of the stabilization or revaluation of the Italian currency, sold short in moments of political or economic crisis. The depreciation of the lira against the French and Belgian francs reflected the relative lack of confidence of foreign investors in Italy. During the four years between the armistice and the March on Rome, the lira was consistently quoted below the two sister currencies of the pre-war Latin monetary union on the exchange markets. Significantly, this trend inverted in late 1922, when the lira stabilized and the French and Belgian currencies began to come under speculative attack.[20]

The ability of the final liberal governments to obtain a broad base of political consensus was circumscribed by Italy's difficulties in restoring equilibrium to its international accounts. Nitti in particular looked to the United States and Great Britain for financial support in order to ease the economic burdens of readjustment and reconstruction. He sought to trade territorial sacrifice in the Adriatic and support for the more conciliatory

---

[20] Giancarlo Falco and Marina Storaci, "Fluttuazioni monetarie alla metà degli anni 20: Belgio, Francia e Italia," *Studi storici*, 16 (1975), no. 1, pp. 57–101.

foreign policy of the anglophone powers *vis-à-vis* Germany and the Habsburg successor states for food, coal, and credits. Indeed, Nitti believed the liberal reformist economic and political project – promoting industrialization and economic development with a view to raising living standards] and broadening the political base of the liberal state by incorporating moderate socialists and progressive Catholics into a liberal-dominated reformist bloc – was contingent on maintaining close economic and political relations with, and receiving financial assistance from the United States and Britain.

Policymakers in the United States and Britain recognized that their continental Allies in general, and Italy in particular, would have great difficulty bringing their international accounts back into equilibrium after the war, and that France, Belgium, and Italy were in need of substantial further credits. However, the proponents of additional government lending to the continental Allies did not enjoy substantial political support in Britain or in the United States. In London the authorities were so concerned about Britain's own critical financial position that they imposed an informal injunction against most medium or long-term private international lending.

In the United States, the authorities hoped that private concerns would step into the gap when government lending ceased in the latter half of 1919. Several American banking houses, most notably J. P. Morgan & Co. demonstrated a keen interest in developing Italian business after the war. Thomas Lamont, a senior partner of J. P. Morgan & Co. was among the cofounders of the Italy–America Society in 1917. But American investment bankers were unwilling to make substantial new financial resources available to continental Europe, prior to general political, budgetary, and economic stabilization, both at home and on the continent. The general reluctance of American bankers to make long-term investments in Europe was heightened by particular concerns regarding the Italian situation. There was the fear that weak and ineffectual left-liberal ministries could be replaced by a right-wing government that would pursue a bellicose foreign policy, delay demobilization and the reduction of war-related state expenditure, and possibly even embroil Italy in a new war with Yugoslavia or Turkey. American investors also worried that left-liberal, reformist governments, in their efforts to secure the support of the moderate wing of the Socialist Party and the Partito Populare Italiano (the Catholic party), would not have the determination to eliminate the bread subsidy and other welfare-related expenditures in order to balance the budget. Although American investors pressed for tax reform, they were alarmed by the confiscatory tax proposals presented by the Nitti government in the fall of 1919, and by the Giolitti government in the summer of 1920.

American interest in Italy's economic promise ultimately benefited Mussolini, rather than the reformist left. In the years 1924–29, Italy was the recipient of more long and medium-term US loans than any other country in Europe, with the sole exception of Germany. In large measure, this was a question of timing, as American investment bankers were not prepared to extend substantial loans to any European country prior to the settlement of reparations claims and inter-Allied war debts, and political stabilization in central Europe. In part, however, it also reflected the sympathy of American bankers for Mussolini's authoritarian regime, which was unbeholden to popular pressures for welfare-related spending, and therefore less susceptible to departure from orthodox monetary and fiscal policy. The American enchantment with Italian fascism, of course, lasted only so long as Mussolini seemed disposed to pursue a moderate foreign policy and promote European political stability. Meanwhile, the Italian extreme right was constrained to abandon, at least for a decade, its expansionist foreign policy, in order to reach a political and financial understanding with the United States and Britain.[21]

---

[21] Gian Giacomo Migone, *Gli Stati Uniti e il fascismo. Alle origini dell'egemonia americana in Italia* (Milan: Feltrinelli, 1980); John P. Diggins, *Mussolini and Fascism: The View from America* (Princeton: Princeton University Press, 1972); Frank Costigliola, *Awkward Dominion: American Political, Economic, and Cultural Relations with Europe, 1919–1933* (Ithaca: Cornell University Press, 1984).

PART 1

GIOLITTIAN ITALY, 1901–1914

1

THE POLITICAL ECONOMY OF GIOLITTIAN ITALY: THE DILEMMAS OF WELFARE, WARFARE, AND DEVELOPMENT

By all accounts the years 1901–14 were a remarkable period in Italy's recent history. It was an era of significant political and social reform, which had its counterpart in the *république radicale* in France, and the radical liberalism of Lloyd George and Asquith in Britain. In Italy these years are usually referred to as the "Giolittian era" because of Giovanni Giolitti's domination of parliament and politics. Giolitti and his collaborators sought to guide Italy through a set of delicate transitions, in many respects comparable to similar processes underway in all European states with liberal parliamentary institutions and traditions in the late nineteenth and early twentieth century: from a parliamentary system based on a restricted franchise to a democratic suffrage; from a repressive to an open system of labor relations; and from a "nightwatchman" state to a rudimentary social welfare state. Nowhere was this process of transition easy, and in many countries – Portugal, Spain, Germany, and Austria, in addition to Italy – in the interwar years parliamentary institutions collapsed under the stress. In Italy during the Giolittian era, however, significant steps toward democratization were taken. Salomone felicitously characterized the political system during these years as a "democracy in the making."[1]

In many respects, Italian politics at the beginning of the century bear greater similarities to the Western democracies than to the more authoritarian political systems of Central Europe. True, Italy's constitution, the Statuto Albertino of 1848, gave the crown important prerogatives in foreign and military affairs independent of parliament; the monarch also was empowered to appoint a prime minister who did not enjoy the confidence of the lower house of parliament, the Camera dei deputati. However, Italian political practice resembled democratic France more nearly than authoritarian Germany. No prime minister of unified Italy ever successfully defied parliament with the backing of the crown over an extended period, in the manner of Bismarck. Significantly, both Latin countries experienced institutional crises at the turn of the century from

[1] A. William Salomone, *Italy in the Giolittian Era: Italian Democracy in the Making, 1900–1914* (Philadelphia: University of Pennsylvania Press, 1960).

which democratic forces emerged triumphant. In France the Dreyfus
Affair raised the question of whether the military was subject to the rule of
law and parliamentary oversight. With the formation of a government of
republican defense by Réné Waldeck-Rousseau in 1899 it was clear that
the rule of law and parliament had prevailed.[2] Italy experienced an
extended political crisis between 1894 and 1900 in which foreign and
domestic problems were intertwined. One of the key issues at stake was
whether the government could pursue an ambitious and expensive foreign
policy without the backing of parliament, and the country. Francesco
Crispi invaded Ethiopia without such backing, and fell, after his army was
defeated at Adowa in 1896; Luigi Pelloux embarked an Italian expeditionary force in China in 1899, which he subsequently withdrew, in the face of
an uproar at home. Another key issue was whether or not the king could
appoint a government which did not enjoy the confidence of parliament.
Sidney Sonnino, a leading conservative, argued that the Statuto Albertino
explicitly recognized the monarch's prerogative in this regard, in an
influential article published in 1897.[3] The third key issue was whether or
not the government could radically restrict civil liberties in order to
preserve public order in the face of increasingly militant workers' and
peasants' movements. Crispi banned radical organizations and arrested
opposition leaders to combat the Fasci movement in Sicily in 1894; Pelloux drafted a bill radically restricting civil liberty, banned socialist parties,
papers, and trade unions, and jailed the leaders of the radical opposition in
1899. These authoritarian measures produced a broad political mobilization in favor of civil liberties and parliamentary government, extending
from moderate conservatives to the socialist left. In June 1900, Pelloux's
second government fell, and Giuseppe Saracco, a moderate conservative,
formed a new government with the backing of the left-liberals. Seven
months later, in February 1901, a left-liberal government was formed,
with Giuseppe Zanardelli as Prime Minister, and Giolitti holding the
strategic portfolio of the Interior. It is from the formation of the
Zanardelli government that the beginning of the Giolittian era conven-
tionally is dated. Giolitti remained at the center of Italian politics from
that time until the spring of 1915: as Prime Minister three times, 1903–5,
1906–9, and 1911–14, and always as the dominant figure in parliament.[4]

---

[2] On the political fallout of the Dreyfus Affair see Madeleine Rebérioux, *La République
radicale? 1898–1914* (Paris: Seuil, 1975).

[3] "Torniamo allo Statuto" (signed "Un deputato") *Nuova antologia*, 32 (1897), vol. LXVII,
pp. 9–67, now in Sidney Sonnino, *Scritti e discorsi extraparlamentari, 1870–1902*, ed.
Benjamin F. Brown (Bari: Laterza, 1972), pp. 575–97.

[4] Among the many studies of the turn-of-the-century crisis, and Giolittian Italy, of particular
interest are: Salomone, *Italy in the Giolittian Era*; Giampiero Carocci, *Giolitti e l'età giolittiana* (Turin: Einaudi, 1961); Umberto Levra, *Il colpo di stato della borghesia: La crisi politica di
fine secolo in Italia, 1896–1900* (Milan: Feltrinelli, 1975); Alberto Aquarone, *L'Italia giolit-*

The failure of the authoritarian experiments of the turn of the century constituted one of the essential preconditions for the politics of Giolittian Italy. After 1900 the principle of parliamentary government and rule by law seemed firmly established. King Umberto was assassinated in July 1900, and replaced by his son Victor Emmanuel III; thereafter prime ministers were appointed strictly in accordance with the wishes of the Camera. Even the leading conservatives, including Sidney Sonnino, reconciled themselves to parliamentary government.

Within this political environment Giolitti developed his grand strategy of broadening the basis of support for the liberal state among Italy's workers and peasants through the political accommodation of reformist socialists and Catholics. In the process the state would acquire new responsibilities – notably in social welfare, and the regulation of labor markets – and parliament would acquire new constituents, while respecting the core institutions and ideology of the established liberal order.

A key component of the ideology of unified Italy was the claim to great power status. The prestige of the monarch, who constitutionally served as commander-in-chief and supreme arbiter of war and peace, was closely bound to great power politics. The military and the Foreign Ministry formed the linchpin of the Italian state, and the higher levels of their bureaucracies were staffed disproportionately by the peninsula's old nobilities.[5]

The withdrawal from Abyssinia after the Battle of Adowa spelled a temporary halt to colonial expansion; however, at no time during the Giolittian era did Italy relinquish its great power aspirations, and these included a colonial sphere of interest. When Libya, already earmarked for colonization before the turn of the century, threatened to slip from Italy's grasp in 1911 Giolitti went to war, despite the stress this imposed on his domestic politics; and despite the destabilizing effects of Turkish defeat on the European balance of power. Giolitti's Foreign Ministers, Tommaso Tittoni, and the Marquis Antonino di San Giuliano, were often the most conservative members of his governments, and their tenure in office was unusually stable.[6]

The unquestioned commitment to great power politics had important implications for economic policy. Since the 1880s the Italian state had promoted the development of a constellation of industries necessary for the domestic production of armaments, including iron and steel-making,

tiana (1896–1915), vol. I, *Le premesse politiche ed economiche* (Bologna: Il Mulino, 1981); Alberto Aquarone, *Tre capitoli sull'Italia giolittiana* (Bologna: Il Mulino, 1987).

[5] Denis Mack Smith, *Italy and its Monarchy* (New Haven: Yale University Press, 1989); Richard J. B. Bosworth, *Italy, the Least of the Great Powers: Italian Foreign Policy before the First World War* (New York: Cambridge University Press, 1979).

[6] Bosworth, *Italy, the Least of the Great Powers.*

shipbuilding, and shipping, in addition to weapons manufacturing *per se*. The centerpiece of Italy's strategic industrial policy was the promotion of basic iron and steel production from iron ore and coking coal. Political leaders from Depretis to Giolitti held it as axiomatic that only a nation with such manufacturing capability could aspire to great power status. Of course the other European states, including second-rate powers like Spain, pursued similar industrial policies, often at considerable expense. However, iron and steel production from coking coal was singularly unsuited to Italy's economy and natural resource endowment. There were no significant deposits of coking coal in Italy or its colonies; therefore the creation of an autarkical heavy industrial base was illusory from the beginning. Basic iron and steel manufacturing was structurally non-competitive, and would remain so until the factor cost of importing coking coal declined significantly after World War II.

Better suited to Italy's resource endowment was the production of steel and steel products from scrap iron, using electricity, and the Siemens-Martins process. Indeed, a multitude of relatively small firms developed in Italy, which transformed scrap iron (much of it imported) in Siemens-Martins furnaces into an array of specialized steel products. They were often highly profitable, and in any event immune from the periodic financial crises which plagued integrated-cycle steel-making. Nevertheless, in 1887 Italy adopted a tariff system which penalized scrap iron imports, and afforded comparatively greater protection to basic iron and steel-making, forcing the shipbuilding, mechanical and engineering industries to rely on a relatively expensive and often technically inferior domestic product. Heavy protection for iron and steel produced only the illusion of strategic self-sufficiency at great economic cost.[7]

This fundamental contradiction in Italy's industrial policy was aggravated by technical deficiency, intrigue and corruption. Heavy protection, and the promise of lavish state contracts attracted speculators, rather than serious entrepreneurs, to the strategic sector. Five enterprises sprang up between the 1880s and the first decade of the twentieth century to produce pig iron and steel in open-hearth furnaces. None of them was large or rich enough to build a complete integrated-cycle production facility, on the model of the most efficient foreign producers. Like other firms in the strategic sector, the steel-makers were highly vulnerable to a political business cycle created by fluctuations in state commissions. Private

---

[7] Franco Bonelli, *Lo sviluppo di una grande impresa in Italia: La Terni dal 1884 al 1962* (Turin: Einaudi, 1975); Richard A. Webster, *Industrial Imperialism in Italy, 1908–1915* (Berkeley: University of California Press, 1975); Antonia Carparelli, "I perché di una 'mezza siderurgia.' La società Ilva, l'industria della ghisa e il ciclo integrale negli anni venti," in Franco Bonelli, ed., *Acciaio per l'industrializzazione: Contributi allo studio del problema siderurgico italiano* (Turin: Einaudi, 1982), pp. 3–158.

demand was incapable of sustaining these industries, and when budget problems forced the government to cut back on military spending and railroad construction, they lurched toward bankruptcy. In 1911, on the eve of the Libyan War, the five open-hearth steel-making firms were merged in the Ilva trust. The new company required extensive refinancing, including loans and guarantees by the Bank of Italy. It was to be the first in a long series of public rescues of strategic industries. Italy's commitment to the maintenance of a non-competitive strategic industrial sector, which was viewed as an essential prerequisite for great power politics, functioned as a heavy mortgage on economic growth, and ultimately on Giolitti's political project of democratization.[8]

In brief, great power politics, the primacy of foreign over domestic policy, and an industrial policy favoring a strategic industrial sector were essential features of the liberal state which Giolitti inherited and sought to preserve and strengthen, even as he developed his program of reform. But he also inherited a tradition of civil liberty, rule by law, and government by parliamentary majority: although Italy still possessed a restrictive franchise; and although the government customarily used bribery and strong-arm tactics to secure the election of its supporters in backward districts, particularly in the South.

With some degree of success, Giolitti sought to reconcile the two major emerging mass opposition movements, socialists and Catholics, with the institutional and political framework of liberal Italy. To the socialists Giolitti offered, more than anything else, organizational freedom for the party (Partito Socialista Italiano or PPI, founded in 1892) and trade unions, and state neutrality in labor disputes. The new attitude of the police and military to strikes was already evident during Giolitti's tenure as Minister of the Interior in 1901. The forces of public order were restrained as a wave of strikes spread among industrial and agricultural workers in the north and center, producing substantial wage increases. Giolitti continued to deal harshly with political strikes, however, and he imposed marshal law when railway workers threatened the functioning of what he believed to be an essential public service in 1902. A second essential aspect of Giolitti's social policy was the funding of public works projects. These were particularly important in the Po Valley, where salaried agricultural workers were well organized in socialist leagues, and where unemployment, except during the sowing and harvesting seasons on the great estates, was endemic. Important pieces of social legislation also were passed: the creation of a Labor Council (Consiglio Superiore del Lavoro) as a forum for business-labor-government discussion of social

---

[8] On the restructuring of Ilva see, Antonio Confalonieri, *Banca e industria in Italia dalla crisi del 1907 all'agosto 1914* (Milan: Banca Commerciale Italiana, 1982), vol. II, pp. 48–135.

legislation, and mediation of labor disputes (1902); the regulation of children's and women's labor (1902, 1907); the expansion of workers' disability insurance (instituted 1898, expanded 1904); the improvement of the financial organization and facilitating expansion of the membership of the voluntary social security program (instituted 1898, expanded and improved repeatedly after the turn of the century); the creation of a mandatory 24-hour weekly holiday (1907); and the creation of a Worker's Inspectorate to supervise the application of labor laws (1912). The capstone of Giolitti's reformism was a bill abolishing the literacy requirement for the vote, and hence introducing universal male suffrage, in 1912.[9]

Giolitti's opening to the left met with some political success. The institutional opposition to liberal Italy of the three parties of the so-called "extreme left," i.e. those that opposed Italy's constitutional arrangements, was substantially weakened. The radicals essentially were coopted into Giolitti's majority; Republicans cooperated with constitutionalists on a case-by-case basis. Although socialist deputies consistently declined to join coalition governments, the party's parliamentary delegation supported three liberal governments (Zanardelli–Giolitti, 1901–3, Sonnino 1906, and Luzzatti 1910–11), either by voting in their favor or by abstention. Moreover, socialist deputies actively supported, and even helped draw up key pieces of social legislation. However, the Socialist Party remained divided between reformists and revolutionaries, and in 1912, after a period of reformist ascendancy, the latter recaptured the party directorate at the congress of Reggio Emilia.[10]

Giolitti pursued a different strategy toward the Catholics. He remained hostile to the popular wing of the the Catholic movement, and its leader, the Sicilian priest Don Sturzo. Catholic trade union organizations were ignored by the Consiglio del Lavoro, and Catholic peasant leagues were shunned by the Ministry of Public Works. Giolitti remained opposed to the creation of a mass Catholic party, determined to draw Catholic voters and politicians as individuals into the orbit of liberal politics. He cultivated conservative Catholic leaders and the Vatican. The Pope responded to his advances by progressively weakening the ban on participation in elections by Catholic voters and candidates, particularly where Catholic–liberal coalitions stood to defeat the left. Hence Giolitti's opening to the Catholics also met with some success. On the other hand, his simultaneous cultivation of the Catholic right and the socialist and anti-clerical left produced hostility and distrust in both camps; and contrary to his desires

[9] On strikes and social reform see, Aquarone, *L'Italia giolittiana*, pp. 199–231, and *passim*; Aquarone, *Tre capitoli sull'Italia giolittiana*, pp. 177–87, and passim; Guido Neppi Modona, *Sciopero, potere politico e magistratura, 1870–1922* (Bari: Laterza, 1969).

[10] Carocci, *Giolitti e l'età giolittiana*.

the mass wing of the Catholic movement gained ascendancy after the war, with the foundation of the Partito Populare Italiano by Don Sturzo in 1919.[11]

But the politics of Giolittian Italy have been studied exhaustively elsewhere, and need not concern us here at length. Nor is it necessary to document in detail how Giolitti encountered growing difficulty in keeping the disparate elements of his coalition together in the final years before the outbreak of World War I, particularly after the Libyan War of 1911–12. The point here is to explore the economic preconditions of the liberal reformist project; the dilemmas in economic policy facing Giolitti and the other liberal leaders during the first fourteen years of the century; and how these dilemmas eventually narrowed political choices.

In addition to the political precondition for liberal reformism, i.e. the failure of the authoritarian experiment at the turn of the century, there were a set of economic preconditions: sustained growth, a favorable international balance of payments, and the stability of state finances. The international economic situation at the beginning of the century was decidedly favorable, and from the late 1890s at least through 1907 Italy's economy grew at a rate decidedly above the European average. According to the rather conservative estimates of the public agency which collects statistical data in Italy (ISTAT), the economy grew at a rate of 3.4% 1899–1907, and 1.8% 1907–13. Industrial production grew even faster: according to ISTAT at 5.9% 1899–1907, and 2.0% 1907–13. Other estimates of the rate of growth of industrial output are even higher. Gerschenkron characterized the first years of the century as the period of industrial "take-off" in Italy, and calculated the rate of increase in manufacturing output at 6.5% 1899–1907, and 3.2% 1907–13, while in a recent study Fenoaltea arrived at rates of 7.1% and 4.1% in these two periods respectively.[12] Whatever the rate of growth, it was during the fifteen years preceding the outbreak of World War I that the key industries of the second industrial revolution – iron and steel, chemicals, electrical engineering, and automotives – became well established in the Italian peninsula.

These figures reveal the relative weakness of Italy's economy after 1907, and in many respects this year represents a crucial turning point in Italy's political economy. The causes and consequences of slower growth after 1907 will be discussed below, in connection with the banking system. However, first it is necessary to review briefly the condition of public finances in Giolittian Italy.

[11] Ibid.
[12] All figures cited in Gianni Toniolo, *Storia economica dell'Italia liberale (1850–1918)* (Bologna: Il Mulino, 1988), p. 163.

Public finances

The first decade of this century was something of a golden age for Italy's public finances. After years of large budget deficits, the Italian state ran a budget surplus in fiscal 1898/99, and (according to official statistics) surpluses continued uninterruptedly until fiscal 1911/12 (see Table 1 Appendix, pp. 297–300).[13] This achievement was more the result of economic growth and rigorous economy in public expenditure than tax reform. Both state expenditure and tax revenues tended to decline as a percentage of gross domestic product between 1900 and 1910, although sustained economic growth permitted gradually rising real tax revenues. Giolitti owed much to his leading conservative political opponent, Sidney Sonnino, for the happy state of public finances during the era of his political ascendancy. The Tuscan statesman had reorganized state finances during his tenures as Minister of Finance and Minister of the Treasury under Crispi, 1893–96, cutting expenditures, and imposing more rigorous accounting on the public bureaucracies. The curtailment of military expenditure after the African disaster in 1896 did the rest. Together, these measures facilitated the moderate increase in social spending required by Giolitti's reforms.[14]

The budget surpluses permitted a series of public debt conversions between 1903 and 1906, which replaced consols bearing 4% and 5% with new securities bearing 3% and 3.5%. It was considered one of the great achievements of the era. The largest conversion promised to spare Italy Lit. 45m. annually on debt service when it became fully operative, at a time when the total annual budget was about Lit. 1,700m.[15] More significant than the financial results of the debt conversion was the prestige value of reducing the interest on the national debt to a level comparable with the

---

[13] As is indicated in Table 1, Francesco A. Répaci calculated that the Italian state began running budget deficits again already in 1909/10. A third statistical series produced by the Ragioneria Generale dello Stato, Italy's general accounting administration, in 1969 shows deficits reappearing as early as fiscal 1905/6. Untangling Italy's public finances in this period is no easy task. As the financial situation deteriorated in the final years of the Giolittian era, the authorities used creative accounting practices to make their annual budgets look better. For example, they spread out payments to contractors over several fiscal years; the contractors in turn borrowed from financial intermediaries using their state contracts as security. In this manner, public borrowing was made to look like private borrowing. None of the statistical series reproduced in Table 1 should be looked upon as definitive. For creative accounting see, Confalonieri, *Banca e industria, 1907–1914*, vol. I, pp. 66–67.

[14] Francesco A. Répaci, *La finanza pubblica italiana nel secolo 1861–1960* (Bologna: Zanichelli, 1962), pp. 28–29, and passim; Confalonieri, *Banca e industria, 1907–1914*, vol. I, pp. 55–93.

[15] Répaci, *La finanza pubblica*, p. 117. On the debt conversions see Marcello De Cecco, ed., *L'Italia e il sistema finanziario internazionale, 1861–1914* (Bari: Laterza, 1990), pp. 39–42, 455–591.

more economically advanced states of Northwest and Central Europe. Giolitti himself was Prime Minister in 1903 and 1906 when the crucial financial operations were undertaken, and he derived considerable personal prestige from their success.

The favorable conditions which had permitted the debt conversion began to disappear, however, almost as soon as the operation was completed. Although hidden in the official statistics, moderate deficits reappeared not long after the 1906 debt conversion was concluded. Then came the Libyan War, which produced very substantial deficits for the first time since the age of Crispi. After 1911 the Italian government was no longer able to meet its financial needs by borrowing at 3.5%. In fiscal 1911/12 the Treasury began issuing 5-year treasury bonds at 4%, in the hope of refunding the debt after a few years at a more favorable rate. This, as we shall see, was not to be.[16]

Tax reform had been long on the agenda in liberal Italy, even before the reemergence of large budget deficits. But prior to the Libyan War, tax reform was more an issue of political and social justice, than of increasing revenues. At question was the large and growing weight of indirect taxation, largely on items of popular consumption, and the absence of progressive income and inheritance taxes. Beginning in 1866, a long succession of bills envisaging the reduction of consumption taxes, and their substitution with progressive income or inheritance taxes were introduced, and defeated in parliament. Giolitti himself long championed fiscal reform, railing in his speeches against a system which was "inversely progressive." However, Giolitti's commitment to fiscal reform was more rhetorical than practical. Twice, in 1893, and in 1909, he proposed progressive tax legislation when support for his cabinet in parliament was weakening for other reasons. This enabled him to fall on a "progressive" issue, and maintain his image as a man of the left. Significantly, when Leone Wollemborg produced a comprehensive tax reform package, including a progressive income tax, as Minister of Finance in the Zanardelli government in 1901, Giolitti opposed him determinedly, leading to Wollemborg's resignation. At that time Giolitti preferred to press ahead with the symbolically rich debt conversion, rather than embarking on a more fundamental and uncertain experiment in tax reform.[17]

With the Libyan War, the terms of the debate on tax reform began to

[16] Confalonieri, *Banca e industria, 1907–1914*, vol. I, pp. 75–83.
[17] For an overview of tax reform proposals, 1866–1914, see, Luigi Einaudi, *La guerra e il sistema tributario italiano* (Bari: Laterza, 1927), pp. 297–301. For a discussion of the role of tax reform in Giolitti's political career see, Nino Valeri, *Giovanni Giolitti* (Turin: UTET, 1971), passim. On Giolitti's political use of tax reform legislation in 1909 see, Carocci, *Giolitti e l'età giolittiana*, p. 65 and passim. On his opposition to Wollemborg's reform see, Aquarone, *L'Italia giolittiana*, pp. 212–13.

change. Increasing government revenue was now as pressing an issue as redistributing the tax burden; naturally, such pressures would only increase with the outbreak of World War I. Substantial new revenues, it was generally agreed, would have to come from increasing the yield of direct taxes: thus fiscal and political imperatives seemed to converge. This makes it necessary to examine Italy's system of direct taxes at some length.

Direct taxes

Italy's taxes were divided into three main categories, each of which was administered by separate administrations within the Ministry of Finance: consumption taxes, "imposte sugli affari" or transactions taxes, and direct taxes. Consumption taxes included tariffs and internal sales taxes, as well as the revenues of government monopolies on salt, tobacco, and lotto. Transaction taxes included various registration and stamp taxes, and the inheritance tax. It is impossible to make sharp analytical distinctions between consumption and transactions taxes; for example, wine and spirits taxes counted as consumption taxes, whereas registration taxes were collected on luxury items such as automobiles and perfumes. Prior to the war, there were three direct taxes: on land, buildings, and *ricchezza mobile* (as opposed to *immobili*, i.e. real estate).

As was noted in the introduction, taxes as a percentage of GNP were higher in Italy than they were in much of the rest of Europe prior to World War I. However, the relative contribution of direct taxes to revenues had been declining before 1914. In the early 1870s, direct taxes had constituted 40% or more of total revenue, and in the years before the turn of the century they still made up 37%–39%; by 1913 their share of total tax revenues had fallen to 27%. During that year transaction taxes accounted for another 15% of revenues, with consumption taxes making up fully 58%.[18]

At the outbreak of World War I, revenue from the land tax was locked in a process of secular decline. At the time of unification, the land tax had been the centerpiece of the direct tax system. It yielded Lit. 128.5m. in 1871 or 40% of direct tax revenues. By 1888 its yield had sunk to Lit. 106m. or 27% of total direct tax revenue and in 1913 it yielded only Lit. 82m. or 16%.[19] The decline in yield of the land tax stood in no proportion to the contribution of agriculture to the gross national product. Rather, the modesty of land tax yields was due to the inefficiency of the system by

---

[18] Paolo Ercolani, "Documentazione statistica di base," in Giorgio Fuà, ed., *Lo sviluppo economico in Italia*, 3rd rev. and enl. ed. (Milan: Angeli, 1978), vol. III, pp. 444–45.
[19] Répaci, *La finanza pubblica*, p. 67.

which it was assessed and to the increasing reliance of the provinces and municipalities on the land tax as their main source of revenue. At the time of Italy's unification, the land tax was collected on the basis of a quiltwork of old land registers inherited from the predecessor states. Some attempt had been made after unification to equalize the tax burden among the provinces, but the land registers had been compiled at various dates and according to radically differing criteria and this led to repeated recriminations of inequality. Finally, in 1886 a law was passed which envisaged the creation of a new, uniform national land register. By 1914, however, this new register was in place in only twenty-one of sixty-nine provinces. The fears and remonstrances of landowners and their political representatives in provinces where the old assessments were relatively light inhibited the progress of revision there. The central government agreed to begin implementing the new register in provinces where local authorities were prepared to put up half of the costs. These were naturally provinces that expected to see their tax obligations reduced as a result of the reassessment. Hence the implementation of the new register actually caused land tax revenues to decline. The total yield of the land tax was further reduced by a law of 1900 which allowed for fiscal deductions of up to 30% for the provinces of southern Italy, which had been hard hit by agricultural depression during the tariff war with France.

Provincial and municipal governments derived a substantial part of their income from surcharges on the state land tax. As provincial and local expenditures for purposes such as road construction and repair, social projects, education, and sanitation expanded, the surtaxes came to weigh more than twice as heavily as the state taxes themselves. Central state authorities concluded that if state taxes on the land were light, the overall burden of land taxes did not permit the extraction of significantly greater sums from the tax.[20]

The building tax was meant to tax the income stemming from all real property that fell outside the purview of the land tax. Agricultural utility buildings were exempt as the income they produced was considered to be already covered by the land tax. Residential buildings were taxed whether or not the owner lived in them. Although provinces and municipalities also imposed increasingly heavy surtaxes on the building tax, it produced steadily increasing revenues for the state in the decades after unification. In 1866 it yielded Lit. 32.5m. or 21% of direct tax revenues, in 1888 Lit. 67.5m. or 17%, and in 1913 Lit. 108m. or 21%.[21]

The third and by far the most important of the direct taxes was that on

---

[20] Einaudi, *Il sistema tributario*, pp. 7–11.
[21] Répaci, *La finanza pubblica*, p. 67; Einaudi, *Il sistema tributario*, pp. 11–12.

ricchezza mobile. Like the other direct taxes, the *ricchezza mobile* was real, rather than personal, although it contained certain features typical of personal taxes. The tax fell on all incomes derived from sources other than real property. Personal income was not taxed as a whole; rather, each individual source of income was taxed separately. The personal aspects of the tax included an exemption for minimum incomes, an exemption from a surtax that had been imposed to raise relief funds after the Messina earthquake of 1908 for somewhat larger incomes, and an exemption for interest payments on debts. A distinction was made between "unearned income" or *redditi di puro capitale* and "earned income" or *redditi di lavoro puro*, as was the case in England after 1907/8. The former was taxed more heavily than the latter. Italian tax tables were in fact divided into a number of further categories, which took into account the relative degree of risk of invested capital, the mixed incomes of the self-employed, which were considered to derive from a combination of capital and labor, and so on. The tax on *ricchezza mobile* had become the mainstay of the Italian tax system by the eve of World War I. It had been created shortly after unification on the basis of a hodgepodge of direct taxes that had been levied earlier by the predecessor states. In 1865, the first year in which it was in place, it yielded Lit. 65.8m. or 33% of direct tax revenues. These figures grew to Lit. 216m. or 55% of direct tax revenues by 1888 and to Lit. 329m. or fully 63% of direct tax revenues by 1913. At this time, the *ricchezza mobile* tax made up roughly one-sixth of total Italian tax revenues.[22]

In its main features, the direct tax system in Italy was clearly less efficient and less equitable than those in place in Great Britain and the United States, as it taxed income-earning activities, rather than total personal income; but it was more efficient and more equitable than the German and French systems. In Germany the central state enjoyed no permanent direct tax revenue at all. Direct taxes had been left as a prerogative to the individual states at the time of German unification. In 1913 the Reich imposed an extraordinary military levy on "increases in wealth," but collection was only beginning at the outbreak of war. France had an array of real direct taxes like Italy, but the system was more fragmented and conceptually less coherent.[23]

The problem with the Italian tax system, at least in comparison with the other continental powers, lay not so much in its conception, but in its

[22] Répaci, *La finanza pubblica*, p. 67; Einaudi, *Il sistema tributario*, pp. 12–16.
[23] On Germany see Fritz Fischer, *Krieg der Illusionen* (Düsseldorf: Droste, 1969), pp. 257–69; on France, Henri Truchy, "How France Met Her War Expenditure," in Gaston Jeze and Henri Truchy, *The War Finances of France* (New Haven: Yale University Press, 1927), pp. 204–6; Alfred Sauvy, *Histoire économique de la France entre les deux guerres*, III (Paris: Economica, 1984), pp. 74–78.

implementation. As Luigi Einaudi pointed out, tax rates were exceedingly high by pre-World War I standards. As was noted in the Introduction, the officials of the Ministry of Finance bargained with citizens about their declared taxable income; the figures agreed upon were usually far lower than real income. Inevitably, these informal agreements resulted in considerable inequality in tax burden borne by individuals and firms. Moreover, because official rates were high, they could not be screwed much higher in wartime without exposing the fictitious nature of assessments. Moreover, because the tax burden was distributed unequally, higher rates would have imposed financial ruin on taxpayers with relatively onerous effective assessments, even though the burden on more modestly assessed taxpayers still would have been very light.[24]

In sum, two reforms would have been necessary to increase substantially revenues from direct taxes: tax assessments would have had to be brought up to date and made more accurate, and a personal income tax would have to be introduced. The latter measure was a necessary precondition for creating a rational system of progressive taxation. Before 1911 these reforms were championed by social reformers, concerned about the inequitable distribution of the tax burden; after the Libyan War, and the massive budget deficits it engendered, tax reform became more pressing for purely fiscal reasons. However, nothing was done before 1914, and Italy – like the other continental powers – entered the conflict with an antiquated tax structure, ill-suited to raising the huge revenues required by total war.

Public borrowing, and the controversy over the Istituto Nazionale delle Assicurazioni

The debt conversions of the Giolittian era were made possible by the existence of segmented credit markets. Postal savings banks, savings banks, and cooperative and popular banks were required to hold a proportion of their assets in state securities. During Giolitti's fourth ministry, 1911–13, the government sought to extend its privileged access to the credit markets by creating a state monopoly on life insurance policies.

The proposal was part of Giolitti's program of establishing the voluntary social security system on a firmer basis. However, the project had another dimension, the significance of which became particularly clear after the Libyan War and the return of large budget deficits. The national life insurance company was to hold primarily government securities in its portfolio. The proposal ran into strong opposition. Antonio Salandra and

---

[24] Einaudi, *Il sistema tributario*, pp. 16–18.

the parliamentary right, supported by the major banking and industrial interests, and almost the entire national press – including papers which normally supported Giolitti – bitterly attacked the proposed life insurance monopoly. In the end, parliament passed a watered-down version of the government's bill, which allowed private companies to continue operating alongside the state-owned company for ten years; thereafter, parliament was to decide whether or not to grant the state company a monopoly based on its performance. This legislation fell short of what Giolitti needed to keep down interest rates on public borrowing, and the celebrated debt conversions of the early century were in danger of coming undone. Moreover, the parliamentary right emerged strengthened from the controversy, and Salandra's stature as Giolitti's principal rival for power was consolidated.[25]

The banking system on the eve of World War I

Gerschenkron was certainly correct to maintain that the German- inspired mixed or universal banks contributed substantially to the development of new industries in Italy during the years of sustained economic growth, 1898–1907; however, he failed to come to terms with the negative consequences of a system of industrial finance based on mixed banking. Gerschenkron's decidedly favorable assessment of the workings of the banking system is belied not only by more recent scholarly work on Italian financial history, but also by the judgments of many commentators during the Giolittian era. The involvement of deposit-taking banks in industrial promotion is inherently pro-cyclical and lends instability to the financial system. This problem has been at the center of recent revisionist studies directed against Gerschenkron's thesis, notably those of Bonelli and Confalonieri, and need be summarized only briefly here.[26]

---

[25] On the financial implications of the proposed national life insurance monopoly see, Antonio Scialoja, "L'Istituto nazionale delle assicurazioni e il progetto giolittiano di un monopolio di stato delle assicurazioni sulla vita," *Quaderni Storici*, 6 (1971), pp. 971–1027. On the policy of creating a privileged credit market for state securities generally see, Confalonieri, *Banca e industria, 1907–1914*, vol. I, pp. 88–93; vol. II, pp. 480–81.

[26] Alexander Gerschenkron, "Economic Backwardness in Historical Perspective," and "Notes on the Rate of Industrial Growth in Italy," in *Economic Backwardness in Historical Perspective: A Book of Essays* (Cambridge MA: Harvard University Press, 1962), pp. 5–30, 72–89; Franco Bonelli, *La crisi del 1907. Una tappa dello sviluppo industriale in Italia* (Turin: Fondazione Luigi Einaudi, 1971); Franco Bonelli, "Osservazioni e dati sul finanziamento dell'industria italiana all'inizio del secolo XX," *Annali della Fondazione Luigi Einaudi*, 2 (1968), pp. 264–71; Antonio Confalonieri, *Banca e industria in Italia (1894–1906)*, 3 vols. (Milan: Banca Commerciale Italiana, 1977–80); Confalonieri, *Banca e Industria, 1907–1914*. On the pro-cyclical bias of mixed banking see also Gianni Toniolo's comments in Banco di Roma, *Banca e industria fra le due guerre. Atti del convegno conclusivo della ricerca promossa dal Banco di Roma in occasione del suo primo centenario* (Bologna: Il Mulino, 1981), p. 132, and passim.

Confalonieri has demonstrated that in the pre-World War I years Italy's universal banks, notably the Banca Commerciale and the Credito Italiano, did not aspire to become holding companies, by retaining majority interests of the industrial concerns whose securities they promoted. Rather, the key goals in the banks' industrial promotion activities were to earn profits through underwriting commissions, and by acquiring the normal, commercial banking business of the firms they sponsored. Nevertheless, the practices of the commercial banks made them almost as vulnerable both to fluctuations in the earning potential and in the equity value of the manufacturing firms they maintained relations with, as if they had owned the firms outright. In addition to underwriting stock and bond issues, the major commercial banks extended substantial loans to the manufacturing firms with which they maintained close relations. The banks not only supplied working capital to industrial firms, but also funds for fixed investments. Frequently, loans for long-term investments were made formally as short-term commercial loans, in order to make the banks' portfolios appear more liquid than they actually were. Such nominally commercial, but in reality illiquid loans were regularly turned over on maturity. Deposit-taking banks thus assumed the high risks associated with industrial promotion. The banks' exposure to their industrial clients left them with little choice but to extend new credits when the latter experienced financial difficulties, in order to protect their original investments.

The stability of the commercial banks was linked directly to the stock market by two additional factors. First, the profits of the banks' underwriting activity depended on the ebullience of the stock market; if the market went down, major new security issues would be precluded, and blocks of shares still in the process of being issued by the banks would remain in their hands. Secondly, the banks encouraged firms with which they maintained close relations to borrow against collateral deposits of their own securities, making the loan portfolios of the banks highly vulnerable to fluctuations in stock values. As a consequence, the banks intervened habitually on the stock markets to support the value of industrial securities which they had underwritten. It is evident that in such a system the banks stood to take significant losses in the event of a major stock market panic.

In brief, the system of industrial finance predicated on mixed banking allowed for rapid economic growth in Giolittian Italy, but also made the banking system exceedingly unstable. The vulnerability of the banking system to financial crises, in turn, threatened to interrupt the process of industrial growth. In this regard, Bonelli has underscored the significance of the economic and financial crisis of 1907, which marked a decisive turning point in Italian industrial development. As was noted above, economic growth slowed significantly after 1907. An important obstacle to continued rapid economic growth after the crisis of 1907 was the failure of the financial system to generate sufficient capital for industrial investment.

The crisis was preceded by an intense stock market boom. Many essentially sound manufacturing firms, including some, like Pirelli and Fiat, that would become leading industrial enterprises, raised significant sums on the market in the boom years 1903–7, and utilized fresh capital for productive investments. But many other poorly organized and technically deficient firms, often founded for speculative purposes, also issued stock and obligations. The commercial banks bore considerable responsibility for this wave of unbridled stock market speculation. As was noted above, they encouraged firms to borrow against collateral deposits of their own securities and intervened on the market to support the value of industrial securities. Particularly the smaller and less conservative competitors of the two largest commercial banks, the Banca Commerciale and the Credito Italiano, were deeply involved in promoting more speculative issues. Worse still, some of the more unscrupulous banks and the stockbrokers close to them engaged in bearish speculation against the securities of firms close to their competitors, creating considerable turbulence and insecurity on the markets.

The Italian stock market boom collapsed in the wake of the international monetary tensions created by the New York financial crisis of 1907. Private investors sustained enormous losses and were reluctant to return to the stock exchanges in subsequent years. The predominance of a few large operators on the stock markets, and their ability to make large speculative profits at the expense of the general investing public created distrust for industrial securities. After 1907, the savings generated by Italy's middle classes were diverted into investments that were perceived as being more secure, including national and foreign government securities, and savings bank deposits, while demand for industrial securities stagnated. The commercial banks, which had also sustained significant losses in the crisis, now were concerned to maintain higher liquidity ratios and became reluctant to finance new industrial investments out of their own resources. Industrial investment and economic growth consequently slowed.

New and less stable financial circuits developed as a partial, but inadequate substitution for the industrial securities market. The commercial banks continued to extend new loans to the least profitable among their larger clients in order to prevent them from becoming insolvent. As had been the case before the crisis, these loans were frequently carried on the banks' books as if they were short term, even though they were actually illiquid and repeatedly had to be renewed. In contrast to the commercial banks, the savings banks were confronted with an excess of resources in relation to the investment opportunities in which they were allowed to engage, according to their statutes. As a consequence, they were increasingly drawn into industrial finance, especially through a type of operation whereby the savings banks made loans to firms against the guarantee of two commercial banks.[27]

Economic commentators during the Giolittian era were sensitive to many of the issues later raised by Bonelli and Confalonieri, as they have been summarized above. In particular, in the years before World War I a debate arose in the financial press about the inadequacies of the mixed banks and the need to develop a more reliable source of investment and venture capital for industry.[28] But the pre-war Italian banking system was not only structurally unstable, but also profoundly riven by political and institutional conflicts. At the heart of these conflicts was the inability of the Bank of Italy to control effectively the national credit market, and its poor relations with the largest commercial banks. The problem of the lack of "bank cooperation," as it was often referred to in the economic literature of the time, excited a second great debate in the financial press.[29] However, contemporary economic historians have shown less interest in this problem, largely because it has no important implications for the Italian banking system today, whereas the problem of the relative weakness of the Italian market for industrial securities remains an issue of great immediate relevance. Nevertheless, the issues raised in the pre-war debate about central bank influence and cooperation among the major financial institutions is critical for an understanding of the history of banking during and after World War I, and in particular the spectacular events of that period: the "parallel wars" between rival financial groups, the liquidity crisis, and the bank failures and rescues of 1921–23.

The Bank of Italy's weakness on the credit markets and its poor relations with the largest commercial banks, was largely a product of events stemming from the financial crisis of 1893. In that year, Italy was beset by a severe bank crisis, which resulted in the failure of the country's two largest commercial banks, the Credito Mobiliare and the Banca Generale, along with the Banca Romana, one of the six issue banks that the Kingdom of Italy had inherited from the predecessor states. The bank reforms of the 1890s restricted the privilege of issuing bank notes to three institutions:

---

[27] On the crisis of 1907 see, Bonelli, *La crisi del 1907*; on the commercial banks after the crisis see, Confalonieri, *Banca e industria, 1907–1914*, vol. I, passim.

[28] Bonelli, "Finanziamento dell'industria italiana all'inizio del secolo XX"; Confalonieri, *Banca e industria 1907–1914*, vol. II, pp. 493–515.

[29] F. S. Nitti, "Il capitale straniero in Italia," in *Scritti di economia e finanza*, ed. Domenico Demarco, vol. III, pt. 2 (Bari: Laterza, 1966), pp. 375–468 (original ed. 1915); "Limiti e caratteri di possibili accordi fra i grandi banchi," unsigned, *Finanza italiana*, 9 June 1917; 'Verso la solidarità fra le banche italiane," unsigned, *Finanza italiana*, 10 November 1917; "L'accordo fra le grande banche italiane," unsigned, *Finanza italiana*, 6 July 1918.

the Bank of Italy, which was formed by amalgamating the pre-existing northern and central Italian issue banks, and two small southern banks, the Banco di Napoli, and the Banco di Sicilia. These three institutions were subjected to a strict code, which limited the kind of financial activities they were allowed to engage in, and set interest penalties for issuing notes above certain reserve ceilings. These measures no doubt produced a more rational and stable financial system, and helped create the basis for the subsequent spurt of investment and economic growth, but they also established the conditions for a new set of tensions in the banking system.[30]

In addition to the Piedmontese and Tuscan issue banks, the Bank of Italy was constrained to absorb the Rome-based Banca Romana, which had been heavily compromised in the financial crisis. Consequently, the Bank of Italy was born with a portfolio of bad loans and over-valued real estate assets, which it was obligated to liquidate gradually over the following two decades. In contrast, the Banca Commerciale Italiana was an institution created *ex-nuovo* by foreign interests after the worst period of financial distress was already over. It was in no wise compromised by the collapse of the earlier commercial banks, although it was able to build up quickly a clientele among the sounder industrial and commercial firms that had previously banked with the failed institutions. The nucleus of the Credito Italiano was a smaller Genoese bank that had been hurt in the crisis, and the new bank had considerable difficulties in its early years; however, it was able to reorganize itself on a strong financial basis in the last years of the nineteenth century and to participate in the first important wave of Italian industrial expansion.[31]

As a result, the Bank of Italy was unable to assume strong leadership in monetary policy or in regulating the financial markets in the first years of its existence, because of its need to reorganize and strengthen its own portfolio.[32] As the Bank of Italy became stronger after the turn of the century, it sought to pursue a more active monetary policy; however, by this time the two major Milanese banks had already achieved a dominant position in the Italian financial world and were ill-disposed to submit to the direction of the premier issue bank. The conflict between the Bank of Italy and the commercial banks in pre-war Italy bears much resemblance to the conflict during the same period between the Bank of England and the major English joint-stock banks. However, whereas in Britain grow-

---

[30] On the bank crisis of the 1890s, and the establishment of the Bank of Italy see esp., Confalonieri, *Banca e industria, 1894–1906*, vol. I.

[31] Ibid., vol. II, pp. 297–417; vol. III, passim.

[32] On the Bank of Italy see Pierluigi Ciocca, "Note sulla politica monetaria italiana 1900–1913," in Gianni Toniolo, ed., *Lo sviluppo economico italiano*, (Bari: Laterza, 1973), pp. 241–82; Confalonieri, *Banca e industria, 1894–1906*, vol. II, pp. 87–211.

ing tensions between the Bank of England and the clearing house banks were caused by the decline in influence and market share of the Bank of England, and the growing importance of its private competitors, in Italy after the turn of the century it was the premier issue bank that was increasing its financial strength and influence on the market and thereby challenging the previously uncontested dominance of the major commercial banks.[33]

The Bank of Italy clashed in its policy goals with the major commercial banks in almost every area. Similar to the English situation before World War I, the fundamental source of tension between the premier issue bank and the major commercial banks was their status as direct competitors on the financial markets. Like the Bank of England, the Bank of Italy was not exclusively a banker's bank, but also did business directly with commercial and manufacturing firms. And like the Bank of England, the Bank of Italy was obliged to remunerate its private shareholders by realizing a profit on its commercial transactions. Sayers' adage for the Bank of England, that it had a duty to be rich, that is, that it had to distribute satisfactory dividends to its shareholders in order to achieve the stability necessary to pursue an active public policy, was no less true for the Bank of Italy. Achieving a satisfactory level of profitability was by no means easy for the Bank of Italy in the early years of the century, burdened as it was with the portfolio of the Banca Romana. At its inception, the Bank paid annual dividends of only Lit. 18 on nominal shares of Lit. 600, although it was able to raise its dividends to Lit. 48 in the final years of peace.[34]

Bank of Italy officials were acutely aware of the commercial banks' competition for its commercial clientele. Bonaldo Stringher, General Director of the Bank from 1900 to 1928 and governor until his death in 1930, told his board in 1905 that the commercial banks were able to offer interest charges on good commercial paper only slightly above their passive interest rates because they could supplement low profits in this business with higher profits on more speculative activities, in which the Bank of Italy was forbidden by law to engage.[35] The Bank of Italy authorities were also dismayed by the inability of the Bank to attract substantial deposits, given the statutory limit of the issue banks' passive interest rates to one-third of the official discount rate, and the considerably higher rates offered by the commercial banks. When Stringher won approval in 1909

[33] On the Bank of England see Richard Sidney Sayers, *The Bank of England, 1891–1944* (New York: Cambridge University Press, 1976); Marcello De Cecco, *Moneta e impero. Il sistema finanziario internazionale dal 1890 al 1914* (Turin: Einaudi, 1979).
[34] Ciocca, "Note sulla politica monetaria italiana 1900–1913"; Banca d'Italia, *Adunanza generale ordinaria degli azionisti della Banca d'Italia* (Rome: Banca d'Italia) (published annually).
[35] Confalonieri, *Banca e industria, 1894–1906*, vol. III, pp. 438–39.

for a modification of this law, which allowed the issue banks to raise passive interest rates to three-quarters of the interest rates paid by the savings banks, the measure elicited protests and disapproval from the directors of the Banca Commerciale.[36]

A second important area of tension stemmed from the unwillingness of the major commercial banks to hold a part of their reserves, and rediscount a significant part of their commercial portfolios with the issue banks. Bank of Italy authorities were eager to encourage the development of the institution's role as a bankers' bank, not only because it promised to increase the Bank's earning potential, but even more importantly because it enhanced the Bank's capacity to influence the credit markets. Similar to the Bank of England, the Bank of Italy was concerned to make its discount rates effective on the market. The Bank of Italy's preoccupation with controlling prevailing interest rates was in fact even greater than that of its English counterpart. Like the Bank of England, it sought to manipulate the discount rate to attract gold to Italy in order to defend the lira during periods of monetary strain, but unlike the English issue bank it also sought to use its discount policy to control the level of domestic business activity. Bank of Italy authorities were bound to take a broader view of their role in regulating the domestic economy than appeared necessary in England, precisely because of the instability endemic to a financial system predicated on mixed banking. Given the intimate involvement of the commercial banks in industrial finance, in times of financial crisis the central bank in Italy was the ultimate source of liquidity not only for the banking system, but for industrial concerns as well.[37]

The directors of the commercial banks, however, resisted all efforts of the Bank of Italy to gain influence over their lending policies. In fact, the major Milanese banks essentially created their own autonomous monetary system by holding the reserves and rediscounting the commercial paper of smaller banks that moved in their orbits. The comparison with the British situation is again instructive: unlike the London clearing house bankers, who demanded a say in the formulation of British monetary policy as a precondition for their cooperation with the Bank of England, the directors of the Milanese banks apparently resisted the idea that the Italian issue banks should actively regulate the credit markets at all. The determination with which the commercial bankers resisted the efforts of the Bank of Italy to regulate the credit markets bears comparison with the imperious behavior of European bankers in Latin America or other semi-colonial environments at the beginning of the century, and it produced a hostility

[36] Confalonieri, *Banca e industria, 1907–1914*, vol. I, p. 136.
[37] On the Bank of England see, Sayers, *The Bank of England*, esp. pp. 37–46; on the Bank of Italy see esp., Confalonieri, *Banca e industria, 1907–1914*, vol. I, pp. 132–41.

among central bankers and political leaders that would have important repercussions during the war and post-war years.

More or less in opposition to the two Milanese banks, the Bank of Italy built up a clientele of smaller banks that cooperated with it by holding their reserves in correspondence accounts and rediscounting a part of their commercial portfolios with the issue banks. Among these the Bank of Italy particularly encouraged the expansion of a third Milanese commercial bank, the Società Bancaria Italiana (SBI), as a competitor of the two larger institutions. But the Bank of Italy's partnership with the SBI proved disastrous. As a relative latecomer to the Milanese commercial banking world – the SBI was founded as the Società Bancaria Milanese in 1899, five years after the Banca Commerciale and four years after the Credito Italiano – the smaller bank was unable to build up an industrial clientele as select or as stable as that of its older and larger competitors. The SBI was formed from the merger of a series of smaller banks, and the central administration never gained a good overview of the activities of the branches. In essence, the SBI was not a large bank, despite its nominal size, but rather a constellation of unamalgamated smaller banks. One of the component parts, the Banca di Sconto e di Seta of Turin, was absorbed by the SBI in 1905, when the former was on the verge of failure. Evidently, the business of the Sconto continued to be a drain on the resources and profitability of the Milanese institution. Moreover, a group of stock market speculators in Genoa bought up shares of the SBI and were able substantially to take control of the Genoa branch, which they then used to approve substantial loans to themselves.[38]

The essential dilemma for the Bank of Italy was that the one larger bank willing to cooperate with it did so because of its inherent weakness. Paradoxically, the Bank of Italy, in its efforts to gain greater control over the Italian banking system in order to promote stability, ended up by making common cause with the most speculative elements in the financial community against the more cautious and stable institutions. Further, in its eagerness to expand its rediscounting business, the Bank of Italy actually encouraged the SBI and other smaller institutions to be less prudent in their commercial lending business than they would have been otherwise. The Bank of Italy's policies thus contributed to the wave of speculation that culminated in the financial crisis of 1907. Not surprisingly, the SBI was the first among the major banks to lose the confidence of depositors during the crisis. As the SBI had rediscounted heavily its portfolio with the Bank of Italy already, its remaining liquid resources were inadequate to meet the run. It was only saved *in extremis* through the intervention of the Bank of Italy, and its directors were forced to devalue its capital from Lit.

[38] On the SBI see, in particular, Bonelli, *La crisi del 1907*, passim.

50m. to Lit. 20m. As a consequence, the SBI virtually lost its position as a serious competitor of the Banca Commerciale and the Credito Italiano.[39]

But the collapse of the SBI did nothing to resolve the underlying conflict between the Banca Commerciale and the Credito Italiano on the one hand and the Bank of Italy on the other. Stringher continued to challenge the Milanese financial establishment, alternately by favoring the Credito Italiano, encouraging it to detach itself from the Commerciale and enter into closer relations with the Bank of Italy, and by supporting the foundation of yet another rival institution. The rise and fall of the Banca Italiana di Sconto during the World War I and post-war years would essentially repeat the history of the SBI at the beginning of the century.

The conflict of the Bank of Italy with the major commercial banks over regulation of the credit markets inevitably led to divergent views on how the banking community should meet a financial crisis. An attentive reader of Bagehot, Stringher was convinced that the Bank of Italy should act as lender of last resort in the event of a crisis. However, he was convinced also that the Bank should not take this function upon itself alone, but rather should act as leader of a syndicate that would include all of the leading financial institutions in the event of a run on deposits or a major bank failure. Not just the Bank of Italy, but the entire banking community should share in the burden of maintaining confidence in the system, given that a depositors' run on a single bank was likely to produce a general crisis of confidence and thus imperil the stability of all banks. Stringher's attitude in this regard was almost certainly influenced by the behavior of the Bank of England in the Baring Crisis in 1890. Being an institution that was charged with extraordinary public duties, but also had obligations to its private shareholders, the Bank of England took care to limit its role in the depositors' run on the merchant banking firm Baring & Co. to assuming a leadership role in the formation of a rescue syndicate, which all of the major merchant bankers were obliged to join.[40]

The leadership of the Milanese commercial banks, in particular the Banca Commerciale, rejected Stringher's views on the obligations of the banking community in the event of financial crisis and argued that the Bank of Italy was seeking to make them coresponsible for the imprudent behavior of their less scrupulous competitors. They suggested that the Bank of Italy's excessive concern to avoid bank failures actually diminished the stability of the system by encouraging a sense of impunity on the part of reckless bank administrators. Not surprisingly, the Banca Commerciale and Credito Italiano directors were loath to participate in a consortium to rescue their ambitious competitor, the Società Bancaria Italiana, in 1907.

---

[39] Ibid., esp. pp. 151–55.
[40] On the Baring crisis see, De Cecco, *Moneta e impero*, pp. 119–35.

Stringher held the two banks responsible for the total loss of public confidence in the SBI because of their hesitation to join a rescue syndicate headed by the Bank of Italy and their tardiness in taking defensive measures. Only when the panic threatened to spread beyond the SBI to the other banks and the stock market in general did the major Milanese banks cooperate in good faith with the Bank of Italy.[41]

A similar conflict between the Bank of Italy and the Banca Commerciale flared up in 1912, when Stringher urged the Milanese bank to acquire the failing Banca di Lecco, stressing the general interest in maintaining public confidence in the banking system. Banca Commerciale director Otto Joel turned down Stringher's request, insisting on his supreme duty to preserve the stability of the Commerciale itself.[42]

Finally, there was a political dimension to the tensions between the Bank of Italy and the major commercial banks. Unlike the leadership of central banks in other European countries, the directors of the Bank of Italy were not drawn primarily from the world of *haute finance*. Stringher and other top officials in the Bank of Italy began their careers as government officials – Stringher had been Director General of the Treasury prior to assuming the directorship of the issue bank – and they were more sensitive to the goals and concerns of the Italian state's political and administrative leadership than they were to those of the financial community. The essential identification of the Bank of Italy with government policy produced conflicts with the Milanese financial community in two important areas: state financial policy, and foreign policy.

Stringher was intimately involved in the conversion of the Italian state debt beginning in 1903. The Bank of Italy seconded government policy by favoring easy money and low interest rates, so as to reduce the attractiveness of alternatives to the new, low-interest government bonds.[43] In later years he played a major role in every government financial operation. In the early years of the century, the Milanese financial elite was more or less favorable to government financial policy, as the reduction in state borrowing freed financial resources for private investment, and the reduction in interest payments on government bonds enhanced the attractiveness of industrial securities for investors. However, the banking establishment began to oppose vehemently government financial policy, and hence the Bank of Italy's measures on behalf of the government, in the final years before World War I.

This change occurred after state budget deficits mounted as a consequence of the Libyan War. The Milanese commercial banks were in the

[41] Bonelli, *La crisi del 1907*.
[42] Confalonieri, *Banca e industria, 1907–1914*, vol. I, p. 137.
[43] Confalonieri, *Banca e industria, 1894–1906*, vol. II, pp. 146–64.

vanguard of opposition to the state monopoly on life insurance after 1911, accusing the government of seeking to establish a privileged market for its own securities to the detriment of private borrowers. Proponents of the life insurance monopoly countered by accusing the banks of putting the interests of their foreign minority shareholders – the majority of the Italian life insurance business was in the hands of foreign, particularly Austrian companies – above Italian national interests. Stringher not only publicly supported the life insurance monopoly, but even agreed to assume the honorific position of President of the Istituto Nazionale delle Assicurazioni (INA, or National Insurance Institute) when it was established in 1913.[44] Throughout the Giolittian era, and indeed throughout his career as a central banker, Stringher acted on the principle that government borrowing requirements represented the foremost national interest, and should be given first priority in periods of capital scarcity. The Milanese commercial bankers, in contrast, accused Giolitti's final pre-war government of seeking to avoid pursuing fiscally responsible policies by creating artificial financial circuits that allowed the state to borrow on the cheap.

In addition to exacerbating tensions with Stringher and the Bank of Italy, the Milanese commercial bankers' determined opposition to the national life insurance monopoly earned them another important enemy within Italy's political elite – Francesco Saverio Nitti. Giolitti had appointed the ambitious young radical deputy Minister of Industry, Commerce and Agriculture in his fourth ministry, and in this capacity Nitti was responsible for drawing up and defending the life insurance bill in parliament. Nitti had already had a brush with the Milanese banks earlier in his political career. As a young deputy from the South, he had campaigned in the early years of the century for public ownership of hydroelectric resources in the river basins surrounding Naples; contrary to his wishes, however, the Società Meridionale di Electricità, a private firm with close ties to the Commerciale, eventually won and developed the major concessions. Now Nitti saw the Milanese banks dilute and compromise the major piece of legislation he sponsored during his first ministerial post. He came away from the experience embittered, and convinced that the Milanese banks held too much economic and political power. As we shall see, it was not the last the directors of the Banca Commerciale would hear of Nitti.[45]

The final area of controversy between the Bank of Italy and the Milanese commercial banks was in foreign policy. The Milanese business

---

[44] On the life insurance monopoly see, Scialoja, "L'istituto nazionale delle assicurazioni"; on the proposal requiring banks to hold fixed proportions of their assets in government securities see, Confalonieri, *Banca e industria, 1907–1914*, vol. II, pp. 478–82.

[45] On Nitti and the hydroelectric concessions in the Naples region see, Francesco Barbagallo, *Nitti* (Turin: UTET, 1984), pp. 116–18; on Nitti and the life insurance monopoly, pp. 165–68.

elite had strongly opposed Crispi's colonial expansionism in the 1890s, and it supported Giulio Prinetti's (Foreign Minister in the Zanardelli––Giolitti government, 1901–3) policy of colonial retrenchment and *rapprochement* with France at the beginning of the century. When, however, the Italian Foreign Ministry began to renew its efforts to expand Italian political and economic influence abroad from about 1908, new tensions arose between the Consulta and the Milanese commercial banks. The Italian government, strongly seconded by Stringher, sought to interest the major commercial banks in the areas in the Mediterranean basin and the Balkans marked out for imperialist expansion.

But despite the imperialist sentiment of broad elements of the Italian middle classes, including many clients of the two banks, the banks' directors were far from enthusiastic about projects proposed by the Consulta primarily for political purposes that offered indifferent or uncertain prospects for economic returns. In fact, the Comit and the Credit were much more interested in developing foreign branches and subsidiaries in London and Latin America, where economic prospects seemed bright, than in the Balkans and North Africa. Both banks participated only reluctantly and very modestly in the share capital of newly formed issue banks in Morocco, Albania, and Abyssinia, under strong pressure from the Italian government.[46] Similarly, the Comit and Credit were pressured by Stringher to participation in a syndicate to finance the ambitious trans-Balkan railway, the cornerstone of the Consulta's policy in that region, in 1912, but the two banks insisted on keeping their investment to a minimum. They were no doubt relieved when political complications delayed the project until the outbreak of war in 1914, at which point it was dropped permanently.[47]

True, the Comit founded two subsidiaries, one to engage in industrial and commercial activities, and the other to engage in banking in the Ottoman Empire in 1907. The Comit leadership seems to have viewed these ventures as potentially lucrative; but in 1911, after the financial results of the Ottoman bank had proven disappointing, the Comit sold its interests to the Banco di Roma, while retaining its control over the commercial and industrial organization.[48]

The willingness of the Comit's directors to invest in properties in Montenegro in collaboration with the adventurist Giuseppe Volpi probably was due more to their concern to maintain the lucrative banking business of Volpi's domestic industrial empire, including the mammoth

[46] On the Moroccan, Albanian, and Abyssinian issue banks see, Confalonieri, *Banca e industria, 1907–1914*, vol. I, pp. 403–6.
[47] Ibid., vol. I, pp. 406–14.
[48] Ibid., vol. I, pp. 414–20.

Società Adriatica di Elettricità (SADE), than to their persuasion that huge profits were to be had in the Dalmatian hinterlands. Volpi himself may have been motivated in his Dalmatian projects more by the advantages to be gained by cultivating the good will of Italy's foreign policy establishment than by his assessment of the earning potential of the Balkan projects themselves. The Montenegrin investments represented in any case a minuscule fraction of the Banca Commerciale's portfolio, and their significance has been vastly overrated by some historians.[49]

Although the Milanese bankers were on the whole reluctant to make investments abroad to further the Consulta's political interests, they were deeply involved in financing domestic industries, such as subsidized navigation lines, shipbuilding, iron and steel, and armaments manufacturing, that profited from the government's bellicose imperialist policies. Indeed, the limited cooperation of the Banca Commerciale and the Credito Italiano with the Consulta's imperialist projects probably owed much to the concern of the Milanese bankers to maintain good relations with the government in order to protect the defense-related contracts and shipping line subsidies of their client firms.

The international financial connections of the major Milanese banks exercised a countervailing influence. The Comit and the Credit had important business relations with leading financial circles in all of the great European powers: their branches in London were highly profitable and allowed them to make use of the London discount market to finance international trade; their relations with French and Belgian banks provided them with ready access to the cheap capital markets of those countries and proved instrumental in developing subsidiaries in Latin America; their relations with German bankers allowed them to make lucrative, low-risk investments in electrical enterprises in Italy originally developed by German companies.[50] Consequently, the Milanese banks were bound to oppose any policy that was likely to lead to a deterioration in Italy's relations with any of the great powers. The Italian commercial banks hence found themselves in the contradictory position of being simultaneously financiers of domestic rearmament and champions of international concord.[51]

Although the share of Comit and Credit stock in foreign hands had declined to a minority interest in the first years of the century, a dis-

[49] My interpretation agrees substantially with that of Confalonieri, *Banca e industria, 1907–1914*, vol. I, pp. 414–20, and contrasts with that of Richard A. Webster, *Industrial Imperialism in Italy*, pp. 310–22, and passim. On Volpi see also Sergio Romano, *Giuseppe Volpi: Industria e finanza fra Giolitti e Mussolini* (Milan: Bompiani, 1979).

[50] Confalonieri, *Banca e industria, 1907–1914*, passim; Peter Hertner, *Il capitale tedesco in Italia dall'unità alla prima guerra mondiale* (Bologna: Il Mulino, 1984).

[51] See, Brunello Vigezzi, "Otto Joel, il principe di Bülow e i problemi della neutralità," in *Da Giolitti a Salandra* (Florence: Vallecchi, 1969), pp. 203–62.

proportionate number of foreign directors still sat on the boards of the two banks. The opposition of foreign directors to participation in Balkan and colonial projects urged on the banks by the Italian Foreign Ministry and Stringher has been documented by Confalonieri.[52] It is noteworthy that the two banks' managing directors were subject to criticism by foreign board members in cases where the bank participated in colonial and imperial ventures to placate Italian government and central bank authorities. Of course, the self-evident interest of the major Milanese banks in peace and international cooperation, and the presence of foreign board members opposing colonial and imperial adventures made the banks vulnerable to charges of a lack of patriotism on the part of the nationalist right. There is evidence that Stringher in part shared such nationalist views. As a life-long government official and native of the border province of Friuli, where irredentist sentiment ran high, Stringher was inclined to equate foreign expansion with the supreme national interest. In 1911 he was even vice-president of the moderately nationalist Dante Aligheri Society.[53]

Significantly, it was the more speculative elements in the Italian financial community that were most disposed to cooperate with the government in its colonial and imperial program. Evidently with the encouragement of the Consulta, the Banco di Roma, a Roman bank with close ties to the black or Catholic aristocracy of the capital, and the Vatican itself, opened a series of branches in Libya in the years prior to the Italian invasion. The Roma also established itself at Alexandria in Egypt and in Constantinople, where it purchased the Comit's affiliate. It made plans for further expansion in the Ottoman Empire, including Asia Minor, Syria, and Palestine. In Egypt and Libya, the Roma invested in local businesses and even directly founded industrial enterprises in which it retained majority interests. It also operated a subsidized shipping line that called at Libyan, and eventually Egyptian ports. Subsequent heavy losses at all of the Roma's Ottoman branches suggest that these businesses were neither well managed nor necessarily conceived of as likely to be profitable in their own right; rather, it appears that the Roma directors hoped to receive subsidies and government financial business in exchange for promoting Italian interests in areas staked out for Italian colonization. The Roma had good reason to believe that the government would see its interests in a favorable light: Tommaso Tittoni, the brother of the Bank's vice-president, Romolo Tittoni, was an eminence at the Consulta, serving

[52] Confalonieri, *Banca e industria in Italia, 1907–1914*, vol. I, p. 316.
[53] Bosworth, *Italy, the Least of the Great Powers*, p. 51, and passim. On Stringher's life see also, Franco Bonelli, *Bonaldo Stringher, 1854–1930* (Udine: Casamassima, 1985); Giuseppe Marchetti, "Bonaldo Stringher," in *Il Friuli. Uomini e Tempi* (Udine, 1959), pp. 676–83.

as Foreign Minister from 1903 to 1905, and again from 1906 to 1909, and as ambassador to France from 1910 until the outbreak of war. After the Italo-Turkish War, it became apparent that the Banco di Roma had so thoroughly mismanaged its investments in Libya that it faced huge losses even after Italian sovereignty over the territory was acquired in 1912. The Roma sought to recoup its losses by demanding compensation from the government for the damages the war allegedly wrought on its business activities there, but its claims were so large that the Consulta could not agree decorously to settle them. On the eve of World War I the Banco di Roma appeared to be on the verge of failure, and its difficulties were only alleviated by the surge in business activity and liquidity produced by the war economy.[54]

At least with regard to its Libyan and shipping interests, the Roma did not act as a bank at all, but rather as an industrial holding company. Despite the size of its share capital (see Tables 13 and 14, Appendix, pp. 317–20), the Roma was not really a serious financial institution at all, and in no wise a serious rival of the Banca Commerciale and the Credito Italiano. Luigi Einaudi's judgment of the Catholic bank, as expressed in a private letter to Luigi Albertini in March 1916, after the bank had already posted huge losses, stands as definitive:

> It's the worst banking scandal since the Banca Romana. The only thing better about it is that it doesn't concern the public purse.
>
> Libya doesn't have anything to do with the ruin of the Banco di Roma, nor do the other excuses adopted by [Ernesto] Pacelli [President of the Roma, and uncle of Eugenio, the future Pius XII] in the past.
>
> But what good does it do to worry about it now? Privately, for years I have been telling my friends and relatives (and no bank has its stock so widely diffused among the owners of small and moderate fortunes, which makes it terrible): don't touch those shares![55]

The Consulta's alliance with the Banco di Roma in foreign policy bears remarkable similarity to the Bank of Italy's alliance with the Società Bancaria to promote its domestic monetary policy. In both cases, the public authorities were confronted with the dilemma that the elements in the financial world most willing to cooperate with them were the most speculative, even to the point of corruption.

In sum, on the eve of World War I Italy's banking system was structurally unstable, because of the role of deposit-taking banks in industrial

---

[54] On the Banco di Roma see Luigi De Rosa, *Storia del Banco di Roma*, vols. I–II (Rome: Banco di Roma, 1983).

[55] Einaudi to Albertini, 26 March 1916, published in Luigi Albertini, *Epistolario, 1911–1926*, ed. Ottavio Barié, vol. II, *La grande guerra* (Verona: Mondadori, 1968), p. 579.

promotion, and also politically unstable, because of the bitter conflicts between monetary authorities, political leaders and the directors of the largest commercial banks.

International accounts

The structure of Italy's international accounts during the Giolittian era was unique not only in comparison to the other major European countries, but also relative to previous and more recent periods in modern Italian history. The influx of financial resources to the center of world Catholicism and revenues from foreign travellers traditionally had allowed Italy to consume more than it produced. In more recent times, emigrant remittances had become another important source of foreign exchange. Imports have exceeded exports almost every year since the creation of a unified Italian state and probably, as the American economist Constantine McGuire surmised, since the fall of Carthage.[56] During the Giolittian era, however, the Italian trade deficit reached unprecedented levels. This was rendered possible by the rapid growth in the two principal positive invisible items in Italy's international accounts, namely emigrant remittances and tourist expenditures.

During the Giolittian era unprecedented economic growth prompted a rapid increase in international trade. Imports increased much more rapidly than exports. With 1901 as a base, Italian imports rose to 184 by 1913, while exports increased to 157. In 1901 exports covered 84% of the total cost of imports; by 1908–13 this figure had fallen to an average of 66%.[57] In Europe, only Portugal paid for a lower proportion of total imports out of exports (46%). Other major European debtor nations ran export surpluses or far smaller trade deficits than Italy. Over the years 1908–13 Russia and Romania ran estimated average surpluses of exports over imports of 129% and 116% respectively and in Spain and Austria-Hungary exports paid for 94% and 82% of imports respectively. Even the leading European capital exporters had higher export to import ratios in these same years: for Great Britain the average figure was 79%, for France 84%, for Germany 85%, for the Netherlands 81%, for Belgium 79%, and for Switzerland 70%.[58] Invisible earnings allowed Italy to sustain a trade

---

[56] For a continuous series of Italian trade statistics see, Istituto Centrale di Statistica (hereafter ISTAT), *Sommario di statistiche storiche italiane 1861–1955* (Rome: ISTAT, 1958), p. 152; Constantine Edward McGuire, *Italy's International Economic Position*, (New York: Macmillan, 1926), p. 26.

[57] Epicarmo Corbino, *Annali dell'economia italiana*, vol. V, *1901–1914* (Città di Castello: Leonardo da Vinci, 1938), p. 192.

[58] B. R. Mitchell, *European Historical Statistics, 1750–1975*, 2nd rev. ed. (New York: Facts on File, 1981), pp. 505–22.

deficit of a size that would have been impossible to finance through foreign borrowing.

Imports increased with particular rapidity in the years spanning the crest of Italian economic growth 1905–8. In the final years before the war, imports continued to grow at a rate higher than in the period before 1905. The rise in imports was stimulated by industrial expansion and rising living standards. Raw materials for industry accounted for a significant proportion of the total import bill. Italy was almost entirely dependent on foreign sources for coal, and in the period 1909–13 coal imports comprised 8.9% of total imports by cost. Raw materials for the textile industries, especially cotton, but also wool and silk, accounted for another 22.1%. Metals and metal products including machines made up 16.8%. Cereal imports, in turn, accounted for about 15.2%. Most of the remainder of Italian imports consisted either of other raw materials for industry including hides and furs, wood and paper, and raw rubber, or capital goods, including chemicals and pharmaceuticals.[59] There was little margin to reduce imports without slowing industrial growth or curtailing basic food consumption.

Exports in the Giolittian era not only lagged behind imports in growth, but also remained more traditional in nature. The structure of Italian exports remained almost unchanged from unification to the eve of World War I. Silk and silk products were still the single most important item, comprising a full 24.1% of Italian exports in the years 1909–13. Agricultural products accounted for a further 29.3%. Manufactures, including silk textiles and processed agricultural goods, made up less than one-third of Italian exports.[60] However, in the years immediately preceding the outbreak of World War I, Italian manufacturers developed new markets for certain industrial goods both in the advanced countries of Northwestern Europe, and in the less developed countries of the Mediterranean basin, Eastern Europe, and Latin America. By 1913 Italy was a net exporter of automobiles, and rubber products, and exported modest quantities of textiles, chemical products, machines, and optical instruments.[61] Italian arms manufacturers, particularly shipbuilders, had achieved some successes in sales to Mediterranean, Latin American, and even Northwestern European countries.[62]

In the Giolittian era, Italy's trade was unbalanced not only in the sense that imports exceeded exports, but also in the sense that imports were economically and strategically more essential for Italy than Italian exports were for its major trading partners. The cost deficit in Italy's agricultural

---

[59] ISTAT, *Annuario statistico italiano* (1914), pp. 221–40.
[60] Ibid.   [61] Ibid.
[62] Webster, *Industrial Imperialism in Italy*, pp. 80, 100–1.

trade was substantially surpassed by the caloric deficit; Italy imported primarily cereals and exported less nutritionally essential commodities such as wine, olive oil, liquors, fresh vegetables and fruits, pasta and tomato conserves. With regard to manufactures, Italy essentially imported coal, ferrous metals, iron and steel products, machines, and chemicals, and exported textiles and automobiles. Even in the textile sector Italy primarily imported raw wool and cotton and exported semi-processed silk.

During the tariff war with France in the years 1887–98, Germany became Italy's largest trading partner. The trade with Germany also differed structurally from Italy's trade with its other major trading partners, Great Britain, the United States, France, and Austria-Hungary. The greater part of German exports to Italy consisted of manufactures, and Germany held the largest share in the Italian import market in such critical sectors as dyes (81% in 1913), optical instruments, office machinery and electrical equipment (61%), boilers, machines and machine parts (55%), iron and steel products (51%), wool textiles (44%), and cotton textiles (43%). By contrast, Italian exports to Germany were primarily semi-processed materials and agricultural products. The single most important items were raw spun silk, and fresh fruits.[63]

Italian imports from Great Britain, the United States, and Austria consisted largely of raw materials for Italian industry. A full 55% of Italian imports from Great Britain in 1913 consisted of coal and coke, of which Britain supplied about nine-tenths of Italy's needs. The major item on Italy's import bill from the United States was raw cotton, which made up 48% of total Italian imports from that country in 1913. The United States was also Italy's major supplier of vegetable oils, petroleum and mineral oil, tobacco, and fats. Prior to the war the United States was not yet a major supplier of cereals to Italy; the bulk of Italian cereal imports came from Russia, Romania, and Argentina. Wood and wood pulp for the building and paper industries comprised 42% of Italian imports from Austria-Hungary. Italian imports from France were more diversified. The typical French luxury products, *haute couture*, jewelry, and perfumes, figured prominently in the Italian import bill; but all the same, the largest single item was raw wool, which accounted for an eighth of total French exports to Italy.[64]

Prior to World War I Italian manufacturers were more successful in British and American than German markets. Whereas Italy exported primarily raw spun silk to Germany, it exported finished silk textiles to Britain, which absorbed nearly half of Italian exports in that category.

[63] ISTAT, *Annuario statistico italiano* (1914), pp. 227–40.
[64] Ibid.

Britain was also Italy's best market for automobiles and fruit conserves. In addition to importing Italian raw silk, the United States, thanks to its large Italian immigrant population, was an important and growing market for Italian processed agricultural goods, including olive oil, fruit and tomato conserves, and pasta.[65]

The structure of Italian foreign trade took on strategic significance at the outbreak of the war: Italy was dependent on the Entente and on neutral countries to which the Entente controlled sea lanes for most vital raw materials. German domination of the Italian market for manufactures and particularly for advanced technological products proved less crucial strategically: imports of this nature from Germany were more or less satisfactorily replaced by domestic production and by imports from Britain, France and the United States.

The size of the Italian commercial deficit and the composition of the invisible items that compensated for it was a subject of intense official and public discussion in the years before World War I. As early as 1899 the significance of tourism as a source of foreign exchange earnings was the subject of a study by Luigi Bodio, the founder of modern statistical studies in Italy.[66] Struck by the growing commercial deficit, the government established a commission in 1910 to study Italy's international balance of payments. The report of this commission, which was written by the director general of the Bank of Italy, Bonaldo Stringher, and published in 1911, has remained the fundamental point of reference for all later studies.[67] With privileged access to government officials and the leading private bankers, Stringher was ideally placed to study international capital movements. He concluded that in the years 1901–5 invisible income not only allowed Italy to meet its commercial deficit, but actually to reduce net foreign indebtedness by a total of about Lit. 320m. Stringher estimated that to a significant degree, the Italian balance of payments surplus was used to repatriate a large proportion of the national debt held abroad. Interest payments on the Italian national debt made in foreign currencies declined from the early 1890s on. In 1891/2 the Italian government paid Lit. 218m. or nearly half of total interest due on the national debt, to foreign bondholders. By 1901/2 this figure had fallen to Lit. 102m. and by 1907/8 to only Lit. 56m., or about one-tenth of total interest payments on the public debt. In addition, these years witnessed a marked build up in Italian currency and precious metal holdings. From 1902 to 1909 Italy

[65] Ibid.

[66] Luigi Bodio, "Sul movimento dei forestieri in Italia e sul denaro che vi spendono," *Giornale degli economisti*, 10 (1899), vol. 20, pp. 54–61.

[67] Bonaldo Stringher, "Gli scambi con l'estero e la politica commerciale italiana dal 1860 al 1910," in *Cinquanta anni di storia d'Italia*, vol. III (Milan: Hoepli, 1911).

imported bullion and specie for a total of Lit. 675m. Much of this represented stocks accumulated by the Treasury and the issue banks. After 1909, when the exchanges turned against Italy, there was a net outflow of bullion and specie, but it came entirely from private sources, while the issue banks and the government continued to augment their reserves. The gold and foreign currency reserves of the three issue banks and the Treasury increased from Lit. 622m. in 1901 to Lit. 3,699m. in 1914.[68] The favorable balance of payments at the beginning of the century also encouraged the growth of a modest current of Italian capital exports. Direct Italian investment abroad remained modest, although some firms, like Fiat and Pirelli, founded commercial outlets and even built factories in other countries.[69] A larger share of Italian direct foreign investments before World War I was in areas marked for imperialist expansion by the Italian Foreign Ministry – in the colonies, Asia Minor and the Balkans – and was of dubious economic significance.[70] But the greater part of Italian capital exports consisted of portfolio investments. Particularly after the debt conversions of 1903 and 1906, many Italian investors preferred to purchase foreign state securities bearing higher interest rates than Italian government bonds. A study undertaken by the Ministry of Finance suggests that Russian, Austro-Hungarian, Turkish, and Latin American bonds were particularly attractive to Italian investors.[71] Stringher estimated total Italian foreign investments from 1901 to 1910 at about Lit. 250m., or about one-tenth of estimated foreign portfolio holdings of state and private Italian securities, and direct foreign investment in Italy at the end of the decade.

After 1906, Stringher estimated that net Italian indebtedness, entirely on the private account, began to grow slowly again. His estimates for Italian international income and payments for 1910 are presented in Table 17 (Appendix, p. 322). The net Italian trade deficit is estimated at Lit. 1,100m. to which must be added further net annual payments of Lit. 135m. for interest on public and private debts to persons residing abroad. Emigrant remittances are the largest positive invisible item. In addition to a net income of Lit. 455m. from this source reported directly in the table, a substantial part of the item "net surplus of postal money orders" may be

[68] Renato De Mattia, ed., *I bilanci degli istituti di emissione italiani 1845–1936* (Rome: Banca d'Italia, 1967), vol. I, part 2, tables 10, 11, 19, pp. 479–88, 609–806.
[69] On Fiat: Valerio Castronovo, *Giovanni Agnelli: La Fiat dal 1899 al 1945* (Turin: Einaudi, 1977), pp. 21, 23, 47–48. On Pirelli: Confalonieri, *Banca e industria, 1907–1914*, vol. II, pp. 411–14.
[70] Webster, *Industrial Imperialism in Italy*.
[71] Ministro della Finanze, "Alcuni indici della entità e della orientazione del capitale italiano investito in titoli e valori esteri durante il periodo dall'esercizio 1900–1901 a tutto il 1922–1923," *Bolletino di statistica e di legislazione comparata*, 23 (1923–24), no. 5, pp. 893–997.

assumed to stem from emigrant remittances. Tourist earnings account for an additional Lit. 450m. The miscellaneous category includes a positive balance for Italy from the international financial transactions of the Holy See, which, however, Stringher did not believe to be exceedingly large.

Stringher concluded that tourist earnings were likely to remain fairly stable and would tend to increase over time; he warned however, that emigrant remittances were potentially more volatile and subject to factors beyond the control of Italian authorities:

> the export of labor is more sensitive to variations in the complex conditions which constitute the domestic and international environments than the export of goods. Italy, which ranks among the chief exporters of labor, will experience the good and bad effects of its position. Up to now Italy has benefited for the most part; through the repatriation of a conspicuous part of the debt it had contracted abroad; through the formation of new reserves of gold and silver; through the satisfaction of the needs of its improving economic and social structures; and even by providing the means for a significant amount of foreign investment. But it is necessary to prepare for an inversion of tendency, which could lead to an appreciable reduction in our foreign exchange earnings. These foreign exchange earnings could not be replaced quickly, but only in stages, and perhaps with painful repercussions, by a compensating transformation of our exports.[72]

The negotiations between the United States and Italy to settle wartime debts in the mid-1920s occasioned further intensive study of Italy's international balance of payments prior to the outbreak of war. Naturally, such studies were not disinterested and tended to present the facts so as to support the positions of the two sides. The negotiations were conducted on the principle that the settlement would reflect Italy's capacity to repay. Further, the disposition of private American banks to make further loans to Italy would depend on their estimate of Italy's ability to service an enlarged foreign debt. Italian economists Pasquale Jannacone and Gino Borgatta drew up new figures on the balance of payments on behalf of their government that tended to present a more sanguine view of Italy's international position prior to August 1914 than Stringher's earlier study.[73] They attributed Italian financial difficulties entirely to the disloca-

---

[72] Stringher, "Gli scambi con l'estero," p. 135.

[73] Borgatta and Jannacone's findings are summarized in, McGuire, *Italy's International Position*, pp. 277–79. Note, however, that McGuire's table reproducing Jannacone's estimates for emigrant remittances on p. 277 contains serious printing errors. The correct figures are indicated in Table 16 of this volume. Jannacone's research was published only in truncated form in Pasquale Jannacone, "La bilancia del dare e dell'avere internazionale con particolare riguardo all'Italia," and, "Relazione fra commercio internazionale, cambi esteri e circolazione monetaria in Italia nel quarantennio 1871–1913," both in *Prezzi e mercato*, 2nd ed. (Turin: Einaudi, 1951). See also, Gino Borgatta, *Bilancio dei pagamenti – Cambio* (Milan: Giuffré, 1933).

tions caused by the war. Jannacone argued that Italian investment abroad had continued to exceed foreign investment in Italy up to the eve of the war. He compiled estimates for emigrant remittances in the pre-war period considerably higher than Stringher's figures. In addition, Jannacone and Borgatta pointed out that Stringher had failed to take into account the earnings of the Italian merchant fleet in his 1912 study. Jannacone also argued that further growth in manufactures exports, which although absolutely small had been developing at a rapid pace in the Giolittian era, would have diminished Italy's commercial deficit after 1914 had the war not broke out.

American economist Constantine McGuire, who was close to US diplomatic and financial circles, tended, in contrast, to reconfirm Stringher's original estimates in a study published in 1926.[74] McGuire acknowledged that allowance had to be made for the earnings of the Italian merchant fleet, which he estimated at about Lit. 100m. in 1910, and Lit. 124m. in 1913. He noted however, that Italy was a net debtor in international financial services and estimated annual payments on this account at Lit. 23m. in 1913. McGuire was skeptical of Jannacone's figures for emigrant remittances prior to the war and used Stringher's lower estimates. He accepted Stringher's contention that Italian net indebtedness to foreigners began to grow again after 1906. As evidence he pointed to the decline in the value of the lira against the French franc after 1908. McGuire concluded that Italy must have met its international payments deficit after 1906 largely by private short or medium-term borrowing in foreign money markets, much as was the case with Germany in the same period. He estimated this floating international debt at some Lit. 500m. by the outbreak of the war. In McGuire's view, the pace of industrial growth had begun to destabilize Italy's international accounts even before the outbreak of the war; at that time, Italy's economic future was, in his opinion, "distinctly problematical."[75]

Significantly, Epicarmo Corbino, a liberal economist, and Minister of the Treasury after World War II, substantially reconfirmed McGuire's estimates in a review of the literature on Italy's pre-World War I international balance of payments published in the late 1930s.[76] Corbino accepted McGuire's conclusion that net Italian foreign indebtedness was increasing in the years just before the outbreak of war and that the short-term debt to foreign bankers stood at about Lit. 500m. by 1914. He noted, however, that the foreign exchange holdings of the Italian Treasury and issue banks were of approximately equal size, and that hence the lira could have been

[74] McGuire, *Italy's International Position*, pp. 21–33, 259–87.
[75] Ibid., p. 265.
[76] Corbino, *Annali dell'economia italiana*, vol. V, pp. 209–24.

defended, under normal circumstances, against a short-term run. In any case, whether one accepts the more optimistic estimates of Jannacone and Borgatta, or the more cautious calculations of McGuire and Stringher for Italy's international balance of payments prior to the outbreak of the war, it is clear that the economic growth of that period was made possible by substantial invisible earnings from emigrant remittances and tourism. Any disruption of these financial currents would have jeopardized growth and entailed drastic economic readjustment.

Italy's ability to finance an enormous commercial deficit through invisible foreign exchange earnings in the Giolittian period had important implications for foreign policy. In the first decades after unification, Italy was constrained to seek foreign support to finance its trade deficit. Italian foreign policy required a close relationship with one of the major powers, not only to compensate for political and military weakness, but also to ensure financial and monetary stability.[77] In the 1860s and 1870s France played this role. French military and diplomatic support was essential in achieving Italian unification; the Paris money market was equally essential in financing Italy's military expenditure, and an ambitious program of railroad construction in the 1870s.

The deterioration of relations with France after the establishment of the French protectorate in Tunisia in 1881, and the signing of the Triple Alliance in May 1882 had immediate financial repercussions. At the insistence of the Quai d'Orsay, French bankers who had earlier played a preeminent role in major Italian loan issues refrained from making new commitments in the mid-1880s. At the behest of the Wilhelmstrasse, German bankers rushed to fill in the gap. German banks took up loans for the city of Rome and the state-financed railways. The Italian *rendita* was quoted on the Berlin stock exchange for the first time. The confrontational policies *vis-à-vis* France pursued by Francesco Crispi, who became Prime Minister in 1887, led to economic rupture and a serious deterioration in Italy's international financial and monetary position. At the beginning of 1888 the Franco-Italian tariff agreement expired and the two countries began a trade war. France was by far Italy's largest foreign market at the time and Italian exports declined precipitately. The French government began a campaign against Italian securities on the Paris stock market and the price of Italian government bonds plummeted.[78]

---

[77] Franco Bonelli, "Il capitalismo italiano. Linee generali d'interpretazione," in, Ruggiero Romano and Corrado Vivanti, ed., *Storia d'Italia* Annali I, *Dal feudalismo al capitalismo* (Turin: Einaudi, 1978), esp. pp. 1224–25.

[78] Herbert Feis, *Europe, the World's Banker 1870–1914* (New Haven: Yale University Press, 1930), pp. 235–42; Bertrand Gille, *Les Investissements français en Italie (1815–1914)* (Turin: ILTE, 1968).

German banks, prompted by the German Foreign Ministry, rescued Italy from a severe financial crisis by taking up government loans in 1888, 1890 and 1891. In 1894, after a series of failures of some of the largest Italian private credit institutions, German bankers, again at the prompting of the German government, associated themselves with leading financial houses in Vienna and Zurich to found what was to become the largest commercial bank in Italy, the Banca Commerciale Italiana. In 1895, another German banking group participated in the foundation of what soon became Italy's second largest commercial bank, the Credito Italiano.[79] In the 1880s and 1890s, Italian financial weakness cemented the Triple Alliance.

The growth of invisible earnings and the transformation of the traditional Italian balance of payments deficit into a surplus after 1900, in turn, weakened Italy's attachment to Germany. Germany was never sufficiently strong financially to assume the role that France had played earlier in Italian finances. German capital exports were modest in relation to those of France, and interest rates in Germany were generally higher. Even in the late 1880s and early 1890s, when Italian relations with France were most strained, and when German financial relations with Italy were most intense, French investors held a greater absolute share of the Italian state debt than German investors. When the credit of the Italian state recovered in the late 1890s, German bankers sold off the greater part of the Italian bonds they had previously acquired; many were bought by French investors.[80] On the eve of World War I, 70% of the relatively modest share of Italy's state debt that was still held abroad was again in the hands of French investors.

In quantitative terms, German portfolio investments in private Italian enterprises and direct investments by German firms were also modest. Although 79% of the share capital of the Banca Commerciale was put up by a German banking consortium at the time of its establishment in 1894, by 1898 German investors held only 18% of the Commerciale's share capital, and in 1904 this figure had sunk to 5%. On the eve of World War I, 63% of the capital of the Commerciale was owned by Italian, 20.5% by

[79] Feis, *Europe, the World's Banker*, pp. 235–42; Hertner, *Il capitale tedesco*, pp. 170–91; Confalonieri, *Banca e industria, 1894–1906*; Gille, *Les Investissements français en Italie*.

[80] In 1908/9, out of total interest payments of Lit. 14.8m. on the Italian state debt made abroad, Lit. 10.5m. were made in France. By 1913/14, such payments had risen to Lit. 43.3m., of which Lit. 40.5m. in France. There is, however, no evidence that foreigners actually acquired a greater share of the Italian national debt between 1909 and 1914. Rather, as the exchange rate of the lira fell below par after 1908, many Italian holders of state securities that had been issued abroad earlier, and could hence be presented for interest payments in foreign currencies, presented their coupons in Paris, so as to take advantage of the exchange premium on the French franc. It seems safe to assume that about 70% of the Italian state securities held abroad remained in French hands. F. S. Nitti, "Il capitale straniero in Italia," p. 399; Corbino, *Annali dell'economia italiana*, vol. V, p. 217.

Swiss, 14% by French, and only 2.4% by German investors. The German banking group which participated in the foundation of the Credito Italiano never held a majority interest, and its relative importance was diminished by subsequent injections of fresh Italian, Swiss, French, and Belgian share capital into the bank.[81] According to government statistics, of just over Lit. 500m. in share capital invested by foreigners in Italian private enterprises on the eve of the Great War, Lit. 182m. was owned by Belgian, Lit. 148m. by French, Lit. 110m. by British, Lit. 46m. by Swiss, and only Lit. 28m. by German individuals and corporations.[82]

Hertner has argued recently that the real significance of German investments in Italy prior to World War I was qualitative, rather than quantitative. The size of German capital investments may have been modest, but German firms introduced new technical and administrative processes in the Italian economy. Firms like Mannesmann, a specialty steel producer, created new industries utilizing high technology. Financial institutions close to the German electrical industry provided the starting capital for ambitious hydroelectric and public utilities projects that Italian investors considered too risky. German managerial personnel in the German-sponsored commercial banks founded in the 1890s modernized Italian financial practices.[83]

What needs to be stressed in this context is that, due to invisible exchange earnings, Italy was able to finance industrial and infrastructural investment after the turn of the century without incurring large foreign debts. Italy no longer had need of a close relationship with a financially and economically stronger power, as had been the case in the 1860s and 1870s, when it had turned to France, or in the 1880s and 1890s, when it turned to Germany. Foreign investment may have served as a conduit of technical know-how and advanced business practices, but it was no longer the critical factor in compensating for Italy's negative trade balance.

The growing importance of emigrant remittances in Italy's international balance of payments after the turn of the century allowed Italy to forswear a close political relationship with a financially stronger state: at the same time, however, the stability of Italy's international position came to depend on the immigration policies of the countries which absorbed the outflow of Italian labor. In the Giolittian era this meant in particular the

---

[81] It should be noted, however, that some of the Banca Commerciale shares registered in Switzerland actually belonged to Germans. Hertner, *Il capitale tedesco in Italia*, pp. 170–91; Confalonieri, *Banca e industria, 1894–1906*, vol. II, pp. 297–319; vol. III, pp. 9–68.

[82] Nitti, "Il capitale straniero," pp. 397–98. These figures tend to mute the real significance of German investments somewhat, as German firms used Belgian and Swiss shell corporations to effect investments in third countries. See, Hertner, *Il capitale tedesco in Italia*, pp. 45–55.

[83] Hertner, *Il capitale tedesco in Italia*.

United States, the source of the greater part of remittances.[84] Even before World War I Italy had, in a sense, exchanged an overt financial relationship with Germany for an invisible financial relationship with the United States. The collapse of the international monetary system in 1914, and the increasing regulation of international financial flows during the war ultimately transformed this invisible financial relationship into political dependency on the Entente.

Conclusion: the economic preconditions for liberal reformism in Giolittian Italy

It should be clear from the discussion above that when Giolitti embarked on his project of political reform he did so under exceptionally favorable economic circumstances. The economy grew at a sustained rate during the entire Giolittian era; between 1898 and 1907 it grew faster than at any time since unification. Invisible foreign exchange earnings allowed Italy to run a large trade deficit, permitting vital imports of industrial raw materials and capital goods, as well as considerable autonomy from the major creditor nations abroad. Rapid economic growth, cuts in the size of the army after the Battle of Adowa, and Giolitti's relatively parsimonious social policy in turn produced ten years of state budget surpluses between 1899 and 1909, another development unprecedented in the history of unified Italy.

But the political economy of Giolittian Italy was under growing stress even before the outbreak of World War I. Economic growth slowed after the financial crisis of 1907. This event exposed the structural weaknesses

---

[84] It is difficult to estimate very precisely the share of the United States in total emigrant remittances to Italy. As was noted above, there is disagreement even about the aggregate total of remittances in this period. It is certain, however, that well over half of total remittances prior to the war came from the United States. In the years 1909–13, 40% of all Italian emigrants, including seasonal emigration to European countries, went to the United States. ISTAT, *Sommario di statistiche storiche 1861–1955*, pp. 65–66. The author of a parliamentary commission report in 1909 estimated average annual savings of Italian emigrants at Lit. 1,000–1,500 in the United States, Lit. 600 in continental Europe, and Lit. 300–350 for a season's work in Germany. Hence, the proportion of remittances from the United States must have been notably larger than the proportion of emigrants absorbed. C. Jarach, *Abruzzi e Molise. Relazione della inchiesta parlamentare sulle condizioni dei contadini nelle provincie meridionali e nella Sicilia*, vol. II, part 1 (Rome: Bertero, 1909), p. 258. Emigration to Latin America declined notably after the turn of the century precisely because wages in the United States were higher and exchange rates more stable. Ercole Sori, *L'emigrazione italiana dall'unità alla seconda guerra mondiale* (Bologna: Il Mulino, 1979), pp. 159–60. Sori states categorically that the greater share of remittances came from the United States (p. 125). The Bank of Naples, which between 1902 and 1913 transmitted about one-tenth of total estimated emigrant remittances, did 69% of its remittance business from the United States. The Bank of Naples was, however, less active in the centers of Italian emigration to Europe than overseas. Francesco Balletta, *Il Banco di Napoli e le rimesse degli emigranti* (Naples: Istitut d'histoire de la banque, 1972), p. 45.

of the mixed banking system, and contributed to growing tensions between public authorities and commercial bankers. Thereafter, the financial problems of industry hampered economic recovery. In particular, the industries of the strategic sector remained in the doldrums, leading in 1911 to the restructuring of the Ilva trust with public assistance. The exchanges also turned against the lira after 1909, and Italy's short-term debt held abroad seems to have mounted thereafter. Finally, beginning in fiscal 1911–12 the Libyan War produced large state budget deficits for the first time in over a decade. The government was forced to borrow more dearly, and its efforts to reorganize Italy's segmented credit markets to its own advantage mobilized the business and financial communities against Giolitti, and raised fears that state borrowing would crowd out the private sector.

In March 1914 Giolitti's fourth government fell. The radicals withdrew their support, after revelations that a majority of the liberal deputies returned to the Camera under universal suffrage the previous autumn had made far-reaching commitments to a Catholic political association, in exchange for the clerical vote. A more conservative cabinet, headed by Antonio Salandra, took its place. Giolitti had taken similar "vacations" from power in the past, allowing the conservatives to try their hand at running the country with the backing of his parliamentary majority in 1906 (Sonnino), 1909 (Luzzatti), and 1910 (Sonnino). No doubt he expected to return to power again, after a short interregnum; however, World War I broke out in August, narrowing the space for domestic political opposition, and strengthening the conservatives' position. Salandra would negotiate Italy's intervention in the war in May 1915; Giolitti, known to favor neutrality, confined himself to the political sidelines for the duration of the conflict. There was undoubtedly a fortuitous element in the collapse of Giolitti's system. However, even before the outbreak of war, the veteran Piedmontese statesman was experiencing growing difficulties holding together the disparate elements of his political coalition. In economic policy, he was also experiencing growing difficulties – balancing the conflicting claims of welfare, warfare, and economic growth.

PART 2

WORLD WAR I, AUGUST 1914 – NOVEMBER 1918

The outbreak of the European war in August 1914 produced major realignments in Italy's domestic politics, which would contribute significantly to the post-war crisis of the liberal state. Above all, it created a rift between neutralists and interventionists, confounding the previous left–right political spectrum. Most of the right, after initial hesitation, rallied behind Salandra and Sonnino – who joined the cabinet as Foreign Minister in November 1914 – in support of intervention. The left, in contrast was divided. The Socialist Party, and the leading exponents of the Catholic movement embraced neutrality unreservedly. Giovanni Giolitti tended to oppose intervention in the war as well. While he conceded that Italy's foreign policy aspirations required that it demand compensation from Austria for any gains made by the Habsburg monarchy in the Balkans as a consequence of the conflict, he believed such compensations could be obtained by maintaining armed neutrality. He feared that Italy's political, economic, social, and military structures would prove too fragile to withstand a major war, and he doubted the Entente would prevail quickly over the Central Powers. Austrian intransigence might force Italy to intervene, he conceded, but he felt every effort had to be made to achieve a satisfactory settlement through negotiation first. However reasonable this program may have been, it left the Piedmontese statesman relegated to the political sidelines once war was declared.

Moreover, others on the left found their way into the interventionist camp. On the extreme left, a handful of "revolutionary interventionists," including Mussolini, advocated making war as a prelude to, and instrument of, domestic social revolution. A somewhat larger group of independent reformist socialists, and republicans – including Leonido Bissolati, Ivanoe Bonomi, Gaetano Salvemini, and Pietro Nenni – supported intervention in a "fourth war of the Risorgimento," to emancipate ethnic Italians in Trieste and the Trentino, and to check the ambitions of the authoritarian powers of Central Europe. Many left-liberals who had worked with Giolitti in the past, including the ex-Garibaldian Paolo Carcano, and Vittorio Emmanuele Orlando, embraced the interventionist

cause for similar motives. Nitti was uncharacteristically cautious in
expressing his views about war during Italy's neutrality; after intervention,
however, he argued that Italian participation had been inevitable, and that
the defeat of Germany was necessary for the progress of democracy in
Europe. The split between neutralists and interventionists would hinder
efforts to reconstruct a reformist political bloc in the post-war era.

The war produced a different kind of fracture within Italy's political
elite with regard to economic policy, and as we shall see, this fracture too
had important consequences during the post-war crisis. Here, the lines of
demarcation between two camps, i.e. fiscal conservatives and "productivists," ran somewhat differently. In his assessment of the economic effects
of the war, Giolitti had much in common with his conservative political
adversaries, Salandra and Sonnino. All three were nervous about the huge
wealth transfers likely to be produced by total mobilization, and about the
consequences of enormous state budget deficits, and unprecedented foreign borrowing. Such concerns reinforced Giolitti's advocacy of
neutrality, or at least of delaying intervention as long as possible. For
Salandra and Sonnino, the enhanced prestige that the monarchy, the
military, and the foreign policy establishment would acquire through victory, and not least the reinforcement of the conservative wing of the
liberal party *vis-à-vis* Giolitti and the left-liberal reformers which intervention promised, proved irresistibly tempting, despite their misgivings
about economic and financial mobilization. They did not foresee, or they
chose not to foresee, the duration of the war, and the scale of economic
mobilization that would prove necessary.

Productivist ideologies also cut across the old ideological divisions.
There were two significant political currents which advocated active state
promotion of wartime industrial expansion and modernization: a group of
left-liberals led by Nitti, and a second group of extreme rightists dominated by the Italian National Association (ANI). Whereas the traditional
conservatives had sought to limit as much as possible the transformative
effects of the war on society, the productivists saw the war as an opportunity to make a qualitative leap in industrial development impossible during
peacetime. The productivists, both of left-liberal and of extreme rightist
persuasion, believed that the benefits of growth and development fully
justified the budgetary and inflationary costs. Nitti aimed to modernize
and transform Italy's industrial base in order to promote domestic political
reform. In his view, industrial development was the key to improving mass
living standards and broadening the base of social consent for a reformed
liberal state. The southern politician believed that maintaining the close
financial, economic, and political ties to the United States and Britain that
developed during wartime would foster growth, and encourage the

development in Italy of political institutions more like those of the English-speaking countries. Nitti visited the United States as part of an Italian goodwill delegation after America's intervention in 1917, and this visit reinforced his conviction that the United States would continue to play a preeminent role in the world economy and finances after the war.

The nationalists, in contrast, looked to Wilhelminian Germany as a model. Although the nationalists supported Nitti's program of exploiting the war to achieve technological emancipation from Germany, they espoused an independent foreign policy predicated on autarky and imperialism. They believed that only an authoritarian government could consolidate Italy's wartime economic gains and implement an expansionist foreign policy. The common allegiance to productivism – and common links to the Ansaldo–Banca Italiana di Sconto group – held the nationalist right and the Nittian left together during the war. However, given the vast differences in the domestic and foreign political programs of the two groups, a rupture was inevitable, and as we shall see, it took place soon after the armistice.[1]

Italy's three wartime governments, headed by Salandra (until June 1916), Paolo Boselli (until October 1917) and V.E. Orlando (through the armistice) mark important divides in policymaking. Both wartime cabinet crises occurred at crucial junctures in the military conduct of the war: Salandra's fall was precipitated by the Austrian offensive in the Trentino in the spring of 1916, and the formation of the Orlando government coincided with the Italian defeat at Caporetto.

During the first phase of the war the traditional right dominated the cabinet. Sonnino and Salandra were reluctant to mobilize fully the Italian economy, for fear of compromising state finances. In foreign policy, they sought to preserve a modicum of economic and financial independence from their allies, in order to strengthen Italy's expansive territorial claims in the Alps and on the Adriatic, as indicated in the Treaty of London, the secret pact which specified the terms of Italy's intervention. Both the domestic and the foreign economic policies of the conservatives were based on the assumption that the war would be short – an assumption which proved fallacious, much as Giolitti had predicted. Munitions shortages on the Isonzo front in the summer and fall of 1915, and even more Austrian advances in the Trentino the following spring forced the government to step up war production, and led to mounting budget deficits and increased reliance on the printing presses. Even during Salandra's tenure in office productivist ideas began to shape government policy. As will be

---

[1] On the Nationalist program see, Alexander De Grand, *The Italian Nationalist Association and the Rise of Facism in Italy* (Lincoln: University of Nebraska Press, 1978); Franco Gaeta, *Il nazionalismo italiano*, 2nd rev. and enl. ed. (Bari: Laterza, 1981).

discussed in greater detail in chapter 2 below, a bill drawn up by Giannetto Cavasola, the Minister of Industry, Commerce and Labor, and adopted by parliament in February 1916 encouraged firms to use war profits to retire debts and make new investments.

At the same time that the domestic strategy of limited economic and financial mobilization was being undermined, the foreign economic policy of Salandra and Sonnino was also being compromised. Invisible exchange and export earnings declined quickly; at the same time, the inexorable demands of the armaments industries, soldiers, and civilians for British shipping, coal, and wool, American cotton and wheat, and Anglo-American munitions, armaments, and machinery – forced Italy into total financial dependence. Even before the collapse of the Salandra government, the traditional conservative's strategy of an economically and financially limited war had miscarried – much as their conception of war in pursuit of limited high political objectives: frontier rectifications, the improvement of Italy's strategic position in the Upper Adriatic, the confirmation of its great power status, and the reinforcement of conservative political institutions – had also miscarried.

The formation of the Boselli government in June 1916 was a direct consequence of the Austrian offensive and the failure of the conservatives' war strategy. Boselli expanded the range of political forces represented in the government at the cost of programmatic clarity. Former supporters of Giolitti who had rallied to the war effort, notably Orlando, and other exponents of the interventionist left, notably Bonomi and Bissolati, took seats in the new cabinet. These individuals advocated significant domestic reforms after the termination of hostilities. General Alfredo Dallolio, who headed the army's procurement agency, was elevated to the rank of minister, signalling the new government's intention to step up war production rapidly, regardless of the financial implications. Sonnino remained at the Consulta, as representative of the conservatives within the cabinet, and as a symbol of continuity in foreign policy. However, he distanced himself increasingly from the formation of economic policy; he also failed to explain how Italy's imperial program in the Adriatic could be reconciled with friendly relations with the United States and Britain, upon which Italy was becoming economically and financially dependent.

The third major political phase of the war began in late October 1917. By coincidence, a cabinet crisis coincided with Italy's worst defeat of the war at Caporetto. Francesco Saverio Nitti was the main architect of the change in government. Nitti had emerged as the major parliamentary critic of the Boselli government's economic policy in the course of 1917. In a series of private letters to Boselli, Sonnino, and other leading political figures, Nitti criticized the government for not proceeding to total mobilization of the economy; for not obtaining greater material and financial assistance from the Allies; and for not making an arrangement with the Allied governments to stabilize the exchange rate of the lira. Although Nitti refrained from openly attacking the government in the Chamber of Deputies until October, his negative views of the government's economic policy, including its foreign economic policy, and his ambition to become either Prime Minister or Minister of the Treasury in a new cabinet were widely known.[2]

It was Nitti who opened the cabinet crisis by bitterly attacking the government in a speech in the Camera on 20 October 1917. Boselli submitted his resignation six days later, after intensive negotiations among the leaders of the parliamentary factions had produced a broad consensus on the composition of the new government. Nitti was to become Minister of the Treasury, over the objections of Sonnino. Nitti made his participation in the new government conditional on the formation of a war cabinet consisting of the Prime Minister, and the Ministers of Foreign Affairs, War, Navy, and Treasury, and the supreme commanders of the army and navy. The war cabinet was to be a sort of super government above the cabinet, following the example of the Lloyd George ministry in Britain. The Minister of the Treasury would be elevated thereby above the other ministers dealing with economic affairs, and be guaranteed wide latitude in shaping all aspects of economic policy.[3]

In the middle of the cabinet crisis, during the night of 27–28 October 1917, the Italian front collapsed at Caporetto, leading to the worst defeat suffered by Italy during the war. The defeat dramatically changed the political climate in Italy: the war of aggression against Austria was converted overnight into a defensive war against an enemy invader, and there was a general tendency among political groupings that had opposed intervention to rally to the government. For the first time, exponents of the moderate wing of the Socialist Party gave reserved support to the war, declaring that they could not be indifferent to the negative consequences for the Italian proletariat of enemy occupation. At the same time, the loss of substantial stockpiles of arms, munitions, and food in the army's retreat from the Isonzo to the Piave greatly intensified supply shortages.[4] The defeat and its political impact inevitably favored Nitti's efforts to take hold of and reshape economic and financial policy: Nitti's call for total economic mobilization seemed appropriate in the wake of the terrible material

[2] Alberto Monticone, *Nitti e la Grande Guerra (1914–1918)* (Milan: Giuffré, 1961), pp. 51–58, 82–132; Francesco Barbagallo, *Nitti* (Turin: UTET, 1984), pp. 216–37; Vincenzo, Nitti, *L'Opera di Nitti* (Turin: Gobetti, 1924), pp. 17–20.
[3] Barbagallo, *Nitti*, pp. 232–33; Monticone, *Nitti e la Grande Guerra*, passim.
[4] Piero Pieri, *L'Italia nella prima guerra mondiale (1915–1918)* (Turin: Einaudi, 1965), pp. 162–65, 168–70.

losses suffered at Caporetto; and his call for closer relations with the Allies seemed inevitable, given Italy's great needs. Einaudi published an article in the *Corriere della Sera*, arguing that Italian withdrawal from the war was unthinkable, in light of its total dependence on Allied provisioning, and Nitti made the argument his own in his public statements.[5]

Nitti's policies flooded Italian industry with new orders, and left the financial markets awash with liquidity. Despite shortages of raw materials and energy, not to say the urgent needs of the troops at the front, many of the major manufacturing concerns initiated massive new investment programs. At the same time, open war broke out on the stock exchanges, despite the fact that they were officially closed, for control of financial institutions, utilities, and engineering firms. Nitti's allies at the Banca Italiana di Sconto and Ansaldo were undoubtedly the most aggressive participants in these "parallel wars," but a mood of euphoria and a sense of almost unlimited economic possibilities was widespread in Italy's business community, even before the Allies' fortunes on the battlefield reversed during the summer of 1918.

The bullish attitudes of the business community coincided with rising expectations on the part of Italy's peasant-soldiers and workers. Prior to Caporetto, the Italian General Staff had paid little attention to troop morale. However, in November 1917 Armando Diaz replaced Luigi Cadorna as Supreme Commander, and the army embarked on an extensive propaganda campaign to rally its soldiers. Although the government avoided making clear promises, peasants were led to believe that land reform and a general revision of agricultural contracts would be undertaken following the Allied victory. Meanwhile, workers' expectations were also rising, buoyed by full employment, high nominal wages, and the Bolshevik Revolution in Russia. As the collapse of Austria became imminent, the right pressed even more extravagant territorial claims in the Adriatic littoral than those contained in the Treaty of London.

Against this background of general euphoria, and in an objectively less favorable economic and financial environment, Italy's post-war liberal-democratic leaders would struggle unsuccessfully to resurrect the cautious reformism of the early century. However, before we turn to the history of the post-war era, it is necessary to examine the three major strands of monetary and financial policymaking during wartime in turn: taxation, state borrowing, and monetary policy.

---

[5] Luigi Einaudi, "La realtà in cifre," *Corriere della Sera*, 10 November 1917, republished in Luigi Einaudi, *Cronache di un trentennio*, vol. IV (Turin: Einaudi, 1961), pp. 582–85. For Nitti's views see Olindo Malagodi's notes on his conversation with Nitti on 19 November 1917, Malagodi, *Conversazioni della guerra 1914–1919*, vol. I, pp. 203–6

2

THE COLLAPSE OF THE ITALIAN FISCAL SYSTEM

The enormous financial requirements of World War I overwhelmed the tax systems of all of the belligerents. None of the major participants in the struggle raised more than a quarter of wartime expenditure through taxes and other forms of revenue. As W.S. and E.S. Woytinsky state in a frequently quoted study, total war expenditure of the belligerents on a gold basis amounted to $200 bn., about five times pre-war expenditure, and the equivalent of five times the total state debt at the beginning of the war. The total outlay represented six and a half times the sum of all the national debt accumulated in the world from the end of the eighteenth century up to August 1914.[1]

Within this generally dismal picture, the performance of Italy, as it is presented in the official budget statistics in Table 2 (Appendix, pp. 297), appears comparatively favorable. Revenue as a percentage of expenditure was consistently higher in Italy during the war years than in Germany and France, and only slightly lower than in Britain. These figures led contemporary observers, and after them historians, to judge the performance of Italy's tax system during World War I in a relatively favorable light. Aldcroft for example, in his classic study of the world economy in the 1920s, gives the following figures for war expenditures covered by revenue among the principal belligerents: France and Germany less than 2%, Italy 16%, Great Britain 20%, and the United States 23%.[2] Einaudi, the author of the standard work on the wartime Italian fiscal system, argued that Italy pursued a more rigorous financial policy than the other continental powers.[3] Although Einaudi savagely attacked the technical imperfections of Italy's wartime tax laws, he reaffirmed the thesis of relative Italian fiscal rigor as late as 1961:

I recognized [in his newspaper articles published during World War I] that

---

[1] W. S. Woytinsky and E. S. Woytinsky, *World Commerce and Governments: Trends and Outlook*, (New York: Twentieth Century Fund, 1955), pp. 743.
[2] Derek Aldcroft, *From Versailles to Wall Street 1919–1929* (Berkeley: University of California Press, 1977), p. 31.
[3] Luigi Einaudi, *La guerra e il sistema tributario italiano* (Bari: Laterza, 1927).

Italy had not reached the ideal, which would have been to cover wartime
needs exclusively with revenues from new taxes and loans. This would have
meant financing the war the old-fashioned way, i.e. through restricting
private consumption, and it would not have been necessary to print money
without backing. Still, I praised the Ministers of the Treasury and Finance
for having, "established new taxes as state expenditures and deficits mounted." Consequently, Italy, although less austere than England, managed to
cover at least a part of its war expenditures with taxes, and this was considerably superior to the policies followed in Germany, France, and the Austro-
Hungarian Empire, where the leaders refused to admit openly to the people
that it was impossible to win the war without [financial] sacrifice.[4]

It will be argued here, however, that the relatively high percentage of
wartime expenditure covered by wartime revenue in Italy reveals little
about the tax system's ability to absorb purchasing power in the private
sector. As state spending came to make up almost 60% of gross domestic
product, most taxpayers and users of government services were in a position to pass taxes and charges back to the state in the form of higher prices
on state contracts. Nominal increases in revenue merely provoked nominal increases in expenditure. Draconian tax laws were passed, but their
effect was vitiated by the inability or unwillingness of government authorities to control the prices paid to state suppliers. In the course of the war,
appearances diverged ever further from reality in Italian public finances.
Higher taxation actually promoted inflation, as it created an ever larger
volume of financial movements that did not correspond to transfers of real
purchasing power.[5] Taxes did not begin to absorb purchasing power in a
significant way again until the volume and structure of public spending

---

[4] Luigi Einaudi, *Cronache economiche e politiche di un trentennio (1893–1925)*, vol. IV
(1914–1918) (Turin: Einaudi, 1961), p. xiv.
[5] Gerd Hardach makes a similar argument about Russian public finance in World War I in,
The First World War, 1914–1918 (Berkeley: University of California Press, 1977), pp.
167–8. About war finance in general Hardach also observes: "A special problem was the
practice of passing on taxes; to do so under conditions of wartime inflation was by no
means difficult and readily produced a vicious spiral. The taxes a manufacturer paid to the
state one day he received the next by increasing the price of his armaments. Where taxes
were wholly passed on to the state, the increased revenue shown in the budget was matched
by a corresponding increase in its own expenditure . . . Although in these circumstances no
effective transfer of purchasing power was achieved, a larger proportion of expenditure was
being met out of revenue. Thus the ratio of fiscal revenue to government expenditure is not
a reliable guide to the efficacy of taxation policy." p. 171.
   Professor Franco Modigliani of MIT has pointed out to me that it is rarely possible to
prove that a particular increase in price charged by a supplier to a customer is in response
to a particular tax increase. As we shall see below, on frequent occasions during World War
I in Italy it is possible to point to a direct relationship, because clauses were inserted in
contracts with state agencies stipulating that the price would rise to cover any tax increases!
However, the main point here is to argue that revenue collections during the war did not
absorb purchasing power to a significant degree.

changed. This occurred *pari passu* with the liquidation of munitions and armaments contracts, substantially in 1919 and early 1920.

The collapse of the Italian fiscal system contrasts markedly with the success of Great Britain in absorbing purchasing power through higher taxation. The British authorities utilized taxation as a complement to a comprehensive system of direct economic controls. Most importantly, the prices paid to government suppliers were fixed in proportion to production costs. Although the centerpiece of wartime Italian fiscal legislation, the Extraordinary Profits Tax, was modelled closely on a British law, the government did not control its costs, and consequently lost control of revenue. France and Germany were no more successful than Italy in controlling costs, but they made less of an effort to collect large, but fictitious revenues.[6] The peculiarities of the Italian experience give rise to the question which will be addressed below: why did the authorities impose draconian taxes during the war that had little real effect?

Finance and high politics: the imperatives of rigore

Italian motivations for entering the war made a rigorous financial policy a political imperative. The German and French governments appealed to their populations at the onset of the war to resist a foreign aggressor. Both countries proclaimed that the war was being waged in self-defense, and that the enemy would be compelled to pay the costs after victory. In making this argument, German and French leaders could look back to the indemnity extracted by Prussia from France after the Franco-Prussian War of 1870–71. Both governments held out to their populations the prospect of enemy reparations as a means of relieving the material burden of war.

The circumstances of the Italian declaration of war precluded such a strategy. The war against Austria was clearly not defensive, and demands for an indemnity would have made the enterprise seem even more like a *Raubkrieg* than it already did. The Italian government sought to portray

---

[6] T. Balderston recently has argued that Britain's tax policy in World War I was "scarcely less inadequate than Germany's," and by extension the other continental belligerents. He points out that if one takes not only the Reich's finances, but also local and state finances into account in Germany, about 16.7% of total government expenditure was covered by revenues, compared with 26.2% in Britain. In his view the markedly greater capacity of the British capital market to absorb public debt, compared with those of the continental nations, was a more important factor in Britain's success in avoiding substantial currency depreciation after the war than differences in tax policy. "War Finance and Inflation in Britain and Germany, 1914–1918," *Economic History Review*, 2nd ser., 42 (1989), no. 2, pp. 222–44. Balderston's point about the importance of the London capital market for Britain's post-war monetary stabilization appears well taken; however, British taxes may have made more of a difference than he allows, because, in the absence of a *partita di giro*, they absorbed private purchasing power more effectively than continental taxes.

World War I as the fourth war of the Risorgimento, and as such as a struggle for the liberation of ethnic Italians in the Trentino, Trieste, Istria, and Dalmatia from foreign domination. The three previous wars of 1859–60, 1866, and 1870, but especially the first two, had been costly, and expenses had been defrayed thereafter by heavy taxation. Italian unification was justified on ideal rather than material grounds and the financial costs of the enterprise were portrayed, like the bloodshed, as a patriotic sacrifice. Hence when the government called up a mass army to fight for the recovery of the "unredeemed" Italian provinces in the east in 1915, it was constrained to make a corresponding appeal to the civilian population for financial sacrifice.

Other domestic and international political considerations also militated in favor of a rigorous financial policy. The Italian government that declared war in May 1915 was led by men who represented the right in the pre-war parliament. They had criticized the lax spending policies and budget deficits of Giolitti's fourth ministry, and meant to demonstrate their relative fiscal austerity.

The Italian government was equally anxious to foster an image of financial rigor with the Allied powers. Antonio Salandra, the Prime Minister, and Sidney Sonnino, his Foreign Minister, sought to limit Italy's financial dependence on its Allies, notably England, so as to gain a free hand to redraw the eastern Italian frontier after the conflict. In allying with Britain, France, and Russia, the Italian government pursued policies not unlike those of the Risorgimento period. In 1866 Italy had joined forces with Prussia against Austria while retaining distinct war aims. In 1870, Italy had exploited the momentary indisposition of France, involved in war with Prussia, to seize the Papal States. In similar fashion, in 1915 Italy joined the Triple Entente in pursuit of purely national objectives. Loans from England were seen as a *quid pro quo*, for the benefits accruing to the Allies from Italy's war against Austria, to be backed by the credit worthiness of the Italian state. Sonnino and Salandra felt that should Italy become a poor credit risk, English loans would lead to political dependency and curtail their freedom of action in foreign policy. Hence an austere fiscal policy was regarded as necessary to impress England with Italy's financial solvency. In this the Italians were, at least until late in the war, on the whole successful. British Treasury documents suggest that officials did not probe all too closely into the weaknesses and contradictions of their Allies' public accounts. As late as November 1916, John Maynard Keynes, who at that time was working for the Treasury, wrote approvingly of wartime Italian financial policy. In a memo produced to brief British diplomats for imminent financial negotiations with Italy, Keynes affirmed that Italian Treasury Minister Carcano, "might be warmly congratulated on the prudence and success with which he has conducted the internal finance of Italy."[7] Italy had, according to Keynes, largely increased taxation and consequently depended less on inflation as an instrument of war finance than any of the other continental belligerents: "The intrinsic condition of Italian public finance is surprisingly sound. It has probably not yet been pressed to the limits of its capacity and should show rapid recovery to equilibrium after the war."[8]

Following Italy's major military defeat by German and Austrian forces at Caporetto in late October 1917, and the appointment of Francesco Saverio Nitti as Minister of the Treasury, which occurred at the same time, Rome's requests for financial and material assistance became more importunate, and Italy's economic dependency on its Allies more evident. But Nitti continued to emphasize the great sacrifices of Italian taxpayers, and the intrinsic solidity of Italian internal finance in his efforts to gain further concessions from the Allies. Throughout the war and into the post-war years, Italian authorities sought to project an image of fiscal rigor in their financial dealings with the Allies, and also with neutrals.

Finance and economic policy: the imperatives of *legerezza*

Although imposing heavy taxes was a high political imperative closely bound up with Italy's domestic and international war aims, another set of policy goals conflicted fundamentally with the line of fiscal austerity, and ultimately subverted it. In particular, the authorities sought to exploit the war as a means of shoring up the financial base of domestic industry, and even promoting industrial growth. The desire to favor industrial development made successive governments reluctant to control the prices charged by suppliers and restrict private investment. Fiscal rigor was undermined by lax spending, and private investments projects competed with government contracts for scarce human and material resources. In the midst of war, the Italian government promoted industrial development that did not directly contribute to the war effort itself. That would appear paradoxical, given that Italian governments had favored industrialization from the 1880s on, as much to obtain an indispensable prerequisite for great power politics as to make the society more prosperous. But, during the war, industrial expansion was regarded as a strategic end in itself, irrespective of its direct contribution to military capabilities. There was a broad consensus within the political leadership on the need to favor industrial growth. Even the social and fiscal conservatives who dominated the Salandra

---

[7] Keynes, internal Treasury memo, 18 November 1916, Public Record Office, London (hereafter PRO), Treasury files (hereafter T-files), T1/12033/5070/17.
[8] Ibid.

government from March 1914 to July 1916 encouraged industrialists to utilize war profits to retire debts, and upgrade plant and equipment. They feared that Italy could win the war militarily, but emerge from it economically weakened, and unable to exploit post-war opportunities. They were particularly sensitive to the weakness of Italy's industrial base in comparison with the other great powers. As we have seen, in the years just before the war Italian industry, particularly heavy industry, had been drifting into stagnation. The war appeared as a kind of *deus ex machina*, allowing industrialists to put their firms on financially sounder footing. The Salandra government sought to avoid unmanageable budget deficits by being niggardly to the army. Much slack remained in the economy by the end of the first year of war, in spite of requests for more arms and munitions from the front. But Salandra was less stringent *vis-à-vis* industry: new laws granting generous tax deductions and promoting investments were put on the books by his government. Most importantly, the Salandra ministry did not set up a viable mechanism to control costs, and in war finance the cost factor was decisive.

The Austrian offensive in the Trentino in the spring of 1916 exposed Italy's economic unpreparedness, and led to the collapse of the Salandra government. The Boselli government which followed (July 1916 – October 1917) stepped up industrial production and introduced new laws favoring investments. As was noted above, with Nitti's appointment to the Treasury in October 1917, the government openly embraced so-called productivist ideas. But even before Nitti's appointment at the Treasury the tax system had been seriously compromised. Italian political leaders were caught between the high political imperatives of fiscal rigor and the productivist imperative of encouraging industrial growth. The collapse of the fiscal system was the result of this dilemma. The authorities resolved the conflicting demands of high politics and industrial policy by pursuing fiscal policies which were substantively lax, but apparently rigorous. Tax revenues came to be largely fictitious and the fiction was willfully cultivated for both domestic and international political consumption.

Einaudi's inflexibility thesis and the problem of controlling costs

The verdict of historiography on the Italian fiscal system during World War I has largely been based, as was noted above, on Luigi Einaudi's work, in particular the volume in the series published by the Carnegie Endowment in 1927, *Il sistema tributario italiano durante la guerra*. In many respects, Einaudi's study was a summary of two decades of scholarly research and political agitation dedicated to the reform of the Italian fiscal system. Fiscal reform had been one of the major themes of Einaudi's journalistic and scholarly writing in the years before the war. During the war itself, Einaudi was a member of a government commission that proposed a comprehensive reform of the fiscal system. The proposal embodied in the final report of the commission, which is usually referred to as the "Meda project" after the name of the commission's chair, Finance Minister Filippo Meda, was substantially the work of Einaudi. The essential aspects of the Meda project were later implemented in the piecemeal reforms enacted by Mussolini's first Finance Minister, Alberto De Stefani in 1922–25. Not surprisingly then, Einaudi's book describes the transformation of an inelastic, ill-distributed and technically flawed fiscal structure into one that was more modern, more elastic, and fairer. However, Einaudi's personal preoccupation with financial theory and fiscal reform led him to neglect important problems peculiar to war finance. In particular, he devoted little attention to the problem of the circularity of tax revenue in a situation where the state purchased up to 60% of national output and failed to controls its costs. For Einaudi, the central problem of war finance was the inflexibility of the pre-war tax system:

> At the outbreak of the war Italy had a tax system inadequate to the great task it needed to accomplish. Suppose that one wanted to cover at least half of total expenditures with taxes … this would not have been absurd if the mechanism of assessing taxes on national income had functioned efficaciously. For this purpose, it would have been necessary for the taxes in place to be few in number, well-distributed, moderate, and therefore elastic. Other nations, endowed with an admirable tax system, succeeded in this endeavor. Italy was unable to reach this goal, because its taxes were many, poorly distributed, and rates were high, and therefore inelastic. The officials had a very imperfect knowledge of the actual incomes subject to the direct taxes. The indirect taxes were flawed by their use for commercial protection. Consequently, during and after the war Italy had a dual task: it had to use loans to find the means necessary for prosecuting the war; and it had to transform its tax system at the same time, in order to make it capable of sustaining, at the end of the war, the increased burden of public expenditure.[9]

Consequently, the resolution of the financial crisis was essentially a function of tax reform:

> At the end of the war, and largely as a consequence of it, Italy finally acquired a tax system which, if not perfect is at least more similar to those of other advanced states, and, because of its greater elasticity, is better adapted to meet the needs of future national emergencies.[10]

Evidently, even if a state possesses few, elastic, equitably distributed and

---

[9] Einaudi, *Il sistema tributario*, pp. 1–2.
[10] Ibid., p. 4.

moderate taxes, it still will not absorb purchasing power through taxation if it acts as a virtual monopoly buyer on the market and is unable to control its costs. In effect, the rigidities of the pre-war tax system would have limited the ability of the Italian state to absorb purchasing power in wartime if it had sought to do so. At most, during the war fiscal rigidities imposed hardships on a relative minority of taxpayers, who were unable to profit from or keep up with the inflationary price spiral, and were nevertheless subject to increased tax assessments. Fiscal inflexibility took on a far greater significance with the liquidation of the war economy. With the drying up of war contracts, producers were no longer able to pass their costs back to the state. The resurgence of a private market caused the high tax rates approved during the war to exact a very heavy fiscal burden from taxpayers accustomed to near total tax evasion. At this point the inequalities in the distribution of taxation provoked real hardship on the part of those with unfavorable assessments. Starting in late 1919, and early 1920, the inequities in the fiscal system denounced by Einaudi became a political as well as a financial issue of great importance.

What primarily distinguished the finance of Italy and other continental states from Britain and the United States in World War I was the inability or unwillingness of the continental powers to control costs. The Italian case is instructive. Despite the fact that nominal revenues never fell below 23% of total nominal expenditure during the war years, the wholesale price index in Italy stood at 364 in 1919 (1913=100), as compared to 242 in Britain, 357 in France and 415 in Germany.[11] When costs are examined, the mysteries of fiscal rigor coexisting with inflation in Italy dissolve and the essentially fictitious character of tax revenue is revealed. Financial battles in World War I were won and lost not in the active but in the passive column of government ledgers. The success, or relative success of British fiscal policy rested on two types of direct economic controls: prices on war contracts were fixed in proportion to production costs, and private consumption and investment opportunities were restricted. Italian finance failed because too much was expected of it; it was seen as the sole instrument for absorbing private purchasing power and directing the flow of production into the war effort. British finance succeeded because taxes came to be used, after an extended period of hesitation and trial, as an auxiliary to direct economic controls.

Britain, like other European states, imposed economic controls reluctantly.[12] Almost invariably, economic controls were imposed as a response

---

[11] Keynes, J. M., "A Tract on Monetary Reform," in Elizabeth Johnson, ed., *The Collected Writings of John Maynard Keynes*, vol. IV (London: Macmillian, 1971), p. 3; Hardach, *The First World War*, p. 172.

[12] On British economic controls see, E. V. Morgan, *Studies in British Financial Policy,*

to crippling shortages. Like the other major belligerents, Britain initially sought to meet its munitions and arms requirements through the utilization of stocks, the production of the four state-owned armaments factories, and a small number of customary private suppliers. The move to direct controls came immediately after the British offensive on Festubert ground to a halt in May 1915, in part due to a lack of munitions. The ensuing "shells scandal," which was fanned in Lord Northcliffe's newspapers, contributed to the collapse of Asquith's all-Liberal government and the termination of the "business as usual" philosophy. The new coalition government created an autonomous Ministry of Munitions, which set about mobilizing the British economy for war production.[13]

The British Ministry of Munitions disposed at its inception of far-reaching legal powers to effect direct economic intervention. The Defense of the Realm Act (DORR) of August 1914 gave the war ministries the right to take control of factories or requisition their output. It said nothing about compensation, but government authorities assumed on the basis of customary usage that they were not obliged to pay for goods requisitioned to meet a national emergency, and could hence set compensation at any level they chose. According to the provisions of the modified DORR of February 1916, dissatisfied parties could take their grievances to a Defence Losses Commission, which acted as an arbiter. On 23 February 1917, the DORR was again modified to specify that:

> ... regard need not be had to the market price, but shall be had to the cost of production of the output so requisitioned and to the rate of profit usually earned in respect to such output before the war, and to whether such a rate of profit was unreasonable or excessive and to any other circumstances of the case.[14]

This was merely an explicit legal sanction for what had long been actual practice. In fact, the Act of February 1916 had already supplied the legal basis for the inspection of firms' accounts, which was undertaken precisely in order to establish production costs. Even earlier, in the second half of 1915, the British government was able to drive down the unit costs it paid its private suppliers for a number of standardized items.

The supervision and imposition of price ceilings was greatly facilitated by the expansion of state-owned and state-controlled armaments produc-

---

1914–25 (London: Macmillan, 1952), pp. 33–66; Kathleen Burk, ed., *War and the State: The Transformation of British Government, 1914–1919* (London: George Allen and Unwin, 1982), passim.

[13] On the Ministry of Munitions see, R. J. Q. Adams, *Arms and the Wizard: Lloyd George and the Ministry of Munitions, 1915–1916* (College Station TX: Texas A and M University Press, 1978); Chris Wrigley, "The Ministry of Munitions: An Innovatory Department," in Burk, ed., *War and the State*, pp. 32–56.

[14] Quoted in Morgan, *Studies in British Financial Policy*, p. 46.

tion. With the powers granted by the Defense of the Realm Act, the British government brought about 70 factories under its direct control by the end of 1915 and about 250 by the armistice. About half of them were constructed *ex nihlo* during the war, in part in collaboration with private manufacturers; the other half consisted of factories commandeered from or surrendered by their private owners. Factories could be seized if production records were deemed unsatisfactory, or if labor disputes threatened to interrupt work. The owners of factories vital for war production also could turn their facilities over to the government for the duration of the war if they so chose: the owners were in that event usually compensated on the basis of pre-war earnings. The expansion of state productive capacity not only allowed the government to control costs for that part of production directly under its own control; it also gave the authorities broad knowledge of the approximate production costs in many areas for its private suppliers.

The British system did not and was not intended to prevent the accumulation of war profits. British authorities structured prices and taxes so as to leave manufacturers with net profit margins ample enough to make them prefer government work to other work, and to spur them to maximize output. British policy, however, was designed to inhibit the accumulation of profits that were in excess of the levels required to attain these goals. In addition, the British sought to limit the opportunities of manufacturers and workers in the armaments industries from directing their accumulated purchasing power to private consumption and investment during the war. Production of consumer goods that competed indirectly with government armaments contracts, such as automobiles and construction, was restricted or suspended. High taxes were applied on available consumer goods such as beer and spirits. New investments were limited sharply. New capital issues on the stock exchange were permitted only when Treasury authorities were persuaded that proposed investments were in the national interest.[15] Such measures contributed to the explosion of private buying, and the consequent inflationary pressures, that followed the armistice and the termination of direct economic controls.[16] Restrictions on investment and consumption did not prevent inflation – they merely suppressed it – but they did prevent the accumulation of private purchasing power from interfering with wartime economic mobilization.

In what came to be a complement to direct controls, the British increased taxation to mop up private purchasing power.[17] As was custom-

[15] Ibid.; J. E. Allen and F. W. Hirst, *British War Budgets* (Oxford: Oxford University Press, 1926).
[16] Susan Howson, "The Origins of Dear Money, 1919–1920," *Economic History Review*, 2nd ser., 26 (1974), no. 1, pp. 88–107.
[17] Morgan, *Studies in British Financial Policy*, pp. 89–121. On the relationship between

ary in Britain in wartime, income tax and death duties were increased substantially. Pre-existing consumption taxes, notably on beer and spirits were also raised. The Excess Profits Duty, which was instituted by Reginald McKenna, the Chancellor of the Exchequer, in September 1915, became a major source of revenue. As the Italian War Profits Tax of 1916 was modeled closely on this English tax, a comparison of the effect of the two taxes illustrates the significance of direct controls. British manufacturers were unable to pass the tax back to the state because their prices were controlled. Prices were set at a level that allowed the most inefficient producers the government wished to attract into a given line of production to earn reasonable profits. The Excess Profits Duty enabled the state to mop up some, but not all, of the far higher earnings that more efficient producers were able to realize. Further, the Excess Profits Duty was collected not just on firms doing state business, but on all earnings that exceeded pre-war levels, thus acting as a supplementary brake to direct controls on non-essential production.

Einaudi's argument about fiscal inflexibilities applies better to Great Britain than it does to Italy. In Britain, the *sine qua non* of successful fiscal policy, price controls, existed. World War II was to prove that a far higher percentage of total wartime government expenditure could be raised through taxation, provided tight economic controls were in place. In World War I, Britain raised approximately 28% of expenditure in taxes, in World War II 53%.[18] In commenting on the relatively poor British performance in World War I, Morgan advanced the inflexibility thesis in a far more convincing context than Einaudi:

> To those who have passed through the sterner days of the Second World War the taxation we have described [in World War I] seems very light, the deficits relatively large, and the complacency with which the situation was regarded by successive Chancellors, little short of fantastic. Similar criticisms were common enough at the time ... Why, then, did successive Governments vie with one another in the half-heartedness with which they tackled the budgetary problem?
>
> The answer lay partly in the technical difficulties of increased taxation, partly in the general climate of opinion and partly in the lack of understanding among Ministers and their advisers of the true principles of public finance. The technical difficulties must not be underrated. Income tax would have needed considerable reform if the rates of the Second World War were

finance and direct economic controls see also, Alan S. Milward, *War, Economy and Society, 1939–1945* (Berkeley: University of California Press, 1977), pp. 105–9.
[18] The figure for World War I is taken from, Hardach, *The First World War*, p. 165. It differs from the figure given by Aldcroft cited above, because Aldcroft separated war expenditure from ordinary expenditure, while Hardach uses total expenditure. The World War II figure is from Milward, *War, Economy and Society*, p. 107.

to be imposed, and, like other taxes, considerable staffs would have been needed to collect it and to check evasion.[19]

Paradoxically, liberal Britain, where state economic intervention in normal times was minimal, was far more successful in imposing direct controls in wartime than were the continental states, where such intervention was a constant.

Germany and France were as unsuccessful as Italy in controlling costs. Organized economic interests easily parried efforts by state officials to regulate profits. General Wilhelm Groener lost his job at the War Office, the administrative body responsible for economic mobilization in Germany, in the latter half of 1917, after he endorsed a memorandum calling for rigid price controls, the restriction of profits, and direct military control of factories. Business interest groups conspired with the Supreme Command to bring about his dismissal.[20] When the French War Ministry sought to force down prices on a number of items in October 1915 on the grounds that the introduction of mass production techniques had lowered unit costs, businessmen responded by threatening to restrict production: the government quickly relented.[21] Significantly, at the same time and for the same reasons, Lloyd George successfully forced down prices on standardized items in Great Britain.[22]

The failure of the Italian government to control costs did not stem from a lack of legal powers on the part of government procurement agencies. In the first year of the war, a series of decree laws gave Italian authorities powers every bit as far-reaching as those of British administrators.[23] R.d. (*Reale decreto* – royal decree) 22 April 1915, no. 506. allowed field commanders to requisition property and also provided for the requisitioning of factories and their output. Under R.d. 26 June 1915, no. 993, state authorities were authorized to constrain private owners to modify or expand production facilities for war purposes and to arbitrarily fix prices. The latter decree, along with R.d. 9 July 1915, no. 1065, R.d. 22 August 1915, no. 1277 and D.l. (*Decreto luogotenenziale* – decree by the king's minister) 26 September 1915, no. 1437, established the basic structure of

---

[19] Morgan, *Studies in British Financial Policy*, p. 94.

[20] Gerald Feldman, *Army, Industry and Labor in Germany, 1914–1918* (Princeton: Princeton University Press, 1966), pp. 391–403.

[21] Gerd Hardach, "Französische Rüstungspolitik, 1914–1918," in Heinrich August Winkler, ed., *Organisertier Kapitalismus* (Göttingen: Vandenhoeck and Ruprecht, 1974), p. 103.

[22] Hardach, *The First World War*, p. 83.

[23] On wartime economic controls in Italy see, Luigi Einaudi, *La condotta economica e gli effetti sociali della guerra italiana* (Bari: Laterza, 1933), pp. 99–130, 139–78; Alberto De Stefani, *La legislazione economica della guerra* (Bari: Laterza, 1926), esp. pp. 403–68; Loredana Mascolini, "Il ministero per le armi e munizioni (1915–1918)," *Storia contemporanea* (1980), no. 6., pp. 933–65; Paola Carucci, "Funzioni e caratteri del ministero per le armi e munizioni," in Giovanna Procacci, ed., *Stato e classe operaia in Italia durante la prima guerra mondiale* (Milan: Angeli, 1983), pp. 60–78.

economic mobilization under the direction of a Bureau of Arms and Munitions, which was a dependency of the Ministry of War until June 1917, and thereafter an independent ministry.[24] This administration was empowered to assign auxiliary status to firms producing armaments and munitions or other strategic supplies; the entire personnel of such firms was placed under military jurisdiction. At first seven and later eleven regional mobilization committees (Comitati regionali di mobilitazione industriale) were given authority to regulate production in factories under their jurisdiction. Finally, D.l. 30 October 1915, no. 1570 established a special commission (Collegio arbitrale) to arbitrate disputes arising out of compensation for requisitions.

In the event, Italian authorities made little or no use of the far-reaching discretionary powers this legislation gave them, at least as a means of controlling costs and production. The Under-Secretary, and later Minister of Arms and Munitions, General Alfredo Dallolio, preferred to elicit the voluntary collaboration of industrialists. As he himself described his practices after the war.

[the procedures for seizing factories were not drawn up] because I was convinced that one would never arrive at this extreme. Requisitioning would have occurred when the industrialists refused to produce with good will the items requested by the government. With the powers conferred on it, the government would have assumed in this eventuality the technical and managerial direction of a factory, substituting the industrialist. But one should not delude oneself. Because of public accounting norms, and because of bureaucratic practices, the government is inevitably a slower, and perhaps also a less efficient industrialist than private individuals, so that in its hands production would have declined, rather than increased, and it would have been more costly. One would have obtained exactly the opposite of the desired effect, at least in the short run. For this reason, and also because I trusted in the patriotism of industrialists and workers, I did not order requisitions or government takeovers. If it had been necessary, one could have done it rapidly.[25]

Although coercive powers were not used to discipline industrialists, they were used to discipline workers.[26] Workers in auxiliary factories were

[24] On successive reorganizations of government procurement agencies see in particular, Mascolini, "Il ministero per le armi"; Carucci, "Funzioni e caratteri del ministero per le armi."
[25] Commissione parlamentare d'inchiesta per le spese di guerra, "Relazione," in *Atti parlamentari. Atti della Camera dei deputati*, 26th legislature, session 1921–23, Documenti III, no. 21–23, vol. 2, p. 111, quoted in Einaudi, *La condotta*, p. 103.
[26] On government intervention in the labor market see, Einaudi, *La condotta*, pp. 105–22; De Stefani, *La legislazione economica*, pp. 20–30, 106, 179–80, 415–22; Procacci, ed., *Stato e classe operaia*, particularly, Luigi Tomassini, "Mobilitazione industriale e classe operaia," pp. 79–102; and Bruno Bezza, "Gli aspetti normativi nelle relazioni industriali del periodo bellico (1915–18)," pp. 103–20.

forbidden to change jobs without permission. Italy, like France, restricted worker mobility and thereby limited pressures for higher wages, in marked contrast to Germany and Britain.[27] As noted, the entire work force in auxiliary factories was subject to military discipline. In addition, a significant number of able-bodied male workers actually were drafted into the army. They remained in the factories because of their skills, but the threat of transfer to the front was consciously used to keep them pliant. Contingents of soldiers from the front were deployed in industrial and agricultural work when military and production considerations rendered this opportune.

Since Italian authorities were unwilling to use coercion or apply direct controls to regulate production, they were constrained to rely on financial incentives to persuade industrialists to convert to the manufacture of war-related items. The decree law of 4 August 1914 (R.d. no. 770) was the first of a series of measures enabling all government administrations acting to meet the war emergency to dispense with normal accounting procedures. R.d. 24 January 1915, no. 42, and D.l. 31 December 1915, no. 1842 gave state administrators the authority to make advance payments on contracts of up to Lit. 200,000 on their own discretion, and for even larger amounts with the consent of the Treasury. Toward the end of the war, D.l. 4 August 1918, no. 1168 actually permitted advance payments of up to 80% of the total value of contracts without Treasury consultation. Other laws were passed allowing for partial payments on deliveries that had been executed fully or partially, but for which a formal contract had not yet been drawn up.[28]

Government purchasing was not only extremely liberal to sellers, but also operationally chaotic. Ministry officials frequently placed orders with oral contracts which were only formalized at or after delivery. The administration often did not have precise records of informal contract terms, cash advances, or raw material deliveries. The parliamentary commission appointed by Giolitti in 1920 to investigate war costs found that state raw materials consignments were a major source of uncontrolled profits during the war. State administrations had only an approximate notion of the amount of materials required to build many items. Unused materials and wastes were used on other state contracts or appropriated privately. The commission report also reveals that the bureaucracy lacked adequate information to judge the production costs of its suppliers. D.l. 30 March 1916, no. 370 expressly directed the Bureau of Arms and Munitions

---

[27] On France see, Hardach, "Französische Rüstungspolitik," pp. 104–6; on Germany, Feldman, *Army, Industry and Labor*, pp. 76–96, 197–249, 308–16; on Great Britain, Hardach, *The First World War*, pp. 191–96.

[28] De Stefani, *La legislazione economica*, pp. 403–6; Einaudi, *La condotta*, pp. 122–26.

to fix prices with regard to production costs, but it was bound to remain a dead letter in the absence of close state regulation, and inspection of private production facilities and processes.[29]

In contrast to Great Britain, the Italian government made no systematic effort to expand the output share of state-owned armaments factories. As was noted, not a single private factory was taken over by the government. Such state-owned facilities as the Fabbrica d'armi of Brescia, which made machine guns, the Fabbrica d'armi of Terni, which made rifles, and the Regio Silirificio of La Spezia, which made torpedoes, significantly expanded their work forces and capacity during the war, but the contribution of private firms to total output for all of these items increased rather than decreased with time.[30]

Although industrialists had little formal authority in the Arms and Munitions administration, their actual influence became substantial. At the central level, a Central Committee (Comitato centrale di mobilitazione industriale), which included civilians and representatives of industry and labor, had a purely advisory capacity. The Regional Committees mentioned above were presided over by career army officers and consisted of military and civilian members. The civilians were for the most part regional notables, while the representatives of industry and labor had a purely advisory role. The Regional Committees had direct authority over the organization of production and the distribution of raw materials among the auxiliary firms in their area of jurisdiction. Most war contracts were signed at this level. With time, the Central Committee came to be more and more preoccupied with the arbitration of labor disputes, leaving the Regional Committees with ever greater autonomy in the organization of production. Although the industrialists sat in the committees in a purely advisory capacity, the civilian members frequently were tied to them, and the military members typically were reluctant to assume a confrontational attitude. Decisions regarding all aspects of production, including prices, thus came to be influenced strongly by industrialists through the structure of the Regional Committees.[31]

The weakness of the Italian state *vis-à-vis* its industrial suppliers was accentuated by the climate of emergency that prevailed at the front. Italy went through a munitions crisis in the summer and fall of 1915 that closely resembled the German and French munitions crises provoked by the

[29] Commissione spese di guerra, "Relazione," vol. 2, pp. 19–80; Alberto Caracciolo, "La crescita e la trasformazione della grande industria durante la prima guerra mondiale," in Giorgio Fuà, ed., *Lo sviluppo economico in Italia*, vol. III, 3rd ed. (Milan: Angeli, 1978), pp. 215–20; Luciano Segreto, "Armi e munizioni. Lo sforzo bellico tra speculazione e progresso tecnico," *Italia contemporanea* (1982), nos. 146/7, pp. 42–44.
[30] Segreto, "Armi e munizioni," pp. 50, 61.
[31] Carucci, "Stato e classe operaia," pp. 65–67.

Battle of the Marne in September 1914, and the British "shells scandal" of May 1915. The first three offensives on the Isonzo River against the Austrians from July to October 1915 were hampered by the lack of artillery pieces and shells. Even in the first offensive, the army was so short of shells that orders were issued to use them sparingly. Supreme Commander General Luigi Cadorna was among the first advocates of total industrial mobilization. He wrote in this sense to Salandra in June 1915, and two months later, after the second battle of the Isonzo, he warned the Prime Minister that the offensive could not be resumed unless munitions supplies were stepped up. Fearing financial disaster, Salandra and Sonnino were initially reluctant to give in to Cadorna's huge requests for material. The conflict between the Supreme Command and the government continued through the fall and winter. In a cabinet meeting on 27 October, Sonnino proposed Cadorna's replacement if he did not limit his demands for equipment. A compromise was worked out in early November, but on 6 January 1916 Cadorna again wrote to the Council of Ministers proclaiming that the artillery he would have at his disposal by spring would be insufficient to mount a viable offensive. Sonnino and Salandra were confronted with the dilemma of renouncing vigorous prosecution of the war or abandoning the policy of financial rigor.[32] The issue was decided by the Austrian offensive in the Trentino in the spring of 1916.[33] The supply problem was transformed into a question of national survival, and controlling costs became a secondary consideration. Salandra was forced to resign, in part because of criticism of his economic policy. Sonnino remained in the new government as Foreign Minister, but he increasingly distanced himself from financial and economic policy.

Dallolio, himself a military man, was less susceptible to budgetary scruples than other cabinet members. Vested with broad discretionary powers, and pressured by urgent requests from the front, he threw financial caution to the winds. In a meeting of the Central Committee for Industrial Mobilization in August 1916, Dallolio even said that, "after the end of the war it will be the task of the Minister of the Treasury to resolve the problem of superprofits," thus renouncing any responsibility of the Bureau of Arms and Munitions for controlling costs.[34]

In early 1917, mounting criticism of high profits on military contracts coincided with a burst of parliamentary discontent at the usurpation of

---

[32] Piero Melograni, *Storia politica della grande guerra, 1915–1918* (Bari: Laterza, 1977), vol. I, pp. 74–76; Ferdinando Martini, *Diario 1914–1918* (Verona: Mondadori, 1966), pp. 529–30, 536–38, 557–59, 565–67, 580, 583, 614–15, 625–28.

[33] Piero Pieri, *L'Italia nella prima guerra mondiale, 1915–1918* (Turin: Einaudi, 1965), pp. 104–10; Segreto, "Armi e munizioni," pp. 44–45.

[34] Carucci, "Stato e classe operaia," p. 68.

legislative prerogatives by the executive. In March 1917, a Consultative Commission for Price Review (Commissione consultive per la revisione dei prezzi) was formed under the leadership of senator Alessandro D'Ancona, and later senator Alberto Cencelli. The commission was authorized to examine contracts stipulated by government procurement agencies and reject them if prices greatly exceeded production costs. Commission members made spot factory inspections in order to determine production costs. The commission examined 405 contracts signed between January 1917 and April 1918, rejecting about half of them. Total savings for the state were calculated at Lit. 300m. The post-war parliamentary committee to investigate war costs praised the work of the commission, as did Luigi Einaudi.[35] The post-war committee sustained in its report that government procurement agencies used more rigorous criteria in negotiating contracts after the D'Ancona–Cencelli commission began its activities. But it is difficult to escape the impression that the overall impact on costs was modest. The military procurement agencies signed some 27,000 contracts in the course of the war, for a total value of Lit. 19.5bn.[36] As a proportion of this amount, the savings realized directly by the D'Ancona–Cencelli commission were evidently minimal. The staggering Italian material losses at Caporetto soon smothered concern about high industrial profits; increasing output and hastening delivery times again became all-consuming imperatives.[37] In the spring of 1918, attacks against the free-spending policies of General Dallolio's Ministry were renewed. Nitti, Minister of the Treasury since October 1917, sent Attilio Prandi, his Inspector General, to check out the accounts of the Ministry of Arms and Munitions in March and April. Several of Dallolio's close collaborators were arrested and later tried on charges of corruption. A deputy, Cesare Nava, presented a parliamentary interpellation in April concerning the irregular accounting procedures of the Ministry. In early May, a decree was promulgated that set up a committee to monitor the accounts of the administration (Comitato per il controllo sulla gestione e contabilità del Ministero, D.l. 9 May 1918, no. 620). A few days later, on 14 May, Dallolio resigned. The Ministry was reconverted into a bureau of the Ministry of War, under the direction of Cesare Nava. Procurement for

---

[35] On the D'Ancona–Cencelli commission see, Commissione spese di guerra, "Relazione," vol. 2, pp. 82–83; Einaudi, *La condotta*, pp. 121–22.

[36] For the number of contracts see, Caracciolo, "La crescita e la trasformazione," p. 218; for the expenditures of the procurement agencies, F. Zugaro, *Il costo della guerra italiana* (Rome: Stabilimento poligrafico per l'Amministrazione della guerra, 1921), p. 19, quoted in Massimo Mazzetti, *L'industria italiana nella grande guerra* (Rome: Stato maggiore dell'Esercito, 1979), p. 16.

[37] Caracciolo, "La crescita e la trasformazione," p. 219; Mazzetti, *L'industria*, pp. 42–43; Pieri, *L'Italia nella prima guerra mondiale*, pp. 176–77.

the Air Force was detached and assigned to a separate bureau, which was placed under the direction of another deputy, Eugenio Chiesa.[38]

Although charges of exceptional war profits precipitated these institutional changes, it is doubtful that pricing policy became more rigorous thereafter. Dallolio's enemies were motivated more by political and industrial rivalries than by genuine concern about high war profits. The Perrone brothers, directors of the huge Ansaldo concern, sought to secure a privileged position with the procurement agencies by intimidating the officials. They produced a series of memoranda accusing ministry officials and rival companies of incompetence, corruption, and even collusion with the Germans. Such accusations were widely disseminated in newspapers directly or indirectly under the control of Ansaldo. Nitti, who was close to the Perrone brothers, had his own reasons for getting rid of Dallolio: he wanted to turn the Treasury into a kind of super economic ministry and the prestige and discretionary powers of the Ministry of Arms and Munitions stood in his way.[39] Nitti demonstrated his concern for rigor in accounting procedures in the spring of 1918 when he signed a contract with Ansaldo for the construction of 100 locomotives over the head of and without consulting the competent Minister of Transportation.[40] Nor was Nitti above personally intervening to secure raw materials and labor supplies for work on the pharaonic Cogne iron, steel and electrical works being built by Ansaldo high in the mountains of the Val d'Aosta. Construction on the Cogne facility began in the spring of 1918, although the requisite raw materials and labor were in extremely short supply, and although it was clear that it would not become operational until years after the end of the war.[41] Significantly, another ministry official, General Pasquale Tozzi, director of Italian military procurement in the United States, was charged by Nitti and his friends with spending too cautiously, rather than too freely. In addition to accusing him of being under the influence of German agents, Tozzi's enemies argued that his budgetary scruples slowed the flow of desperately needed supplies to Italy and to the

[38] On the events leading up to Dallolio's resignation see Mascolini, "Il ministero per le armi e munizioni," pp. 953–55; Carucci, "Stato e classe operaia," pp. 72–77; Fortunato Minniti, "Alfredo Dallolio (1853–1952)," in Alberto Mortara, ed., *Protagonisti dell'intervento pubblico* (Milan: Angeli, 1984), pp. 186–88; Luciano Segreto, "Statalismo e antistatalismo nell'economia bellica. Gli industriali e la mobilitazione industriale (1915–1918)," in Peter Hertner and Giorgio Mori, eds., *La transizione dall'economia di guerra all'economia di pace in Italia e in Germania dopo la prima guerra mondiale* (Bologna: Il Mulino, 1983), pp. 326–28.

[39] On the relations of Nitti and the Perrone brothers with Dallolio see, in addition to the sources cited above, Alberto Monticone, *Nitti e la grande guerra (1914–1918)* (Milan: Giuffré, 1961), pp. 199–256.

[40] Ibid. pp. 237–46; Franco Bonelli, "Riccardo Bianchi (1854–1936)," in Mortara, ed., *I Protagonisti*, pp. 84–86.

[41] Monticone, *Nitti e la grande guerra*, pp. 219–26.

front. Tozzi was forced to resign and defend himself in front of a parliamentary committee.[42]

The huge stocks of material in the hands of the government at the time of the armistice, and the contracts in the process of being executed were liquidated in the first year of peace in a manner entirely commensurate with the purchasing policies pursued during the war. In December 1918, the Bureau, or General Commissariat of Arms and Munitions – as it had been rechristened after yet another administrative reorganization – and the General Commissariat of Aeronautics were dismantled. Responsibility for pending contracts fell to a new bureau of the Ministry of the Treasury, while another bureau, dependent on the Ministry of Industry, Commerce, and Labor, assumed responsibility for the disposal of excess government stocks of war materials. Ettore Conti, a prominent Milanese industrialist, assumed control of industrial demobilization. As head of the former bureau he was given the title of Under-Secretary of the Treasury; he also chaired an interministerial committee for the restructuring of war industries (Comitato interministeriale per la sistimazione delle industrie di guerra) that received overall responsibility for the liquidation of the war economy.[43] In November 1918 the government was forced to call on private firms with pending military contracts to provide the Treasury with basic information on the nature of the contracts they were working on (D.l. 17 November 1918, no. 1696).[44] Government records were so disorganized that they were unusable as a basis for negotiating the settlement of pending business. Conti later boasted that he saved the Treasury a conspicuous sum by talking down private suppliers from the total of Lit. 7.5bn. they originally claimed to only Lit. 4.5bn.; but given the circumstances under which these negotiations took place, it is difficult to believe that private suppliers fared particularly poorly.[45] As for the liquidation of war stocks, Conti's performance was later qualified by Luigi Gasparotto, a member of the Parliamentary Commission of Inquiry into War Expenditures, as one of the greatest scandals of the post-war period.[46]

[42] The Ministry of Foreign Affairs assembled a copious file on the case. Archivio Storico, Ministero degli Affari Esteri, Archivio Politico (1915–1918), "Italia," 104/15. Sonnino and the Italian ambassador in the United States, Vincenzo Macchi di Cellere, defended Tozzi. More details about the case are in Justus (pseudonym), *Macchi di Cellere all'Ambasciata di Washington. Memorie e testimonianze* (Florence: Bemporad, 1920). Monticone makes only passing references to the Tozzi affair.

[43] Carucci, "Stato e classe operaia," pp. 76–77.

[44] Antonia Carparelli, "Uomini, idee, iniziative per una politica di riconversione industriale in Italia," in Hertner and Mori, eds., *La transizione dall'economia di guerra*, pp. 222–23.

[45] Ettore Conti, *Dal taccuino di un borghese*, 3rd ed. (Bologna: Il Mulino, 1986); Carucci, "Stato e classe operaia," p. 77.

[46] Commissione spese di guerra, "Relazione," vol. II, p. 799, quoted in, Giorgio Rochat, *L'esercito italiano da Vittoria Veneto a Mussolini (1919–1925)* (Bari: Laterza, 1967), p. 65.

Lack of information impeded the government from recovering or securing payment for the raw and semi-finished materials it had consigned to private industry. But Conti was equally negligent in disposing of the huge stocks of material and equipment in the possession of the military services, the procurement agencies, and other government departments at the end of the war. Proper inventories of government stocks did not exist at the termination of the war, and Conti made no effort to have them drawn up. Not surprisingly, allegations of corruption and thievery were widespread. Even worse, in the course of 1919 government materials were sold off hastily with little concern either for economic reconversion or state revenue. Much of the material was disposed of in individual deals rather than through public auction, creating opportunities for middlemen and speculators. Fourteen consortia, dominated by the largest firms, were formed to take responsibility for the liquidation of stocks of distinct materials. Not surprisingly, the parliamentary commission concluded that the consortia tended to put the interests of member firms above those of the state or the economy as a whole.[47] Conti, who had just been appointed to the board of the Banca Commerciale and was soon to become president of the major Italian business association, the Confindustria, clearly acted as a fox sent to guard the henhouse. If some industrialists, like the Perrone brothers of Ansaldo, complained about his administration, it was because they faulted him for partiality in the division of the spoils.[48]

The financial and economic consequences of Conti's maladministration are evident if one compares his record with the liquidation of Italian and Allied war stocks in Italy under the direction of Ernesto Rossi after World War II. Rossi was determined to avoid the débâcle that took place after World War I. His "Azienda per il rilievo e l'alienazione dei residuati," or ARAR, spread the sale of war stocks over a five-year period, with the greater part of the sales concentrated in the first three years (1946–48). Rossi saw to it that special units of *carabinieri* guarded government stockpiles to prevent pilfering. Accurate inventories were drawn up. Materials were auctioned off in relatively modest quantities, so as to enable smaller firms to compete effectively. In timing sales, Rossi sought to balance the state's need for revenue with more general economic considerations; he promoted economic recovery and diminished inflationary pressures by maintaining a steady offer of basic raw and semi-finished materials on the market.[49]

Not surprisingly, the Italian liquidation of war stocks after World War I

---

[47] Commissione spese di guerra, "Relazione," vol. II, pp. 754–802; Carparelli, "Uomini, idee, iniziative," pp. 229–47.   [48] Conti, *Dal taccuino di un borghese*.

[49] On Rossi and the ARAR see, Antonia Carparelli, "Ernesto Rossi (1897–1967)," in Mortara, ed., *I protagonisti*, pp. 618–46.

compares unfavorably with the British performance as well. As Chancellor of the Exchequer, Austen Chamberlain made revenues from the sale of war materials a cornerstone of his 1919 budget. He expected the Treasury to realize £st. 254m. on the sale of excess stocks that year out of a total estimated revenue of £st. 1,201m.; in the event, receipts from sales of stocks actually exceeded this figure. The British government spread the bulk of sales over a period of two years, whereas Conti had largely liquidated his stocks by mid-summer of 1919.[50]

The Italian government not only failed to control the prices of its suppliers, it also failed to use direct economic controls to block alternative forms of consumption and particularly investment. State costs were driven higher by private competition for scarce resources. During the war, much was made of increases in private consumption. Conservatives were appalled at the appreciable rise in popular consumption in the course of the war. In effect, Barberi has calculated that total consumption rose during the war because of the increase in consumption of primary necessities (food, clothing, shelter, heat), but particularly food. Secondary and luxury consumption, in contrast, fell.[51] But conservatives did not take into account that the primary cause of increased popular consumption was the demand for soldiers and the increased demand for labor. Italy's mass army in World War I was drawn to a disproportionate degree from the urban and particularly the rural poor. Military rations were often far superior, nutritionally and calorically, to the fare that draftees had been accustomed to in civilian life. It is not that Italian military rations were particularly generous – their caloric content was less than the average rations in the American, British, and French armies – pre-war consumption was simply very low.[52] The civilian population ate better on the whole too during the war. The elimination of unemployment and underemployment inevitably put more purchasing power in the hands of the poorest strata of society. Total consumption increased because Italy's surplus population, for the first time, now was needed, and had to be properly fed and to some degree also properly clothed. This phenomenon was not unique to Italy in World War I: the literature suggests that in France too popular consumption increased during the war, although pre-war living standards in France were much higher than in Italy.[53]

---

[50] On Britain, Morgan, *British Financial Policy*, p. 95; Allen and Hirst, *British War Budgets*, pp. 246–47, 298.

[51] Benedetto Barberi, *I consumi nel primo secolo dell'unità d'Italia (1861–1960)* (Milan: Giuffré, 1961).

[52] Melograni, *Storia politica della grande guerra*, p. 319. Italian military rations actually had a slightly higher caloric content than those in France until December 1916.

[53] See the review article, Patrizia Dogliani, "Stato, imprenditori e manodopera industriale in Francia durante la prima guerra mondiale," *Rivista di storia contemporanea*, 11 (1982), no. 4, pp. 536–37.

Italian governments also had an important political reason for ensuring a satisfactory level of popular consumption: they knew the war was not popular and hoped to pacify the population by guaranteeing the food supply. Keynes remarked on the importance the Italian government set on food supplies in the memo written for the British Treasury quoted above. He noted the clear Italian preference for using scarce foreign exchange and shipping resources for cereal imports above other kinds of imports.[54] Financing increased popular consumption was the price the Italian authorities paid for fighting a total war that the greater part of the population was never enthusiastic about.

Government opponents on the left decried the ostentation and consumerism of the rich, particularly the war profiteers. But the rich were relatively few in number, and the economic impact of luxury consumption declined steadily in the course of the war. As was noted above, total private consumption of goods other than primary necessities declined. Government demand, and later, government control over the allocation of transportation and raw materials eventually cut the quantity of luxury goods available on the market.

The real problem in Italy was private investment. A series of deductions and exemptions modified the regime of ordinary and extraordinary direct taxes in order to encourage investment. The shipbuilding industry was the primary benefactor. The so-called Arlotta decree of 10 August 1916 (no. 1031) granted exemption from direct taxes on the earnings of freighters purchased abroad for the first three years of operation, and five years of tax exemption for freighters built in Italy. Critics at the time noted that the law encouraged ship construction in Italy at a time when military imperatives should have induced the government to restrict it. Domestic shipbuilding required imports of most of the requisite raw materials, such as coal and scrap iron. More scarce shipping space was taken up by imports of materials for ship construction than was gained by new shipping capacity coming on the line during the war.[55] The law epitomizes the attitude prevalent at the time that strengthening industry and particularly strategic industries was a desirable end of financial policy in itself. Other industries that were favored by tax exemptions or deductions included domestic coal mining, electricity, plant located in or near Rome, and facilities built or rebuilt in the invaded provinces of the northeast.[56] From 1915, generous

[54] PRO, T-files, T1/12033/5070/17.
[55] On the special legislation for shipbuilding see, Einaudi, *Il sistema tributario*, pp. 190–95; Einaudi, *Corriere della Sera*, 27 January 1917, republished in, *Cronache*, vol. IV, pp. 419–23.
[56] Einaudi, *Il sistema tributario*, pp. 197–98; Ministro delle Finanze, Direzione Generale delle Imposte Dirette, *La gestione delle imposte dirette dal 1914 al 1925* (Rome: Provveditorato Generale dello Stato, 1926), p. 51.

deductions on investments undertaken to increase production of armaments and munitions were granted. Naturally, one purpose of such legislation was to encourage conversion for war production. But the provisions of the laws, particularly after they were modified by D.l. 18 January 1917, no. 145, were so generous that new plant which later could be converted to non-military purposes enjoyed considerable fiscal privileges. The law did not encourage industrialists to undertake investments of maximum utility to the war effort, but rather to make investments that offered the greatest likely utility in peacetime. D.l. 24 November 1919, no. 2164 pushed even farther in this direction: because all profits in excess of 1914 levels were subject to the war profits tax, it was reasoned, all investments in sectors where such profits prevailed ought to be eligible for the exemptions envisaged by the earlier law.[57]

The most representative piece of wartime productivist financial legislation was the so-called Legge Cavasola, D.l. 7 February 1916, no. 123. The law restricted the distribution of annual dividends to 8% of invested capital for firms which had existed at the outbreak of the war and to 10% for firms which were constituted thereafter. Only firms that had already distributed higher dividends in the last three years of peace were allowed to exceed these limits, at a level commensurate with earlier profits. The law was promulgated by Giannetto Cavasola, Minister of Industry, Commerce, and Agriculture, rather than by the Minister of Finance. Its purpose was to, "safeguard the future of business, strengthening its property base during the current exceptional circumstances." The intent of the law was not to curtail purchasing power in the hands of shareholders and hence to restrict consumption, but to encourage firms to use war profits to retire debts and make new investments. The law provoked considerable controversy that reveals much about the productivist attitudes prevalent in the government, and in broad sectors of public opinion. Some critics on the left wanted the reserves accumulated under the provisions of the law to be invested in state securities or some other form of liquid assets. There was in particular a fear that the reserves could be employed to raise share capital, which then would enable firms to distribute larger dividends. The law itself was worded highly ambiguously. Cavasola declared publicly that his sole intention had been to reinforce the financial structure of firms, leaving administrators free to employ their reserves as they wished. Liberals like Luigi Einaudi came to the defense of Cavasola, insisting that firms should be allowed to use the reserves to make investments. Ultimately, Cavasola was constrained to compromise. D.l. 3 September 1916, no. 1108 modified the earlier law; firms were now obliged to invest

[57] Einaudi, *Il sistema tributario*, pp. 167–68, 174–90.

one-third of the special shareholders' reserves in state securities, but they were free to utilize the other two-thirds as they saw fit, including new capital issues.[58]

Italian government regulation of the stock market stands in striking contrast to British policy.[59] Whereas in Britain the market was reopened quickly after the financial crisis of August 1914, the Italian market was not reopened until the beginning of October 1917. Official trading was suspended quickly again in the wake of the Caporetto disaster less than a month later, and it was not allowed to resume until after the armistice. But whereas in Britain new stock issues were prohibited without Treasury permission – which rarely was granted – in Italy new stock and bond offerings were not restricted in any way. By the end of 1915 the booming business climate induced Italian firms to take ample advantage of the benign attitude of the authorities. Fiat increased its share capital in November 1915 by utilizing undistributed profits. Two of the major four commercial banks, the Credito Italiano and the newly formed Banca Italiana di Sconto, increased their capital in 1916. Bachi noted the renewed interest of all of the large commercial banks in underwriting stock and bond issues in 1916. By 1917, the high level of liquidity and economic activity generated by the war provoked a flood of new stock and bond issues. All four major commercial banks increased their capital. Ansaldo successfully sold obligations for Lit. 100m. The investment boom expanded in 1918. Again, all four major commercial banks raised their share capital. In the summer, Ansaldo made a spectacular stock issue to increase its share capital from Lit. 100m. to Lit. 500m. All four of the major commercial banks participated in the underwriting syndicate. The subscription campaign was carried out, in Bachi's words, "with sonorous propaganda, which made some think it was a patriotic undertaking, analogous to the national loan subscription campaigns."[60]

Einaudi and others decried the evident incompatibility of huge stock and bond issues with the financial needs of the state.[61] Finally, D.l. 24 March 1918, no. 382 subjected new issues to the approval of a commission

---

[58] On the Legge Cavasola see Einaudi's articles in the *Corriere della Sera*, 15 February 1916; 24 February 1916; 6 October 1916; 7 October 1916; 8 October 1916; 11 November 1916; 25 January 1917, *Cronache*, vol. IV, pp. 298–334; Cesare Vivante, "La limitazione dei dividendi," *Il Sole*, 28–29 February 1916; Angelo Sraffa, "Alcune note sul decreto limitante i dividendi," *Il Sole*, 10 March 1916; Roberto Pozzi, "La limitazione dei dividendi. Altri quesiti," *Il Sole*, 13–14 March 1916.

[59] On Britain see, Morgan, *British Financial Policy*, p. 52; on Italy, Riccardo Bachi, *L'Italia economica nell'anno 1915*; *L'Italia economica nell'anno 1916*; *L'Italia economica nell'anno 1917*; *L'Italia economica nell'anno 1918* (Città di Castello: S. Lapi, 1916–19).

[60] Riccardo Bachi, *L'Italia economica nell'anno 1921* (Città di Castello: S. Lapi, 1922), p. 55.

[61] See Einaudi's articles in, *Corriere della Sera*, 8 March 1918; 25 July 1918, *Cronache*, vol. IV, pp. 619–31.

formed under the control of the Minister of Industry, Commerce, and Labor. New issues were to be judged on the basis of the soundness of the firm, and the importance of the purpose for which the funds were intended. Far from restricting new issues, the commission actually seems to have encouraged them. Bachi protested that commission approval was regarded as a kind of government certification of the soundness of capital issues and actually increased their popularity.[62]

The legislation discussed above indicates the unwillingness of successive governments to restrain industrial investments, even where these investments conflicted with the goal of maximizing war production. The Italian government failed to utilize taxation to absorb purchasing power in the private sector in part because it did not wish to absorb purchasing power. At the most, it sought to divert purchasing power from consumption to investment. Strategic investments were understood not in the narrow sense of investments that were likely to enhance the fighting capacity of the Italian and Allied armies during the war, but in the broadest sense of investments that were likely to strengthen the Italian industrial base for the future.

Direct taxes during the war

The experience of industrialized nations in the twentieth century suggests that if an appreciable proportion of wartime state expenditure is to be covered by current revenues, the greatest part of the burden must fall on direct taxes. The performance of Great Britain, the European power by far most successful in increasing tax revenue during both world wars, is exemplary. In the final three budgets preceding World War I, 1911/12–1913/14, direct revenues in Britain accounted for from 25% to 32% of total tax revenues; in the final three wartime budgets 1915/16–1917/18, direct taxes accounted for from 60% to 66% of total tax revenues. In the final three peacetime budgets prior to World War II 1936/37–1938/39, direct taxes made up 37%–43% of total British tax revenues. In the three budgets 1942/43–1944/45 that figure climbed to 55%–57%.[63]

In Italy, as we have seen, even prior to the outbreak of war debates about fiscal reform focused on raising direct tax revenues, and this was the area in which the major wartime innovations occurred. During the last three years of peace 1912–14 direct taxes made up 27%–29% of total Italian tax receipts; by 1919 they constituted 38%. The contribution of transactions

---

[62] Bachi, *L'Italia economica nell'anno 1918*, pp. 71–75.
[63] B. R. Mitchell, *European Historical Statistics, 1750–1975*, 2nd rev. ed. (New York: Facts on File, 1981), p. 762.

taxes held relatively steady at about 14% of total tax revenue during the war years, while consumption tax receipts fell in real terms by more than half between 1914 and 1919, and from 56% to 48% of total tax returns (see Table 22, Appendix, p. 327). As we shall see, direct taxes were passed back to the state most easily.

The authorities pursued two strategies to increase direct tax revenues during World War I: they increased tax quotas, and they created an array of new, extraordinary war taxes. A surtax on each of the three permanent direct taxes of 2% that had originally been imposed in 1908 to finance reconstruction after the Messina earthquake was raised to 5% in October 1914. In December, a 10% increase in all direct taxes was approved by parliament.[64] Two years later, the authorities undertook a far more drastic, and irrational, restructuring of the traditional direct taxes. D.l. 9 November 1916, no. 1525 introduced progressivity into land and *ricchezza mobile* tax assessments, despite the fact that these taxes had single income- producing activities, rather than total individual or family income as their object. Land taxes only were graduated according to assessments within individual tax districts, so that a landowner with property scattered across several districts would pay at a lower rate than a second landowner with an equivalent property assessment within a single district. The 1916 law introduced only a moderate degree of progressivity into the *ricchezza mobile* tax; assessments continued to be graduated also on the basis of the pre-war distinction between "unearned," "mixed," and "earned" income. D.l. 9 September 1917, no. 1546 imposed a fully progressive regime on both the building and the *ricchezza mobile* taxes. The same technical flaws that marred the progressivity of the land tax now applied to the building tax. The *ricchezza mobile* tax was no less flawed. Two independent sources of income to an individual would be assessed separately. The *ricchezza mobile* made no distinction between corporations and individuals, to the considerable disadvantage of collective enterprises.[65] Quotations ranged as high as 20% for the upper brackets, but this must be set against the plethora of other extraordinary direct taxes that were assessed on the same income. Hence, by the latter stages of the war the Italian authorities had perverted completely their pre-war system of direct taxation by imposing progressivity on real taxes. The operation was much criticized by economists and by the minority of taxpayers whose incomes were insufficiently elastic to offset tax increases. The authorities justified the measures solely on the basis of increased government need for revenue.[66]

To supplement the revenues from the traditional direct taxes – and to

[64] Direzione Generale delle Imposte Dirette, *La gestione*, p. 135.
[65] Ibid., pp. 86–144; Einaudi, *Il sistema tributario*, pp. 79–86.
[66] Direzione Generale della Imposte Dirette, *La gestione*, pp. 86–144.

satisfy public opinion that war profiteers were being taxed – the authorities instituted a series of extraordinary taxes. The most important of these was the so-called Extraordinary War Profits Tax. It was decreed in late 1915 (R.d. 21 November 1915, no. 1643) and conformed closely to the British Excess Profits Duty, which became law in December 1915, although it had been proposed earlier than the Italian tax. Unlike the British tax, the Extraordinary Profits Tax was to be levied only on profits stemming directly or indirectly from the war. The burden of proof that high profits realized after 1 August 1914 did not stem from the war was left, however, to the taxpayer. Extraordinary war profits were defined as profits over 8% except in cases where firms or individuals could demonstrate that they had realized higher average profits in the three years before the war; in that case profits up to the previous level were not subject to the tax. War profits were taxed at rates of up to 60%, and after R.d. 24 November 1919, no. 2164, 80%. Eventually it was established that the tax was to apply to all earnings of industrialists, merchants, and intermediaries up to the end of June 1920.[67]

In addition to the war profits tax, Italian authorities created a number of other, less important extraordinary direct taxes. Some functioned in practice merely as an addition to existing direct taxes. In order to prevent corporations from evading regulations limiting the distribution of dividends, special taxes were imposed on corporate directors and administrators. A tax on the income of administrators of limited liability corporations was decreed on 12 October 1915 (R.d. no. 1510). Later, a separate tax was imposed on non-salary emoluments to the directors and upper management echelons of corporations (D.l. 28 February 1918, no. 237).[68] Various taxes were imposed on males of military age who for one reason or another had not been called up to serve, or who served in non-combat positions. These taxes cost much to collect, yielded little, and eventually were discontinued.[69] Finally, there were the *centesimi della guerra*, or "war pennies" (R.d. 21 November 1915, no. 1643, in effect from 1 January 1916). The *centesimi* legislation set up two distinct taxes. One part consisted of an additional surtax of 2% on the three permanent direct taxes, similar to the earlier earthquake *centesimi*. The other tax was a charge levied on all payments of the state and other public administrations to private parties for services rendered. In other words, government agencies only were to pay first Lit. 99, then Lit. 98 (1 July 1916), and finally Lit. 97

---

[67] Ibid., pp. 47–53; Einaudi, *Il sistema tributario*, pp. 129–37.
[68] Direzione Generale delle Imposte Dirette, *La gestione*, pp. 27–33; Einaudi, *Il sistema tributario*, pp. 71–128.
[69] Direzione Generale delle Imposte Dirette, *La gestione*, pp. 7–11; Einaudi, *Il sistema tributario*, pp. 107–21.

(4 June 1918) on contracts stipulated at Lit. 100. This was the easiest and the most obvious direct tax to evade by passing costs back to the state.[70]

As Table 23 indicates (Appendix, p. 327), increases in direct tax revenue lagged behind inflation until fiscal 1920/21. Nevertheless, inflation-indexed direct tax revenues declined less than consumption and transaction taxes. Extraordinary war taxes came to make up an ever greater part of direct tax revenues (see Tables 5 and 6, Appendix, pp. 304–5). By 1918/19 the war profits tax yielded more than the tax on *ricchezza mobile*. The land and building taxes declined to insignificance as a proportion of total revenue.

The greater part of wartime direct tax revenue was vulnerable to evasion by passing costs back to the state. This was most true of the extraordinary taxes levied on war profits, but it was also true to a large degree of the *ricchezza mobile*. According to ISTAT figures, state spending made up 12% of gross national income in 1913/14, 25% in 1914/15, 45% in 1915/16, 53% in 1916/17, 59% in 1917/18 and 58% in 1918/19; hence most direct taxes were paid on earnings accruing from the sale of goods and services destined directly or indirectly for state consumption, at a time when state costs were uncontrolled.[71] Nor was this structural problem of taxation unknown at the time. The *centesimi della guerra*, which were deducted from payments on public contracts, were notoriously ineffective, and they were singled out for criticism by Bachi and Einaudi.[72] This did not prevent Ferdinando Bocca, president of the Turin Chamber of Commerce, from proposing in November 1915 that the newly established extraordinary profits tax be abandoned, and the rate of the *centesimi* be increased instead.[73] Pasquale D'Aroma, Director General of Direct Taxes in the Finance Ministry in the years following the war, wrote the definitive requiem of the *centesimi*:

> for it [the *centesimi* tax on payments made by the state and other public administrations] the transfer from the private taxpayer to his debtor, the state administration, must have been normal, and often explicitly recognized. Cases were not infrequent in which state administrations, in calculating prices for requisitions, took account of the *centesimi* by adding it to the total amount paid.
> Often, in state contracts there was a clause which envisaged their revision, in case of increases in taxes.

[70] Direzione Generale delle Imposte Dirette, *La gestione*, pp. 12–15; Einaudi, *Il sistema tributario*, pp. 94–99.
[71] Paolo Ercolani, "Documentazione statistica di base," in, Giorgio Fuà, ed., *Lo sviluppo*, vol. III, p. 443.
[72] Bachi, *L'Italia economica nell'anno 1916*, p. 333; Einaudi, *Il sistema tributario*, pp. 96–97.
[73] On Bocca see, Luigi Albertini, *Epistolario, 1911–1926*, ed. O. Barié (Verona: Mondadori, 1968), pp. 503–4.

With regard to the state, therefore, this tax on state contracts represented a *partita di giro* [circle play], when it was not the cause of even greater profit for the contractors, who shrewdly used it to justify even bigger price increases.

In conclusion, the *centesimi* seems in retrospect to have been inefficient, if not actually harmful, when applied to state contracts.[74]

Bocca was unjustifiably worried that other forms of direct taxation would prove considerably more difficult to evade, but no doubt he, like other industrialists, was soon pacified as the dynamics of the fiscal *partita di giro* became clear. The difficulty of absorbing purchasing power with the war profits tax in a regime of uncontrolled prices on state contracts was evident to more perspicacious observers from the beginning. Even before the decree establishing this tax was promulgated, Einaudi criticized the legislation privately in a letter to *Corriere della Sera* director Luigi Albertini: "For me: the war profits tax is stuff for the theater, Giolitti-style: the serious and *truly productive* [emphasis L.E.] measure is the reform of tax assessments."[75]

Albertini, who at that time was close politically to Salandra's government, responded with revealing candor: "Unfortunately, taxes must be considered not only from a strictly scientific standpoint, but also from a political standpoint. Politically, the tax on war profits [is] necessary . . ."[76]

Political considerations undoubtedly explain why Einaudi's commentary on the war profits tax that later appeared in the *Corriere della Sera* was considerably more muted than the opinion he had expressed privately earlier. In the midst of an overall positive judgment of the government's new financial measures, he nevertheless allowed the following observation to escape:

> yet it is unclear whether real revenues will not end up being greatly inferior to apparent revenues, because of the almost ineluctable tendency the tax will have to become a *partita di giro* between the Ministries of War and the Treasury, with little real effect on the apparent taxpayers (industrialists and intermediaries).[77]

Political considerations continued to inhibit the liberal economists from exposing the fictive character of a substantial part of government revenue. Although liberals like Einaudi only partially accepted the productivist logic that justified leaving fabulous war profits in the hands of industrialists, they were reluctant to make public statements that would damage the

---

[74] Direzione Generale delle Imposte Dirette, *La gestione*, p. 16.
[75] Einaudi to Albertini, 4 November 1915, Fondazione Einaudi, Turin, Archivio Luigi Einaudi, Carteggio.
[76] Albertini, *Epistolario*, pp. 503–4.
[77] Einaudi, *Corriere della Sera*, 27 November 1915, *Cronache*, vol. IV, p. 267.

credit of the state internationally or domestically. Einaudi's liberal ideological orientation made him unwilling to espouse rigid state controls on
production, and the extension of fixed prices throughout the arms and
munitions sector. Although Einaudi praised the British Ministry of Munitions for realizing economies on war-related items, he never advocated
using Lloyd George's methods. In reality, Einaudi was closer to the
theoretical position of the ultra-liberal critics of British government
policy, such as Hartley Withers, the director of *The Economist*. Withers
argued that efficient mobilization could have been accomplished without
direct controls, using financial incentives alone, and that the requisite
funds could have been raised exclusively through state borrowing from
real savings and taxation.[78] Neither Withers nor Einaudi ever fully came
to grips with the dynamics of the *partita di giro*. The other Italian liberal
economists were equally reluctant, for ideological reasons, to advocate
systematic economic controls. Patriotic economists were willing to criticize specific technical aspects of government fiscal policy, but they drew
back from suggesting that state revenues were largely fictitious.

Einaudi returned to the argument of the *partita di giro* again only in
February 1918 to counter government resistance to implementing the
Meda project, which proposed to restructure fundamentally the perma-
nent direct tax system:

> The financial bureaucracy imagines that the war allows it to commit a few
> *coups de main* with impunity, to grind out a few millions here and there,
> wherever it is easiest, without any rationalization, so long as it finds the
> millions.
>   It is painful to note that one does not make millions like that, one loses
> millions. The apparent revenue figures grow, one throws sand in the eyes of
> the public: but effective, restorative [sic] revenues do not grow. How much
> sand in the eyes of the public is there in the hundreds of millions of the
> centesimo, in the stamp tax on war contracts, in the war profits tax![79]

Einaudi took up the problem once more in August 1920, at a time when
the *Corriere della Sera* was waging a bitter campaign against Giolitti's last
government and its financial proposals. With the return of peace and the
termination of Allied credits, *raison d'état* no longer restrained him from
formulating a franker judgment about wartime taxation:

> When it is possible to make a final account, one will see that this whole
> business of the extraordinary profits tax was a colossal *partita di giro*. The

---

[78] Hartley Withers, *Wartime Financial Problems* (New York: Dalton, 1920), p. 43, quoted in,
Morgan, *British Financial Policy*, p. 34. Einaudi professed his esteem for Withers and his
ideas in, *Corriere della Sera*, 1 February 1916, 8 January 1918, *Cronache*, vol. IV, pp. 289,
462.

[79] Einaudi, *Corriere della Sera*, 26 February 1918, *Cronache*, vol. IV, p. 536.

state will have taken back a part of the excess of what it gave in the first place, and the contractors made sure they got too much anticipating confiscatory taxes. The net result will be an enormous waste of energy and resources.[80]

Remarkably, the problem of fictive revenues is accorded only modest attention in Einaudi's 1927 monograph on the Italian tax system during the war. Here all of the emphasis is on the technical deficiencies and the resulting incongruities of wartime taxation: the neglect in updating tax assessments, and the (largely post-war) injustices perpetrated against the taxpayers because of excessively high rates. Einaudi mentioned the *partita di giro* here only in connection with the *centesimi della guerra*, and not in his discussion of the war profits tax. The fact that Einaudi, as is noted above, reaffirmed as late as 1961 that Italy pursued a more rigorous financial policy than the other continental powers leaves one to suspect that the preoccupation to affirm Italy's financial sacrifice in the "fourth war of the Risorgimento" remained a constant among erstwhile interventionists. Einaudi's reasoning in 1961 derives straight from Hartley Withers: he suggests that state expenditures should and could have been met solely out of borrowing from real savings and taxation. War profits should not have been allowed to form in the first place; but Einaudi does not hint that this goal should have been achieved by direct production and price controls. Rather, there is every reason to assume that, for Einaudi, excess profits were merely the consequence of, "incompetence, frivolity, and the habit of letting things go of the functionaries in making purchases and drawing up contracts for the state," as he had put it in a *Corriere della Sera* article in 1916.[81]

In reality, most of the direct taxes during the war were evaded as easily as the *centesimi della guerra* and for the same reasons. D'Aroma's verdict on the war profits tax holds for the entire system:

> For many incomes dependent on state contracts, when it was not a question of taxes being assessed on annual profits, they were eluded in large measure – because the contractor was able to make the state pay by increasing his prices.
>
> There were cases in which special clauses were inserted in contracts, whereby the state was obliged to pay the war profits tax, or, more simply, taxes were itemized among the contractors' costs.[82]

Given that government payments were generally prompter than tax assessments, taxes became a sort of interest-free loan to war contractors.

[80] Einaudi, "Le ritorsioni de 'La Stampa'," *Corriere della Sera*, 6 August 1920, *Cronache*, vol. V, p. 780.
[81] Einaudi, *Corriere della Sera*, 6 October 1916, *Cronache*, vol. IV, p. 310.
[82] Direzione Generale delle Imposte Dirette, *La gestione*, p. 61.

In a period of brisk inflation, this situation brought notable advantage to the taxpayer. The substantial revenues collected by the state on the war profits tax in the four fiscal years following its abolition in June 1920 is an indication of just how long these loans could be.

The end of hostilities, and the winding up of state contracts, meant winding up the fiscal *partita di giro*. Manufacturers who had looked upon wartime expedients such as the imposition of progressive rates on real taxes, and the introduction of a panoply of new extraordinary taxes with relative equanimity, were bound to change their views once the state was no longer willing to purchase everything they produced at almost any price, and they were forced to compete for customers on competitive markets. At the same time, the government still had to cope with huge budget deficits, and it was more anxious than ever to increase tax collections. Tax reform could not be postponed much longer: but as we shall see, liberal political leaders found it difficult on the one hand to impose draconian taxes on a business community reeling from the shocks of raw materials shortages, labor unrest, and beginning in mid-1920 world recession; while socialists and Catholics, on the other hand, were unwilling to settle for the moderate tax reforms proposed by the Meda Commission, particularly after witnessing the huge wealth transfers engendered by the war economy.

3

THE LIMITS OF STATE BORROWING
CAPACITY

A universal consequence of the prodigious increase in government expenditure and the considerably more moderate growth in revenue collections during World War I was huge increases in the size of national debts. Not only did the national debts of all the major belligerents expand to unprecedented size during the war, but the structure of the debt also changed unfavorably, with the growth of floating debts outpacing that of consolidated debts. The enormous growth of the floating debt would become an issue of grave concern throughout Europe in the post-war era, as political leaders worried about the willingness of investors to roll over their holdings of short-term securities, and about the monetization of the debt in the event they did not.

A large floating debt bedeviled post-war Italy too, but on the basis of official statistics, Italy's situation looked relatively favorable compared to that of the other belligerents, and only slightly worse than Britain's. Using UN statistics, Ettore Gatti arrived at the following estimates for floating debt as a percentage of total internal debt:[1]

	Britain	France	Germany	Italy
1914	1.8	17.9	4.6	5.9
1918	23.7	45.2	31.7	34.0
1920	19.7	38.8	51.8	29.8

Italian statesmen at the time, most notably Nitti, who as Minister of the Treasury in 1918 and Prime Minister in 1920 presided over the issue of the two largest consolidated war loans, were well aware of these figures, and they pointed to the nominal success of the consolidated war loans as evidence of Italy's financial solidity.

In this chapter it will be argued, however, that nominal yields of Italian government loans in World War I bore little relationship to their real

[1] Ettori Gatti, "Appendice statistica," in Antonio Confalonieri and Ettori Gatti, *La politica del debito pubblico in Italia, 1919–1943* (Bari: Cariplo-Laterza, 1986), p. 474.

effectiveness as an instrument for absorbing private purchasing power. Loan subscribers evaded surrendering purchasing power to the state by means of a financial *partita di giro* that closely resembled the "circle play" whereby taxpayers passed their costs back to the state in the form of higher prices. Italian Treasury and central bank authorities had sufficient influence to coerce large institutional investors into making generous subscriptions to the national loans, but banks and manufacturing firms quickly recovered their former liquidity positions by selling securities on the market or by using them as collateral for loans from banks. Both of these actions reduced state borrowing capacity. When institutional investors dumped state securities on the market shortly after loan drives, it provoked a quick decline in their market value. Smaller savers, who retained the securities in their portfolios, suffered an immediate capital loss that made them more reluctant to subscribe to future government loans. Low market values for state securities naturally constrained the government to accept steadily more onerous terms on successive loans. The increasing use of state securities as collateral for bank advances amounted to the indirect monetization of the national debt. Government borrowing provoked steadily larger increases in commercial credit, and a corresponding increase in the money supply. Like taxes, to an increasing degree the war loans came to have inflationary effects.

These limitations on state borrowing capacity were not unique to Italy. All belligerents experienced a steady decline in the market value of long-term state securities, and were constrained to offer higher rates of return on successive issues. Monetary authorities in other countries offered modest interest rates for advances on state securities, so as to enhance their attractiveness to subscribers. In all countries, including the United States and Great Britain, greatly expanded state borrowing led to an expansion of bank credit during and particularly after the war. The locus of Italy's unique difficulties was not in financial or monetary policy, but rather in the unwillingness of the authorities to control private invest-ment. The fundamental contradiction between harnessing national financial and economic resources to prosecute the war and encouraging industrial expansion limited the extent, and undermined the effectiveness of government borrowing. In Britain, where private consumption and investment were more effectively limited by a comprehensive system of direct economic controls, private savers had little choice but to invest in government securities. In Italy, private investments were not only tolerated, but actively encouraged, with the consequence that state bor-rowing capacity was reduced correspondingly.

As was the case with tax revenues in the course of the war, the nominal yield of government loans diverged ever farther from the effective capacity of state security issues to absorb private purchasing power. Successive loan drives were organized with ever more publicity and patriotic fanfare, and nominal subscription yields were ever more impressive; but an increasing proportion of successive security issues were monetized by commercial borrowing from the issue banks. Like tax revenues, yields from the sale of government securities became increasingly fictitious, and the fiction was willfully cultivated for political reasons.

Government policies produced two distinct types of investor in state securities. A first group, composed predominantly of individual, small savers, bought government securities as a long-term investment. These investors incurred substantial capital losses in the war and post-war years through the inflation tax and the decline in the market value of state securities. A second group of predominantly large, institutional investors bought short and medium-term government securities as liquid, but inter-est-bearing assets, and was coerced into buying long-term securities by central bank and Treasury authorities. The behavior of this second group of investors was inimical to the interests of the first group. Larger, institutional investors dumped securities on the market after war loan subscription drives, causing their value to decline. In addition, the larger investors borrowed against short and long-term securities, stimulating inflation. This situation produced a dilemma for the authorities. Government officials coerced large institutional investors into making greater subscriptions to national loans than they actually wished, to keep the cost of state borrowing below market rates, and to make the loan drives appear more successful than they actually were. However, such policies ultimately alienated the mass of small savers who were prepared to hold state securities as a long-term investment. Steadily greater nominal successes for state loan drives were obtained at the cost of increasing discontent among the strata of the population that generated real savings. With time, small savers lost confidence not only in government securities, but also in the existing political leadership and institutions.

Italian state borrowing falls roughly into two periods, with the fourth national loan drive in early 1917 representing a transitory phase. State borrowing in the earlier period was characterized by the relative financial conservatism of the Salandra government. The sums raised in the first three national loans of January 1915, July 1915, and January 1916 – Lit. 1,000m., Lit. 1,145m., and Lit. 3,018m. respectively – were relatively modest in relation to subsequent war loans, and reflected the reluctance of the Salandra government to incur debts of a magnitude that would make post-war funding problematic (see Table 9, Appendix, p. 308). The first three loans did not provoke a significant long-term rise in the volume of commercial credit extended by the issue banks. Before each of these three loans, issue bank commercial credit expanded as subscribers borrowed funds in order to make down payments on the new government securities. The authorities encouraged national loan subscribers to take out short-term loans in order to make subscriptions in excess of current cash reserves. After the subscription periods were over, issue bank commercial portfolios contracted again, as loan subscribers repaid their advances from current income (see Figure 1, p. 328).

The problem with the first three loans was that market quotations rapidly declined to below par after the end of the subscription periods (see Table 8, Appendix, p. 307). Contemporary testimony suggests that institutional investors, which had been pressured into making large subscriptions by government and issue bank authorities, sought to regain their former liquidity positions by selling the new securities, even though they were constrained to accept capital losses. The very banks which participated in the underwriting syndicates in some cases sold off the national loan paper.

From early 1917 a different pattern emerges. Nominal subscriptions to the fourth, fifth, and sixth national loans of February 1917, January 1918, and January 1920 – Lit. 3,612m., Lit. 5,926m., and Lit. 20,591m. respectively – far exceeded those of the early loans. More sophisticated and extensive propaganda campaigns accompanied the subscription drives than had been heretofore the case. The huge fifth and sixth loans were closely associated with Francesco Saverio Nitti. As Minister of the Treasury in 1918, and Prime Minister in 1920, he committed his personal prestige and the prestige of his government to raising far larger sums than previous subscription drives had yielded.

In contrast to the earlier loans, the market quotations of the fourth and fifth loans remained at or above par in the months following the subscription drives. Presumably, at this point the issue banks began intervening consistently to sustain the war loans on the market. At the same time, a new relationship between bank of issue commercial portfolios and loan drives emerges from early 1917, which indicates that government securities were used increasingly as collateral for bank credit. Issue bank commercial credit increased in the weeks before the opening of subscriptions for the fourth loan on 5 February 1917, as had been the case in the previous three loan drives. Thereafter, issue bank commercial portfolios declined again, but they stabilized at a level far higher than that of the months prior to the loan drive. After the fifth loan, issue bank commercial portfolios continued to rise. The sixth loan brought about a spectacular rise in commercial credit. The commercial portfolios of the issue banks increased by a factor of 2.4 between October 1919 and June 1920, and the rate of increase was sharpest during and immediately after the loan drive. Greater sales of state securities provoked higher levels of private borrowing. Far from exercising a stabilizing effect on the money stock, the sale of state securities exercised a multiplier effect on it. The government either spent the proceeds of consolidated loans or deposited them in banks. Institutional investors subscribing to government loans took state securities to the issue banks as collateral security for new commercial credits.

The first three war loans, January 1915 – January 1916

War finance was from the beginning a highly charged political issue. The government was reluctant to offer a rate of return on long-term securities that reflected market rates in the uncertain war climate. Salandra and his allies on the parliamentary right had criticized Giolitti for deficitary spending, and the growth of the floating debt in the years after 1911. However, after the conservatives came to power in March 1914, they did not effect a radical change in financial policy. Salandra's Minister of Finance, Luigi Rava, approved only modest tax increases in early 1914. Just before the outbreak of the war in July 1914, the government issued a new series of 5-year Treasury bonds at 4% for Lit. 150m. By the end of 1914, a total of Lit. 1,233m. of 5-year bonds were in circulation, amounting to about 13% of the total national debt.[2] Salandra was as reluctant as his predecessor to offer a long-term security at more than 3.5% and incur the opprobrium of having undone the debt conversion.

By January 1915, however, rearmament expenditures drove Salandra to issue a new long-term security. The loan was limited to Lit. 1,000m. It was in the form of 25-year obligations at 4.5% with the state guaranteeing that it would not undertake a conversion for 10 years. The subscription price was Lit. 97, making the effective interest rate 4.76%. It was to be paid in installments with 10% down, and the balance due by 1 October 1915. The Bank of Italy formed an underwriting syndicate of over 200 financial institutions that guaranteed the loan for up to Lit. 500m. It was a failure. Only Lit. 881m. were subscribed by the general public, leaving the underwriting syndicate to take up the remaining Lit. 119m. Commentators at the time believed that most of the loan was taken up by small savers. Institutional investors apparently held back in the belief that financial needs soon would force the state to issue a new loan on more advantageous terms. According to Bachi, neutralist circles boycotted the loan to discourage Italian intervention in the war.[3] Einaudi believed the government could have raised a far larger amount if it had offered better terms. At the

---

[2] Luigi Einaudi, *Corriere della Sera*, 26 December 1915, republished in Luigi Einaudi, *Cronache economiche e politiche di un trentennio (1893–1926)* (Turin: Einaudi, 1961), vol. IV, p. 108.
[3] Riccardo Bachi, *L'Italia economica nell'anno 1914* (Città di Castello: S. Lapi, 1915).

beginning of December he had written to Luigi Albertini, the director of the *Corriere della Sera* and a close confidant of Salandra, that the moment was propitious for a long-term loan: "It would have considerable success. I have been talking to bankers and foreign exchange dealers; they too are of this opinion. In Italy there is a lot of capital that is waiting for this. Why delay in using it, and fall into chaos."[4]

Despite the alleged liquidity of the capital market, the price of the new security plummeted to Lit. 95.32 by late May, at the time of the first official quotation.

As early as April 1915, even before the Italian intervention in the war, the government began preparing a second war loan. Einaudi took part in the discussions along with Salandra, Eduardo Daneo, Minister of Finance since November 1914, Paolo Carcano, Minister of the Treasury, and Bonaldo Stringher, General Director of the Bank of Italy. Einaudi persuaded the government to remedy what he perceived to be an important defect in the first war loan. Subscribers to the new loan were promised more favorable conditions if any should be offered on new loans through 1916; this provision, it was felt, would prevent investors from holding back from the market in the hope of more advantageous terms later. Subscribers to the previous loan also were offered the new security at a special rate. Einaudi was, however, unsuccessful in convincing the government to issue the new security at 5%. Salandra and the other ministers were reluctant to return openly to the interest rate level that had prevailed before Giolitti's debt conversion. Instead, the government issued 25-year obligations at 4.5%, but at an issue price of Lit. 95. Hence the net rate of interest was 4.74%. Subscribers to the first loan were offered the new security for an amount equal to their previous subscription at Lit. 93 or at a net interest rate of 4.84%. Einaudi and Albertini feared that the government's attempt to conceal the real rate of return on the new security by issuing it under par would succeed only too well; they thought the low nominal interest rate would elicit scarce enthusiasm among the general public. Throughout the spring they pleaded with the government to issue the loan at 5%. Shortly before the decree authorizing the loan was published, Einaudi wrote to Albertini desolately noting that the government had persisted with the 4.5% project. Carcano had assured him that the Treasury needed to raise only Lit. 1 bn. or less and Einaudi conceded that the project was likely to bring in that amount, "although one shouldn't delude oneself into expecting a brilliant result."[5]

[4] Einaudi to Albertini, 4 December 1914, Fondazione Einaudi (henceforth FE), Archivio Einaudi, Carteggio.
[5] Einaudi to Albertini, 28 April 1915; Albertini to Einaudi, 29 April 1915, Luigi Albertini, *Epistolario 1911–1926*, ed. Ottavio Barié (Verona: Mondadori, 1968), vol. I, pp. 345–46,

The second loan was for an unlimited amount with the underwriting syndicate agreeing to take up a fixed sum of Lit. 200m. The subscription period was 1–18 July 1915 in Italy, and slightly longer in the colonies. At first subscriptions proceeded slowly. A coupon was attached to the loan entitling the bearer to a discount on future security issues. The coupons were detachable and soon began to circulate independently at a price far below par.[6] At this point the Bank of Italy probably intervened, as Einaudi argued it should, buying up sufficient quantities of the coupons to bring their price back up to par. Remarks in Albertini's correspondence suggest that the Bank of Italy also applied pressure on the major banking and industrial firms to make larger subscriptions, informing them that if the loan were unsuccessful the government would be constrained to resort to a forced loan.[7] Einaudi had drafted a project for a forced loan on the basis of direct tax assessments and corporate dividends in May at the behest of the government.[8] Bachi noted that industrialists and merchants, including those working on government contracts, took up a significant part of the second loan, whereas they had hardly subscribed to the previous loan in January.[9] The loan yielded about Lit. 1,145.8m., including the Lit. 200m. taken up by the underwriting syndicate.

Despite the reservations of Einaudi and Albertini, the government apparently was satisfied with the yield of the loan. Stringher characterized the result as, *veramente bene*, in the meeting of the board of the Bank of Italy on 26 July 1915.[10] As had been the case after the first loan, market prices quickly plummeted. The first official quotation of the new obligation at the end of September was Lit. 93.92, and it continued to decline in the fall (see Table 8, Appendix, p. 307). Presumably, many institutional investors which had been coerced by the government and the Bank of Italy into making larger subscriptions than they desired quickly sold the new security.

To spur subscriptions to the first and second loans, the issue banks were authorized to make advances against the new obligations for amounts greater than was generally allowed on long-term securities. L. (legge – law) 31 December 1907, no. 804 authorized the issue banks to make advances on short-term Treasury bills for up to 100% of the nominal

---

346–47; Einaudi to Albertini, 4 May 1915; Einaudi to Albertini, 7 May 1915; final citation from Einaudi to Albertini, 14 June 1915, FE, Archivio Einaudi, Carteggio.

[6] Einaudi to Carcano, 1 July 1915, FE, Archivio Einaudi, Carteggio (a copy of this letter is included in a letter of Einaudi to Albertini of the same date).

[7] Albertini to Einaudi, 11 July 1915, Albertini, *Epistolario*, vol. I, p. 421.

[8] Einaudi to Albertini, 7 May 1915, FE, Archivio Einaudi, Carteggio.

[9] Riccardo Bachi, *L'Italia economica nell'anno 1915* (Città di Castello: S. Lapi, 1916), p. 282.

[10] Archivio Storico, Banca d'Italia (henceforth ASBI), fondo 9.2, Consiglio Superiore, verbali, 26 July 1915.

value and on consolidated and medium-term state securities for up to 90% of their *market* value. The banks of issue were authorized to make advances on the first war loan at 4.5% for up to 95% of the nominal value of the loan. In the event, the issue banks practiced more restrictive policies. With the fall in the market value of the first loan the issue banks would otherwise have run the risk of absorbing the entire issue in their commercial portfolios.[11] For the second loan, the issue banks were authorized to make advances for up to 95% of market value. This norm was rigorously enforced. On 11 August 1915, when the market value of 4.5% securities had dipped to nearly Lit. 93, Stringher issued a directive to branches of the Bank of Italy requiring them to limit advances on 4.5% state obligations to Lit. 88 per Lit. 100 of nominal capital. If branch offices had made advances for proportionally greater sums, they were to require borrowers to increase their collateral or reduce their debt.[12] This policy, although more liberal than the norm, was hardly calculated to support the market price of the second loan.

Albertini worried that the rapid decline in the market value of the first two national loans would make government borrowing more difficult in the future:

> I think that the security was issued at too onerous a price. They should have had the courage to go down to 90 or at least to 93.5 and 90, instead of 95 and 93. Now the damage is done; but it is clear that what worries the subscribers most is this: within a short time, between one or two months, won't it be possible to buy these bonds on the market at 88 and at 90, while they cost 95 or 93 [now]? Nothing discredits a loan more than market quotations below the issue price just after subscriptions close.[13]

Further increases in military spending following the munitions crisis in the summer and fall of 1915 brought the government back to the long-term financial market at the beginning of 1916. Preparations for the third national loan indicate that Treasury authorities had learned from some of the technical failures of the earlier loans, and from the experiences of the other European countries. The loan was in the form of twenty-five-year obligations convertible by the state after 10 years, similar to the previous two war loans, but the interest rate was 5%, and the issue price Lit. 97.5, making the effective interest rate 5.13%. Einaudi praised this innovation, and later ascribed the loan's relative success to the adoption of the 5% security over the 4.5% nominal obligation issued earlier.[14] Propaganda for

[11] Bachi, *L'Italia economica 1915*, pp. 279–80.
[12] Circular letter, 11 August 1915, ASBI, Fondo 13, "Sconti, Anticipazioni, Corrispondenti," bob. 47, pratica 296.
[13] Albertini to Einaudi, 11 July 1915, Albertini, *Epistolario*, vol. II, p. 421.
[14] Einaudi, *Corriere della Sera*, 10 March 1916, *Cronache*, vol. IV, pp. 115–116.

the third loan was, in the words of Bachi, "truly ample, well-organized, varied," indicating that the Italian authorities had learned the value of a concerted publicity campaign from France, Germany, and Great Britain.[15] The formalities required for obtaining the new security were reduced to a minimum. Payment for the first loan had been accepted exclusively in installments, and provisional certificates had been issued prior to the final payment. The entire balance for securities of the second loan could be paid at once, but subscribers were still obliged to make three separate trips to the bank: to make payment, to exchange a receipt for a provisional certificate, and finally to exchange the provisional certificate for the bond itself. The bonds for the third loan were issued immediately against payment in full. In addition, cooperative banks and other savings banks offered a range of financing packages for installment purchases.[16] For the first time Treasury securities were accepted for up to half the amount of subscriptions. In addition to the so-called "ordinary" Treasury bills maturing in 3 to 12 months, the 5-year bonds that had been issued in 1912 and 1913 were accepted at Lit. 99 and Lit. 97.8 respectively, prices somewhat above the market rate; 5-year bonds issued after January 1914 were not eligible for conversion.

The underwriting syndicate agreed to take up at least Lit. 300m. of the new security and guaranteed an additional Lit. 200m. if public subscriptions fell short of Lit. 1,500m. This arrangement was the result of a compromise, as Stringher had wanted the bankers to take up a larger fixed sum instead of extending a guarantee. After the subscription drive began, Stringher persuaded, or coerced, the underwriting syndicate to take up another Lit. 150m. of the loan for a total of Lit. 450m.[17]

A major confrontation developed between the large commercial bankers and the industrialists on the one hand, and the government on the other, in late December, when the final preparations for the new loan were being made. The bankers and industrialists wanted a provision to be included in the new loan guaranteeing subscribers any more favorable conditions that would be offered on future war loans. Such a clause had been included in the second war loan, and the government was now prepared to convert the bonds of the second loan into the new security for an additional fee of Lit. 2.5. The first loan contained no such provision, and the government now refused, against the objections of the industrialists and bankers, to write a clause into the law authorizing the new loan that would allow the earlier security to be converted. Albertini and Einaudi sided with the bankers and

---

[15] Bachi, *L'Italia economica 1915*, p. 283.
[16] Ibid., p. 283; Einaudi, *Corriere della Sera*, 26 December 1915, *Cronache*, vol. IV, p. 106.
[17] ASBI, fondo 9.2, Presidenza e Giunta del Consiglio Superiore riunite in Comitato (henceforth Comitato), verbali, 28 December 1915; 24 January 1916.

industrialists on this issue and put pressure on Salandra to change the provisions. Albertini's correspondence suggests that Sonnino was particularly adamant about the conversion clauses, and that Stringher tended to sympathize with the bankers:

> ... bankers returning from Rome tell me that the government is determined not to make either one of the two concessions. Stringher is very upset about it. Sonnino is responsible for these two colossal errors, having opposed any changes with his usual obstinacy. The bankers have the impression that under these conditions the loan will be a disaster.[18]

Albertini asked Einaudi to write an article for the *Corriere della Sera* denouncing the lack of a conversion clause, and threatened to publish it if the government persisted.[19] But the government, presumably owing to Sonnino's resistance, refused to back down and the subscription drive was opened without conversion clauses. Einaudi's critical article was published in the *Corriere della Sera* on 30 December 1915, eliciting a personal protest from Salandra to Albertini. The controversy notwithstanding, the government refused to alter the provisions of the loan and Einaudi, and the *Corriere* later rallied to support the loan.[20] Stringher's initial willingness to compromise with the bankers about the amount and form of the underwriting syndicate's participation in the loan may have been motivated by the fear that the quarrel about conversion clauses could have compromised the success of the loan. Once the subscription drive was opened, and it became evident that the government's goal of Lit. 1.5 bn. would be surpassed easily, Stringher became tougher with the syndicate and forced them to take up a larger amount of the loan.

But the government was forced to yield on conversion rights for the first war loan. Quotations for the first loan fell rapidly when it became clear it would not be accepted for conversion into the new security. The government felt constrained to issue new directives accepting the first loan in payment for up to one half of subscriptions to the new loan, with payment of a Lit. 5 supplement.[21]

The bankers and industrialists may have been bluffing when they predicted failure for the loan without the conversion clauses. The market was extremely liquid by early 1916, and the other features of the new security were exceptionally attractive. When the loan drive ended on 1 March 1916 (it had opened on 10 January) the government had collected

---

[18] Albertini to Einaudi, 30 December 1915, Albertini, *Epistolario*, vol. II, p. 524.
[19] Ibid.
[20] Einaudi, *Corriere della Sera*, 30 December 1915 (not republished in *Cronache*); *Corriere della Sera*, 26 December 1915, *Cronache*, vol. IV, pp. 103–9; *Corriere della Sera*, 6 February 1916, *Cronache*, vol. IV, pp. 109–14. See also, Salandra to Albertini, 31 December 1915, Albertini, *Epistolario*, vol. II, pp. 526–27.   [21] Bachi, *L'Italia economica 1915*, p. 283.

Lit. 2,281m. in cash and short-term securities and an additional Lit. 148m. in 5-year Treasury bonds. Most of the first and second loans were converted in spite of the supplements and other limitations. As had been the case in the past, the new loan quickly fell under par; its first official quotation at the end of July was 95.49; and by the end of October it was at 93.70. Commercial borrowing from the issue banks rose sharply prior to the subscription period, but then declined again to exceptionally low levels from March to October 1916.

The third war loan marked the end of the first phase of wartime borrowing policy. Up to that point the government had sought to meet budget deficits by maintaining a rough balance between short-term and long-term borrowing. The authorities did not try to absorb the greatest possible share of national savings in consolidated loan drives, but only enough to just meet or not even meet current borrowing requirements. Evidently, Salandra and Sonnino continued to hope for a quick victory that would enable them to float a post-war loan under more favorable financial conditions. The reluctance of the government to order total economic mobilization was reflected in its reluctance to order total financial mobilization. In order to keep real interest rates lower than market conditions would have permitted otherwise, the government and the issue banks pressured the more important financial and industrial firms into making larger loan subscriptions than they wished. Private investors subsequently divested unwanted securities, causing their market value to fall below par. Capital losses on war loans embittered small savers and raised the cost of borrowing on successive issues.

Short and medium-term borrowing

After the third war loan the government waited a year before issuing a new consolidated security. In the course of 1916 the relative size of the floating debt grew correspondingly. As was noted above, a total of Lit. 1,233m. in 5-year Treasury bonds had been issued in 1912–1914. In September 1915 a further issue of Lit. 100m. in 5-year Treasury bonds at 4% was approved. The sale of 5-year bonds was suspended during the subscription period for the third war loan, but in May 1916 the government began selling 5% 3-year and 5-year bonds at issue prices of 100 and 98.5 respectively. Conversion of these bonds into consolidated securities at par was guaranteed through 1917. Essentially, 3- year and 5-year Treasury bonds, along with "ordinary" bills, were available "on tap" for the remainder of the war. The decrees authorizing short and medium-term security issues set an upper ceiling to the amount of Treasury paper that could circulate, but when sales approached the maximum authorized level a new decree would be drawn up raising the ceiling; 3-year and 5-year bond sales were regularly suspended during consolidated loan drives. The sale price on 3-year bonds was lowered to 99.25 in December 1916, but otherwise the prices of medium-term securities remained stationary.

The amount of ordinary Treasury bills in circulation also grew rapidly in the period following the third loan. A series of decree laws from September 1915 to June 1916 successively raised the legal ceiling of ordinary Treasury bills in circulation. D.1. 16 July 1916, no. 878 effectively authorized the Treasury to make unlimited issues to meet war financial needs. The same decree also authorized the issue of bearer bills maturing in six months or less for the first time. D.1. 24 December 1916, no. 1811 extended a provision earlier adopted for 3-year and 5-year Treasury bonds to ordinary bills: they could be converted now also into consolidated securities at par.

In April 1918, the government issued a new series of 1-year bearer Treasury bills at 5% in denominations of only Lit. 25, as a means of absorbing the savings of the most modest social classes. Bachi feared the certificates could circulate like money, similar to US Treasury issues during the American Civil War; but in actual fact they found little favor with the public.[22] Einaudi later ascribed the failure of the issue to lack of publicity.[23]

Lit. 1 bn. of ordinary Treasury bills that figured in the government debt during the war years were not taken up by the financial markets at all; rather, the Treasury discounted these bills with the Bank of Italy for cash advances. The cash paid out figured in Bank of Italy accounts as an increase in the commercial note circulation. These advances were arranged in addition to open Treasury borrowing from the issue banks. Legislation adopted at the beginning of the war allowed the Treasury to obtain emergency advances for essentially unlimited amounts from the issue banks against a special series of Treasury bills bearing only 0.25% interest. As will be discussed in further detail below, this provision was amply used, and by June 1915 the so-called "note circulation on account of the state" already exceeded the commercial circulation. The Treasury began borrowing from the Bank of Italy and the Bank of Naples surreptitiously in July 1916 in response to an emergency shortage of cash, and in order to disguise the extent to which the government had recourse to the printing press.[24] The policy was unpopular with the shareholders and

---

[22] Riccardo Bachi, *L'Italia economica nell'anno 1918* (Città di Castello: S. Lapi, 1919), pp. 258–59.

[23] Einaudi, *Corriere della Sera*, 1 April 1919, *Cronache*, vol. V, p. 184.

[24] Stringher to Carcano, 29 June 1916; Carcano to Stringher, 29 June 1916; Stringher to Nicola Miraglia (Director general of the Bank of Naples) 29 (?) June 1916, ASBI, Carte Stringher, 20/302/1/02.

members of the board of the Bank of Italy. The Bank had to pay a fine equal to the discount rate on commercial note circulation that exceeded a 40% metallic reserve requirement. Shortly after Caporetto, the commercial circulation of the Bank of Italy exceeded the reserve requirement for the first time since the Bank's foundation in 1894. Stringher felt obliged to reveal the existence of the secret Treasury advances to his board in order to defend his own lending policies.[25] The secret soon became an open one, although some uncertainty as to the extent of the advances apparently persisted. Bachi noted the, "deplorable practice of the state directly placing vast quantities of Treasury bills with the issue banks," in his yearbook for 1918. He concluded that the Treasury discounted bills with the Bank of Naples and the Bank of Sicily in this manner too; but the sums borrowed from the southern issue banks must have been comparatively modest, and the operations must have been liquidated earlier.[26]

The initial operation in the summer of 1916 appears to have been for Lit. 175m. (Lit. 125m. from the Bank of Italy, and Lit. 50m. from the Bank of Naples). Stringher first alluded to the existence of covert advances to the Treasury to his board of directors (Consiglio Superiore) on 18 June 1917. On 18 November 1917, at a meeting of the Bank's executive committee (Presidenza e giunta del consiglio superiore riunite in comitato), Stringher read into the minutes a long letter to Nitti, the Minister of the Treasury, denouncing the practice. On that date, Stringher put the figure secretly advanced to the Treasury at Lit. 959,652,000.[27]

Despite repeated protests by individual members of the board of the Bank of Italy, the Treasury advances were continually renewed until June 1919. Stringher himself eliminated the practice during his tenure as Minister of the Treasury in the Orlando government, 18 January – 23 June 1919. Only four days before Orlando was defeated in a parliamentary vote of confidence, Stringher, who presumably anticipated the fall of the government and his imminent return to the Bank of Italy, issued a decree creating a new state circulation of Lit. 1 bn. to replace the Lit. 1 bn. in Treasury bonds perennially discounted with the Bank of Italy.[28] His successor at the Treasury, Carlo Schanzer, implemented the measure in the following months, but, according to a recent study, only after Stringher, once again General Director of the Bank of Italy, had agreed to make new surreptitious advances to the Treasury against bills![29] On 24 May 1920

[25] ASBI, fondo 9.2, Consiglio Superiore, verbali, 18 June 1917.
[26] Bachi, *L'Italia economica 1918*, pp. 248–49.
[27] ASBI, fondo 9.2, Comitato, verbali, 18 November 1917.
[28] Ibid., 28 July 1919.
[29] Paolo Frascani, *Politica economica e finanza pubblica in Italia nel primo dopoguerra (1918–1922)* (Naples: Giannini, 1975), p. 291.

Stringher noted that such advances again figured in the commercial circulation for over Lit. 1 bn.[30]

Bachi suggests that Lit. 120m. of the commercial portfolio of the Bank of Italy at the end of 1920 represented bills directly discounted by the Treasury. According to him, for most of the year the volume of such operations was closer to Lit. 300m.[31] If true, this would represent yet another form of covert Bank of Italy advances to the government against Treasury securities, because the Lit. 1 bn. discussed above figured in the commercial circulation, but not in the commercial portfolio of the Bank.

In addition to ordinary, 3-year and 5-year treasury bonds, the government authorized the issue of so-called *buoni per i fornitori* or contractor bonds with D.l. 18 October 1915, no. 1498. The Treasury issued these special bills to contractors against bills of payment issued by the military procurement agencies. In other words, government suppliers, subject to mutual agreement, could be paid all or in part in Treasury securities rather than in cash. It was evident from the beginning that such bills would be used promptly as collateral security for advances from banks, and would in turn be rediscounted with the issue banks, provoking an increase in the money supply. The government utilized this procedure to limit its direct reliance on advances from the issue banks, and make the increase in the money supply appear to be due in part to increased commercial demand. The economists naturally saw through the stratagem and denounced it: "it is probable that many of these securities have collected in the portfolios of the issue banks, causing the note circulation to increase, exactly as if the state had borrowed directly from the issue banks."[32]

By April 1916 the government was sufficiently embarrassed by such arguments to lower the circulation limit for contractor bonds to Lit. 100m.; but two months later D.l. 22 June 1916, no. 754 raised the ceiling back to Lit. 300m., and D.l. 7 January 1917, no. 24 eliminated a ceiling on the issue of such bills altogether. The June 1916 decree also allowed the administration to pay contractors with 3-year and 5-year Treasury bonds.

Short and medium-term securities made up 2% of the total value of all government securities issued between 1 July 1914 and 30 June 1915, 20% between 1 July 1915 and 30 June 1916, and 58% between 1 July 1916 and 30 June 1917. On 30 June 1917 government figures indicate that Lit. 5,591m. in Treasury securities were in circulation in Italy. The actual figure was higher, as the Lit. 1,232m. in 5-year bonds issued from 1912–14, because of yet another case of accounting legerdemain, never figured in the national debt, and most of these bonds were still in circula-

---

[30] ASBI, fondo 9.2, Consiglio Superiore, verbali, 24 May 1920.
[31] Riccardo Bachi, *L'Italia economica nell'anno 1920* (Città di Castello: S. Lapi, 1921), p. 61.
[32] Bachi, *L'Italia economica 1915*, p. 285.

tion. After the fifth war loan in early 1918, the size of the floating debt in relation to the consolidated debt declined somewhat.

The steady rise in the commercial portfolios of the issue banks beginning in May 1916 was a direct result of the increasing volume of government securities on the market. With the expansion of the war economy, ordinary commercial paper all but disappeared, and lending operations came to be made increasingly against government securities. As was noted above, the issue banks could make advances against short-term Treasury securities for up to 100% of their nominal value. In practice, credits were made available for the full nominal amount less the interest earnings of the bills during the period of the lending operation, and taxes. This policy was continued even in periods of financial panic, such as August 1914 and November 1917, when the issue banks applied more restrictive criteria for advances against other securities. The issue banks normally were required to restrict advances against other state securities to 90% of their market value; however, in 1914 the government promised that this margin would not apply on 5-year Treasury bonds issued that year. Until the financial crisis of August 1914, Stringher apparently also lent against the 5-year treasury bonds issued in 1912 and 1913 without applying a margin.[33] No such provisions were offered or applied on later medium-term Treasury bond issues. During the financial panic of November 1917, Stringher raised the margin on loans against 3-year and 5-year Treasury bonds to 15%.[34] Advances against contractor bills were made on conditions identical to the ordinary bills.

Remarking on the transformation in the character of commercial borrowing in the course of 1916 and 1917, Bachi described it as in part "a hidden and therefore more menacing form of inflation, indirectly determined by state financial operations: presumably in this manner a non-trivial part of the commercial note issue actually is issued for the state."[35] A year later he noted that "The often repeated statement, that the copious issue of Treasury securities prevents the issue of banknotes, does not seem to be completely true: in part at least it is only an accounting device."[36]

A significant part of the short and medium-term Treasury securities in circulation were held by the larger banks and industrial firms. In 1918 two of the four major commercial banks, the Credito Italiano and the Banca Commerciale Italiana, indicated the amount of Treasury securities in their

[33] Or so one would conclude from Stringher's remarks in, ASBI, fondo 9.2, Consiglio Superiore, verbali, 24 August 1914.

[34] ASBI, fondo 9.2, Consiglio Superiore, verbali, 19 November 1917.

[35] Riccardo Bachi, *L'Italia economica nell'anno 1917* (Città di Castello: S. Lapi, 1918), pp. 35–36.

[36] Bachi, *L'Italia economica 1918*, p. 36.

portfolios in their annual reports. Extrapolating from these figures, Bachi estimated the four largest commercial banks together held approximately Lit. 2,800m. of the Lit. 10,845m. in Treasury paper in circulation on 31 December 1918.[37] Interest rates on Treasury securities were about 40% higher than savings deposit rates, ensuring the banks a large and virtually risk-free profit.

Curiously, whereas Riccardo Bachi argued in his economic yearbooks for 1916, 1917, and 1918 that Treasury issues were highly inflationary and almost counterproductive, Albertini and Einaudi repeatedly pressed the government to stimulate sales by making Treasury securities more attractive to investors. They urged the government to raise interest rates, create smaller denominations, and vary maturity dates.[38] On one occasion, in May 1916, Carcano prevailed on Albertini to refrain from publishing an article by Einaudi in the *Corriere della Sera* advocating larger and more varied short-term Treasury issues, on the grounds that the policy could lead to vast savings deposit and current account withdrawals, and destabilize the banking system.[39] But it is not at all evident that Einaudi was primarily concerned with eliminating the profits the banks obtained by mediating between the Treasury and depositors. Rather, Einaudi seems to have held fast to the notion that selling securities was an intrinsically less inflationary form of public finance than issuing bank notes. His advocacy of short-term security issues may have been influenced by British financial policy. After the third war loan in early 1917, the British government refrained from issuing further long-term securities until after the armistice. Long-term interest rates had risen above short-term rates, and the authorities chose to finance the current deficit with Exchequer Bonds. But Exchequer Bonds absorbed real purchasing power in Britain to a greater degree than in Italy because direct economic controls blocked other forms of investment.[40] In Italy industrialists borrowed from banks against Treasury securities to finance private investments. The situation became particularly acute in the fall of 1917 when an unprecedented wave of stock speculation commenced. Industrialists and financiers sought to increase

[37] Ibid., p. 51.
[38] Albertini to Einaudi, 13 November 1915, Albertini, *Epistolario*, vol. II, pp. 494–95; Albertini to Einaudi, 22 November 1915, FE, Archivio Einaudi, Carteggio; Albertini to Einaudi, 30 May 1916; Albertini to Einaudi, 18 July 1918, Albertini, *Epistolario*, vol. II, pp. 601, 953; Einaudi to Albertini, 26 July 1918; Einaudi to F. S. Nitti, 11 July 1919, FE, Archivio Einaudi, Carteggio; Einaudi, *Corriere della Sera*, 26 June 1916, *Cronache*, vol. IV, pp. 356–59; *Corriere della Sera*, 10 March 1917, *Cronache*, vol. IV, p. 123; *Corriere della Sera*, 1 September 1918, *Cronache*, vol. IV, pp. 714–19.
[39] Albertini to Einaudi, 30 May 1916, Albertini, *Epistolario*, p. 601.
[40] On British policy see, E. V. Morgan, *Studies in British Financial Policy 1914–1925* (London: Macmillian, 1952), pp. 112–13.

their liquidity margins to make or protect themselves from hostile take-over attempts.

To summarize, the Salandra government sought to stabilize the floating debt as a relatively small proportion of the total national debt until early 1916. Beginning with the third war loan of January 1916, Treasury securities could be converted into new consolidated securities; but only in the following period was a concerted effort made to use Treasury bills as an intermediate stage in absorbing national savings between consolidated loan issues. The size of the floating debt both absolutely and as a proportion of the total national debt grew precipitately from the spring of 1916. The floating debt became increasingly inflationary, as billholders used their investments as loan collateral. This practice was encouraged by the government as early as November 1915, with the creation of contractor bills.

The fourth and fifth national loans, February 1917 – March 1918

In February 1917 the Boselli government issued a fourth war loan. Its conditions were considerably more favorable than those of the third loan. It was a perpetual rent, or consol, as the old 3.5% security had been, and the government promised not to convert it for fifteen years. The issue price was Lit. 90, signifying a net interest rate of 5.56%. Earlier war loans could be converted into the new security with the payment of a supplement of Lit. 2.5 for the first two loans, and Lit. 3 for the third. All short and medium-term Treasury securities were accepted in payment for the new loan. In addition, for the first time a limited number of foreign securities were made exchangeable for the new loan.

To the great satisfaction of the bankers, as well as Einaudi and Albertini, subscribers were promised any more favorable conditions that should be granted on future war loans. The banks of the underwriting syndicate were not obliged to retain any of the new loan in their own portfolios. Perhaps because of this, the government, at the insistence of Sonnino, insisted that the banks accept a commission of only Lit. 0.20 instead of the customary Lit. 0.40. At least one of the major commercial banks, the Credito Italiano, threatened to suspend its participation in the underwriting syndicate because of the dispute. As had been the case at the time of the third loan, the government refused to back down, and the commercial banks eventually cooperated in the loan drive despite their objections.[41]

The results of the new loan easily surpassed those of earlier war loans. About Lit. 2,500m. was collected in cash, Lit. 1,100m. in short and

[41] Einaudi to Albertini, 29 January 1917, FE, Archivio Einaudi, Carteggio.

medium-term Treasury obligations, in addition to Lit. 4m. in the colonies, and Lit. 182.2m. abroad. Nevertheless, holders of short and medium-term Treasury securities remained reluctant to exchange them for the new loan; Einaudi estimated that only about one-sixth of such securities in circulation were converted.[42] In contrast to the earlier experience, the market quotation of the fourth loan stabilized at a level slightly above the issue price in the months following the subscription drive. This was probably due to Bank of Italy intervention on the market. In the latter part of June 1917, before the market price of the new security had been set officially for the first time, the fourth loan was apparently being exchanged informally at less than Lit. 90. According to Einaudi, the underwriting syndicate dumped the loan paper remaining in its hands after the closing of the subscription period at below par.[43] In late June 1917 Einaudi bitterly criticized Stringher and Carcano for allowing yet another national loan to slip quickly below par: "I am struck very much by the carelessness of the Treasury and the Bank of Italy. They have allowed a very dangerous financial situation to form, which will wrench us considerably."[44]

Einaudi was concerned particularly that continued capital losses would alienate further the mass of small savers who subscribed to the loan as a long-term investment and thus represented the ideal clientele of the state. On another occasion in mid-1918, when the market value of the 5% war loan turned downward again, Einaudi remarked:

> The medium and petty bourgeoisie constitutes the fundamental nucleus of the state's clientele for securities; a clientele which is preferable to all others, because it does not sell the securities it purchases. But it sees the value of its savings clipped, and becomes disgusted by the capital losses it is subjected to after every new subscription.[45]

But in actual fact the fourth and fifth war loans rarely traded below par. The biweekly figures provided by Bachi show only one quotation for the fourth loan below par between mid-July and the end of December 1917, and only two quotations of the fifth loan below par between January 1918 and December 1919.

With the fourth loan a new problem emerged: for the first time the issue of a new consolidated loan provoked a significant permanent expansion of commercial credit on the part of the issue banks, and hence an expansion of the money stock. The commercial portfolios of the issue banks had expanded before and during previous subscription drives as

[42] Einaudi, *Corriere della Sera*, 10 March 1917, *Cronache*, vol. IV, p. 123.
[43] Luigi Einaudi, *La condotta economica e gli effetti sociali della guerra italiana* (Bari: Laterza, 1933), p. 54.
[44] Einaudi to Albertini, 24 June 1917, FE, Archivio Einaudi, Carteggio.
[45] Einaudi to Albertini, 5 May 1918, FE, Archivio Einaudi, Carteggio.

subscribers took out short-term loans to pay for the new security. However, after the first three subscription drives closed, issue bank commercial portfolios tended to contract to previous levels over a period of two or more months. After the fourth loan, the total volume of issue bank commercial loans declined only moderately, stabilizing at a level considerably higher than the average in late 1916. The total volume of issue bank commercial credit on 30 November 1916 was Lit. 1,010m.; on 31 May 1917 it was Lit. 1,250m.; and on 31 July 1917 Lit. 1,305m. Cash subscriptions to the fourth war loan of Lit. 2,500m. were an overriding factor in the increase of Lit. 250m. to Lit. 300m. in issue bank commercial credit at a time when the issue banks presumably were making substantial market interventions to keep 5% state securities above the February 1917 issue price of Lit. 90.

For the first time, a long-term security issue had an inflationary impact similar to that of short-term Treasury bill issues. This development was not lost on contemporary observers. Bachi noted in his yearbook for 1917 that the fourth and fifth war loans, unlike the earlier loans, had been taken up in large part by the bigger institutional investors: "The volume of subscriptions in that milieu [large institutional investors], after the pressures which were exerted, caused an inflow of securities into bank vaults as collateral for loans, leading indirectly to inflation."[46]

The fifth war loan of February–March 1918 led to an even greater expansion of bank credit than the fourth. The loan was issued only two and a half months after Caporetto. The military defeat caused a brief financial panic and the volume of commercial credit extended by the issue banks in the course of October 1917 expanded from Lit. 1,650m. to Lit. 1,970m. State credit was also shaken by the defeat: 5% consols fell from Lit. 91.47 to Lit. 88.40 in the first half of November. At the same time, state financial needs expanded greatly as the military procurement agencies sought to replace quickly the huge material stocks lost in the retreat from the Isonzo to the Piave River. Despite unfavorable financial conditions, Nitti, the new Minister of the Treasury, resolved to spur subscriptions to the fifth loan to unprecedented levels. Shortly after Caporetto, Nitti met with the directors of the large commercial banks and announced his intention to issue a new loan for Lit. 6 bn. Nitti's son Vincenzo later recounted that the bankers were shocked by his plan, arguing that not more than Lit. 2 bn. possibly could be obtained; they were reluctant to guarantee the loan for more than Lit. 1.5 bn.[47]

But Nitti persisted in his proposal to make the fifth war loan an exem-

[46] Bachi, *L'Italia economica 1917*, p. 254.
[47] Vincenzo Nitti, *L'opera di Nitti* (Turin: Piero Gobetti, 1924), pp. 27–28, quoted in Alberto Monticone, *Nitti e la grande guerra (1914–1918)* (Milan: Giuffré, 1961), p. 182.

plary and unprecedented success. In reality, Nitti's objectives were as
much political as financial. The fourth war loan had already demonstrated
that spurring subscriptions beyond a certain point would merely provoke
the expansion of bank credit; but Nitti hoped to achieve a political success
by obtaining unprecedented nominal subscriptions. In the months before
Caporetto, he had attacked the Boselli government for pursuing economic
mobilization with insufficient vigor. After becoming Minister of the
Treasury, he declared that the negligence of his predecessor, Paolo Carcano, had left him with an emergency situation upon taking office.[48] Nitti
sought to demonstrate his administrative effectiveness, and enhance his
political stature through organizing the loan drive. He also believed that
he would have more success in obtaining generous new credits from
Britain and the United States if he achieved a striking success with the
domestic loan.[49]

Nitti organized an unprecedented propaganda campaign during the
subscription period. He gave over a hundred speeches in all of the major
urban centers of the peninsula, including Milan, Florence, Genoa, Turin,
Naples, and Bologna. They were widely commented on in the newspapers,
and several were reprinted in pamphlets. Prominent economists and
political figures, including Einaudi and Stringher, made speeches and
wrote articles urging subscriptions to the loan.[50] Even the Catholic
Church was enlisted to support the subscription drive. The remarks of
Monsignor Federico Tedeschini, the Vatican Secretary of State, to
newspaper publisher Olindo Malagodi suggest that many clergy urged
loan subscriptions from the pulpit, with the full blessing of the Vatican.[51]
The loan drive was an ideal instrument for Nitti's personal political
advancement. Public criticism of the war loans was virtually non-existent,

[48] Olindo Malagodi, *Conversazioni della guerra 1914–1919*, ed. Brunello Vigezzi (Milan and
    Naples: Ricciardi, 1960), vol. II, p. 398 (notes on a conversation of Malagodi, the editor of
    the Roman newspaper *La Tribuna*, with Nitti, 27 September 1918); Monticone, *Nitti e la
    grande guerra*, pp. 181–90; Nitti, *L'opera di Nitti*, pp. 26–28.
[49] Nitti insisted on the need for large subscriptions to the fifth war loan to enhance his
    negotiating position *vis-à-vis* the Allies in his public speeches. In a speech in Turin, for
    example, he stated that: "Italy, in order to live today, and in order to prosper tomorrow,
    needs aid from the Allies: cordial and sincere aid ... The war, as is natural, has worsened
    our situation ... After the war, only the powerful assistance of the Allies, and especially
    the United States of America, will allow us to recover. We have to merit the confidence of
    the Allies." In Bologna Nitti solicited subscriptions by arguing: "*Resistance* [Nitti's
    emphasis] means securing for ourselves the assistance of the Allies, in other words the
    means of surviving and living; it means avoiding enemy invasion, of which we know the
    bitterness, and the horrors; it means giving Italy success tomorrow, and afterwards
    affluence." Quoted in Monticone, *Nitti e la grande guerra*, p. 187.
[50] "5° prestito nazionale," Archivio Centrale dello Stato (henceforth ACS), Archivio Nitti,
    V/18/44.
[51] Malagodi, *Conversazioni della guerra*, vol. II, pp. 318–19 (conversation with Monsignor
    Tedeschini, 7 April 1918).

despite the frequent and bitter recriminations between bankers, industrial-ists, economists, and government officials in private. Even the *Giornale d'Italia*, the newspaper of Sidney Sonnino, Nitti's foremost political enemy, gave the Minister of the Treasury ample favorable publicity during the loan campaign.[52] By identifying himself closely with the fifth and largest war loan, Nitti meant to associate himself with the national will to resist, and become a symbol of national unity – an Italian Clemenceau, in the words of Ansaldo director, Pio Perrone.[53]

The new loan was in practical terms a further issue of the 5% perpetual security introduced the previous year. The subscription price was lowered to Lit. 86.5, making the net interest rate 5.78%. Loan subscriptions were inflated by an offer of the National Insurance Institute to issue life insurance policies against payment in the new security at par, rather than at the issue price. All short and medium-term Treasury securities were accepted in payment for the new loan.

Patriotic fanfare notwithstanding, Nitti's correspondence with String-her in January and February 1918 reveals that the more traditional tech-nique of central bank pressure on financial and industrial firms was instrumental in achieving the subscription goal of Lit. 6 bn. When loan subscriptions began to falter in late January, Nitti demanded that String-her intensify his efforts to obtain the conversion of Treasury issues, notoriously in the hands of institutional investors.[54] Nitti intimated in his speeches that if subscriptions proved mediocre, a forced loan inevitably would follow. The loan was scheduled to close on 3 February, but Nitti, still far short of his goal, had subscriptions prolonged until 10 March. Ultimately, Lit. 3,586.8m. was collected in cash domestically (Lit. 3696.6m. nominally in the new security); together with Lit. 1,941.9m. in securities, mostly Treasury bills; Lit. 10.6m. in the colonies; Lit. 440m. abroad; and Lit. 875m. in insurance policies. Total nominal subscriptions, at Lit. 6,245m., exceeded Nitti's goal. But the nominal success of the loan far exceeded its real capacity to absorb private purchasing power. The volume of issue bank commercial credit, already swollen to unprecedented levels in the weeks following Caporetto, stabilized at only slightly lower levels in the months following the termination of the loan drive. Issue bank commercial credit rose from Lit. 1,420m. in September 1917 to Lit. 2,030m. in June 1918, with advances being made overwhelmingly against state securities. Bachi noted:

[52] Monticone, *Nitti e la grande guerra*, p. 183.   [53] Quoted in ibid., p. 207.
[54] Nitti to Stringher, 14 February 1918, ACS, Archivio Nitti, V/17/37/5. Monticone quotes another letter of Nitti to Stringher, 4 February 1918: "The banks do not put the necessary ardor into [the loan drive], perhaps believing they can cover themselves with collective responsibility. The four biggest commercial banks, and particularly the smaller banks could do more. Will you stimulate them?" *Nitti e la grande guerra*, p. 189.

The size of these advances is very substantial, much larger than the level before the war: the increase is due largely to state securities and is connected closely with the big financial operations of the state: a non-trivial part of the loan subscriptions, particularly by industrial firms, is made with bank loans, a dangerous technique.[55]

We will return to Nitti's sixth war loan, which was issued in early 1920, and had even more inflationary consequences later. In effect, the policies pursued by the Treasury and the issue banks during the later war loan issues presented subscribers with a choice between making a long-term investment or paying an indirect tax on currency holdings. If subscribers sought to regain their former liquidity positions, they paid an immediate tax of 10% equivalent to the margin requirement of the issue banks for advances on long-term state securities plus or minus the difference between the discount rate and the interest rate on the national loans. During a period of brisk inflation, unprecedented stock speculation, and feverish industrial investment many subscribers chose the latter course. The government, in addition to collecting the "tax," directly through subscriptions and indirectly through participations in the profits of the issue banks and fines on excess commercial circulation, derived an indirect, political benefit from this fictitious borrowing. State borrowing capacity appeared greater, and state financial solidity seemed firmer than was actually the case. The extent of government recourse to the printing press was camouflaged by increases in private borrowing and the "commercial" note circulation.

During October 1918, as the approaching defeat of the Central Powers became evident, the market value of 5% consols rose more than four points to above Lit. 91. Bachi later argued that the state should have seized the occasion to issue a new consolidated loan, as was done in France, and persistent rumors circulated at the time that such an issue was in the offing.[56] In fact, Nitti ordered the preparation of a new loan, and the bonds were even printed and distributed among the branches of the Bank of Italy.[57] Evidently, Nitti hesitated to launch the loan drive because of political dissension in the government. Nitti demanded that Orlando restructure his cabinet, removing Nitti's arch-rival Sonnino from the Foreign Ministry, and giving the Minister of the Treasury control over all important aspects of economic policy. Capitalizing on his success with the fifth war loan, Nitti implicitly threatened Orlando with financial ruin if he did not accede to his political demands:

[55] Bachi, *L'Italia economica 1917*, p. 38.
[56] Bachi, *L'Italia economica 1918*, pp. 258–59.
[57] Frascani, *Politica economica*, p. 286.

It is necessary to make a huge loan, and make it soon. I, or my successor, really should do it right away . . . The Treasury's deficit is very grave . . . It is necessary that the new loan be made in a state of calm, by a strong ministry which inspires confidence, otherwise everything will fall apart, and we will go into a paper money regime. I cannot take responsibility for issuing a loan unless I can guarantee the public a secure situation, and I do not feel I can guarantee that now.[58]

Bachi suggests that Nitti was also reluctant to float a new loan after the armistice, because it would perforce have been more modest than the fifth loan, and hence of uncertain political value.[59] Orlando, in any case, was prepared to placate his Minister of the Treasury through partial concessions, but not to dismiss Sonnino, and become a figurehead in a new government in which Nitti would play the *éminence grise*. The latent cabinet crisis and resulting administrative paralysis persisted until 15 January 1919, when Orlando finally accepted Nitti's resignation. By the time Bonaldo Stringher, the former and future General Director of the Bank of Italy, had succeeded Nitti at the Treasury on 18 January, 5% consols had fallen back to Lit. 86.12. Stringher decided at this point against a new consolidated loan. He later justified his course of action on the grounds that it would have been inopportune for the state to lock itself into long-term interest payments of over 5.7% at a time when the cost of long-term state borrowing was expected to fall.[60] From his experience at the Bank of Italy he was naturally also aware that a significant part of the fifth loan was still held by the issue banks as collateral in their commercial portfolios. A letter from the director of the Bank of Italy branch in Bergamo to Stringher in December 1918 reveals that industrialists and bankers, anxious not to reduce their liquidity during the delicate transition to a peace economy, strongly opposed a new consolidated loan issue.[61]

Einaudi supported Stringher's decision to rely on short and medium-term borrowing to meet the budget deficits of 1919. Although he acknowledged the possibility that the government could be faced with a financial crisis if short-term billholders refused to renew their investments, he believed this outcome was more theoretical than practical in the financial and economic climate of early 1919: "*in concreto*, what can bill- and bond-holders do, if not be happy that they can buy another bill or bond for another 3 or 6 months, or one year or three years?"[62] In 1918, Einaudi had

---

[58] Nitti to Orlando, 14 January 1919, published in Monticone, *Nitti e la grande guerra*, pp. 424–29.   [59] Bachi, *L'Italia economica 1918*, pp. 258–59.

[60] Stringher, Adunanza generale ordinaria degli azionisti della Banca d'Italia, 31 March 1920, republished in Banca d'Italia, *Sulle condizioni della circolazione e del mercato monetario durante e dopo la guerra* (Rome: Casa Editrice Italiana, 1920), p. 170.

[61] Frascani, *Politica economica*, p. 287.

[62] Einaudi, "I buoni ordinari del tesoro. Per i buoni ad interesse progressivo," *Corriere della Sera*, 1 April 1919, *Cronache*, vol. V, p. 183.

already written that the state had paid too dearly for the fifth war loan; he now advocated waiting until market conditions permitted a new long-term security issue at interest rates of 5% before attempting to consolidate the floating debt.[63]

It is interesting to note that the authorities in Great Britain made a series of attempts to consolidate their floating debt from June 1919 to April 1921 at unprecedentedly high interest rates and with only modest success. The decline in long-term interest rates from mid-1921 has led Morgan to conclude that British Treasury officials were excessively preoccupied with the size of the floating debt in the immediate post-war period, and ought to have pursued a course of action similar to that advocated by Einaudi.[64] But, of course, the decline in long-term interest rates on state borrowing in Britain was a consequence of fiscal rigor and post-war budget surpluses. In Italy, spending had not yet been brought under control, and delays in tax reform precluded debt conversion.

[63] Einaudi, *Corriere della Sera*, 30 January 1918, *Cronache*, vol. IV, p. 131.
[64] Morgan, *British Financial Policy*, p. 118.

4

MONETARY POLICY AND THE BANKING
SYSTEM

Monetary policy, 1914–1922

Italian monetary policy in the period between the outbreak of World War
I and the March on Rome falls into three phases. The first phase lasted
from the outbreak of war until approximately the end of 1914. During this
time, monetary authorities were primarily preoccupied with restoring
stability to the financial markets in the wake of the panic caused by the
outbreak of war, and the breakdown in international payments and trade.
During the second phase, which lasted until the end of the first post-war
inflationary cycle in late 1920, monetary policy was largely subordinated
to the exigencies of the Treasury. The issue banks were enlisted in support
of war finance by favoring the placement of war loans, and by making
direct advances to the Treasury. In the third phase, which lasted until the
March on Rome, and indeed into the first months of 1923, the Bank of
Italy was forced to respond once again primarily to the grave liquidity
crisis experienced by industry and the banks, by assuming its responsibilities as lender of last resort, and guarantor of financial stability.

Phase 1: Domestic aspects of the financial crisis of July–August
1914

In Italy, as was the case elsewhere, panic enveloped the foreign exchange
markets in the final week of July 1914, as the outbreak of war became
imminent. But whereas in most of Europe and in North America the
financial crisis of July and August 1914 was primarily connected with the
breakdown of international payments and trade, in Italy it tended to
expand into a crisis of the mixed banks, and the manufacturing and commercial firms associated with them. The panic on the exchange markets
quickly produced an abrupt decline in the market prices of domestic
securities. The collapse of stock prices in turn threatened to undermine
the basis of the entire Italian financial system. Industrial firms were heavily
indebted to the banks, and a significant part of these debts were held

125

against collateral deposits of industrial stocks; therefore, any significant decline in the value of industrial securities threatened to undermine the country's largest commercial banks. Significantly, the price of bank shares fell more dramatically on the market than those of manufacturing firms. The collapse in stock and bond prices soon produced a run on bank deposits. The commercial banks were consequently induced to turn to the issue banks with extraordinary rediscount requests. In contrast to Britain, France, and Germany, but similar to Austria, restrictions on withdrawals from current and savings accounts were imposed.[1]

Despite, or perhaps because of, the gravity of the situation, the leading private bankers in Milan were soon locked in a bitter dispute with the Bank of Italy and the government about how to respond to the financial crisis. The Milanese bankers advocated a permissive monetary policy, and public guarantees for commercial bills pending at the time of the financial panic; Stringher and Salandra above all sought to limit the liabilities of the Treasury and the issue banks, and avoid inflation.

The foreign exchange and securities markets were closed by order of their respective governing commissions in response to the panic in late July. The issue banks were given powers to expand the note circulation to meet extraordinary demands for liquidity. Stringher's initial response to the crisis reflected a curious admixture of adherence to Bagehot's principles, that a central bank should lend freely but dearly during a liquidity crisis, and his fears that the issue banks themselves could be ruined by locking up their resources through rediscounting the nominally liquid, but in reality essentially illiquid, commercial portfolios of the mixed banks. On 31 July, the issue banks eliminated all discount operations under the official rate of 5%. The following day, in accordance with the Minister of the Treasury, the discount rate was raised to 6%. On 2 August, Stringher recommended raising the discount rate to the unprecedented level of 7%, imitating the Bank of England, which had raised its rate to 8% on 31 July, and 10% on 1 August. Probably fearing that this action would cause the financial panic to become uncontrollable, Giulio Rubini, the Minister of the Treasury, vetoed Stringher's proposal, and the discount rate remained at 6%.[2]

At the same time that Stringher sought to make money dearer to borrowers from the issue banks, he sent instructions to the directors of the Bank of Italy's branches urging them to be selective in accepting bills for

---

[1] Riccardo Bachi, *L'Italia economica nell'anno 1914* (Città di Castello: S. Lapi, 1915), pp. 90–91, and passim; Banca d'Italia, Consiglio Superiore, verbali, 24 August 1914, in, Gianni Toniolo, ed., *La Banca d'Italia e l'economia di guerra, 1914–1919* (Bari: Laterza, 1989), no. 30, pp. 132–46.

[2] Banca d'Italia, Consiglio Superiore, verbali, 24 August 1914, in Toniolo, ed., *La Banca d'Italia e l'economia di guerra*, no. 30, pp. 132–46.

rediscount. The branch directors were enjoined to "make sure that the large and small institutes of credit, and the savings banks do not burden the Bank [of Italy] with bills representing the mobilization of industrial credits, thereby improving their own positions at the expense of our portfolio."[3]

Stringher also raised the margin on advances against collateral deposits of state securities from the statutory minimum of 10% to 20%. On 4 August, the first in a series of decrees was announced that substantially raised the legal limits of the three issue banks' note circulation.[4]

However, the run on bank deposits showed no sign of abating, and even began to spread from the commercial banks to the savings banks and the Monti di Pietà. On 4 August Stringher abandoned the policy of meeting the crisis solely by injecting liquidity into the market. The government now took the extraordinary step of freezing bank accounts. Withdrawals were limited to 5% per bank account for sums over Lit. 50 during the period 4–20 August. Subsequent decrees stipulated that another 5% could be withdrawn by 10 September and yet another 5% by the end of September. Withdrawals of 10% per month for October through December were authorized and 20% per month from January to March 1915. Bank accounts were to be unfrozen completely by 31 March 1915. The severity of the freeze was subsequently reduced by a series of decrees making allowances for larger withdrawals for paying salaries, purchasing raw materials, paying taxes, and, in December, for subscriptions to the government's first war loan.[5]

Further, the issue banks were authorized by decree on 18 August 1914 to make special advances of up to Lit. 300m., not subject to ordinary restrictions on commercial lending, to savings banks and Monte di Pietà against collateral deposits of state securities. The government feared that the run on deposits would induce the savings banks and Monte to liquidate a part of their vast holdings of government securities. Naturally, such action would have had disastrous consequences for the price of state securities. The mere announcement of this decree was sufficient to calm the depositors of the savings banks and the Monti, and they were able to weather the new withdrawals allowed after 20 August without making substantial recourse to the emergency funds.[6]

[3] Stringher to branch directors of Bank of Italy, circular letter, 1 August 1914, in Toniolo, ed., *La Banca d'Italia e l'economia di guerra*, no. 21, pp. 116–18.
[4] Banca d'Italia, Consiglio Superiore, verbali, 24 August 1914, in Toniolo, ed., *La Banca d'Italia e l'economia di guerra*, no. 30, pp. 132–46.
[5] Bachi, *L'Italia economica nell'anno 1914*, pp. 236–38; Banca d'Italia, Consiglio Superiore, verbali, 24 August 1914, in Toniolo, ed., *La Banca d'Italia e l'economia di guerra*, no. 30, pp. 132–46.
[6] Banca d'Italia, Consiglio Superiore, verbali, 24 August 1914, in Toniolo, ed., *La Banca d'Italia e l'economia di guerra*, no. 30, pp. 132–46.

On 4 August, the same day that bank accounts were frozen, another decree was issued allowing debtors to postpone repayment on outstanding commercial bills until 20 August free of additional interest charges. Initially, the two moratoria seem to have been welcomed by the Milanese financial community. Luigi Della Torre, director of Zaccaria Pisa & Co., a private bank in Milan which maintained close relations with the Comit and Credit, wrote to Stringher on 5 August, reporting on a meeting of the leading bankers. He noted that while businessmen had been hurt by the freezes, they were unanimous in recognizing the utility of the measures. He added: "Without the decree, we would have been ruined, to no constructive purpose."[7]

However, when Stringher proposed extending the original moratoria decrees beyond 20 August, opposition in financial and industrial circles began to mount, leading to another bitter battle between Rome and Milan. Commercial credit had been reduced to a trickle by the freezes on bank accounts, and the repayment of commercial bills. The Milanese bankers wanted the Bank of Italy to follow a policy similar to that adopted by British authorities on 13 August. The Bank of England agreed to accept all commercial bills drafted before the onset of the crisis, and hold them (against interest payments) until the end of the war. The British government in turn made available to the English central bank a special currency issue to cover advances for this purpose. These measures restored commercial credit, but at the price of a massive increase in the money stock.[8]

Stringher resolutely opposed a similar initiative in Italy. He argued it would allow the private banks to unload their bad loans on the state and the issue banks at no cost to themselves, while creating substantial inflationary pressure. Above all, Stringher wanted to prevent the issue banks from incurring new obligations, without the full backing of the government, and compensations from the state. The Bank of Italy was paying substantial fines already for increases in the note circulation above the statutory limits since late July.

Salandra also favored a restrictive monetary policy. He was more concerned about inflation than recession, and particularly anxious to limit state spending. Consequently, a new decree was issued on 16 August which created a moratorium of forty days for commercial bills maturing

---

[7] Della Torre to Stringher, 5 August 1914, in Toniolo, ed., *La Banca d'Italia e l'economia di guerra*, no. 23, pp. 120–22.

[8] On British monetary policy see, R. S. Sayers, *The Bank of England, 1891–1944* (New York: Cambridge University Press, 1976), pp. 77–78. For the views of Italian bankers see, Banca d'Italia, Consiglio Superiore, verbali, 24 August 1914; Vittorio Rolandi Ricci to Stringher, 18 September 1914, in Toniolo, ed., *La Banca d'Italia e l'economia di guerra*, nos. 30 and 33, pp. 132–46, 151–54; Otto Joel, unsigned, undated letter [but to Rolandi Ricci, probably in late September], Banca Commerciale Italiana, Archivio Storico, (hereafter ASBCI) Carte Joel, Cartella 16.

before 30 September 1914. Those availing themselves of the provision were to be charged 6% interest, and required to repay 15% of the principal by the bill's original date of maturity. Payment on bills falling due after the end of September, but before 31 December, could be postponed until 31 March 1915, but stiffer interest penalties were applied. The latter date marked the final termination of the commercial bill moratorium. However, the private bankers, joined by some business associations, continued to call for the termination of the moratorium, and its substitution with a liberal rediscounting policy by the issue banks.[9]

Meanwhile, the Milanese bankers took steps to evade the freeze on bank deposit withdrawals. In early August they began offering so-called "B" accounts, which they assured the public would be free from any subsequent moratorium legislation. In the third week of August, Federico Balzarotti, director of the Credito Italiano, announced that his bank would no longer avail itself of the moratorium, allowing all of its depositors to make unlimited withdrawals from their accounts. For prestige considerations, the Comit and other important banks prepared to follow suit. Stringher feared the moratorium would come unraveled, and the weaker institutions would be compromised irreversibly. Moreover, he found it unconscionable that the commercial banks proposed to stop making use of the moratorium legislation at a time when they were relying heavily on rediscounting operations with the issue banks for liquidity. Stringher instructed the Bank of Italy's Milan office to refuse any additional rediscount requests from the Credito Italiano, and on 19 August Balzarotti backed down.

Milanese bankers continued to criticize the government's policies, however. Discussions even took place in Milan in early September about bringing down the Salandra government, and replacing it with a new administration disposed to pursue a less restrictive monetary policy. Giannetto Cavasola, the Minister of Agriculture, Industry, and Commerce, dissented from his cabinet colleagues, taking the side of the Milanese business community; but Stringher and Salandra held firm.[10]

---

[9] Bachi, *L'Italia economica nell'anno 1914*, pp. 239–40; Stringher to Rubini, 19 September 1914, in Toniolo, ed., *La Banca d'Italia e l'economia di guerra*, no. 34, pp. 154–56.

[10] Cavasola to Salandra, 8 September 1914; Rolandi Ricci to Stringher, 18 September 1914; Stringher to Rubini, 19 September 1914; Stringher to Domenico Gidoni, director of the Turin branch of the Bank of Italy, 21 September 1914; Salandra to Cavasola, 22 September 1914, in Toniolo, ed., *La Banca d'Italia e l'economia di guerra*, nos. 32, 33, 34, 35, 36, pp. 148–59. It is clear from these documents that Balzarotti, Della Torre, and Giuseppe Toeplitz, a director of the Comit, were far more vocal in their opposition to Stringher, and his policy of continuing the moratoria, than were Otto Joel and Federico Weil. The latter two had been the leading personalities at the Comit since its founding in 1894. Both Joel and Weil would soon resign their positions at the bank, due in part to age and ill-health, but also due to the violent campaign against them in the nationalist press, because of their German birth and neutralist sympathies. This left Toeplitz effectively at the helm

As a sop to the Milanese, Salandra replaced Rubini at the Treasury with Paolo Carcano in early November. Rubini's rigid fiscal orthodoxy, his opposition to increased military spending, and his unwillingness to mitigate the fines paid by the issue banks on excess note circulation, alienated even Salandra and Stringher. Carcano proved more pliant. He had been chosen by Zanardelli and Giolitti to replace Wollemborg at Finance in 1901, when the latter resigned because of the government's failure to support his ambitious tax reform proposal. During World War I, Carcano exhibited once again his "ministerial" qualities; the initiative in monetary policy quickly passed to Stringher, with whom it remained until Carcano's death, and Nitti's appointment as Minister of the Treasury in October 1917.[11]

Meanwhile, Italian manufacturers began receiving orders from the belligerent powers, and soon also from the Italian government, as domestic rearmament got underway. By the end of 1914 at least in some sectors the slump was turning into a war-driven boom, eliminating the main cause of contention between the government and the financial and business communities. Italy's intervention in May 1915 did not produce another depositors' run on the banks, although Stringher remained apprehensive through the spring about the condition of some provincial banks, and most of all the Banco di Roma.[12]

Despite uneven economic recovery beginning in the final months of 1914, considerable skepticism prevailed as to whether the stock exchanges could be reopened again safely on 31 March 1915, as was envisaged by the moratorium legislation. Stocks and even government securities were traded informally in August at prices far below the last official exchange quotations. In effect, the stock exchanges were not reopened until September 1917, whereas in most of the other European belligerent nations they were functioning normally again by mid-1915, a fact which further underscores the particular vulnerability of the Italian financial system to fluctuations in stock prices.

Even though the government decided to keep the stock exchanges closed during most of the conflict, it took two important measures in December 1914 to firm up stock prices. First, firms, including financial institutions, were authorized to carry stocks in their portfolios at their market values on 30 June 1914 in their annual financial statements.

---

of the Comit after March 1915. Joel was deeply concerned about Toeplitz's poor relationship with Stringher, as is clear from a letter to Senator Vittorio Rolandi Ricci (a corporate lawyer who often acted as an intermediary between via Nazionale and Piazza della Scala) on 20 September 1914. ASBCI, Carte Joel, Cartella 13.

[11] On Stringher's relationship with Rubini, Carcano and Nitti see Toniolo's introduction in Toniolo, ed., *La Banca d'Italia e l'economia di guerra*, passim.

[12] Stringher to Carcano, 21 May 1915, in Toniolo, ed., *La Banca d'Italia e l'economia di guerra*, no. 44, pp. 172–74.

Secondly, a new financial institution was created by a banking syndicate led by the Bank of Italy, which was authorized to make advances to non-financial institutions against stock deposited as collateral at a margin of 50% of its market value on 31 July 1914, or 90% of its nominal value.[13]

The Consorzio per Sovvenzioni su Valori Industriali (CSVI, Industrial Securities Finance Consortium), as this new institution was called, was to charge interest rates equivalent to the official discount rate of the issue banks. It was authorized to rediscount its portfolio with the issue banks at 1.5% less than the official discount rate. The issue banks were exempted from paying penalties on increases in their note circulation above the maximum ceilings fixed by law, insofar as such increases stemmed from rediscounting the portfolio of the CSVI. The entire profit of the CSVI, and half of the profits earned by the issue banks by rediscounting its portfolio, were to form a reserve fund to cover eventual losses. The CSVI began functioning in February 1915 with a capital of Lit. 22m., which had been subscribed by the three issue banks, two old public banks – the Monte dei Paschi of Siena, the Banco di San Paolo of Turin – and the Savings Banks of Milan (Cassa di Risparmio delle Provincie Lombarde or CARIPLO), Turin, Genoa, Bologna, Florence, and Palermo. At the time of Italian intervention in May 1915, the CSVI's capital was raised to Lit. 40m., with the major commercial banks taking minority interests. It was authorized by statute to make advances for up to ten times its capital.[14]

The CSVI was clearly the brainchild of Stringher and represented an attempt to create a new institutional framework for dealing with the financial crises endemic to the Italian system of industrial finance predicated on mixed banking. The association of the Savings Banks and similar institutions, such as the Monte di Paschi and the Banco di San Paolo, in the new organization reflected Stringher's long-term concern to extend the responsibility and risk associated with maintaining the stability of the financial system beyond the Bank of Italy to all major financial institutions. In effect, the CSVI created a new financial circuit that allowed Stringher to establish a direct rapport with financially distressed manufacturing firms, bypassing the mixed banks.

The CSVI had its direct precedents in the "voluntary" bank syndicates that were formed under pressure from Stringher in the spring of 1907 to defend the prices of stocks on the Milan and Genoa exchanges during the period of greatest stress. The 1907 syndicates had, however, included only

[13] Bachi, *L'Italia economica nell'anno 1914*, pp. 240–44; Archivio Storico, Banca d'Italia (hereafter ASBI), fondo 9.2, Presidenza e Giunta del Consiglio Superiore riunite in Comitato (hereafter Comitato), verbali, 20 December 1914.
[14] Riccardo Bachi, *L'Italia economica nell'anno 1915* (Città di Castello: S. Lapi, 1916), p. 242; ASBI, fondo 9.2, Comitato, verbali, 31 May 1915.

smaller private banks, and their scope of action was relatively limited. Moreover, the statutes of the Bank of Italy did not allow it to provide direct financial assistance to these syndicates to support their interventions on the stock exchanges. In the fall of 1907, when the collapse of the Società Bancaria threatened to provoke a general crisis of confidence in the Italian financial system, Stringher had conceived the imaginative idea of dramatically expanding the strength of these syndicates by uniting them, and persuading the CARIPLO, and the Società per le Strade Ferrate Meridionali (an investment bank) to join. The latter two institutions possessed large stocks of railway obligations that the Bank of Italy could make advances against, allowing it to indirectly put its resources at the disposal of the syndicate. The CARIPLO and the Meridionali could not, however, be persuaded to participate in a venture with such dubious financial prospects. Stringher was ultimately constrained to intervene on behalf of the SBI in association with the Credit and the Comit; as was noted above, the latter two institutions cooperated with Stringher only reluctantly, and after ensuring that their intervention only would become effective after the SBI had almost entirely lost the confidence of its depositors, and therefore its status as a serious competitor of the other two major commercial banks.[15]

The CSVI avoided many of the inconveniences of the earlier syndicates promoted by Stringher. The law which established it expressly authorized it to rediscount its portfolio with the issue banks. The fact that the CSVI could lend up to ten times its capital afforded it ample scope for intervention. Moreover, Stringher had himself appointed the first director of the new institution, thereby ensuring his own direct control over its activities.

But the CSVI neither remedied Italy's fragile financial structures nor protected the Bank of Italy from locking up its resources in the event of a collapse of stock prices and a major run on the commercial banks. With its modest share capital, the CSVI hardly divided the risk of meeting a financial crisis. The CSVI represented only a paper wall between illiquid firms and the issue banks, as the latter were expected to rediscount the CSVI's acceptances. In practical terms, the main function of the CSVI was to create a mechanism whereby the issue banks could make loans to industry in the event of a liquidity crisis without violating the issue banks' statutes, which forbade loans against anything other than first class commercial paper or collateral deposits of state and state-guaranteed securities.

By the time the CSVI began operating in February 1915, the recession of the previous fall had turned into a war-related boom. Informal prices of

---

[15] On the 1907 bank syndicates see, Bonelli, *La crisi del 1907.*

industrial securities began to rise again, and firms had little reason to make use of the credit facilities of the CSVI. The CSVI's operations were modest during the war years, both in relation to the maximum level of business it was allowed to conduct, and to the total commercial business of the issue banks. It is therefore all the more striking that Stringher seized every opportunity to prolong the life of the institution and increase its share capital. At the time of Italian intervention in May 1915, Stringher championed new legislation that raised the CSVI's share capital to Lit. 40m., and the maximum volume of operations it was allowed to undertake to Lit. 400m. The CSVI also now was allowed to extend loans to firms against collateral consisting of raw materials or semi-manufactures. In November 1916 a new decree authorized the CSVI to extend its activities to credits for the construction of merchant shipping. In December 1918, when the original charter of the institution was due to expire, a new decree prolonged its life for an additional six months; in June 1919 its charter was renewed again until December 1920.[16] It seems likely that Stringher intended to make the CSVI the institutional centerpiece of his plans for meeting an eventual financial crisis arising out of post-war reconversion; as we shall see, it was precisely during the financial crisis of 1920–3 that the CSVI finally became a critical instrument of monetary policy.

Phase 2: The issue banks and state finances

As was the case with the central banks of all other belligerent nations, the policy of the Italian issue banks during the war and immediate post-war years was almost entirely subordinated to the Treasury's need to finance extraordinary budget deficits. The issue banks supported government financial policy by selling Treasury securities; heading war loan placement syndicates; "preparing" the financial markets for new war loan offers through open market operations; lending against state securities; and pursuing a permissive money policy, which kept interest rates on government debt issues relatively low, as was described in detail in chapter 3 above. But like central banks in all other belligerent nations, the Italian issue banks performed the additional essential function of making direct advances to the Treasury, that is, of printing notes to bridge the gap between the government's expenditures and the total sums it raised through loans, taxes, and other revenues.

Prior to the war, the issue banks were obligated to make advances of up to Lit. 155m. to the Treasury against special Treasury bills bearing only

---

[16] ASBI, fondo 9.2, Comitato, verbali, 31 May 1915; Alberto De Stefani, *La legislazione economica della guerra* (Bari: Laterza, 1926), pp. 154–55.

1.5% interest in exchange for the privilege of holding the Treasury's active balances. Already in September 1914, the ceiling on these so-called "ordinary" advances to the Treasury was raised to Lit. 485m. In June 1915, a new form of so-called "extraordinary" advances was created to meet the needs of war finance, on which the Treasury was obliged to pay only 0.25% interest. The ceiling on extraordinary advances was originally fixed at Lit. 200m., but it was repeatedly raised, until a maximum figure of Lit. 4,850m. was set in June 1918. Additional extraordinary advances of Lit. 1,000m. were authorized by decree in June 1919 in substitution for an equal amount of ordinary Treasury bills that the government had surreptitiously put up as collateral against commercial loans from the issue banks during the war, as was discussed above in chapter 3.[17]

In addition to this borrowing from the issue banks through ordinary and extraordinary advances, which were duly inscribed as debts in the government's annual budget, the Treasury borrowed additional sums from the issue banks that did not appear in the budget. This was accomplished by creating the so-called *gestioni fuori bilancio*, or administrations outside the budgets (for details see the note on sources to Table 1, Appendix, pp. 297–300). The size of the issue banks' advances to the Treasury under this system reached a maximum of Lit. 3,350m. in September 1919. Although outside the budget, advances to these agencies were duly noted in the 10-day and annual statements of the issue banks.[18]

The expansion of the note issue reached a peak at the end of December 1920, at 708, with 31 December 1913 as 100. Ercolani's figures for M1, the note issue plus deposits, similarly show a peak at the end of December 1920, at 493. Figures for the annual rate of expansion of the note issue during the wartime inflationary cycle are as follows: 1914 23%; 1915 31%; 1916 27%; 1917 59%; 1918 38%; 1919 34%; 1920 17%.[19] As is evident, the pace of monetary expansion was brisker in the final years of war, and in 1919, than in earlier years. The financial panic following Caporetto accounts for the exceptionally high figure for 1917. Noteworthy is the sharp decline in the rate of monetary expansion during 1920, despite the persistence of large state budget deficits, an indication of the beginning of monetary stabilization.

[17] De Stefani, *La legislazione economica della guerra*, pp. 380–81.
[18] On the *gestione fuori bilancio* see, Francesco A. Répaci, *La finanza pubblica italiana nel secolo 1861–1960* (Bologna: Zanichelli, 1962), pp. 128–29; Francesco A. Répaci, "Il costo finanziario della prima guerra mondiale in Italia," *Studi in onore di G. Pietra*, vol. II, special ed. of *Statistica*, 14 (1954), no. 4, pp. 579–93.
[19] All figures elaborated from, Paolo Ercolani, "Documentazione statistica di base," in, Giorgio Fuà, ed., *Lo sviluppo economico in Italia*, vol. III, 3rd rev. ed. (Milan: Angeli, 1978), p. 470. Note however that there is an error in columns a and c for 1918: the correct figures are 15.90 and 35.08 respectively. For the correct data see, Renato De Mattia, ed., *I bilanci degli Istituti di emissioni italiani*, 2 vols. (Rome: Banca d'Italia, 1967), Tables 2, 5, and 23.

Phase 3: Stabilization and financial crisis, 1920–1922

At the risk of anticipating some of the themes of the final chapters of this study, it seems useful to set out here the main lines of monetary policy during the post-war period of stabilization. Italy was the only continental ex-belligerent to exploit the favorable international conditions created by the post-war world economic recession to stabilize its state budget and the rate of monetary growth. The defeated powers – Germany, Austria, Hungary, and Russia – continued to inflate until hyperinflation and the complete destruction of their national currencies forced them to return to budgetary and monetary orthodoxy. France continued to run large budget deficits until the collapse of the mark focused bearish speculation on the international currency markets on the franc; and until the failure of French efforts to collect reparations by force made it clear that budget deficits could be brought under control only by raising taxes.[20]

Britain and the United States of course eliminated their budget deficits, and even began running budget surpluses in the latter half of 1919. With the elimination of state budget deficits, the way was clear in England and America for higher interest rates, and central bank discount rates were raised in the fall of 1919, and again in the spring of 1920. In April 1920 the Bank of England raised its bank rate to the extraordinarily high level of 7%. One month later world commodity prices broke, and the post-war recession began.[21] The break in world commodity prices, and the impact of deflationary policies in the United States and Britain tended to relax pressure on the exchange rates of continental European countries. The lira began to recover in May 1920, after a period of prolonged weakness on the exchange markets (see Figure 3, p. 330). Even the German mark was temporarily buoyed.[22]

At this point the Italian government was able to reduce drastically its reliance on the printing presses, even though net state borrowing in fiscal 1920–21 was about as large as in fiscal 1919–20. This singular achievement was brought about by a corresponding increase in the issue of government

[20] On France see, Stephan A. Schuker, *The End of French Predominance in Europe: The Financial Crisis of 1924 and the Adoption of the Dawes Plan* (Chapel Hill: University of North Carolina Press, 1976), pp. 31–56.

[21] On monetary and financial policy in the United States and Britain and the onset of the world economic recession see, Milton Friedman and Anna Jacobsen Schwartz, *A Monetary History of the United States, 1867–1960* (Princeton: Princeton University Press, 1963), pp. 221–76; Lester V. Chandler, *Benjamin Strong, Central Banker* (Washington DC: Brookings Institution, 1958), pp. 135–87; Susan Howson, "The Origins of Dear Money, 1919–1920," *Economic History Review*, 2nd ser. (1974), no. 1, pp. 88–107; Susan Howson, *Domestic Monetary Management in Britain, 1919–38* (Cambridge: Cambridge University Press, 1975), pp. 9–24; Sayers, *The Bank of England*, pp. 115–26.

[22] On the German mark see, Carl-Ludwig Holtfrerich, *Die deutsche Inflation, 1914–1923* (Berlin: De Gruyter, 1980), p. 188, and passim.

short and medium-term Treasury securities. The willingness of private
investors to buy new Treasury issues was increased greatly after Giolitti
introduced new tax proposals in July. Giolitti wanted to require the
registration of private stocks and bonds and long-term government securities, in order to prevent tax evasion. This provoked a break in the stock
market and enhanced the attractiveness of short and medium-term
Treasury issues, which Giolitti's proposals would have made the only
remaining bearer securities in Italy. Two additional factors further but-
tressed the market for short and medium-term Treasury issues in the
winter of 1920–21: first, the recession in America and Britain produced a
downturn in Italian manufacturing toward the end of 1920, aggravating
the flight of capital from private to state securities; and second, the abolition of the bread subsidy by decree in February 1921 augmented confidence in state finances.[23] By the spring of 1921 the state budget deficit
actually was declining, and the Treasury was able to retire loans from the
issue banks with the proceeds of new Treasury issues.[24]

The moderately deflationary influence of state financial policy on the
money supply deepened the economic recession, and transformed it into a
liquidity crisis for commercial banks and industrial firms. The financial
crisis entered a critical phase in the spring and summer of 1921. As will be
discussed in detail in chapter 7, the Ilva and Ansaldo iron and steel and
engineering concerns were essentially bankrupt. The two giant Italian
heavy industrial concerns were financially restructured by syndicates
headed by the major commercial banks, the Credito Italiano and the
Banca Commerciale in the case of Ilva, and the Bansconto in the case of
Ansaldo. The issue banks actively cooperated in these salvage operations
by rediscounting the illiquid portfolios of the commercial banks. The
CSVI now came into its own, acting as the main intermediary in making
central bank credit available to industrial firms. The commercial loan
portfolios of the issue banks swelled by 27.5% during the period of
greatest financial stress, between 1 October 1921 and 1 May 1922.[25] Such
generous public support enabled the Credit and the Comit to survive the
recession; but the Bansconto–Ansaldo group, which had undertaken a far

[23] See, Paolo Frascani, *Politica economica e finanza pubblica in Italia nel primo dopoguerra (1918–1922)* (Naples: Giannini, 1975), pp. 327–32.
[24] Official figures for the annual state budget are unhelpful, due to the incorporation of the losses of the *gestioni fuori bilancio* in the budgets of fiscal 1920/21, and 1921/22. A more accurate indication of the decline of the deficit is the volume of state borrowing as is indicated in Table 9 (Appendix, p. 308). See also, Luigi Einaudi, "Dove se tenta di calcolare il disavanzo del bilancio italiano," *Corriere della Sera*, 25 April 1923, *Cronache*, vol. VII, *1923–1924* (Turin: Einaudi, 1966), pp. 210–14.
[25] On issue bank commercial credit see, De Mattia, *I bilanci degli Istituti di emissione*, Tables 15 and 16; on the CSVI see, Riccardo Bachi, *L'Italia economica nell'anno 1921* (Città di Castello: S. Lapi, 1922), pp. 34–36, and passim.

more daring program of expansion during the war, was compromised irremediably. As we shall see below, the Bansconto collapsed in a depositors' run in late December 1921 and early January 1922, despite the efforts of the Bank of Italy to keep what was now the country's second largest commercial bank solvent.

The expansion of bank credit produced by the Bank of Italy's rescue operations largely compensated for the retirement of issue bank loans to the Treasury. The note issue declined by 4% in 1921, an additional 8% in 1922 and 7% in 1923. However, M1 declined by only 3.5% in 1921, and increased by 1% in 1922, and by a further 14% in 1923.[26] Therefore, in contrast to the United States and Great Britain, where large budget surpluses followed quickly on large wartime deficits, and where inflationary monetary policy in wartime was followed by severe deflation, in Italy stabilization was achieved through a gradual reduction in state budget deficits, and by an only moderately deflationary monetary policy. However, because of the structural instability of the banking system and rapid wartime industrial expansion, even moderately deflationary policies produced a relatively severe financial crisis in Italy.

It is worth drawing attention to the apparent paradox that Italy began the process of financial and monetary stabilization long before France, despite the gravity of the Italian political and institutional crisis. The absence of anything comparable to French reparations illusions in Italy certainly accounts in part for the relative speed with which the final liberal governments initiated the stabilization process, even though they alienated the socialists and Catholics in the process. More importantly, the Italians simply had less freedom of maneuver than the French. The French government was able to mobilize a far greater pool of domestic savings to finance budget deficits than existed in Italy.[27] The Italian balance of payments position was much weaker than that of France, and the threat of a complete collapse of the lira on the exchange markets, on the order of the central European currencies, correspondingly greater. Moreover, the relative severity of the post-war recession in Italy, and particularly its impact on the financial markets and the banks facilitated stabilization: in a first phase, beginning in the summer of 1920, capital flight from private to short and medium-term state securities allowed the Treasury to retire loans from the issue banks, easing and ultimately terminating monetary expansion one year before the state budget deficit significantly contracted; in a second phase, beginning in the summer of 1921, the very severity of the liquidity crisis convinced the authorities that stabilization was imperative to prevent the crisis of confidence in the major Italian commercial

[26] Ercolani, "Documentazione statistica di base," p. 470.
[27] Schuker, *The End of French Predominance in Europe*, pp. 31–56.

banks and manufacturing firms from growing into a general crisis of confidence in the Italian economy, the lira, and state finances.

The impact of the war on the structure of the banking system

In many respects, the structural changes in the banking system in the course of World War I represented the continuation of trends already underway in the Giolittian era. Most importantly, the commercial banks, particularly the largest commercial banks, continued to increase their share of the total assets and deposits of the banking system, largely at the expense of the savings banks and the postal savings banks, at about the same rate as had been the case in the pre-war years. In 1913, the commercial banks held 25% of both the assets and the deposits of the banking system, while the savings banks and postal savings banks held about 30% of the assets and 57% of the deposits. At the end of 1923, the commercial banks had increased their share of the total assets of the system to 39% and of deposits to 43%, while the share of savings institutions had fallen to 22% and 43% respectively. This tendency is in line with structural changes in the banking systems of most other industrialized countries.[28] In fact, the commercial banks in Italy held a smaller share of the total assets of financial intermediaries, both in the Giolittian era and on the eve of the world economic crisis in 1929, than in other industrialized countries. The explanation for this seemingly paradoxical relative weakness of the commercial banks in a country where they played an exceptionally important role in industrial finance lies in part in the long succession of Italian bank failures. The largest commercial banks of the first decades of this century, the Banca Commerciale and the Credito Italiano, had begun as relatively small institutions in the last years of the nineteenth century, and had not built up asset portfolios of anything like the size of the older, respectable commercial banks in Britain, France, or Germany. Previous bank failures also led many savers to place greater trust in savings banks, which in part explains the extraordinary relative weight of savings institutions in the Italian banking system.

Even though the commercial banks improved their relative position in the banking system during the war years, they did not achieve absolute gains, either in the real values of their assets or of their capital and reserves. When adjusted for inflation, the reported assets of the commercial banks declined in the course of the war, and figures higher than 1913 values were not posted until 1923. Similarly, the real value of

[28] Anna Maria Biscaini Cotula and Pierluigi Ciocca, "Le strutture finanziarie: Aspetti quantitativi di lungo periodo (1870–1970)," in Fausto Vicarelli, ed., *Capitale industriale e capitale finanziario. Il caso italiano* (Bologna: Il Mulino, 1979), pp. 61–136.

deposits at commercial banks fell below 1913 levels until 1918, and only began to rise significantly above pre-war figures after 1922. In Italy, as elsewhere in continental Europe, the banking system as a whole was a net loser in the war and post-war inflationary process.

The relative decline of the savings banks and postal savings banks during the war and post-war years was due in part to their particular vulnerability to inflation; their assets consisted largely of long-term, fixed-yield securities, particularly state bonds. Nevertheless, the savings banks' share of the total assets of Italy's financial intermediaries in 1929 was still far higher than in other industrialized countries. This persistent strength of the savings banks was undoubtedly due in part to the continued preference of small savers for the relative security of savings banks' accounts, despite their low yield. The distrust of small savers for the commercial banks was presumably reinforced by the collapse of the Banca Italiana di Sconto in 1921.

Both before and after World War I the issue banks held a relatively large share of the assets of financial intermediaries in Italy compared to other developed countries. This fact was hardly an indication of the issue banks' strength; in the Giolittian period it was due rather to three factors: the relative weakness of the commercial banks; the real estate and loan portfolio that the Bank of Italy had inherited from the failed Banca Romana in the 1890s; and the non-issue bank activities of the Banks of Naples and Sicily in southern Italy. During the war the issue banks' share in total bank assets rose further, due to their role in financing the state deficit against deposits of government bonds. In the post-war economic crisis, the issue banks' portfolios were further swollen with rediscounted commercial paper.

The most catastrophic losses in the Italian banking system during the war inflationary cycle were posted by the mortgage banks. More than any other type of financial institution, the mortgage banks were squeezed by the growing disparity between the unchanging value of their assets, and the increase in prices. Popular banks were also hit hard during and after the war. Their difficulties were due in part to the weight of fixed-return securities in their portfolios. Catholic and socialist banks were also compromised by imprudent loans to cooperatives moving within their respective political orbits. The already fragile structure of the socialist and Catholic popular banks was further damaged, in many cases irremediably, by the depredations wrought by fascist squads in 1921 and 1922 on the cooperatives (see Tables 11 and 12, Appendix, pp. 310–16).[29]

---

[29] Ibid. On the Catholic banks see, Anna Caroleo, *Le banche cattoliche dalla prima guerra mondiale al fascismo* (Milan: Feltrinelli, 1976).

The commercial banks

Any conclusions about the activities of the commercial banks during the war and post-war years must remain highly tentative at this time. The Italian commercial code notoriously allowed the banks to file annual reports and monthly statements that contained little substantive information about their business. Even the little information provided by the commercial banks was often misleading. In the manner of British banks, the Italian commercial banks were adept at practicing "window dressing," i.e., building up cash reserves at the end of the month in time for bank statements, which were rapidly depleted again thereafter. But more significantly, as was noted above, the Italian commercial banks habitually extended long-term credits which were carried in their books as short-term loans, but regularly rolled over. During the war years, the commercial banks' statements became even more cryptic than had been the case previously. In 1919, for example, only the Credito Italiano separately itemized its holdings of Treasury securities.[30] But despite the lack of firm evidence, broad trends in the banks' activities can be deduced from the limited quantitative data available, the statements of contemporary observers, and comparisons with the activities of commercial banks in countries with similar financial structures, notably Germany and Austria.[31]

From the beginning of the war, the banks were confronted with a decline in their ordinary commercial business. The economic recovery caused by defense-related contracts did not lead to a substantial recovery in commercial lending, as manufacturers were able to demand large advances from the state, and became extraordinarily liquid. At the same time that the traditionally most liquid form of business of the commercial banks dried up, depositors manifested a much stronger preference for highly liquid assets: time deposits declined, and current account deposits increased. Hence the banks were constrained to find new, highly liquid investments in order to replace their declining commercial business, and guard against a sudden run on deposits. As was the case for banks in other belligerent countries, this need was filled largely by "ordinary" Treasury bills, i.e. bills maturing in three to twelve months, which the government obligingly issued in ever greater volume (see Table 9, Appendix, p. 308). Extrapolating from the Credito Italiano's indications of its holdings of

---

[30] Riccardo Bachi, *L'Italia economica nell'anno 1919* (Città di Castello: S. Lapi, 1920), p. 70, and passim.

[31] On Germany see Karl Erich Born, "Vom Beginn des Ersten Weltkrieges bis zum Ende der Weimarer Republik (1914–1933)," in, Ernst Klein et al., eds., *Deutsche Bankengeschichte*, vol. III (Frankfurt a.M.: Knapp, 1983), pp. 17–146; on Austria see, Eduard März, *Austrian Banking and Financial Policy: Creditanstalt at a Turning Point, 1913–1923* (London: Weidenfeld and Nicolson, 1984).

Treasury bills in its annual report for 1919, Bachi estimated that the four largest commercial banks together held approximately Lit. 4,975m. of a total of Lit. 21,759m. of Treasury bills in circulation.[32] In Italy, as in other ex-belligerent countries, the size of the floating debt and the concentration of Treasury bill holdings in the portfolios of the largest banks later would be perceived as a significant threat to the stability of government finances; but at least during the war the banks had little choice but to roll over their holdings of Treasury bills.

Recent work on the history of Austrian commercial banks underscores the importance of exchange speculation, normally a marginal activity, as a source of profits during the war inflationary cycle.[33] In Italy too, there were persistent rumors that the banks had reaped huge profits from exchange speculation, even though the figures posted for revenues from "commissions and exchange transactions" in the banks' annual statements showed only modest nominal increases, that did not even keep pace with inflation. It is difficult to take the banks' official representations on this subject seriously.

The major banks played an important role, of course, in underwriting the war loans. However, as was noted in chapter 3, they showed great reluctance to hold substantial amounts of the war loans in their own portfolios. After each of the first three war loan subscription drives in December 1914, July 1915, and January 1916 respectively, they quickly divested themselves of their holdings, even if it meant taking a loss; in the final three war loans in February 1917, January 1918, and January 1920 the banks were pressured by the government into taking up substantial portions on their own account; however, they quickly regained their former liquidity positions by rediscounting the loan with the issue banks. Indeed, the success of the commercial banks in improving their relative position in the banking system with respect to the savings banks during the inflationary years, was in no small measure due to their avoidance of huge capital losses on the war loans.

The war boom allowed industrial firms to retire substantial debts to the banks, rescuing them from what appeared to be an imminent liquidity crisis in the year and a half prior to August 1914. Presumably, many industrial firms went from being debtors to being creditors of the banks, as they retired loans and deposited a portion of their huge wartime profits in current accounts with the commercial banks. Large industrial groups also engaged in stock speculation and in three important cases – Ansaldo with the Banca Italiana di Sconto, Ilva with the Società Mediterranea, and Fiat with the Credito Italiano – bought up substantial shares of financial

---

[32] Bachi, *L'Italia economica nell'anno 1919*, p. 70.
[33] März, *Austrian Banking and Financial Policy*, pp. 152–53, 357.

institutions, gaining a major voice in the banks' affairs.[34] However, in some instances the expansion of industrial firms outstripped their very substantial wartime earnings, and they soon became indebted to the banks again. In the most spectacular of the three cases cited above, the domination of the Bansconto by Ansaldo, the industrial group sought to gain control of the bank not so much because it held an excess of liquid funds, but because it wished to use the Bansconto's resources to promote its own extravagant expansionary plans. Even manufacturing firms that remained highly liquid during the war became quickly indebted to the banks again in the post-war years: as they sought to complete investments begun in the heady climate of the war; or to reconvert to peacetime production, after state contracts began to dry up. It has been argued that industry emancipated itself from the banks during the war, but emancipation often lasted only until the post-war recession.

The commercial banks were active in underwriting stock issues during the war, and during the expansionary phase immediately following the armistice. Bachi noted that new stock issues by industrial firms in the immediate post-war years were often undertaken at the insistence of the banks, presumably in order to convert bank debts into equity capital.[35] März observes that Austrian bankers pursued a similar policy with respect to their industrial clients in the same period.[36]

With regard to deposits and assets, the Italian commercial banks would appear to have recovered much more completely, and much more rapidly from the wartime inflationary cycle than banks in Germany and Austria. Although the Italian banks had to weather a far more severe economic storm in the immediate post-war years than their counterparts in the Allied nations, they were not exposed to the horrors of hyperinflation and revolution, and they did not face the near-total loss of their foreign investments, as was the case in East Central Europe. Nevertheless, the failure or near-failure of all the major Italian commercial banks in the 1920s and early 1930s, similar to the German and Austrian banks, suggests that their underlying structural problems were similar. In one crucial respect, the ratio of own to outside resources, the Italian commercial banks were severely weakened in the course of the war. In the Giolittian era, the major commercial banks had maintained capital plus reserves to deposit ratios of about 1:3; by the immediate post-war years this ratio had fallen to 1:10.6 for the Banca Commerciale, 1:11.3 for the Credito Italiano, 1:11.6 for the

---

[34] Riccardo Bachi, *L'Italia economica nell'anno 1918* (Città di Castello: S. Lapi, 1919), pp. 48–49, and passim; Valerio Castronovo, *Giovanni Agnelli. La Fiat dal 1899 al 1945* (Turin: Einaudi, 1977), pp. 104–9; Franco Bonelli and M. Barsali, "Massimo (Max) Bondi," *Dizionario biografico italiano* (1969).

[35] Bachi, *L'Italia economica nell'anno 1919*, p. 93, and passim.

[36] März, *Austrian Banking and Financial Policy*, pp. 356–57.

Banca Italiana di Sconto, and 1:12.6 for the Banco di Roma.[37] Although the banks were able to improve their own to outside capital ratios in subsequent years, they never again approached pre-war levels. Worse, the equity capital of both the Banca Commerciale and the Credito Italiano was essentially symbolic after 1920. In order to defend themselves against hostile take-over attempts in the wake of the Perrone brothers' attempt to capture the Commerciale, the two banks formed financial concerns that held the majority interests in their stock. The majority interests in these financial concerns were in turn owned by firms in which the two banks themselves held controlling interests. Therefore, through a circular pattern of ownership links, dubbed "Chinese" or "Japanese boxes" in Italian financial parlance, the two banks essentially owned themselves.[38] The negative implications of this ownership structure for the stability of the banks is obvious.

Moreover, the stability of the commercial banks continued to be a function of the stability and profitability of the industrial concerns with which they were associated, just as had been the case before the war. The Banca Italiana di Sconto foundered in 1922 after Ansaldo became insolvent during the post-war reconversion crisis. The Credito Italiano and the Banca Commerciale similarly were constrained to seek government assistance in restructuring their assets in 1930 and 1931 respectively because of the losses suffered by their industrial clients during the world depression.

The Milan–Rome conflict and the "war between the banks"

Important episodes in the history of the Banca Italiana di Sconto, notably its creation in 1914–15, and the two hostile take-over bids against the Banca Commerciale in 1918 and 1920, have been studied intensively elsewhere.[39] This discussion is therefore limited to illustrating how the

---

[37] Elaborated from tables in, Umberto Bava, *I quattro maggiori istituti italiani di credito* (Genoa: Valugani, 1926).

[38] Ettore Conti, *Dal taccuino di un borghese*, 3rd ed. (Bologna: Il Mulino, 1986), pp. 301–2; Giovanni Malagodi, "Il 'salvataggio' della Banca Commerciale nel ricordo di un testimone," in, Gianni Toniolo, ed., *Industria e banca nella grande crisi 1929–1934* (Milan: Etas Libri, 1978), pp. 270–83, esp. pp. 275–76.

[39] Ernesto Galli Della Loggia, "Problemi di sviluppo industriale e nuovi equilibri politici alla vigilia della prima guerra mondiale: La fondazione della Banca Italiana di Sconto," *Rivista storica italiana*, 82 (1970), no. 4, pp. 824–86; Anna Maria Falchero, "Banchieri e politica. Nitti e il gruppo Ansaldo–Banca di Sconto," *Italia contemporanea* (1982), nos. 146/7, pp. 67–92; Anna Maria Falchero, "Il gruppo Ansaldo–Banca Italiana di Sconto e le vicende bancarie nel primo dopoguerra," in Peter Hertner and Giorgio Mori, eds., *La transizione dall'economia di guerra all'economia di pace in Italia e in Germania dopo la prima guerra mondiale* (Bologna: Il Mulino, 1983), pp. 543–71; Anna Maria Falchero, *La Banca Italiana di Sconto, 1914–1921: Sette anni di guerra* (Milan: Angeli, 1990).

financial turbulence of the war and post-war years was a product of the conflict that had developed in the Giolittian era between the major commercial banks in Milan and central banks and Treasury authorities in Rome; and how the struggle between the Bansconto and the Milanese banks lacerated the liberal political elite.

The effort to found a third major commercial bank, to contest the predominance of the Banca Commerciale and the Credito Italiano, predated the outbreak of war. Nitti, who returned to his law practice in March 1914, after the fall of the fourth Giolitti ministry, in which he had been Minister of Agriculture, Industry, and Commerce, was involved in the initiative in its early stages. However, the European war broke out before the new bank opened its doors, and its foundation took place in the context of a nationalist campaign against the allegedly German-dominated Milanese banks during the period of Italian neutrality. The Bansconto began operating on 31 December 1914, with a modest share capital of Lit. 15m. In July 1915 the institution was enlarged by merger with the Società Bancaria Italiana, and another commercial bank, the Società di Credito Provinciale, which was itself the product of an earlier merger between two local banks, the Banca di Busto Arsizio (in Lombardy) and the Banca di Verona. The merger raised the share capital of the Bansconto to Lit. 65m. In addition to the interests associated with the component banking institutions – including two French banks, Dreyfus & Cie. and the Crédit Français, which held minority equity interests in the SBI and Credito Provinciale respectively – Pio and Mario Perrone, the directors of the Ansaldo iron, steel, and engineering concern, held a minority interest in the Bansconto from the beginning.[40]

Riccardo Bachi was certainly correct when he observed that: "It was evident that the government favored the creation of the Sconto in opposition to the Commerciale."[41] The Salandra–Sonnino government went so far as to present a bill in the Camera in March 1915, modifying the commercial code, so as to facilitate the merger of the Bansconto with the Credito Provinciale and the SBI. The bill, which evidently had been drafted by Nitti, was approved by the Camera with a wide majority.[42] There also can be little doubt that Stringher favored the establishment of the new bank, given his earlier support for the SBI as a rival to the Commerciale and the Credito.[43]

[40] Galli Dalla Loggia, "La fondazione della Banca Italiana di Sconto;" Falchero, "Banchieri e politica."

[41] Bachi, *L'Italia economica nell'anno 1921*, p. 53.

[42] Galli Dalla Loggia, "La fondazione della Banca Italiana di Sconto," p. 852; Falchero, "Banchieri e politica," pp. 71–72.

[43] Galli Dalla Loggia argues that the Quai d'Orsay was convinced of Stringher's support for the Bansconto in February 1915. "La fondazione della Banca Italiana di Sconto," p. 851.

The hostility of the Salandra–Sonnino cabinet to the Banca Commerciale is further demonstrated by the participation of newspapers close to the government in a press campaign against the Commerciale, which was initially instigated by extreme nationalist circles, and papers close to the Ansaldo–Bansconto group. The newspapers accused high officials of the Commerciale, notably Otto Joel, Federico Weil, and Cesare Mangili, of being sympathetic to German interests, and their resignations were demanded. However, the government was unwilling to support the plan of the Bansconto leadership to place its own men on the board of directors of the rival institution. When Joel and Weil stepped down from their posts as executive directors, and when Mangili resigned as president of the Commerciale during the shareholders' meeting in March 1916, Salandra and Sonnino seemed prepared to make their peace with the Commerciale.[44] Sonnino's *Giornale d'Italia* would later become hostile to the Bansconto, perhaps in part because of the association of the *banca italianissima* with Nitti, the Foreign Minister's archrival.[45]

Galli della Loggia has demonstrated that the Bansconto leadership's plan to take over the Commerciale dated from the fall of 1915, at the latest.[46] The extent to which leading political figures supported the Bansconto and the Perrone brothers in this enterprise is less certain. Nitti's relationship with the Bansconto in particular has been the subject of acrimonious debate, both in his own time, and among contemporary historians. During the war, Nitti and the newspapers controlled by him argued that excessive competition among the major commercial banks was deleterious to the national interest; instead, the southern Italian politician advocated "bank cooperation," and the subordination of the commercial banks to the monetary and economic policy of the Bank of Italy and the Treasury.[47] Nitti always insisted the bank cooperation implied government impartiality with regard to interests of rival groups, but his political opponents accused him of partisanship for the Bansconto.[48] Even though Nitti's critical role as legal counsel to the Bansconto in 1914–15 has been well documented, Nitti's biographers, Monticone and Barbagallo, have

Documents in the French Ministry of Foreign Affairs confirm this, although Stringher was, as usual, cautious in his support for the Bansconto. Quai d'Orsay, Correspondence politique, nouvelle serie, 1896–1918, Italie, finances, banques, bourse, II, 1908–1914.
[44] Galli Dalla Loggia, "La fondazione della Banca Italiana di Sconto," pp. 863–71.
[45] Falchero, "Banchieri e politica."
[46] Galli Dalla Loggia, "La fondazione della Banca Italiana di Sconto."
[47] F. S. Nitti, *Il capitale straniero in Italia*; "Limiti e caratteri di possibili accordi fra i grandi banchi," unsigned, 9 June 1917; "Verso la solidarità fra le banche italiane," unsigned, 10 November 1917; "L'accordo fra le grande banche italiane," unsigned, *Finanza italiana*, 6 July 1918.
[48] Nitti's defense against his critics is set out exhaustively by his son Vincenzo in *L'opera di Nitti* (Turin: Gobetti, 1924), pp. 50–57.

upheld the southern Italian politician's denials of complicity in the Bansconto's hostile take-over attempts on the Commerciale in 1918 and 1920.[49] In contrast, Falchero has insisted, correctly in my view, that Nitti not only continued to maintain close relations with the Ansaldo–Bansconto leadership during his tenure as Treasury Minister in 1917–18, and as Prime Minister in 1919–20; but also that the take-over bids represented a fundamental component of his program of bank cooperation.[50]

Nitti was in any case fully informed by Pio Perrone of the latter's intentions with regard to the Commerciale well before his appointment as Minister of the Treasury. The Director General of Ansaldo outlined his plan for "Italianizing" the Comit to Nitti in a letter dated 2 July 1916. He made clear that the success of a take-over bid would require the presence of a favorably disposed person in the cabinet, and there is little doubt that he regarded Nitti as the individual in question.[51] Monticone discusses this letter at length, and it is hard to disagree with Falchero, when she suggests that Monticone's own evidence tends to undermine his contention that Nitti was extraneous to the affair.[52] Significantly, the first hostile take-over bid on the Commerciale was made in the late spring of 1918, at the first suitable moment, one is tempted to conclude, after Nitti's appointment as Minister of the Treasury – that is, immediately following the issue of Nitti's fifth War Loan.

Although I was able to find only scarce reference to the "war between the banks" in the archive of the Bank of Italy, the minutes of the board for 17 June 1918, at the height of the struggle for ownership of the Commerciale, indicate at a minimum that Stringher was unwilling to intervene against the Perrones. Eugenio Ambron, a board member, suggested that the take-over attempt could threaten the stability of the entire banking system and asked Stringher whether he felt the Bank of Italy should take measures to impede it. Stringher replied that one might well think the take-over attempt was deplorable, but that it was a typical phenomenon in times of excessive paper money circulation, and added: "one should not exaggerate either the significance or the consequences [of the take-over], and the director general does not believe the Bank can take any action."[53]

[49] Alberto Monticone, *Nitti e la grande guerra (1914–1918)* (Milan: Giuffré, 1961), pp. 246–53; Barbagallo, *Nitti* (Turin: UTET, 1984), pp. 373–75.

[50] Falchero, "Banchieri e politica. Il gruppo Ansaldo–Banca Italiana di Sconto nel primo dopoguerra."

[51] Perrone to Nitti, 2 July 1916, Archivio Centrale dello Stato, Archivio Nitti, 28/2.

[52] Monticone, *Nitti e la grande guerra*, pp. 203–8; Falchero, "Banchieri e politica," pp. 82–83.

[53] Banca d'Italia, Consiglio Superiore, verbali, 17 June 1918, in Toniolo, ed., *La Banca d'Italia e l'economia di guerra*, no. 55, pp. 206–9.

In the presence of Cesare Paris, who attended the meeting as the Treasury's representative, Stringher continued:

> The government may take some protective measures, but if it does not do so, it means that it believes there is no need, and that it is better to let a new arrangement come into being naturally. As far as the Bank of Italy is concerned, it must limit itself to being vigilant and prudent ... taking into account events as they occur, and the situation which it may confront once peace is concluded.[54]

Stringher's statement suggests the Treasury enjoined the Bank of Italy not to interfere in the take-over bid. The Bank almost certainly could have impeded the Perrones' take-over bid by restricting credit to the Bansconto.

The "escalade" on the Commerciale ended two days later with the signing of an accord between the two rival groups dictated by Nitti. The accord envisaged an increase in the share capital of the Commerciale from Lit. 156m. to Lit. 208m., with the Ansaldo–Bansconto group being guaranteed a minority interest, and a seat on the board of directors of the rival institution. The agreement did not give the Bansconto group control over the Commerciale, and thus did not satisfy the Perrone brothers. Nitti and his followers insisted that the accord represented a compromise, and furnished proof that the Minister of the Treasury stood above the conflicting parties, a position which has been echoed in the recent literature.

Falchero, in contrast, argues that the Perrone brothers lacked sufficient shares, and sufficient liquid capital to dislodge the old controlling interests from the leadership of the Commerciale, and that under the circumstances the compromise arranged by Nitti was by no means disadvantageous to them. She points out that the Perrone brothers were at least successful in securing the participation of the Comit in an issue of Ansaldo stock in the summer of 1918, which raised its share capital from Lit. 100m. to Lit. 500m., enabling the firm to continue its vast program of investment and expansion. The deal may have included two additional concessions to Ansaldo: (1) friendly control of the Società Elettrica Negri, which controlled the major hydroelectric facilities in the Genoa region, and which the Comit's allies had battled to control; and (2) ownership of Fiat San Giorgio, the marine division of the Turinese engineering firm, which was now rechristened Ansaldo San Giorgio.[55]

Several days later, Nitti persuaded – or forced – the directors of the four major commercial banks (the Comit, the Bansconto, the Credit, and the

---

[54] Ibid.
[55] Falchero, "Banchieri e politica"; Falchero, *La Banca Italiana di Sconto*, pp. 123–35.

Banco di Roma) to sign another accord. The text of this agreement has
remained secret, but it was described in the following terms by the directors of the Credito Italiano:

> These accords are nothing more than the extension, with a few additions
> and variations, of those we reached with the Banca Commerciale in 1907.
> They regard the conditions for loans and deposits, agreements on reciprocal
> respect of employees, common participation in financial operations with the
> state, provinces, municipalities, and other public administrations, as well as
> affairs with private firms which exceed a certain sum, and the exchange of
> information on the opening of new branches at home and abroad. The
> details of these accords will be fixed in September, and their extension to
> include smaller banks, as well as the foundation of an Association of Banks
> and Bankers is under study.[56]

To Luigi Einaudi, a more or less disinterested observer, it was self-
evident that this accord favored the interests of the Bansconto above those
of the Commerciale and the Credito, and that Nitti was partial to the
former group. In his articles in the *Corriere della Sera* Einaudi condemned
the accord on the basis of his liberal economic principles, as it tended to
reduce free competition, without reference to the contending political and
business interests.[57] In his private correspondence with Albertini, he was
more direct. On 1 July 1918 he wrote:

> Nitti is becoming abominable. How much farther can he go in his bad faith
> ... forcing the best banks to make common cause with the bad ones. In my
> opinion, he is a true national threat, and it is necessary to say: *principi obita*. If
> this goes on, all of Italy will fall into the hands of Pogliani [Director General
> of the Bansconto], Perrone, Beneduce [Director of the National Insurance
> Institute, and a protégé of Nitti], and Giuffrida [Director of the Commis-
> sariat for Provisions and other supply committees, also a protégé of Nitti],
> with Nitti behind them.[58]

Whatever the extent of Nitti's collaboration with the Perrone brothers in
1918, the bank accord represented an attempt to impose greater government control over the commercial banking sector, and was sufficient in
itself to provoke the uncompromising hostility of the Milanese bankers to
Nitti, and ensured that the Rome–Milan conflict would continue to divide
Italy's political and economic elites after the armistice.

[56] Archivio Storico, Credito Italiano, Consiglio d'Amministrazione, verbali, 3 August 1918.
[57] Luigi Einaudi, articles in *Corriere della Sera*, 4 June 1918, 2 July 1918, in *Cronache*, vol. IV,
     pp. 683–91.
[58] Einaudi to Albertini, 1 July 1918, Fondazione Einaudi, Turin, Archivio Einaudi,
     carteggio.

5

INTERNATIONAL ACCOUNTS: ITALY'S
LOSS OF FINANCIAL INDEPENDENCE

**The Italian economy and international accounts during the period
of neutrality**

The financial crisis of August 1914, and the collapse of the system of
international payments based on London had a profound impact on Italy's
foreign trade. The major Italian commercial banks, the Banca Commerciale and the Credito Italiano, were deeply involved in financing Italy's
foreign commerce, but they relied heavily on the London acceptance
market. Both banks had branches in London, and most Italian commercial
bills on the United States and Latin America were drawn up in sterling
and presented for acceptance or rediscount in London.[1] Italian cotton
imports plummeted from 208,000 quintals in July 1914 to 94,360 quintals
in August, and 67,060 quintals in September.[2] In addition to the crisis in
the international financial system, Italian trade suffered from the general

---

[1] Interesting documentation regarding the importance of the London branches of the Commerciale and the Credito for financing Italian overseas trade emerges from an audit of the
two bank branches conducted by the British Treasury in the fall and winter of 1914. The
audit was undertaken to determine whether the two bank branch offices engaged in illegal
transactions with enemy countries, as was widely alleged. The auditors cleared both banks
of such charges and expressed their satisfaction with the cooperation offered by Comit and
Credit officials during their investigation. At the beginning of 1915, Siegfried J. Bieber and
other Commerciale and Credito officials with German citizenship were forced by British
authorities to resign their posts. Public Record Office (PRO), Treasury files (T-files),
T1/11955/20334/16. However, documents in the Fred I. Kent papers suggest that Bieber,
the Comit's London director, did in fact evade British laws forbidding financial transactions with German banks. The Bankers' Trust Co. of New York opened a correspondence
account with the Banca Commerciale in the second half of September 1914 on behalf of a
New York Bankers' Committee established to aid American tourists stranded in Europe by
the breakdown in international payments. Immediately thereafter, Fred I. Kent, who was in
London, was able to remit sums to American tourists in Germany by utilizing the Comit as
intermediary. Bieber avoided violating British laws directly by having Kent telegraph
transfers directly to Milan. Kent requested that sums be credited in Milan to the account of
"Smith's bank" and "Hardina's bank" (the Deutsche Bank and the Dresdener Bank), to
evade British military censors. Kent to Benjamin Strong, 21 September 1914; Kent to
Strong 23 September 1914; Strong to Kent, 24 September 1914; Strong to Kent, 26
September 1914, Kent Papers, Seely Mudd Manuscript Library, Princeton University.
[2] Riccardo Bachi, *L'Italia economica nell'anno 1915* (Città di Castello: S. Lapi, 1916), p. 24.

climate of uncertainty in the business community. Recovery was underway in key economic sectors by October or November, with war-related contracts coming to Italian businesses from both belligerent camps and from the Italian government.[3] The cotton and wool industries, along with iron and steel, engineering, and of course armaments manufacturing, were the earliest and greatest beneficiaries of the war-related boom. With the British naval blockade of the German North Sea ports, Genoa became an essential artery for German, Austrian, and Swiss imports from overseas. Activity in the port increased rapidly, creating a major congestion problem by February 1915.[4]

But the impact of war on the Italian economy was not unequivocally favorable. The outbreak of the war produced a dramatic decline in invisible exchange earnings. Tourists all but vanished from the peninsula even before Italian intervention. Emigrant remittances were frozen momentarily by the collapse of the international financial system, and they did not return to anything like their former levels for the rest of the war. Jannacone's figures show a fall of remittances in constant prices from Lit. 828m. in 1913 to Lit. 606m. in 1914, and Lit. 390m. in 1915 (see Table 16, Appendix, p. 321). The swift repatriation of seasonal Italian workers from Germany, Austria, Switzerland, and France after the outbreak of the war probably brought about a temporary influx of foreign exchange, but it was not enough to compensate for the decline in remittances from transoceanic emigrants. Currency fluctuations and economic recession in Argentina and Brazil discouraged remittances from those two countries; and Italians in the United States apparently chose to hold their savings in dollars until the Italian political and economic situation stabilized. After the outbreak of war, repatriation consistently exceeded new emigration, and the savings capacity of the Italian communities abroad diminished correspondingly.[5]

During the period of neutrality the total volume of Italy's trade declined. The decline in imports, however, greatly exceeded the decline in exports. Military demand reduced the disposition of Italy's European trade partners to export strategic raw materials and manufactures. The European powers began to impose export bans on particularly vital commodities. At the same time, foreign demand for Italian manufactures was

---

[3] Bachi, *L'Italia economica nell'anno 1914* (Città di Castello: S. Lapi, 1915), p. vii.
[4] Luigi Einaudi, *Corriere della Sera*, 15 March 1915; 18 March 1915; 2 April 1915, reprinted in *Cronache economiche e politiche di un trentennio (1893–1925)* (Turin: Einaudi, 1961), vol. IV, pp. 138–54.
[5] Istituto Centrale di Statistica (hereafter ISTAT), *Sommario di statistiche storiche 1861–1955* (Rome: ISTAT, 1958), pp. 65–66; Ercole Sori, *L'emigrazione italiana dall'unità alla seconda guerra mondiale* (Bologna: Il Mulino, 1979), p. 401; Francesco Balletta, *Il Banco di Napoli e le rimesse degli emigranti* (Naples: Istitut d'histoire de la banque, 1972), pp. 58–61.

unprecedented. Italian cotton and wool manufacturers, who previously had not enjoyed great success in Northwestern and Central European markets, were now flooded with orders for uniforms. Fiat and other Italian auto and auto parts manufacturers did considerable business, especially building trucks for the French army. During the ten months of neutrality, Italy ran a surplus of exports over imports of manufactured goods for the first time.[6]

Another factor that fundamentally affected the structure of Italian trade was the closing of the Dardanelles as a result of Turkish intervention in the war in October 1914. The near-total interruption of trade with Russia and Romania cut off Italy from its major pre-war foreign sources of cereals, and an important secondary source of petroleum products. The Italian cereal trade shifted in part to Argentina, but largely to the United States. Italy became totally dependent on US companies for petroleum.[7] Hence, at a time when Italian dependence on the United States for crucial raw materials was accentuated, the decline in emigrant remittances and tourist receipts reduced Italian dollar holdings. Italy's trade deficit with the United States grew even though the overall trade deficit was narrowing. The great rise in shipping and insurance costs made Italian food products uncompetitive in American markets, and the military factors that stimulated European demand for Italian manufactures were inoperative in the United States.

The financial and economic transformations during the months of neutrality thus had an equivocal impact on Italy. War-related demand in the belligerent countries offered Italian manufacturers new export opportunities. The war also allowed Italian manufacturers to wrest a greater share of the home market for advanced technological goods and iron and steel products from foreign, particularly German, producers. The wool and cotton industries emerged from a period of prolonged recession and experienced a boom in which only the scarcity of raw materials limited production and sales. Similar conditions obtained in iron and steel manufacturing, and engineering. Other more traditional industries and crafts, however, such as stone quarrying and cutting, flower growing, linen textiles, paper, glass and ceramics production, and the building trade, suffered either because of the scarcity of vital imports, the collapse of foreign markets, domestic inflation, and economic uncertainty, or some combination of these factors. Despite the prosperity of the more advanced industrial sectors, unemployment remained high throughout the period of neutrality.[8]

---

[6] Bachi, *L'Italia economica 1915*, p. 17.
[7] Ibid., pp. 19, 42.
[8] Ibid., pp. 16–51, 143–60.

Financial negotiations with the Entente

Already in August 1914, the French and British governments unofficially let Italian diplomats in their respective capitals know that loans could be arranged in the event of Italian intervention.[9] Marquis Guglielmo Imperiali, the Italian ambassador to Britain, was even quoted a figure of £st. 20m. by his confidants in the City.[10] Apparently, Marquis Antonino di San Giuliano, the Italian Foreign Minister at the outbreak of the conflict, instructed his ambassadors to inquire whether Italy could borrow on the capital markets in Paris or London while remaining neutral. The British and French replies were negative.[11] The British offer of a loan in the event of Italian intervention was reiterated, this time officially, by Sir James Rennell Rodd, the ambassador in Rome, in a conversation with San Giuliano on 19 September 1914.[12] There can be no doubt, therefore, that from the beginning both the Italian and the Allied governments fully expected that a loan to Italy would be negotiated in the event of Italian intervention in the war.[13]

The government refrained from making specific inquiries regarding loans until a complete list of Italy's demands for intervention in the war was presented to Sir Edward Grey, Britain's Foreign Minister, by Imperiali in London on 4 March 1915. Article 14 of the Italian draft treaty called for British government support for an Italian loan of £st. 50m. on the London market.[14] This figure was accepted subsequently by the British government without discussion, and formed the premise of the first financial accord between Britain and Italy, which was arranged in Nice at the beginning of June 1915. As Salandra and Sidney Sonnino (who became Foreign Minister in November 1914, after the death of San Giuliano) were fully aware, the credit arranged through the Nice Accord was

---

[9] Imperiali to San Giuliano, 21 August 1914; San Giuliano to Tommaso Tittoni (Italian Ambassador to France), 20 September 1914; Mario Ruspoli di Poggio Suasa (Chargé de Affaires, Italian embassy, Paris) to San Giuliano, 22 September 1914, published in Ministero degli Affari Esteri, *I documenti diplomatici italiani* (hereafter *DDI*), 5th ser. 1914–1918, vol. 1 (Rome: Ministero degli Affari Esteri, 1954), nos. 370, 753, 772.

[10] Imperiali to San Giuliano, 21 August 1914, *DDI*, ser. 5, vol. 1, no. 370.

[11] San Giuliano to Salandra, 22 August 1914, *DDI*, ser. 5, vol. 1, no. 391.

[12] San Giuliano to Imperiali, 19 September 1914, *DDI*, ser. 5, vol. 1, no. 750.

[13] David Garnett, a writer, and member of the Bloomsbury group, gives interesting testimony as to the British attitude regarding credits to Italy in a diary entry on 1–2 February 1915. In summarizing a recent conversation with Keynes, who was preparing to attend the first Allied financial conference in Paris, Garnett noted: "[Britain was to lend Italy] a large sum which simply means bribing [it] to come in [to the war] … fearfully immoral." Quoted in Robert Skidelsky, *John Maynard Keynes: Hopes Betrayed 1893–1920* (New York: Viking, 1986), p. 298.

[14] Published in, Antonio Salandra, *L'intervento (1915). Ricordi e pensieri* (Milan: Mondadori, 1930), pp. 156–60; Mario Toscano, *Il Patto di Londra* (Bologna: Zanichelli, 1934), pp. 83–86.

inadequate to meet government purchases abroad even in the first months of the war. The size and modality of the credit to be demanded of Britain were determined without consulting financial experts, and even without informing Paolo Carcano, the Minister of the Treasury.[15] Salandra and Sonnino had originally meant to ask for even less. In the famous Telegrammone, or long telegram, containing a draft list of Italian war demands, which was sent to Imperiali on 16 February 1915, the figure specified was only £st. 40m.[16] It was Imperiali who proposed increasing the sum to £st. 50m.[17]

Documents recently published by the Italian Ministry of Foreign Affairs reveal in detail how the Italian proposals formulated in the Telegrammone were drawn up at the Consulta beginning in December 1914.[18] The total inattention to financial matters is striking. Salandra and Sonnino chose to keep credit demands at a minimum for fear of undermining their territorial and political objectives. The Italian leadership's assessment of financial problems in relation to the negotiations with the Entente is well illustrated in an exchange of letters between Sonnino and Salandra on 19 February 1915. Salandra was scheduled to meet Arthur James Balfour, First Lord of the Admiralty, and former British Prime Minister, shortly thereafter, and he considered raising the question of an Italian loan with him. Salandra passed on to Sonnino a letter from the conservative economist Maffeo Pantaleoni regarding the urgency of reaching a financial agreement with Britain. He noted that the Sicilian financier Guido Jung, who later represented Italy in interallied economic organizations and at the Paris Peace Conference, had earlier made similar observations to him.[19] Sonnino's reply is characteristic. While noting that Giorgio Mylius, president of the Association of Cotton Manufacturers, had recently sought to meet him – also in order to urge the negotiation of a financial accord with Britain – he advised Salandra not to raise the question formally with Balfour:

> It might be useful for you to see sig. Balfour, but only to chat in general terms about possible financial assistance. I would not initiate any serious negotiations, even in general terms, before Imperiali presents all of our demands, as formulated in the Telegrammone. The fragmenting of negotiations cannot serve us, because it diminishes the impression that has to be given to Grey, that *c'est a prendre ou a laisser*, in other words that we feel perfectly free to take either course of action [i.e. intervening or remaining

[15] This is clear from a letter of Salandra to Sonnino on 19 February 1915, *DDI*, ser. 5, vol. 2 (1984), no. 827.
[16] Sonnino to Imperiali, 16 February 1915, *DDI*, ser. 5, vol. 2, no. 816.
[17] Imperiali to Sonnino, 24 February 1915, *DDI*, ser. 5, vol. 2, no. 859.
[18] *DDI*, ser. 5, vol. 2.
[19] Salandra to Sonnino, 19 February 1915, *DDI*, ser. 5, vol. 2, no. 827.

neutral], and that our decision in favor of war depends exclusively on whether or not the Entente will accept all of our conditions as they stand. It is the only way to make them take us seriously. . . .

I would not begin anything that seems like a negotiation or gives the impression that we desire or need anything because of decisions already taken or considered inevitable.[20]

Italian financial needs could not be represented in their true gravity for fear that this would reduce the disposition of the Allies to make political and territorial concessions to Italy.

Salandra and Sonnino's neglect of financial problems in the London negotiations stands in marked contrast to the growing alarm not only of the Italian business community, as is reflected in the letters of Pantaleoni, Jung, and Mylius mentioned above, but even of the Treasury and the Bank of Italy. In the course of spring 1915 Stringher's difficulties in providing foreign exchange to the Treasury to support the government's rearmament and supply program were becoming increasingly acute. On 19 April 1915, just before the signing of the Treaty of London, Stringher summarized the critical situation of the government with regard to foreign exchange. On 3 April the Bank had transferred the equivalent of FFr. 35m., probably for the most part in sterling and dollars, to the Treasury. Since then, the Treasury had requested another FFr. 71.7m. in foreign exchange from the Bank of Italy. Up until the date of the letter, the Bank had collected an additional FFr. 12m., but Stringher warned that additional sums could not be obtained without gravely depressing the exchange markets, or drawing down the gold reserves of the Bank of Italy.[21] On the eve of intervention, the Italian government was increasingly hard-pressed to finance even the most essential imports for rearmament.

Salandra and Sonnino's failure to secure greater and more explicit commitments of financial and material support from the Allies at the time of intervention was the object of much criticism by their political opponents during the war.[22] On the other hand, Salandra and Sonnino were probably

---

[20] Sonnino to Salandra, 19 February 1915, *DDI*, ser. 5, vol. 2, no. 829.

[21] Stringher to Carcano, 19 April 1915, ASBI, fondo 3, bob. 78, pr. 217.

[22] Nitti's views, as expressed in a letter to Prime Minister Paolo Boselli on 25 January 1917, are characteristic: "When the honorable Salandra said that Italy would not bargain its intervention, and that he felt it dishonorable to bargain, I was quite distressed. I would have bargained: it was a necessity, and a duty. Wars are fought with feeling, but also with arms, and provisions." Fondazione Einaudi, Archivio Nitti. Giolitti condemned the government's handling of supply and financial problems in similar terms as early as September 1915. Olindo Malagodi, *Conversazioni della guerra* (Milan and Naples: Ricciardi, 1960), vol. I, conversation with Giolitti, 30 September 1915, pp. 70–71. All financial accords signed by the Allies during the war, like the Pact of London itself, were kept secret. The precise entity of the British credits was therefore unknown to the public, but the continued decline of the value of the lira on exchange markets was an evident

correct in their judgment that the Entente would have been less inclined to consent to Italy's extravagant territorial claims in the Adriatic if they had demanded greater material assistance. Later in the war, when the Italian government was constrained to apply for new credit advances, the British government did not hesitate to press Italy for political concessions. Undeniably, the credit provisions of the Treaty of London reflected Salandra and Sonnino's unrealistic conception of a short war, to be waged independently by Italy against Austria, and also their total lack of communication with the officials responsible for financial policy. Carcano and Stringher certainly knew nothing of the financial proposals in the Telegrammone in February 1915, and most probably, they did not learn the terms of the financial clauses of the Treaty of London until after it had been signed. In the subsequent financial negotiations with the British in May and June, Carcano and Stringher were forced to make the best arrangements possible in the context of a treaty that had been worked out without their participation or knowledge.

International trade and finance and Italian intervention

It has been suggested that the structure of Italian commercial and financial relations in 1914 made war against the Central Powers and alliance with the Entente inevitable.[23] Certainly, Italy was in a position to sustain a longer and more intensive war effort in alliance with the Entente than with Germany and Austria. Britain alone could provide Italy with the minimum coal supplies necessary not only for belligerency, but even for

---

indicator of persistent financial weakness. Moreover, it was clear that the government had received no guarantees regarding coal and cereal deliveries or shipping. When the Camera debated the government's wartime economic policies for the first time in March 1916, the socialists attacked the government for not having taken precautionary economic measures in the expectation of having to fight only a short war. Many members of the majority associated themselves with these criticisms. *Atti della Camera dei Deputati*, sessione 1913–14, leg. 24, discussioni 9, meetings of 13 March to 16 April 1916. Even the diplomatic historian Mario Toscano, who was sympathetic with the political orientation of the government, eventually judged Salandra and Sonnino severely on this point in his study of the Pact of London. See, Mario Toscano, *Il Patto di Londra Storia diplomatica dell'intervento italiano (1914–1915)* (Bologna, Zanichelli, 1934), pp. 164–65.

[23] "The way in which Italian heavy industry grew up in the narrow, inhospitable peninsula, so thin in resources and poor in home markets, set an early pattern of imbalance, of foreign ties and enmities, that by 1914–15 had become decisive: on one side, links with the French and Belgians, a few vital partnerships with British industry, and good development prospects in the Balkans and Asia Minor; on the other, continual rivalry with Germany on the Italian industrial market itself and increasing competition with Austria-Hungary on the high seas and in Italy's foreign markets. To Italy's unsteady industries the Entente offered financing and raw materials, while the Germans attempted financing and technical control. Italy's foreign policy from 1911 to 1915, however subject it may have been to considerations of military and diplomatic balance, admirably fitted the interests most dependent on the state." Webster, *Industrial Imperialism in Italy*, p. 42.

armed neutrality. Italian dependence on North American cotton and, after the closing of the Dardanelles, cereals and petroleum, also implied dependence on British shipping and British – and ultimately American – dollar credits. To be sure, the isolation of Italy from German firms producing advanced technological equipment, iron and steel products, and chemicals created economic hardship, but it also allowed Italy to achieve greater self-sufficiency in these sectors. Similarly, the loss of wood and paper pulp supplies in Austria-Hungary produced difficulties for the paper, printing, and construction industries. During the war, domestic forests were ruthlessly cut, causing severe ecological damage. Italian importers were constrained to pay far higher prices for the modest quantities of wood and pulp they were still able to import from neutral countries, especially Switzerland and Sweden. But Austrian wood and paper pulp were clearly less essential and more easily replaceable than the commodities Italy imported from Britain and America.

It is however far from clear that economic considerations of this nature strongly influenced Italian foreign policymakers in the months of neutrality. Salandra and Sonnino counted on a short war when they signed the Treaty of London in April 1915, and they did not foresee how crucial supply questions would become subsequently. The economic dimensions the war would assume were not yet clear to many of the participants. Although Germany and France took the first steps toward massive economic mobilization after the Battle of the Marne in the fall of 1914, British economic mobilization only began in earnest in the weeks following Italian intervention. The first serious Italian efforts at mobilizing the economy began only after the failure of the offensives on the Isonzo in the summer and fall of 1915. The modesty of the British credit obtained under the terms of the Pact of London demonstrates how little importance Salandra and Sonnino attributed to financial questions at that time. The Italians neither demanded nor received specific commitments regarding coal deliveries or the use of British merchant ships in the negotiations preceding intervention. Diplomatic papers and correspondence, the memoirs of Salandra, and the diaries of Sonnino underscore the predominance of territorial, strategic and internal political considerations in the decision to make war on Austria.[24]

---

[24] Antonio Salandra, *La neutralità italiana (1914). Ricordi e pensieri* (Milan: Mondadori, 1928); Salandra, *L'intervento*; Pietro Pastorelli ed., *Sidney Sonnino. Diario 1914–1916* (Bari: Laterza, 1972); Pietro Pastorelli, ed., *Sidney Sonnino. Carteggio 1916–1922* (Bari: Laterza 1975); Alberto Monticone, "Salandra e Sonnino verso la decisione dell'intervento," *Rivista di studi politici internazionali*, 24 (1957), no. 1, pp. 64–89; Edgar Rosen, "Italiens Kriegseintritt im Jahre 1915 als innenpolitisches Problem der Giolitti-Ära. Ein Beitrag zur Vorgeschichte des Faschismus," *Historische Zeitschrift*, 187 (1959), no. 2, pp. 289–363; Leo Valiani, "Le origini della guerra del 1914 e dell'intervento italiano nelle ricerche e nelle pubblicazioni dell'ultimo ventennio," *Rivista storica italiana*, 78 (1966), no. 3, pp.

At most, the economic and financial advantages of alliance with the Entente may have influenced certain sectors of Italian public opinion, creating an atmosphere in which the government's decision to intervene enjoyed broader political support. Castronovo has suggested that many Turinese businessmen who initially advocated neutrality were reconciled to intervention in the winter of 1914–15 because of increasing concern about obtaining supplies and credit from the Western powers.[25] The growth of supply and credit bottlenecks in this period certainly alarmed the business community. The rise in freight costs and the dependence of Italy on foreign, particularly British shipping worried industrialists. Freight and insurance costs for coal deliveries from Cardiff to Genoa increased fourfold from July 1914 to May 1915.[26] But economic questions were not necessarily preponderant in shaping elite opinion regarding intervention or neutrality. Vigezzi has noted a shift to a pro-interventionist, or less adamantly neutralist, position on the part of many Milanese liberals in the same period described by Castronovo, but he attributes this change to domestic political, rather than economic preoccupations. Vigezzi argues that as neutrality became increasingly identified with Giolitti and the democratic left, and intervention with Salandra and the right, the Milanese liberals aligned themselves according to their conservative domestic political preferences.[27]

To the extent that Italian businessmen hoped intervention would ease supply difficulties, they must have been disappointed. Coal imports in the first seven months of belligerency actually declined slightly from the last seven months of neutrality.[28] Cotton imports were up, but the severe congestion of the port of Genoa in the early spring of 1915, and the subsequent easing of the problem in the late spring and early summer probably exerted a greater influence on the volume of Italian imports in this period than any increase in economic cooperation among the Allies after Italian intervention.[29] A comprehensive Allied shipping agreement did not exist before early 1916, although the British government placed

584–613; Brunello Vigezzi, "La 'classe dirigente' italiana e la prima guerra mondiale," in *Da Giolitti a Salandra* (Florence: Vallecchi, 1969), pp. 53–110; Richard J. B. Bosworth, *Italy and the Approach of the First World War* (London: Macmillan, 1983); Luciano Segreto, "Aspetti delle relazioni economiche tra Italia e Germania nel periodo della neutralità (1914–15)," *Annali della Fondazione Luigi Einaudi*, 18 (1984), pp. 455–517.

[25] Valerio Castronovo, "Le relazioni tra la Fiat e il governo francese durante la guerra," in Pierre Guillen, ed., *La France et l'Italie pendant la première guerre mondiale* (Grenoble: Presses Universitaires de Grenoble, 1976), pp. 335–38.

[26] Einaudi, *Corriere della Sera*, 12 January 1916, *Cronache*, vol. IV, pp. 155–61.

[27] Brunello Vigezzi, "I 'liberali' milanesi nel 1914–15: Salandra, Giolitti, la pace e la guerra," in *Da Giolitti a Salandra*, pp. 263–89.

[28] Bachi, *L'Italia economica 1915*, p. 40.

[29] Ibid., p. 24; Einaudi, *Corriere della Sera*, 15 March 1915, 18 March 1915, 3 April 1915, *Cronache*, vol. IV, pp. 138–54.

some ships at the disposal of the Italian and French governments at below market rates on an *ad hoc* basis prior to then.[30] The sterling credits obtained in the Treaty of London eased the shortage of foreign exchange to some degree, but the lira continued to fall on international currency markets at about the same rate as it had before intervention.

To summarize, while it is clear that in the long run Italian economic activity was maintained at a higher level than otherwise would have been possible thanks to Allied economic cooperation, that cooperation was still embryonic in the spring of 1915, and had little immediate impact. Moreover, at the time of intervention, the Italian government was concerned to avoid mortgaging its territorial war goals through excessive economic and financial dependence on Great Britain, and hence was inclined to neglect the needs of national industry for raw materials and foreign credits.

The violent campaign of the nationalist press against German economic interests in Italy, and particularly against the two Milanese commercial banks founded in the 1890s with German capital, the Banca Commerciale Italiana and the Credito Italiano, raises the question of whether the promise of technological and commercial emancipation from Germany did not influence elite opinion in favor of intervention.[31] Certainly, hostility to German financial and economic interests had been intense in Italy, as in many other European countries prior to the war. Feis aptly wrote:

> the close partnership of effort between the government and the banks [in Germany] was discerned; the government was felt to be the driving power in much of German foreign investment. Hence the idea grew that this investment was not merely a private venture but part of an official scheme, aiming at commercial, perhaps political, hegemony.[32]

Isolation from the German economy during the war clearly favored the maturing of the Italian capital goods sector. There is no evidence, as the nationalists alleged, that the directors of the Banca Commerciale and the Credito Italiano, several of whom were German citizens or naturalized

---

[30] J. A. Salter, *Allied Shipping Control. An Experiment in International Administration* (New York: Oxford University Press, 1921), pp. 136–38.

[31] Ernesto Galli Della Loggia, "Problemi di sviluppo industriale e nuovi equilibri politici alla vigilia della prima guerra mondiale: La fondazione della Banca Italiana di Sconto," *Rivista Storica Italiana*, 82 (1970), no. 4, pp. 824–86; Anna Maria Falchero, "Banchieri e politica. Nitti e il gruppo Ansaldo–Banca di Sconto," *Italia contemporanea* (1982), nos. 146–47, pp. 67–92; Brunello Vigezzi, "Otto Joel, il principe di Bülow e i problemi della neutralità," in *Da Giolitti a Salandra*, pp. 203–62; Giorgio Mori, "Le guerre parallele. L'industria elettrica in Italia nel periodo della grande guerra (1914–1919)," in, *Il capitalismo industriale in Italia* (Rome: Riuniti, 1977), pp. 141–215; Renzo De Felice, "Giovanni Preziosi e le origini del fascismo (1917–1931)," *Rivista storica del socialismo*, 5 (1962), no. 17, pp. 493–555.

[32] Feis, *Europe, the World's Banker*, pp. 187–88.

Italians of German origin, were in any way beholden to the German foreign ministry; but the two banks and the industrial firms that moved in their orbit had prospered through intense relations with German firms and financial institutions. Informal bonds between the directors of the two Milanese banks and German industrialists and bankers may well have influenced the structure of Italian trade prior to the war.[33]

But the problem of relations with Germany divided, rather than united, the Italian business community, and even the pro-interventionist camp. In Milan, due to geographical location and established patterns of trade, germanophile sentiment was predominant. In Turin there was little anti-German sentiment, although a flood of French contracts during the period of neutrality may have influenced public opinion in a pro-Entente sense. Genoa, with an economy dominated by heavy industry, and an important armaments manufacturing sector, was the most ardently interventionist industrial city. It was the home of Ansaldo, the shipbuilding and engineering firm, which was the major financial backer of the nationalist daily *L'Idea Nazionale*, an active participant in the press campaign against the Milanese banks.[34] Ansaldo's financial support for the press campaign was not disinterested; it was the major rival of the iron and steel trust Ilva, which was close to the Commerciale and the Credito. Undoubtedly, the Ansaldo directors sought to undermine the position of their rivals under the cloak of patriotism.

The attack on the Commerciale and the Credito caused embarrassment and divisions within nationalist and interventionist circles. Dante Ferraris, an ardent interventionist, who in addition to being general manager of Fiat had interests in a number of Turinese mechanical firms, was constrained to resign from the board of directors of the corporation which owned the *Idea Nazionale* because of Fiat's close financial ties to the Credito and the Commerciale.[35] Although the executive directors of the

---

[33] Among the most perceptive discussions of the nature of German influence at the Commerciale are two memos written by Gaston Guiot, vice-president of the Banque Privée (an institution with close ties to the Banque de Paris et des Pays-Bas), who was sent by the French government to Italy in 1915 as Minister Plenipotentiary, to work out an arrangement between the French and Italian governments, and French and Italian financial-industrial groups, which would draw the Comit closer to France. Guiot to Aristide Briand (Prime Minister of France), memo, 8 November 1915; Guiot to Briand, memo, 6 December 1915, Quai d'Orsay, Correspondence politique, Nouvelle serie, 1896–1918, Italie, Finances, banques, bourse, II, 1908–14. This bizarre and inconclusive initiative is described in Galli della Loggia, "La fondazione della Banca Italiana di Sconto;" and, Pierre Milza, "Les Relations financières franco-italiennes pendant le premier conflit mondial," in Pierre Guillen, ed., *La France et l'Italie pendant la première guerre mondiale*, pp. 298–304.

[34] On differences in public opinion regarding intervention in these three cities see, Castronovo, "La Fiat e il governo francese durante la guerra," pp. 335–39.

[35] Ibid., pp. 338–40.

Milanese banks were neutralist, many businessmen close to the Commerciale favored intervention.[36]

During the same period Nitti promoted a campaign against German economic interests in Italy and the Milanese banks that was distinct from, and more measured than that of the nationalists.[37] Despite his earlier political confrontations with the Milanese banks about public ownership of hydroelectric resources in the Naples region and the national life insurance monopoly, as a corporate lawyer, Nitti had occasionally worked for the Commerciale prior to the war. However, shortly after the fall of the Giolitti government in March 1914, Nitti broke all professional ties to the Milanese banks and began intense work as legal counsel for the Banca Italiana di Sconto.[38] During this period, Nitti also gave a series of public lectures on foreign investments in Italy, which he later worked into a book.[39] He pointed out that German capital in Italy was modest in relation to Belgian, French, and British investments. Nevertheless, he suggested, German influence in the Italian economy, especially through the presence of German citizens or naturalized Italians of German origin in executive positions in the major Milanese banks, was very considerable. He proposed a law prohibiting foreigners from holding executive positions in Italian financial institutions. Nitti also argued that the war provided an extraordinary opportunity for Italy to reduce its technological dependence on foreign producers. In his writings prior to Italian intervention, Nitti suggested that even continued neutrality, but on the condition that the banking system was "nationalized," would be compatible with economic growth and technological emancipation.

It is noteworthy that both the rightist and the left-liberal attacks on German influence in the Italian economy during the period of neutrality were spearheaded by persons close to the Ansaldo–Banca Italiana di Sconto group. But this is not to say that there was not a wider public resentment of the German economic presence in the Italian peninsula. Even an independent observer like Riccardo Bachi, the Roman professor of economics, could not reject out of hand accusations that the executives of the Banca Commerciale had favored German interests – in the management of navigation lines, in influencing purchases of electrical equipment

---

[36] Giorgio Candeloro, *Storia dell'Italia moderna*, vol. VIII, *La prima guerra mondiale, il dopoguerra, l'avvento del fascismo* (Milan: Feltrinelli, 1978), pp. 77–78; Vigezzi, "Otto Joel e il principe di Bülow."

[37] Falchero, "Banchieri e politica." Francesco Barbagallo, in his recent biography of Nitti, inordinately minimizes Nitti's hostility to the Commerciale, *Nitti* (Turin: UTET, 1984), pp. 189–202.

[38] Falchero, "Banchiera e politica," pp. 72–73; Barbagallo, *Nitti*, pp. 189–202.

[39] Francesco Saverio Nitti, "Il capitale straniero in Italia," in *Scritti di economia e finanza*, ed. Domenico Demarco, vol. III, pt. 2 (Bari: Laterza, 1966).

and machinery for the cotton industry, and in pursuing Italian interests in the Levant and the Balkans. Bachi too recommended limiting by law the presence of foreign nationals on the boards of the commercial banks.[40] Indeed, the Banca Italiana di Sconto enjoyed wide public and political support when it was founded precisely because of widespread hostility to the two large Milanese banks. As was noted above in chapter 4, the Salandra government openly favored the Bansconto group. When Nitti introduced legislation in the Chamber in January 1915, to facilitate the merger of two regional banks with the newly constituted Sconto, the government supported him, ensuring passage of the bill. In late 1915 and early 1916 the Salandra government exerted pressure on members of the board of the Commerciale to retire several executives who were either of German descent or reputed to be excessively close to German economic interests.[41] Independently of the government, Bonaldo Stringher, the director of the Bank of Italy, clearly favored the founding of a new large commercial bank that would dispute the predominance of the Milanese *haute banque*.[42] It is, however, difficult to disentangle the extent to which Nitti, Salandra, and Stringher respectively were concerned specifically with German influence in the Commerciale or more generally concerned with the enormous power wielded by that institution in the economy, and in the political process. Most probably, in their separate ways, all three sought to take advantage of the anti-German sentiment of late 1914 and early 1915 to reduce the power and independence of the Milanese bank. The visionary Nitti aimed to create a productivist and *dirigiste* regime wherein the major banks would become pliant instruments of government economic policy; Stringher sought to augment the ability of the Bank of Italy to control the credit system and the money supply; and Salandra feared the Commerciale could sabotage important government initiatives, as it had on several occasions in the Giolittian era.

The reluctance of the Salandra government to declare war on Germany, despite a general commitment made to the Allies at the time of intervention, belies excessive government concern with German influence in the Italian economy. Salandra and Sonnino hoped that Italy could prosecute the war against Austria without unduly disrupting traditionally close relations with Germany.[43] Italy declared war on Germany only in August 1916, after the Salandra government had fallen, and under intense press-

---

[40] Bachi, *L'Italia economica 1914*, pp. 246–49.
[41] Galli Dalla Loggia, "La fondazione della Banca Italiana di Sconto," pp. 853–68; Pierre Milza, "Les Relations financières franco-italiennes pendant le premier conflit mondial," pp. 298–304.
[42] Ibid.
[43] Josef Muhr, *Die Deutsch–italienischen Beziehungen 1914–1922* (Göttingen: Musterschmidt, 1977), pp. 41–47.

ure from the Allies.[44] Until that time, the government encouraged covert exports of silk and citrus fruit to Germany through Switzerland.[45] Many of the firms involved in this trade were close to the Banca Commerciale.

To summarize, although resentment of German economic influence in Italy was a significant political factor in the period of neutrality, it did not directly influence the government decision to intervene in the conflict. On the contrary, the Salandra government sought to minimize the damage to Italo-German relations caused by the war against Austria. Until the summer of 1916, the government covertly supported the continuation of limited commercial relations with Germany through neutral Switzerland. The campaign against the alleged German influences in the Banca Commerciale Italiana served a number of private economic and political ends that had little to do with curbing German economic influence. The Ansaldo–Banca di Sconto group promoted the campaign to dispute the Commerciale's preeminent position in commercial banking, heavy industry and shipping; Nitti, Salandra and Stringher, each in their separate ways, sought to utilize anti-Commerciale sentiment to increase state control over the private banking system.

British financial predominance: the agreements of 5 June and 19 November 1915

Salandra and Sonnino's objective to preserve an element of Italian economic and financial autonomy in the prosecution of the war proved unrealizable within six months of intervention, and Italy became totally dependent financially on Great Britain. In the negotiations leading up to the Treaty of London, Italy had asked for a credit of £st. 50m. from Britain. The British Foreign Office readily agreed, but the details of the financial agreement were not even broached. After the treaty had been signed, Sonnino discovered to his dismay that British terms would be substantially harsher than he had expected. In particular, the British insisted that the Bank of Italy deposit gold in London as a precondition for any loan. The British Treasury had already imposed the principle of gold deposits in London as a precondition for British credits in agreements with Russia and France, and it was not prepared to make concessions to Italy on this point.

---

[44] Lance T. Ventry, "Considerazioni sulla decisione italiana d'intervenire nel conflitto contro la Germania," *Archivio storico italiano*, 130 (1972) vol. 475, pp. 469–94.

[45] PRO, Foreign Office (hereafter FO) 382/1840/18; 382/1841/18; 382/1843/18. See also, Silvio Crespi, *Alla difesa d'Italia in guerra e a Versailles. Diario 1917–1919* (Milan: Mondadori, 1937), pp. 58–59; James Rennell Rodd, *Social and Diplomatic Memories*, vol. III, *1902–1919* (London: Edward Arnold, 1925), pp. 300–3.

Carcano was forced to conclude a financial agreement substantially on British terms, when he met with Reginald McKenna, the Chancellor of the Exchequer, at Nice on 5 June 1915. Against a total credit of £st. 60m. Italy was required to make gold deposits at the Bank of England for £st. 10m. In addition, the Italian government was to present Treasury bills, denominated in sterling, to the British Treasury for a total of £st. 50m. The British Treasury sold bills in like amount on the London financial market at the rate of interest obtaining on the day the credit was drawn upon. The Italian bills were to mature in six months, and bore an interest rate identical to the British bills. They were renewable for successive six-month periods up to one year after the conclusion of a general peace treaty, again at prevailing interest rates for British Exchequer bills. Italy was not to draw more than £st. 2m. weekly on the credit, indicating that the loan was meant to last for about seven months, i.e. until the end of 1915. Although the treaty made no provision for new credits in the event the war lasted longer, there was apparently an implicit understanding that if necessary a new loan would be negotiated after the exhaustion of the Nice credits.[46]

But Sonnino and Salandra's financial policy essentially was predicated on the assumption of a relatively rapid Allied victory; Italy would not be constrained to assume substantial debts in London in the course of a war that, it was hoped, would last only one season. Further, borrowing in Britain would be supplemented by loans from banks in the United States. Both premises of the Italian government's financial policy, quick victory and American credits, proved delusory by the fall of 1915. After prolonged negotiations in the United States, the Italian government was able to secure a loan of only $25m., on relatively onerous terms, from the Boston investment banking house Lee, Higginson & Co. in October 1915. Italy was forced to look primarily to Britain for credits to finance American imports. In the course of the summer and fall, Italian authorities also concluded that the credits arranged in the Treaty of London would prove woefully inadequate. In the offensives on the Isonzo the Italian army experienced a munitions crisis similar to the shells shortages of the French and German armies in the fall of 1914, and the British army in April and May of 1915. It became clear that vigorous prosecution of the war would require intensive industrial mobilization, and that imports of raw materials, machinery, and armaments from abroad would have to be stepped up drastically.

Meanwhile, as Italian financial needs grew, the British Treasury became

---

[46] The text of the accord has been published in, Gianni Toniolo, ed., *La Banca d'Italia e l'economia di guerra, 1914–1919* (Bari: Laterza, 1989), no. 58, pp. 221–24.

less disposed to grant substantial additional credits to the Allied governments. During the British munitions crisis in the spring of 1915, a bitter struggle broke out inside the British cabinet that pitted Reginald McKenna, the Chancellor of the Exchequer, and his adviser, John Maynard Keynes, against David Lloyd George, Minister of Munitions, and Lord Kitchener, the Secretary for War. The Treasury opposed Lloyd George's program for vast industrial mobilization on the grounds that the export industries would be damaged, and Britain's ability to earn foreign exchange to finance British and Allied purchases overseas compromised. Similarly, the Treasury opposed Kitchener's plan for the radical expansion of the British army on the grounds that large-scale recruitment would aggravate the labor shortage and diminish production. In essence, the Treasury argued that new commitments to a greater British military effort could only come at the expense of British financial and material support to the Allies. The Treasury favored a more traditional policy, with Britain assuming the role of paymaster and supplier for the armies of the continental Allies, while maintaining only relatively modest forces on the front. However, when the views of Lloyd George and Kitchener prevailed in the cabinet in the spring and summer of 1915, and the British government committed itself to industrial mobilization and the formation of the new armies, the Treasury began seeking to lessen Britain's financial burden by adopting a more stringent attitude in negotiations with the Allies.[47]

It was under these changed circumstances that an Italian delegation led by Stringher arrived in the British capital in early November 1915 to negotiate a financial agreement supplementary to the Nice Accords. Stringher wanted a substantial increase in Italy's monthly credit allotment. McKenna insisted that Italy's monthly credit be kept at £st. 8m. through March 1916; from April through December 1916 the monthly allotment would be raised to £st. 10m. for a total of £st. 122m. The Bank of Italy was required to make additional gold deposits for one-tenth of the total amount of the credit. In order to limit its foreign liabilities, the British stipulated that not more than £st. 65m. of the total credit be spent in the United States. Moreover, McKenna drafted a letter to Carcano, which was appended *extra tractatum* to the agreement signed on 19 November 1915, stating that dollar credits to Italy could be suspended after March 1916, if the Treasury was unable to obtain adequate resources in the United States. The other technical aspects of the agreement were similar to the Nice Accords of June 1915.[48]

---

[47] Skidelsky, *John Maynard Keynes*, pp. 305–15; Keith Nielson, *Strategy and Supply: The Anglo-Russian Alliance, 1914–17* (London: George Allen and Unwin, 1984), passim.

[48] The text of the accord, and McKenna's letter, have been published in Toniolo, ed., *La Banca d'Italia e l'economia di guerra*, nos. 61, 62, pp. 227–31.

This agreement served as the basis for Italy's financial relations with Britain until the fall of 1916. In June 1916 the British Treasury used McKenna's letter to justify reducing Italy's dollar allowance from $14m. to $10m. monthly. During the course of 1916, British authorities constrained Italy to turn over authority to make most of its overseas purchases to Allied supply organizations, which were essentially emanations of British government departments. As partial compensation for this tightening web of British control, in July 1916 McKenna offered Carcano a £st. 1m. monthly "free credit," which could be used to support the lira on the exchange markets.[49]

Shipping and supply bottlenecks

Until the final months of 1915, the scarcity of financial resources was the crucial factor limiting both Italian purchasing abroad and, more generally, Allied purchasing in neutral markets. From about the time of the second Anglo-Italian financial agreement in November 1915, however, shipping and supply bottlenecks began to emerge as additional significant limiting factors. Consequently, supply problems, in addition to finance, became major issues in Allied economic diplomacy in the course of 1916.

The most serious problems were shipping and coal. Shortages in both of these areas inevitably led to greater Italian dependence on Great Britain. As we have seen, Italy imported almost all of its coal before the war. In peacetime over 90% of Italian coal imports came from Britain, while most of the remainder came from the Ruhr.[50] After intervention, dependence on Britain was absolute. By 1916, British coal production had been pushed to the limits, and the problem of allocating coal between British domestic consumers and the Allies became acute. For the rest of the war, coal deliveries would be a major issue in Anglo-Italian diplomacy, with Italy invariably as the beggar.

British ascendancy in shipping was nearly as complete. Before the war, Britain owned almost half the world's merchant fleet, or 20,831,000 gross tons out of a world total of 42,416,000 gross tons. Italy was in sixth place, behind Germany, the United States, France, and Japan, with a modest 1,514,000 gross tons.[51] Even in peacetime Italy relied on chartered British and other foreign vessels for imports of coal, grain, and other essential commodities. The growing shortage of tonnage from late 1915, and the

[49] "Second Supplementary Financial Agreement Between the British and Italian Governments," 15 July 1916, Bank of England, archive, C40/215 1586/4. For a more detailed discussion of Anglo-Italian financial relations in this period see, Douglas J. Forsyth, "The Politics of Forced Accumulation: Monetary and Financial Policy in Italy, 1914–1922," Ph.D. dissertation, Princeton University (1987).
[50] ISTAT, *Annuario statistico italiano* (1914), p. 232.   [51] Salter, *Allied Shipping Control*, p. 8.

gradual extension of British shipping controls gave London an additional important instrument of economic and political leverage over Italy and the other Allies.

To be sure, the shipping shortage in 1916 derived not so much from an absolute lack of tonnage, as would become the case after Germany declared unrestricted submarine warfare in February 1917, but rather from an inadequate system of shipping controls. Salter estimates total tonnage in British service remained about equal from July 1914 to mid-summer 1915, although Allied demand grew considerably during this time.[52] A sudden surge in demand, triggered by the requirements of the British and French expeditionary forces in Gallipoli and Salonika, led to sporadic shortages in tonnage at the end of 1915. The situation worsened in March 1916, when severe congestion at New York, the major American Atlantic port, caused long delays for freighters bound for Europe.[53] The British government began adopting new, more stringent measures to control shipping, and forced France and Italy to follow suit. In November 1915, a Ship Licensing Committee was formed in Britain to deny licenses to tramp steamers judged to be engaged in relatively expendable activities. A certain number of steamers were immediately assigned to carry wheat on the North Atlantic run, to meet a deficit in British grain supplies.[54] Italy and France also ran up against a shortage of shipping to carry grain, but the British government let several months pass before additional tonnage for Allied grain carriage was allocated. Although Italy did not experience a severe grain shortage at this time, the government was constrained to cancel an advantageous contract with the Canadian government due to lack of shipping.[55]

Italy was compelled by British pressure to requisition German ships that had sought refuge in Italian ports in late 1915. At the beginning of 1916, the British government insisted that Italy and France requisition the whole of their respective merchant fleets in order to continue receiving requisitioned British tonnage at low, Blue Book rates. The Italian government complied, and in early February 1916 a Commissione Centrale del Traffico was established with jurisdiction over the entire Italian merchant fleet.[56]

[52] Ibid., p. 46.
[53] Kathleen Burk, *Britain, America and the Sinews of War, 1914–1918* (Boston: George, Allen and Unwin, 1985), pp. 37–38.
[54] Salter, *Allied Shipping Control*, pp. 49–51.
[55] Vincenzo Giuffrida and Gaetano Pietra, *Provital. Approvigionamenti alimentari d'Italia durante la grande guerra, 1914–1918* (Padua: CEDAM, 1936), pp. 146–47; internal British Treasury memo, J. M. Keynes, 10 December 1915, PRO, T-Files, T1/11962/22595/16.
[56] Commissione parlamentare d'inchiesta per le spese di guerra, "Relazione," in, *Atti parlamentari. Atti della Camera dei Deputati*, 26a legislatura, sessione 1921–23, Documenti

The shipping problem became acute for Italy once again in the summer of 1916, this time due to a shortage of colliers. British government policy contributed directly to Italy's difficulties. In May 1916, the Ship Licensing Committee, based on an assessment of British civilian needs, recommended that British tonnage in the service of the Allies be limited to the level on 1 April 1916. At about the same time, Britain demanded that vessels carrying coal to Italy be obliged to carry mineral ores from Spain and North Africa on the return voyage, considerably lengthening the transit time for colliers. Minimum monthly ore shipment quotas were stipulated in exchange for continued use of British colliers on the runs to Genoa and Naples.[57] The Italian supply situation was further aggravated by the German decision to shift the center of gravity of submarine warfare from the North Atlantic to the Mediterranean in early 1916, in response to public outcry over sinkings in the United States.[58]

By August 1916, Italian coal supplies had fallen so low that the government felt obliged to make a major diplomatic initiative *vis-à-vis* Britain. The British government seized on the occasion to force Italy to make significant political and economic concessions. Walter Runcimann, President of the Board of Trade, travelled to Italy in August 1916 to negotiate a coal agreement. He met with Giuseppe De Nava, the Italian Minister of Commerce, Industry, and Labor, and Enrico Arlotta, Minister of Transportation, at Pallanza, on Lago Maggiore. In exchange for fixing Italian monthly coal allotments at 850,000 tons, or about 250,000 tons more than previous monthly deliveries, the British insisted that Italy take more vigorous measures to interdict trade with Germany. Although Italy made no formal political undertakings with regard to Germany at the conference, war was declared on 28 August 1916, just two weeks later. Ventry, who has studied these events closely, concluded that British concessions on coal deliveries were tied closely to the Italian declaration of war.[59] British pressure on Italy to declare war on Germany in August 1916 in exchange for coal undoubtedly represented the most extreme case of the use of economic pressure to secure political ends in Anglo-Italian diplomacy during the war.

Runcimann also brought to Pallanza proposals for the expansion of the British financial and commercial presence in Italy after the war. The President of the Board of Trade had overseen the creation of a joint venture between leading British financial institutions and the Credito Italiano in May. Two related companies, the British–Italian Corp. and the

---

III, nos. 21–23, vol. II, pp. 167–68. On the requisitioning of German ships in Italian harbors see Forsyth, "The Politics of Forced Accumulation," pp. 348–51.
[57] Commissione spese di guerra, "Relazione," vol. II, p. 179.
[58] Giuffrida and Pietra, *Provital*, pp. 126–27.
[59] Ventry, "Considerazione sulla decisione italiana d'intervenire."

Compagnia Italo-Britannica, were organized in London and Milan respectively to serve as conduits for financing future British exports and investments in Italy. Runcimann intended the organization to become a vehicle for substituting German commercial predominance in Italy with British primacy. At the Pallanza conference, Runcimann did not hesitate to use the coal question to win Italian government support for the Anglo-Italian banking venture.[60]

Actual British coal shipments to Italy never approached the totals agreed at Pallanza, but deliveries were stepped up sufficiently at least to ease the Italian supply situation during the final months of 1916. However, no sooner had the coal situation been ameliorated than grain shortages became acute once again. By mid-November the shortfall in grain imports had become so serious that Giovanni Raineri, the Minister of Agriculture, was dispatched to London to seek additional British tonnage for wheat.[61]

The Italian grain shortage in late 1916 was symptomatic of a more general strain on Allied shipping. In the months just before the German declaration of unrestricted submarine warfare, Allied supply programs began to exceed total available tonnage. The shipping bottleneck was the catalyst for a series of measures that brought shipping and cereal supplies even more tightly under Allied government, and hence essentially British, supervision. On 29 November 1916 Raineri, Runcimann, and Etienne Clémentel, the French Minister of Commerce, signed an agreement creating the Wheat Executive, an inter-Allied organization with considerably greater authority than the Joint Committee, which had been established in January 1916. The Wheat Executive assumed responsibility for all Allied cereal purchases in neutral markets. It was also given authority over French and Italian vessels engaged in wheat carriage.[62]

In January 1917, an Inter-Allied Shipping Committee was formed to coordinate shipping resources globally.[63] The Committee had hardly begun to function when the German submarine campaign offered a new and far more serious challenge to the Allied supply program. A period of critical strain on Allied supply lines ensued, during which the outcome of the war seemed in balance. Losses from German submarines reached their apex in April, when one out of four Allied ships leaving port on the North Atlantic run failed to return. Thereafter, losses were rapidly contained through introduction of the convoy system. The supply crisis coincided

---

[60] Ibid.; on the British Italian Corp., and the Compagnia Italo-Britannica see also, Luciano Segreto, "La City e la 'dolce vita' romana. La storia della Banca Italo-Britannica 1916–1930," *Passato e presente*, 13 (1987), pp. 63–95.

[61] Forsyth, "The Politics of Forced Accumulation," pp. 391–95.

[62] A copy of the accord is published in Italian in, Giuffrida and Pietra, *Provital*, pp. 176–78.

[63] Salter, *Allied Shipping Control*, p. 140–41.

with the moment of greatest Allied financial strain in the three or four months prior to American intervention.

British and Italian financial difficulties prior to US intervention

The four months prior to US intervention represented the period of maximum financial strain for Italy and for the Allies as a whole during the war. The critical factor was the deterioration in Britain's international financial position. The collapse of British credit in the United States, which had been predicted by McKenna and Keynes as early as the fall of 1915, now seemed imminent, and indeed, probably would have occurred in the spring of 1917, if not for direct assistance from the US Treasury.

By November 1916, the Allied financial position was so alarming that J. P. Morgan & Co. advised Britain to risk an unlimited issue of short-term, unsecured Treasury bills on the US financial market. Shortly afterwards, the US Federal Reserve issued a warning to American investors about the possible illiquidity of nominally short-term foreign securities.[64] This is not the place to discuss the complex political and financial considerations that motivated the Federal Reserve's action; the consequence was, however, a crisis of confidence in British, and by extension Allied credit, which precluded further financial operations in the United States.[65] An unprecedented run on the Allied currencies ensued. The lira dropped to record lows against sterling as well as the dollar (see Figure 3, Appendix, p. 330), while the British Treasury was able to defend sterling parity only by radically depleting its gold reserves. The sealing off of the North American emporium to the Allies, and loss of the war through financial collapse appeared possible.[66]

Alarmed by the extent of the damage wrought on Allied finances by the 28 November statement, William Harding, Governor of the Federal Reserve, made a public statement on 14 December 1916, ostensibly to clarify, but in reality to attenuate the earlier announcement.[67] It was the first in a series of steps toward American *rapprochement* with, and eventually armed intervention on the side of the Allies. In January 1917 Britain was again able to issue a secured loan for $250m. in the United States with the approval of the American government. At the end of January, Ger-

---

[64] Burk, *Britain, America and the Sinews of War*, pp. 82–84; Yves-Henri Nouailhat, *France et Etats-Unis, août 1914–avril 1917* (Paris: Sorbonne, 1979), pp. 371–73.

[65] See the discussions in Nouailhat, *France et Etats-Unis*, pp. 375–78; Burk, *Britain, America and the Sinews of War*, pp. 84–85.

[66] On the financial crisis in Britain see Keynes's reminiscences from 1939 in, Keynes, "Notes on Exchange Control," in, Johnson ed., *The Collected Writings of J. M. Keynes*, vol. XVI, pp. 210–14.

[67] Burk, *Britain, America and the Sinews of War*, p. 86; Nouailhat, *France et Etats-Unis*, p. 382.

many declared unrestricted submarine war, to which the United States responded by breaking diplomatic relations. By early March, the Allied governments were informed that the United States was preparing to inter-vene in the war, and that US financial support for the Allies would be forthcoming. In the meantime, Britain was allowed to issue yet another secured loan for $250m. in March.

Despite improving diplomatic relations between the United States and the Allies from mid-December 1916, the Allied financial position remained critical until the eve of US intervention. Britain was reaching the end of its financial resources by early 1917, irrespective of the attitude of the Federal Reserve. Burk is certainly correct in stating that: "without American production and financial aid Britain would have been simply unable, after April 1917, to continue fighting on anything like the scale to which it had become accustomed."[68] This observation holds of course equally for Italy and the other Allies.

Under these extreme circumstances, it was only natural for the British Treasury to assume a more uncompromising attitude *vis-à-vis* Italy. McKenna ordered an immediate moratorium on all new Allied and British orders in the United States after the Federal Reserve announcement of 28 November 1916.[69] Since by now all Italian, and indeed Allied purchases with British dollar credits were effected through British government departments, the order was easy to enforce. At about the same time, British authorities took the additional step of informing Italian representa-tives in London that due to acute pressure on the sterling–peso exchange, British credits could no longer be used in Argentina. Italy, it was sug-gested, could seek the resources to finance necessary imports from Argen-tina among the Italian immigrant community there.[70] The Italian Minister of Transportation found himself in a difficult situation, as he was suddenly deprived of the financial resources to pay for cargoes awaiting loading on ships in Italian service in or near Plata ports.[71] Although Britain made small additional sums in pesos and dollars available in January, repeated Italian diplomatic representations in London to the effect that Italy was no longer able even to pay for the most necessary grain imports during January and February suggest the situation did not improve greatly until the eve of US intervention.[72] On 26 January 1917 Andrew Bonar Law, the

---

[68] Burk, *Britain, America and the Sinews of War*, p. 10.

[69] Ibid. p. 87.

[70] Paolo Conte (Italian Treasury representative in London) to Carcano, 3 January 1917, Ministero degli Affari Esteri, Archivio Storico (hereafter ASMAE), Rappresentanze diplomatiche Londra, 423.

[71] Conte to Carcano, 3 January 1917; Conte to Carcano, 17 January 1917, ASMAE, Rap-presentanze diplomatiche Londra, 423.

[72] Conte to Carcano, 17 January 1917; Malcolm Ramsay (Assistant Secretary to the Treasury) to Conte, 24 January 1917; Conte to Ramsay, 26 January 1917; Sonnino to

conservative parliamentary leader who had replaced McKenna as Chancellor of the Exchequer in the new Lloyd George cabinet in December, wrote to the Italian ambassador acknowledging that British dollar credits were inadequate, but stating that Britain simply had no more dollars to give.[73] The months of January and February were marked by frantic and largely unsuccessful Italian efforts to obtain pesos and dollars independently of the British government.[74]

American financial predominance, April 1917 – November 1918

The intervention of the United States in the World War in April 1917 eliminated finance as a major difficulty for the Allies. Prior to American intervention, the danger that the Allies might soon exhaust their means of payment in the United States, and consequently be forced to drastically reduce essential imports, had been real and immediate; in the early months of 1917 the financial bottleneck had become every bit as critical for the Allies as the supply bottleneck engendered by unconditional submarine warfare. After April 1917, however, the mobilization of the resources of the US Treasury ensured that the only significant factors limiting the availability of vital US supplies would be the productive capacity of the US economy, and shipping resources. Consequently, the center of gravity of Allied economic diplomacy shifted inexorably from financial problems to supply problems.[75] To be sure, initially US Treasury authorities were unprepared and reluctant to advance the immense sums required by their Allies. For a time in mid-June 1917, it appeared that the first Liberty Loan drive in the United States might fail, and that Allied supply programs might have to be cut back. US delay in making credits available to Britain to buy sterling on the exchange markets during June and July nearly drove the British Treasury to suspend efforts to defend the system of pegged sterling and franc exchange rates; if they had done so, Allied commerce would surely have been disrupted. But this misfortune was averted, and the US Treasury soon recognized that the American

Conte, 31 January 1917; Conte to Carcano, 21 February 1917; Conte to Carcano, 3 March 1917, ASMAE, Rappresentanze diplomatiche Londra, 423; Imperiali to Sonnino, 26 January 1917; Carcano to Sonnino, 29 January 1916, ASMAE, Archivio politico, 1915–18, Gran Bretagna 87/14; Imperiali to Sonnino, 26 January 1916, *DDI*, 5th ser., vol. 7 (Rome: Ministero degli Affari Esteri, 1978), no. 162.

[73] Imperiali to Sonnino, 26 January 1917, ASMAE, Archivio politico, 1915–18, Gran Bretagna, 87/14.

[74] The Italian Treasury sought, apparently unsuccessfully, to negotiate a loan in Argentina through the intermediation of the Credito Italiano and its Latin American affiliate, the Banque Brésilienne Italo-Belge. Conte to Carcano, 10 January 1917, ASMAE, Rappresentanze diplomatiche Londra, 423.

[75] Salter, *Allied Shipping Control*, p. 3.

interest in the vigorous prosecution of the war required it to make sufficient advances to support the Allied supply programs.[76]

There remained of course the problem of finding adequate financial resources in the remaining neutral markets. American officials were consternated by the fall of the dollar against the strongest neutral currencies, especially the Spanish peseta and the Swiss franc, beginning in July 1917. Not surprisingly, the bitterest conflicts between Italy and its British and American paymasters erupted over credits for Italian purchases in neutral countries. There was considerable ambiguity as to the extent to which the United States was prepared to finance Allied purchases in neutral countries until at least the middle of 1918. But the economic significance of neutral markets for Italy in particular, and for the Allies as a whole, was marginal in comparison with the significance of the American market; even though Italian authorities were worried in late 1918 that a failure to secure new American credits for frozen meat supplies from Argentina could lead to food riots.

But apart from the problem of Allied credit in neutral countries, the main issues at stake in Allied financial relations after US intervention were really issues of power within the Allied and Associated bloc. Chief among them was the extent to which the United States could use its financial leverage to influence the allocation of scarce resources among the Allies. The will of William McAdoo, US Secretary of the Treasury, to gain control over the allocation of American resources was manifest from the beginning. McAdoo demanded that the Allies consolidate their purchasing missions in the United States and establish a bureaucratic machinery which would allow the United States to review their supply programs and set priorities between the needs of the Allies and the needs of the US Army. As the Allies came to rely increasingly on US assistance to effect purchases in the remaining neutral markets, the US Treasury sought to gain control over Allied purchasing outside the USA, and over the allocation of shipping as well. In brief, the United States sought to exploit its financial predominance to wrest control of the Allied supply machinery from Britain, much as the British had established control over Allied supply earlier due to their financial predominance. The British, however, held several trumps in their hands that enabled them to resist American efforts to achieve total control over Allied economic decisionmaking. First, the British continued to dispose of the largest Allied merchant fleet, and they steadfastly rejected American proposals to put Allied shipping under the authority of an Inter-Allied committee, which would have

[76] Kathleen Burk, "J. M. Keynes and the Exchange Rate Crisis of July 1917," *Economic History Review*, 2nd ser., vol. 32 (1979), no. 3, pp. 405–16; Burk, *Britain, America and the Sinews of War*, pp. 195–207.

included American representatives. Second, the American government only gradually and imperfectly developed an administrative machinery capable of effectively replacing the Allied purchasing apparatus which had been set up in London, under the control of British government departments. The US Treasury exercised supervision over most Allied armaments and munitions purchases in America by the end of 1917, and of cotton purchases by the middle of 1918; but until the end of the war purchases of other important commodities, including cereals, continued to be made by London-based organizations that were essentially emanations of British government departments. At the time of the armistice the United States was taking measures to increase its control over Allied purchasing programs, and US control undoubtedly would have become more complete if the war had continued into 1919.[77]

The Italians became haplessly embroiled in the struggle between the United States and Britain for control of the Allied purchasing machinery. The US Treasury demonstrated increasing reluctance to make credits available to Italy in order to reimburse British government departments for purchases allegedly made on behalf of Italy in the United States. At the same time, the British repeatedly threatened to suspend new purchases on behalf of Italy if dollar reimbursements were not forthcoming, and needed supplies could only be obtained through British government departments. The Italians were thus put in the unfortunate position of not being able to act in good faith *vis-à-vis* both of their Allies at the same time.

Another issue that had an important impact on Allied financial relations was the international distribution of war costs for post-war society. As the war progressed and the magnitude of British, French, and Italian war debts mounted, it became increasingly clear that the repayment terms stipulated in the various international financial accords could not be honored, and that a general renegotiation of Allied debts after the conflict would be necessary. In the wake of American intervention, Allied financial negotiations hence not only lost their material immediacy, insofar as supplies and tonnage were now more scarce than means of payment; but they also took on an unreal quality, insofar as it became increasingly clear that a general debt settlement would have to be negotiated after the war, and that it would be far more favorable to the debtor countries than the wartime agreements.

Nevertheless, there was a widespread perception that the terms of the wartime agreements would have a bearing on the post-war financial settlement. The British government, which alone among the Allies considered full repayment of US loans, was particularly concerned to limit its interna-

---

[77] Burk, *Britain, America and the Sinews of War.*

tional liabilities. The British Treasury was especially concerned to extricate itself from acting as a lender of dollars to France and Italy. The US Treasury objected to dollar reimbursements by Italy to British government departments; as the war progressed, the British demanded such reimbursements for a growing list of products. The British argued, for instance, that all British steel exports to Italy merely forced Britain to import other steel products from the United States, and that Italy therefore should pay for steel in dollars. The British Treasury also began to scrutinize carefully British manufactures exported to Italy, and bill Italy in dollars for the value of materials or components allegedly imported or requiring replacement from the United States. The American government suspected the British Treasury of exploiting Italy's desperate need for supplies to extract dollars that would be used for entirely extraneous purposes, and repeatedly held up approval for reimbursements. The British government responded by threatening to stop purchases on the Italian government account if dollar reimbursements were not forthcoming.[78]

A further area of disagreement after American intervention stemmed from expectations that wartime financial arrangements would have an impact on the post-war international economic and financial system. United States officials sought to use wartime American financial predominance to promote New York as an international financial center, while British authorities sought to minimize the damage wrought by British financial weakness on the prestige and workings of the London financial market.[79] Anglo-American rivalry in this area also had repercussions for Italy: in June 1918 the US Treasury insisted that if the United States were to finance Italian cotton purchases, cotton bills must be drawn on New York, rather than London, to the consternation of the British; and in July 1918, Keynes and his associates at Whitehall were reluctant to follow the American lead in tightly regulating lira transactions, for fear of driving the financing of Italy's foreign trade from London to New York.[80]

[78] Among the numerous documents referring to these issues of particular significance are: Count Vincenzo Macchi di Cellere (Italy's ambassador to Washington) [to Nitti?], 28 February 1919 [but really 1918], tel.; Alessandro Ceresa (representative of Italian Treasury in London) to Carlo Conti Rossini (Director General of the Treasury), 16[?] October 1918; Bonar Law to Nitti, 17 October 1918, ASBI, fondo 3, bob. 108, pr. 313; "Financial Relations between the Italian, French, British, and U.S. Governments; Readjustment between Advances made by the British and U.S. Governments," internal Treasury memo, J. M. Keynes, 20 March 1918, Johnson ed., *The Collected Writings of J. M. Keynes*, vol. XVI, pp. 274–85; Bonar Law [written by J. M. Keynes] to Lord Reading in Washington, 25 March 1918, PRO, T- files, T1/12151/16227/18.

[79] Carl P. Parrini, *Heir to Empire: United States Economic Diplomacy, 1916–1923* (Pittsburgh: University of Pittsburgh Press, 1969), pp. 101–37.

[80] Robert Lansing (US Secretary of State) [but prepared by Crosby] to Paul Cravath (US legal consul to Inter-Ally Council for War Purchases and Finances), de la Chaume

To summarize, Italian financial diplomacy in the final phase of the war was complicated by disputes between the United States and Great Britain, which only indirectly were related to Italian government policies. Italian authorities were on the whole supportive of American efforts to rationalize and reconstitute the Allied purchasing machinery, and they had no particular sympathy with London's efforts to maintain its own position of preeminence; but the British purchasing authorities kept the Italians on a short leash, and for the most part they felt constrained to plead with US Treasury officials to transfer funds to Britain as requested.

Nitti at the Treasury: the realignment of monetary and financial policy

As was noted above, Nitti's appointment as Minister of the Treasury in the Orlando cabinet on 31 October 1917 produced a sea change in monetary and financial policy. In foreign economic policy, Nitti's first aim was to persuade the Allies to expand greatly their level of material and financial assistance to Italy. However, in Nitti's view increases in Allied aid could be secured only if Italy demonstrated its resolve to take tough measures to mobilize domestic economic and financial resources. Thus, on 5 November, even before the Italian front had restabilized, Nitti held a meeting with representatives of the issue banks, and leading commercial banks to announce his intention to establish a foreign exchange bureau that would monopolize all foreign exchange transactions. At the same time he declared he would launch a major war loan drive as soon as the front stabilized.[81]

Referring to his measures to mobilize domestic resources, Nitti made appeals to the British, French, and American governments for greater assistance, arguing that continued Italian participation in the war was essential to Allied victory, and that it could be secured only through massive doses of new material aid.[82] Nitti's appeals were not without effect: in the immediate aftermath of Caporetto, even before Nitti officially assumed his ministry, the US Treasury approved new credits for

(French Ministry of Finance), and Nitti, 14 June 1918, ASBI, fondo 3, bob. 108, pr. 313; "Paraphrase of cable to Cravath from Crosby," 27 June 1918, attached to, Cravath to Keynes, tel., 28 June 1918; internal Treasury memo, J. M. Keynes, 20 July 1918, PRO, T-files, T1/12197/36036/18; internal Treasury memo, Oswald T. Falck (Keynes's subordinate at the "A" Division of the Treasury, 9 August 1918, PRO, T-files, T1/12201/37127/18.

[81] Barbagallo, *Nitti*, pp. 238–39.
[82] Nitti to Crosby, 19 November 1917, Archivio Centrale dello Stato (hereafter ACS), Archivio Nitti, Ser. V/17/38/1; conversation with Malagodi, 9 December 1917, Malagodi, *Conversazioni della guerra*, vol. I, p. 233; Barbagallo, *Nitti*, pp. 241–45; Monticone, *Nitti e la grande guerra*, pp. 144–49.

$230m.; soon after Nitti's formal appeal the US Shipping Board promised to step up grain shipments.[83] From 29 November to 3 December, Nitti participated in an inter-Allied financial conference in Paris, where French and British representatives evidently expressed their willingness in principle, if not in detail, to step up aid to Italy.[84]

Whereas previous Italian governments had been preoccupied with the political consequences of accumulating large debts, and had always exercised restraint in borrowing from the Allies, Nitti argued that a high level of indebtedness was actually politically opportune, as it would increase the Allies' stake in Italy's post-war economic recovery:

> We have to prepare ourselves as much as possible for the post-war era; in the meantime, we must not fear making requests from our Allies ... In the situation in which we find ourselves, I am not afraid of big debts: on the contrary, they are preferable to small ones. Carcano may have been worried when our first loan in America, for twenty-five million dollars, fell due: I think that if we have one or two billions of debts the United States will be interested to send us raw materials for our industries even after the war, because only by working will we be able to repay them ... [85]

Or again: "In any event, I am calm with my billions of debts in America; I know that it is in their interest to protect and help us."[86]

The impact of the war economy on post-war reconstruction was Nitti's obsession. On another occasion Nitti expressed himself in less optimistic terms about the likelihood of continued Allied economic assistance in peacetime, and suggested that Italy should seek to accumulate imported raw materials during the final phase of the war, not only in order to meet the immediate needs of the armed forces and the armaments industries, but also as a reserve for post-war reconstruction:

> For me the major preoccupation is the post-war era. In this final phase of the war, whether it lasts six months or one or two years, we have to create the basis for Italy to make it alone, in energy and food, as soon as peace comes, when everyone will start thinking about themselves, and we will have to compete for provisions even with our current enemies.[87]

The contrast between Nitti's productivism and his willingness to incur large debts in America and elsewhere in order to promote wartime economic expansion, and the views of much of the rest of Italy's traditional

[83] Luigi Borsarelli di Rifreddo (Undersecretary, Ministry of Foreign Affairs) to Imperiali, 28 November 1917; Cellere to Sonnino, 11 November 1917, *DDI*, 5th ser., vol. IX, (1983), nos. 411, 567.
[84] See Nitti's conversation with Malagodi, 7 December 1917, Malagodi, *Conversazioni della guerra*, vol. I, p. 233; Barbagallo, *Nitti*, pp. 244–45.
[85] Malagodi, 10 January 1918, *Conversazioni della Guerra*, vol. II, p. 257.
[86] Malagodi, 27 September 1918, *Conversazioni della Guerra*, vol. II, p. 399.
[87] Malagodi, 22 January 1918, *Conversazioni della Guerra*, vol. II, p. 267.

political elite, including not only exponents of the traditional right, such as Sonnino and Salandra, but also many Giolittians, was complete. Giolitti voiced his concern that Italy had mortgaged its political future to Britain and America because of the war debts in two conversations with Malagodi shortly before, and shortly after the signing of the armistice:

> On our account, I am not worried about the domestic debt, for which we will do what we can. What concerns me is the foreign debt, which has reached an enormous sum. How are we going to pay it? We will have to have a long grace period, and then it will take two generations . . . And we will need a lot of tact and firmness to pass from the state of war to peace.[88]

And:

> What worries me is our foreign debt. With fifteen billion lire of debt, which will become perhaps twenty by the time peace is concluded, we will have to find seven-hundred million gold lire to pay the interest every year. Where are we going to find that? I see that some people hope the American financial market will remain open to us, and that we can make the interest payments by contracting new debts. But debts have two inconveniences: first, you have to repay them, which is the lesser; second, at a certain point you can't borrow any more, which is the greater.[89]

However, the actual impact of Nitti's new economic diplomacy on Allied supply programs was limited. Despite British and French expressions of goodwill, and new American credits, there was little room for drastically stepping up aid to Italy. Coal shipments to Italy, which had fallen from an average of 672,000 tons monthly in 1916 to an average of 426,000 tons in the six months before Caporetto, increased only modestly, to a monthly average of 473,000 tons in the following six months (see Table 8, Appendix, p. 307). Monthly statistics for Italian imports of other commodities are not readily available, but it is clear that shipping and supply bottlenecks inhibited any drastic increase in Allied assistance. Count Vincenzo Macchi di Cellere, Italy's ambassador to Washington, noted in early December 1917 that the supply needs of the growing US Expeditionary Force in France already were cutting into commitments made to Italy in November.[90] After participating in a second Allied financial conference in Paris from 2 to 3 January 1918, Nitti confided to Malagodi: "[The Allies] are prepared to give us all the money we need. The problem, however, is the usual one: the transport of goods."[91]

The impact of the shipping and coal shortages was particularly acute in the winter of 1917–18, when drought reduced the output of Italy's

---

[88] Malagodi, 7 October 1918, *Conversazioni della Guerra*, vol. II, p. 412.
[89] Malagodi, 23 November 1918, *Conversazioni della Guerra*, vol. II, p. 458.
[90] Cellere to Borsarelli, 5 December 1917, *DDI*, 5th ser., vol. II, no. 632.
[91] 10 January 1918, Malagodi, *Conversazioni della guerra*, vol. II, p. 255.

hydroelectric installations.[92] The limitations of *produttivismo* and Allied economic cooperation were painfully apparent, and Nitti was driven to work all the more insistently to obtain Allied support for the exchange rate of the lira.

Exchange controls and regulation of foreign commerce

Nitti's bid for office in October 1917 was reinforced by the persistent weakness of the lira on the exchange markets, and public criticism of Stringher and Carcano for their unwillingness to impose exchange controls. Italy was the only belligerent to allow its currency to float more or less freely on the exchange markets in 1916 and early 1917. Britain and France had pegged their currencies to the dollar in January and April 1916 respectively.[93] Germany, Austria-Hungary, and Russia were unable to stabilize the rates of their currencies on foreign exchange markets, but all three countries, to varying degrees, centralized exchange transactions under government control or supervision in the course of January and February 1916.[94]

The exchange value of the lira declined inexorably, not just against the major neutral currencies, but also against the dollar, the pound, and the French and Belgian francs. Further, the existence of a free exchange market in Italy caused relatively minor, but violent oscillations in exchange rates, and provided opportunities for exchange speculation. In the course of 1916 and early 1917, Stringher and Carcano were exposed to steadily mounting pressure from industrialists and bankers, the financial press, economists, and leaders of the political opposition (notably Nitti) to regulate the exchange markets. But Stringher deeply distrusted the leading commercial bankers, and was reluctant to take measures that would require close cooperation with them. In a memo written for Carcano on 9 February 1916, Stringher pointed out that the German Exchange Bureau functioned only because it had been possible to institute tight controls, which in turn required, "an attitude of firm discipline on the part of the banks, which [in Italy] does not exist."[95] Public criticism of the banks for

---

[92] Riccardo Bachi, *L'Italia economica nell'anno 1917* (Città di Castello: S. Lapi, 1918), p. 128.

[93] Richard Sidney Sayers, *The Bank of England, 1891–1944* (New York: Cambridge University Press, 1976), pp. 83–94; Johnson, ed., *The Collected Writings of J. M. Keynes*, vol. XVI, passim.; Lucien Petit, *Histoire des finances éxtérieures de la France pendant la guerre (1914–1918)* (Paris: Payot, 1929), pp. 210–16; Charles Blankart, *Devisenpolitik während des Weltkrieges (August 1914–November 1918)* (Zurich: Füssli, 1919), passim.

[94] Blankart, *Devisenpolitik*, pp. 73–84; Eduard März, *Austrian Banking and Financial Policy: Creditanstalt at a Turning Point, 1913–1923* (London: Weidenfeld and Nicolson, 1984), pp. 197–200.

[95] Stringher to Carcano, memo, 9 February 1916, ASBI, fondo 3, bob. 78, pr. 217.

exchange speculation became so intense that Giuseppe Toeplitz and Federico Balzarotti, the executive directors of the Banca Commerciale, and the Credito Italiano respectively, drew up their own proposal for a voluntary central exchange bureau in June 1917, but Stringher let the matter drop.[96]

Nitti announced his intention to impose rigid exchange controls almost immediately on assuming office. The collapse of the lira exchange following Caporetto seemed to underscore the need for vigorous measures. In exchange policy too, however, Nitti's dynamism was soon checked. The Ministry of the Treasury was bereft of personnel with experience in foreign exchange and commerce, and Nitti was therefore forced to rely on Stringher, whose opposition to exchange controls was well known, and the Bank of Italy, to implement his policy. Not only was the personnel of the newly established Istituto Nazionale per i Cambi con l'Estero (INC) drawn almost entirely from the Bank of Italy; even the decree establishing the institute had to be written by Stringher. Despite his personal reservations, Stringher dutifully accepted the new policy, although his reluctance to commit his own personal prestige, and that of the Bank of Italy, to the INC drew out the process of selecting officials until the end of February. Ultimately, Stringher himself became president; Arrigo Rossi, previously responsible for foreign exchange operations at the Bank, became Director General; and the Bank's representatives in London and New York, Joe Nathan and Domenico Gidoni, were put in charge of the INC's operations abroad.[97]

Nitti made no effort to conceal his desire to use the INC as an instrument to obtain greater control over the major commercial banks. In November he threatened to cut them out of the exchange institute altogether and requisition their personnel:

> I have the impression that the administrators of the commercial banks are not anxious to serve the state with regard to exchange transactions.
>
> This is a bad sign, and not exactly praiseworthy conduct.
>
> If everything is not organized with their consent by the end of the week, I'll do without them, and requisition their personnel. I've already prepared the decree.[98]

The Minister of the Treasury was particularly disrespectful to Giuseppe Toeplitz, the Comit's executive director. All of the major commercial banks proposed to appoint their highest executive officers as their representatives on the board of the INC; but Nitti let Commerciale offi-

---

[96] Stringher to Carcano, memo, 2 June 1916, ASBI, fondo 3, bob. 78, pr. 217.
[97] ASBI, fondo 9.2, Presidenza e Giunta del Consiglio Superiore riunite in Comitato (hereafter Comitato), verbali, 24 February 1918.
[98] Nitti to Stringher, 20 November 1917, ACS, Archivio Nitti, Ser. V/17/37/5.

cials know that he opposed Toeplitz's nomination, because of his non-Italian origins. Instead, he suggested that Pietro Fenoglio be appointed as the Comit's representative. Fenoglio also held the title of executive director of the Commerciale, although Toeplitz had emerged quickly as the leading personality at the bank after Otto Joel's retirement. This was more than Toeplitz could take. He must have reasoned that if Nitti succeeded in keeping him off the board of the INC, he would end up ruining his reputation altogether. He rallied support among the Comit's senior officers and had Senator Luigi Canzi, the bank's President (an essentially honorific post) write to Stringher, insisting that Toeplitz be allowed to serve on the INC. Canzi pointed out that Toeplitz was not a German at all, but a native of Russian Poland, i.e. of an Allied country. Moreover, he had been a naturalized Italian citizen since 1912. Did the government intend to forbid citizens of Allied nations, by birth, to serve on the boards of companies?[99]

Stringher's hesitations, and the row between Nitti and the Banca Commerciale delayed the formation of the INC for several months. Stringher's decree establishing the institute was submitted in late December. The INC was to have an initial share capital of Lit. 10m., to be subscribed by the three issue banks and the four largest commercial banks: the Banca Commerciale Italiana, the Credito Italiano, the Banca Italiana di Sconto, and the Banco di Roma. Only member institutions were allowed to engage in exchange transactions, and only at rates fixed weekly by the board of the INC. Member banks were required to provide the Institute with detailed information concerning their foreign business; all exchange transactions required approval by the INC. Smaller banks engaged in international commerce could avoid divulging information about their business to the major commercial banks by dealing directly with the Bank of Italy.[100]

The creation of an exchange monopoly necessitated the extension of government controls over all aspects of foreign commerce. To that end, the Giunta Tecnica Interministeriale (GTI) was established on 14 January 1918 to license all imports.[101] Vincenzo Giuffrida, a protégé of Nitti's from the latter's days as Minister of Agriculture, Industry, and Commerce in the fourth Giolitti cabinet, was appointed head of this all-important committee.[102] Exporters were later required to cede their foreign exchange earnings to the INC.[103]

[99] Canzi to Stringher, 6 February 1918, ASBI, Carte Stringher, 20/302/1/03.
[100] ASBI, fondo 9.2, Comitato, verbali, 20 December 1917.
[101] Giuffrida and Pietra, *Provital*, p. 110.
[102] On Giuffrida see, Barbagallo, *Nitti*, pp. 167, 175–77; Sabino Cassese, "Le istituzione amministrative nella storia dell'Italia unita," in, *Esiste un governo in Italia?* (Rome: Officina edizioni, 1970), pp. 61–72.
[103] De Stefani, *La legislazione economica della guerra*, pp. 251–52.

Nitti wanted the INC and GTI machinery in place and functioning as quickly as possible in order to strengthen his position *vis-à-vis* the United States and Britain in negotiating support for the lira exchange. From November 1917 until early March 1918, he bombarded Stringher with repeated demands that the exchange monopoly be introduced expeditiously, despite the INC's near total lack of exchange reserves. Nitti became peremptory in March, with the approach of a scheduled visit to Rome by Oscar Crosby, Assistant US Secretary of the Treasury, to discuss US exchange support. Finally, on 11 March 1918, independent exchange transactions were proscribed and the INC began to function. The immediate result was a near total breakdown in what remained of Italy's private international commerce. Foreign exchange could only be obtained from the INC, which held very modest reserves. The more fortunate Italian manufacturers were able to negotiate contracts with foreign suppliers in lire, albeit frequently at below market rates. Such transactions, already in use before the imposition of the exchange monopoly, naturally contributed to the further decline of the lira.[104]

Despite the critical situation created by the imposition of the exchange monopoly, Nitti failed to obtain American commitments to support the lira during Crosby's visit. The American Undersecretary of the Treasury demanded detailed information on all aspects of Italy's foreign trade and balance of payments, information which the Italian authorities found it impossible to produce. Significantly, Italian officials were unable to provide data on the foreign exchange transactions of the major commercial banks. Silvio Crespi, Undersecretary in the Ministry of Provisions and a cotton textile manufacturer with close ties to the Banca Commerciale, suggested to Crosby that some banks (i.e. the Bansconto) were not cooperating fully with the INC. An implacable enemy of Nitti, Crespi found the opportunity of discrediting the Minister of the Treasury and casting doubts on the honesty of his rivals at the Banca di Sconto irresistible.[105] Crosby was clearly irritated by his hosts' bickering and unpreparedness and quickly departed, stopping only briefly in Paris before

---

[104] Unsigned, undated memo [but by Stringher] on activities of INC, perhaps from the end of June 1918, ASC, Archivio Nitti, Ser. V/17/39; Antonio Musso, untitled article in *Il popolo d'Italia*, 4 October 1918.

[105] Caracciolo to Nitti, undated [but from late March or early April 1918], ACS, Archivio Nitti, Ser. V/17/38/1. Crespi's suggestion that the Banca Italiana di Sconto was acting disloyally *vis-à-vis* the INC was also voiced by less interested parties. On 1 May 1918 Conti Rossini wrote to Stringher noting that he had spoken to Giuffrida that morning: "He noted that commendatore Pogliani [Director of the Banca di Sconto] had told him he had got the knack of speculating, by selling small amounts of lire in Paris on Friday and Saturday to influence exchange rates there, and hence the rates of the INC, so that he could sell back foreign exchange to the INC later at a profit. I couldn't refrain from observing that the B di Sc. had sold substantial sums in lire in Paris recently!" ASBI, fondo 3, bob. 108, pr. 313.

proceeding to Washington for consultations. The hapless Prince Mario Caracciolo di Melito, who was married to Crosby's daughter, and whom Nitti had arranged to have appointed as liaison with Crosby, informed Nitti of his father-in-law's attitudes in a telegram that summarizes in lapidary fashion all of the weaknesses of Nitti's exchange policy:

> The fact that we didn't respond to precise questions addressed to us, and that we didn't explain why we couldn't respond, created the impression of our inability to come to grips with our own situation, or of our reluctance and laziness in cooperating, or of the lack of communication between our Treasury, the Bank of Italy, and the other banks, or possibly all of these factors combined. It was noted unfavorably that we limited ourselves to asking for money, without presenting a concrete plan, waiting instead for others to study the issue for us.
>
> Crosby undoubtedly came to Italy prepared to resolve the issue favorably, and the fact that we were not able to reach an accord certainly won't weigh in our favor. When the American delegation was in Italy they saw an abundance of decrees, but no mechanism to implement them. Crespi's statement at a meeting that our private bankers weren't placing their exchange reserves at the disposition of the INC produced a bad impression, as it seemed to confirm that the INC was unable to impose its authority [this sentence underlined by Nitti]. Nevertheless, Crossby [sic] is perfectly aware of the financial and political importance of the issue, and he is going to America now with the best intentions in our regard.[106]

In fairness, it must be added that the British and French governments were also frequently hard pressed to produce detailed financial information demanded by US Treasury officials.[107] It is unlikely that the US Treasury itself disposed of the kind of exhaustive information about all aspects of the American balance of payments that Crosby demanded in Rome. INC officials spent much of the following weeks trying to assemble data on the Italian balance of payments to present to Crosby. Stringher finally produced a satisfactory memo on 20 April.[108] Thereafter negotiations on support for the lira resumed in ernest, this time in New York and Washington.

Accords with the Allies to support the exchange value of the lira

Little more than two months after Crosby's abrupt departure from Rome, US Treasury and Federal Reserve officials and Domenico Gidoni, the INC's representative in America, worked out an agreement for controlling

---

[106] Caracciolo to Nitti, undated [but from late March or early April 1918], ACS, Archivio Nitti, Ser. V/17/38/1.
[107] Burk, *Britain, America and the Sinews of War*, passim.
[108] Stringher to Crosby, memo, 20 April 1918, ASBI, fondo 3, bob. 107, pr. 312.

the dollar–lira exchange in New York. In essence, the agreement involved subjecting all aspects of Italo-American trade and financial relations to the supervision and regulation of a joint committee established by the INC and the Federal Reserve Bank of New York (FRBNY). Italy's commercial and financial transactions with the United States were to be sealed off hermetically from those with the rest of the world, and the US Treasury would assume responsibility for financing Italy's commercial deficit with the United States, while the Federal Reserve would make available up to $100m. to support the exchange rate of the lira against the dollar. Initially, the lira was stabilized at 9.10, a rate slightly above the market rate at the time the agreement went into effect (mid-June 1918). The accord was envisaged as the first step in a general agreement among the Allies regulating the lira exchange and, by extension, all aspects of Italian foreign trade. American officials expected France and Britain to make similar commitments to finance Italy's balance of payments deficits with them. Lira exchange arbitration between the three markets would be prohibited. Britain and the United States would share equally the burden of financing Italy's trade deficit in neutral markets.[109]

American and Italian officials gambled that the cost of stabilizing the lira would be moderate or zero. Even though they estimated that Americans held lira balances worth the equivalent of approximately $100m., Federal Reserve and Treasury officials believed that emigrant remittances would soon create a net demand for lire on the private market. Remittances from the United States had all but ceased in the months after Caporetto, but once the two governments indicated their determination to halt the decline of the lira on the exchange markets, it was reasoned, Italian immigrants in the United States would resume remittances, and the pent-up demand for lire, at least in the United States, would soon drive exchange rates up again. All that was needed, in the opinion of Fred I. Kent of the FRBNY, and Gidoni, was a public announcement that the Federal Reserve was prepared to buy up to $100m. in lire at the rate of 9.10. The stabilization and moderate rise in the lira's exchange rate against the dollar in June and July vindicated this analysis.[110] Gidoni's New York office of the INC became a net seller of lire almost from the beginning.

In exchange for stabilizing the lira, American policymakers were able to drive a hard bargain with respect to Italy's independent exchange resources in the United States: net dollar balances earned by the INC

[109] Lansing [but prepared by Crosby] to Cravath, de la Chaume, and Nitti, 14 June 1918, ASBI, fondo 3, bob. 108, pr. 313; H. Parker Willis (Professor at Columbia University, and adviser to Strong) to Benjamin Strong (Governor, FRBNY), 31 May 1918, FRBNY, C261.
[110] See McAdoo's retrospective justification of his lira exchange policy, McAdoo to Woodrow Wilson, 9 October 1918, US National Archives (NA), Treasury, RG 39/143.

through the sale of lire in New York were earmarked as a first charge against Italy's private debts in the United States, with US Treasury advances making up the difference. The arrangement, in other words, eliminated any discretionary use of dollars acquired by the Italian government outside the framework of US Treasury advances.[111] The agreement worked out between the INC and the Federal Reserve at the end of May also served broader US policy goals. The total subjugation of Italy's commercial and financial transactions with the United States to Federal Reserve supervision and control reinforced the Treasury's long-standing aim of extending American control over the levers of Allied economic decisionmaking.

The agreement was also a response to a British Treasury proposal in March that the United States eliminate Britain's role as a financial intermediary between America and the other Allies, by increasing its direct monthly financial assistance to France and Italy by approximately $110m., and reducing its advances to Britain by an equal amount.[112] But whereas the British Treasury proposed that the additional credits in favor of France and Italy be transferred to London, to reimburse British government departments for purchases allegedly made on behalf of the two continental Allies, the Kent–Gidoni agreements aimed at reducing the role of the London supply committees in allocating US commodities among the European Allies. The Wheat Executive would continue to purchase wheat supplies for Italy, and the US Treasury would make requisite funds available in London; but commercial and financial arrangements for other important commodities would henceforth be made over New York, rather than London.

By far the most important of these commodities was cotton. US government officials and bankers regarded capturing the financing of cotton exports as a major prize in their efforts to establish New York as a world financial center. Despite the war, and the extension of Allied government regulation of raw materials imports, in early 1918 the greater share of US cotton exports, including nearly all exports to Italy, continued to be financed by bills drawn on London acceptance houses. According to the terms of the Gidoni–Kent arrangements, the US Treasury would henceforth relieve Britain of the burden of financing Italian cotton imports, but all new cotton bills would be drawn on New York, rather than London.[113]

---

[111] Italian and American officials later differed as to whether the agreement permitted the INC to transfer dollars earned through the sale of lire in New York to London and Paris to defend the lira exchange rate. See below.

[112] Bonar Law (composed by Keynes) to Lord Reading (British ambassador and high commissioner in the United States), 24 March 1918, in, Johnson, ed., *The Collected Writings of J. M. Keynes*, pp. 274–85.

[113] Lansing to Cravath, de la Chaume, and Nitti, 14 June 1918, ASBI, fondo 3, bob. 108, pr. 313.

The major difficulty with the Kent–Gidoni accords was that, in order to be successful, they required the cooperation and participation of Britain. In British perspective, the virtues of the accord from the American point of view were a measure of its unattractiveness. Oswald T. Falck, Keynes's subordinate at the "A" Division of the Treasury, worried that if Britain applied equally restrictive measures to transactions in lire, it would compromise London as an international exchange market.[114]

Despite ernest entreaties from Nitti, British cooperation in the lira support scheme had not been secured by mid-June, when Kent and Gidoni decided to proceed unilaterally, in order to halt the steady decline of the lira. After interventions on the New York market began, a gap developed between New York and London quotations of the lira, and it became all the more imperative to secure British cooperation in the scheme. US and Italian officials increased their pressure on the British Treasury to extend the exchange monopoly to London. Nevertheless, Keynes continued to raise objections to the agreements and to stall British participation through June and July. Keynes's ostensible objection was that excessive regulation would do Italy more harm than good. In a telegram that went out under the Chancellor of the Exchequer's signature on 21 June, Keynes argued that:

> So far as I understand, the arrangements set up in New York for regulating offerings of lire exchange may serve to protect fairly completely the interests of the United States Treasury, and so far as British interests are concerned I should see no objection to adopting similar arrangements here. I fear, however, that such action, if I understand it rightly, would be disastrous to Italian credit and instead of assisting Nitti we should be pressing him into even greater distress than at present.[115]

The telegram went on to note that the bulk of commercial bills drawn on London were from all over the world, and that the adoption of New York procedures would cause the collapse of Italy's international credit system. The closing of the New York bill market to Italy was not disastrous as long as London remained open, although the affect of the New York measures had been to depress the lira *vis-à-vis* sterling. Keynes's real concern was transparent: that the imposition of an exchange monopoly in London would drive the financing of a significant part of Italy's foreign trade, in particular imports from the United States, from London to New York.

British objections to the provision that Italian cotton bills be drawn on New York rather than London in the future betrayed that their real

---

[114] Falck, internal Treasury memo, 9 August 1918, PRO, T-files, T1/12201/37127/18.
[115] Bonar Law (drafted by Keynes) to Lord Reading, 21 June 1918, PRO, T-files, T1/12165/24820/18.

concern was for British and not Italian interests. Crosby responded by
noting:

> If sterling against our cotton were allowed to go forward it would throw on
> Great Britain a financial burden which is more properly ours . . . It is to be
> remembered that the control of all bills drawn by Italian nationals has been
> placed by the government in the Institute of Exchange. Certainly Italy's
> credit cannot be injured by placing at its disposal funds which it did not have
> before.[116]

Neither American nor Italian officials were impressed with the British
Treasury's arguments.

But, in the long run, the British were not in a position to oppose US
efforts to shore up the lira, when they were dependent on American
assistance to support the pound. By July Keynes had given up opposing the
extension of the INC's activities to London. Nitti arranged to visit
London in the latter half of the month, in order to sign a trilateral accord
with Bonar Law and Crosby. By that time, however, the British Treasury
was calling for a general re-examination of Anglo-American financial relations, with a view to shifting the greater part of Britain's foreign financial
responsibilities to the United States. Although reluctant to drag out the
Italian question any longer, Keynes wrote, in the memo preparing Bonar
Law for the negotiations, that:

> the present proposals fall so far short of our main proposals to the United
> States that it ought to be made plain that this present settlement would be
> without prejudice to the major question, and would be made as an interim
> arrangement to meet the pressing necessities of the Italian Treasury.[117]

Britain was now prepared to extend the regime of controlled lira exchange
rates to London and, at least provisionally, share equally with the United
States the burden of financing Italy's purchases in neutral markets.

The first and only trilateral financial agreement between Britain, the
United States, and Italy was signed on 27 July 1918. In it Britain reaffirmed its commitment to make available to Italy £st. 8m. monthly, of
which £st. 1.5m. was as a "free credit," for use outside the British Empire.
Financing for Australian wool, East Indian hides, and raw rubber from the
British Empire was to be transferred from the free credit to the general
credit. In earlier months, Britain had demanded that financing for these
commodities be taken out of the "free credits" on the grounds that exports
to Italy led to increased British purchases of similar products in neutral
markets or the United States. In exchange, the United States was to make

---

[116] Cravath to Keynes, 28 June 1918. Cravath sent Keynes a "paraphrase of a cable from
Crosby to Cravath." PRO, T-files, T1/12197/36036/18.
[117] Keynes, internal Treasury memo, 20 July 1918, PRO, T-files, T1/12197/36036/18.

$10m. monthly available to Italy for purchases in neutral markets; with the approval of the Inter-Ally Council on War Purchases and Finance, chaired by Crosby, some of this credit could be transferred to British government departments to make purchases on Italy's behalf. In addition, the British government would place the so-called "secondary credits," i.e. the sterling equivalent of sums advanced by the Italian government to Britain in lire to meet British requirements in Italy, at the disposal of the INC in London to support the lira exchange. The principle of "constructive supply and re-supply," which allowed Britain to charge Italy in dollars for wheat imported from India, so that Britain could import a matching quantity of wheat from the United States, was reaffirmed.[118]

The American credit of $10m. monthly, plus the British free credit of £st. 1.5m. monthly and the "secondary credits" were calculated to be sufficient to cover Italian financial needs in neutral markets, providing that Italy negotiated a loan in Argentina. Informally, United States and British Treasury officials agreed to divide responsibility for Italy's remaining neutral purchases, with the United States financing Italy's balance of payments deficit with Bolivia, Greece, Spain and Switzerland, and Britain doing likewise for Chile, the Netherlands, and the Scandinavian countries.

This agreement, together with a Franco-Italian accord which Nitti signed with Louis Klotz, the French Finance Minister in Paris on 4 August, represented the high point of the Italian Treasury Minister's initiatives in financial diplomacy. A general agreement for the stabilization of the exchange rate of the lira had been achieved, and Kent and Gidoni were soon able to bring up its value from 9.10 to 6.35 to the dollar. A trilateral accord with Italy's two major creditors, the United States and Great Britain, had been signed, which seemed to protect Italian interests from Anglo-American financial rivalry. Moreover, Nitti had persuaded British and American officials to write a clause into the accord of 27 August which committed the two nations to consider making additional financial resources available to Italy, should existing arrangements prove inadequate.[119]

In exchange, Nitti made concessions with respect to Allied supervision and regulation of Italy's foreign trade and monetary policy that would have been unacceptable to Paolo Carcano, his predecessor at the Treasury. Nitti was prepared to make these concessions because he had committed totally his personal political prestige to reaching an exchange agreement with the Allies. Of equal importance, the extension of state exchange and commercial controls dovetailed with Nitti's own economic *dirigismo*, and

---

[118] "Memorandum on Financial Arrangements between Italy and the British and American Treasuries," copies in PRO, T-files, T1/12197/36036/18, and; ASBI, fondo 3, bob. 108, pr. 313. [119] Ibid.

he considered the INC and the Giunta Tecnica Interministeriale as powerful instruments in his armature for post-war reconstruction and economic planning.

Nitti lost no time in exploiting the domestic political capital he had earned by signing the accords, to the consternation of his critics at home.[120] Nitti's special relationship with the Allies, he suggested, made him the natural inheritor of Giolitti's mantle as leader of the moderate reformist parliamentary majority in the post-war period. In January 1918 Malagodi recorded that Nitti had told him: "With regard to Giolitti, he expressed to me the opinion that he was soft in the brain [sia rammollito]. He added that [Giolitti] couldn't do anything, even after the war, because he wouldn't be able to find anyone who would give him even a ton of coal."[121] Nitti had now demonstrated his ability to obtain both coal and dollars from the Allies.

Relations with the Allies to the armistice, 4 November 1918

The agreement of 27 July was meant to define American and British financial responsibilities with respect to Italy and thereby protect Italian interests from Anglo-American rivalry; in actual fact it merely shifted the terrain of Anglo-American conflict to the interpretation of the two countries respective commitments under the terms of the accord. Allied military successes in autumn, and the imminence of victory diminished the imperatives of financial cooperation and exacerbated disputes. Italian officials found themselves pressed from both sides, with the Americans and the British interpreting the accords in what they considered a restrictive and ungenerous sense. Two main areas of controversy emerged by late September, concerning: (1) the extent to which the INC's foreign exchange reserves in New York could be used to defend the lira in

---

[120] J. H. Nixon, a subordinate of Keynes in the British Treasury's "A" Division, wrote to the famous economist: "I am informed that Nitti's visit was intended as a political coup for domestic purposes." PRO, T-files, T1/12197/36036/18. Einaudi, referring to Nitti's repeated comparisons between his own dynamism and his predecessor Carcano's inability to reach an exchange agreement with the Allies, wrote bitterly to Albertini: "Who knows why Nitti was still slandering Carcano recently, saying that when he arrived at the Treasury no accord had been concluded, while Bonar Law asserted that the accord for exchange rates *with England* [Einaudi's emphasis] had been concluded already in July '17, and that in July '18 the only thing which was added were accords with the United States and France?" Bonar Law was referring evidently to a British bank credit for Italian industry. In his letter to Albertini, Einaudi went on to mock Nitti for going to London to recount the suffering of the Italian people, when, with the exception of some middle-class groups living on fixed incomes and the soldiers in the field, levels of consumption were higher than before the war. Surely, he suggested, the Allies too must be aware that official Italian statistics to the contrary were false. 9 August 1918, FE, Carte Einaudi, Carteggio.
[121] Malagodi, 10 January 1918, *Conversazione della guerra*, vol. II, pp. 255–60.

London; and (2) how Italy's balance of trade deficit with neutral countries
– which quickly exceeded the monthly credits allocated by Britain and the
United States – was to be financed.

The INC monopoly on exchange transactions in London and Paris
finally became operative on 15 August 1918. It had been the intention of
Kent and Gidoni to raise the rate of the lira gradually in New York
thereafter. However, the New York office of the INC soon found itself
under heavy pressure to raise the lira rate quickly, as emigrants and Americans doing business with Italy moved to cover their lira requirements
before the rate increased substantially. The Italian Treasury was particularly insistent that the rate be raised quickly, as it was selling lire through
the INC at 9.10 to the dollar, but evidently would soon be able to sell at
less than 7.00. Nitti, moreover, hoped to reap the maximum political
prestige from a rise in the lira exchange rate. British and French officials,
in contrast, expressed reservations about raising the lira rate too fast,
fearing it would encourage exchange arbitration between New York,
London, and Paris, and that the new rate would prove costly to defend. In
the United States there was pent-up demand for lire, stemming largely
from the immigrant communities; in Britain and France, in contrast,
officials feared that a sudden rise in the lira exchange rate would induce
firms and banks holding large lira balances to sell rapidly. After signing the
27 July accords, Britain had agreed to make the "secondary credits" of
approximately £st. 500,000 monthly available to Italy for exchange arbitration; British officials felt that any additional sums necessary for defending
the lira in London at rates set by Gidoni and Kent in New York, should be
provided by the INC's New York office.

US officials were initially understanding of the British position. Gidoni
and Kent fixed the lira at 6.35 on 28 August, while agreeing to transfer
exchange reserves to London to purchase up to Lit. 20m.[122] But pressure
on the lira in London remained strong throughout September, as holders
of lira balances in neutral countries – particularly Latin Americans – sold
in the British capital. By the end of the month Nathan had exhausted the
exchange reserves made available to him by the British government and
appealed to the Federal Reserve to authorize the transfer of additional
exchange reserves from the INC's New York office.[123] Italian officials
expressed their understanding that the Italo-American agreement of 14
June envisaged the transfer of the INC's dollar reserves accumulated in
New York abroad to defend the lira. As Nathan noted, on 30 September,

[122] Robert Chalmers (Joint Secretary to British Treasury) to Hardman Lever (Representative of British Treasury in New York), 2 September 1918, PRO, T-files,
T1/12210/40542/18.
[123] Nathan to Gidoni, 30 September 1918, ASBI, fondo 3, bob. 108, pr. 313.

once interventions on the New York market to bring up the lira rate began, it was evident the new rate would have to be defended in London as well. Up to then, exchange market interventions had not cost the United States a single dollar; but now the Americans were not even prepared to allow Italy to dispose freely of the dollar resources the INC had accumulated by selling lire in New York.[124] US Treasury officials, however, insisted that Britain had undertaken on 27 July to defend the lira exchange in London with its own resources, and they refused to authorize the INC to make additional dollar transfers to London.[125] Nathan was hard pressed to sustain the exchange rate of the lira at 30.25 during the last week of September, and the first two weeks of October. He feared that the INC could lose control of the situation at any time, but the British and American Treasuries persisted in their brinkmanship, each confident that the other would give in at the last moment. On one occasion in early October, Gidoni transferred the equivalent of Lit. 10m. in dollars to Nathan without Kent's authorization, for which he received a severe tongue-lashing.[126] Collapse was averted in mid-October when demand for lire at the INC's London office began to exceed offers: buoyed by Allied military successes, exchange operators in London and in neutral countries moved to augment their holdings of Italian currency.[127]

Another concern for Italian officials was the dispute that broke out between the British and American Treasuries about the financing of Italian purchases in neutral countries at the end of September. The combined resources placed at the disposal of Italy for purchases in neutral countries in the 27 July agreements – $10m. monthly by the United States and approximately £st. 2m. monthly by Great Britain – were estimated as sufficient to meet Italian payments outside of Argentina. Italy, however, was unable or unwilling to conclude a loan agreement with Argentina in the course of the summer, and the new dispute centered on the financing of Italian frozen meat purchases in the Plata. The controversy began when Keynes handed a note to the Italian Treasury representative in London demanding that the total US credit to Italy earmarked for spending in neutral countries for August and September ($20m.) be transferred to London as repayment for expenditures made on behalf of Italy by British government departments. Keynes claimed that Britain was spending more than £st. 4m. monthly on Italy in neutral countries, i.e. more than the combined US and British credits earmarked for such purposes. Further

---

[124] Ibid.
[125] Albert Rathbone (US Assistant Secretary to the Treasury) to Crosby, 27 September 1918, NA, Treasury, RG 39/143.
[126] Rathbone to Crosby, 7 October 1918, NA, Treasury, RG 39/143.
[127] Nathan to Stringher, 15 October 1918, ASBI, fondo 3, bob. 108, pr. 313.

British requests for transfers of the US monthly credit of $10m., he alerted, would be forthcoming. Although Keynes declined to provide detailed accounting for British overseas expenditures on Italy's behalf, he offered to sign a statement to the effect that total British expenditure for Italy in neutral markets exceeded £st. 4m. monthly.[128] In essence, Keynes was arguing that the United States should be made to pay as much as possible, while Britain should retain control of expenditure and supply allocation among the European Allies, with as little accountability to the Americans as possible.

As was the case with the exchange dispute, the controversy quickly developed into a test of wills between the American and British Treasuries, with Italian officials caught in the middle, threatened by the collapse of their supply programs. Bernardo Attolico, an Italian representative on the Inter-Ally Council on War Purchases and Finances, managed to persuade Crosby to approve the transfer of $10m. to Britain, but the imperious Keynes was soon demanding further transfers, and this time Crosby refused to make additional concessions.[129] In mid-October Keynes ordered a British-dominated Allied supply organization to suspend shipments of frozen meat from Argentina to Italy due to lack of financing.[130] Nitti worried that the disappearance of meat from Italian military and civilian rations would soon lead to disorders, and perhaps also discredit the architect of the Allied financial accords. Bonar Law responded to Nitti's urgent entreaties that financing be found to meet Italy's supply program, as approved by Allied committees, by conceding that the accords of 27 July had indeed proved inadequate to meet Italy's needs; he added, however, that no revision could be undertaken without American participation and approval.[131]

On the eve of Allied victory, Italian officials were preparing for a new round of financial negotiations with Great Britain and America. Nitti chose not to participate personally in the talks. The prospects for success, and for the domestic political prestige to be gained thereby, were dimmer than in July. Moreover, Orlando's ministry appeared to be coming apart over the question of post-war relations with Yugoslavia, and Italy's northeastern border. Nitti's ambition to play a leading role in a new ministry, and possibly to replace Orlando, depended on his remaining in the capital.[132] The dubious task of representing Italy in London therefore fell upon Stringher. He left Rome at the beginning of November, with the

[128] Ibid.
[129] Attolico to Nitti, undated [but marked, "fine settembre 1918" on back], ASBI, fondo 3, bob. 108, pr. 313.
[130] Ceresa to Conti Rossini, 16[?] October 1918, ASBI, fondo 3, bob. 108, pr. 313.
[131] Bonar Law to Nitti, 17 October 1918, ASBI, fondo 3, bob. 108, pr. 313.
[132] Monticone, *Nitti e la grande guerra*, pp. 299–346; Barbagallo, *Nitti*, pp. 276–89.

financing of Italy's frozen meat supplies still in abeyance. Before he arrived in London, the Austro-Italian armistice was signed at Villa Giusti, followed shortly thereafter by the Allied armistice with Germany. As a consequence, his task was made yet more difficult, as both the United States and Britain were determined to keep their post-war financial commitments to the continental Allies to a minimum.

PART 3

THE POST-WAR CRISIS,
NOVEMBER 1918 – OCTOBER 1922

6

A DIFFICULT READJUSTMENT: THE POLITICAL ECONOMY OF THE ORLANDO AND NITTI GOVERNMENTS, NOVEMBER 1918 – JUNE 1920

Much of the shock of readjustment to a peace economy fell on the governments of Orlando (which fell in June 1919), and Nitti (June 1919–June 1920). Above all, Orlando and Nitti had to contend with the cessation of Allied lending and exchange support. The American and British Treasuries discontinued lending to the Allied governments relatively rapidly after the signing of the armistices with the Central Powers in October and November 1918. The United States continued to make advances to Italy and the other European Allies for foodstuffs and certain other commodities through the summer of 1919, while cancelling credits for most other purposes. Britain made a total of £st. 65m. in fresh credits available to Italy for the period after the armistice, of which £st. 5m. was earmarked for use in neutral markets. These credits undoubtedly buffered Italy, as well as France, Belgium and Britain itself, during the period of post-war economic readjustment. Thanks in part to such credits, the Allies were spared the monetary chaos and economic paralysis pervasive in the new and defeated nations of East-Central Europe. However, the post-armistice financial assistance of the British and American Treasuries was insufficient in both amount and time to prevent major disruption in trade and economic activity.

Readjustment was far more difficult in Italy than in France and Belgium, to say nothing of Britain and the United States. The pre-war trade deficit in Italy had been considerably larger than in Belgium and France, and the principal invisible items in Italy's international accounts, emigrant remittances and tourism, recovered slowly and incompletely. In contrast to France and Belgium, Italy was almost entirely dependent on imported coal. Italy's pre-war caloric trade deficit was substantial, in contrast to France. Relatively low living standards reduced Italy's margin to absorb politically and economically the shock of readjustment and recession.

US policymakers differed in their assessment of the need for, and the political opportunity of, making further credits to Italy. Norman Davis, of the Treasury, and Paul Cravath, legal consul of the Inter-Ally Council of War Purchasing and Finances, concluded that two or three years would elapse before Italy would be able to reestablish a satisfactory equilibrium in its balance of payments, and both advocated substantial additional financial assistance.[1] Other US officials, including Crosby and H. Bartlett Harris, the New York Federal Reserve Bank's representative in Rome, were less favorably disposed toward Italy. A fervent Wilsonian, Crosby argued that further US financial assistance would allow Italy to sustain a large army in the field and menace Yugoslavia. Harris suggested that if Italy demobilized, its agricultural sector would recover rapidly, and its balance of payments deficit disappear.[2]

In the event, despite the deterioration in relations in the spring of 1919 over Fiume, the United States did not treat Italy appreciably worse financially than the other Allies. The United States withdrew support for the exchange rates of sterling, the French franc, and the lira at the same time in mid-March 1919; and the US Treasury announced the future termination of financial assistance to the Italian and French governments simultaneously in late April 1919. US officials concluded that it would be politically maladroit to cut off aid to the Allies during the Paris Peace Conference or utilize American economic leverage too overtly in forcing concessions on major political questions. Nevertheless, the reality of Italian economic dependence on the United States remained a significant factor in shaping Italo-American relations during and after the Peace Conference. The US Treasury repeatedly reminded Italy of its dependence in subtle ways, threatening on several occasions to cut off aid because of relatively minor disputes with Italian officials. After Wilson's ill-fated appeal to the Italian people for moderation in the Adriatic, and the departure of Orlando and Sonnino from Versailles in late April, Italian economic policymakers were inclined to interpret every unfavorable action by US Treasury and Federal Reserve officials as politically motivated. In some instances, the Italians clearly overestimated the influence of political considerations, and underestimated the influence of economic factors in the American refusal to consider further loans from late 1919.

British policy towards Italy was no more generous, but it was determined almost exclusively by economics, and not by politics. Shortly after the armistice, Keynes advocated terminating British financial

---

[1] Davis to Rathbone, 5 December 1918; Crosby to Rathbone, 7 December 1918, US National Archives (hereafter NA), Treasury Papers, RG39, box 143.
[2] Crosby to Glass, 7 January 1918; H. Bartlett Harris, memo, 11 January 1918, NA, Treasury, RG39/143.

assistance to Italy as quickly as was, "compatible with avoiding a rupture of friendly relations," and this remained the cornerstone of the Treasury's policy.[3] In fact, Keynes and the permanent civil servants in the Treasury tended to take a harder line than the Chancellor, discouraging him from acceding to Stringher's urgent pleas for more generous aid in late November 1918. At the height of the Fiume dispute in late April 1919, J. H. Nixon, Keynes's successor and former subordinate at the "A" division, asked the Foreign Office, unsolicited, if the political situation warranted a change in financial policy (i.e. immediate termination of all lending).[4] Such credits as Italy succeeded in obtaining from Britain after the armistice were accorded over the objections of Treasury officials, owing to the concern of British political leaders to maintain good relations with Rome, and minimize social and political upheaval in the Italian peninsula.

In Italy good relations with the English-speaking powers and fresh credits soon were perceived as incompatible with a program of expansive territorial claims in the Adriatic. The extreme right and the moderate left divided neatly on this issue, with left-liberals favoring renunciation in the Adriatic and the extreme right espousing Orlando's battle cry, that Italy would "know famine sooner than dishonor." Orlando's own position was considerably more ambiguous than this statement, spoken in excitement after his withdrawal from the Peace Conference, would suggest. Neither Orlando nor Sonnino, his Foreign Minister, wished to sacrifice good relations with the United States and Britain. At the same time they were convinced that a peace treaty that did not give Italy domination over the Adriatic would discredit not only the government, but more importantly, the core institutions of the Italian state: the monarchy, the military and the Foreign Ministry. The Orlando–Sonnino cabinet collapsed as a result of this dilemma in mid-June 1919; unwilling to accede to American demands in the Adriatic, Orlando and Sonnino were equally unwilling to act unilaterally, and burn Italy's bridges to Washington and London.

Nitti formed a new government with the policy of trading territorial sacrifice in the northeast for food, coal, and credits from the English-speaking powers. Securing new British and American credits to finance Italian reconstruction remained one of Nitti's primary policy goals throughout his twelve months in office. Indeed, Nitti believed that his grand scheme for political and economic reform in Italy – promoting industrialization and economic development with a view to raising living

[3] Keynes to John Bradbury (Joint Permanent Secretary to the Treasury), 14 November 1918, British Public Record Office (hereafter PRO), Treasury files (T-files), T1/11234/46337/18.
[4] Nixon to R. P. M. Gower (Bonar Law's secretary), 29 April 1919, PRO, T-files, T1/12367/35324/19.

standards, and broadening the political base of the liberal state by incorporating moderate socialists and progressive Catholics into a liberal-dominated reformist bloc – was contingent on maintaining close economic and political relations with, and receiving financial assistance from, the United States and Britain.

But neither the Treasuries nor private investors in Britain and America were prepared to offer Nitti substantial support in the second half of 1919, and the first half of 1920. True, economic policymakers in both the United States and Britain concluded that Italy would need additional credits to finance its trade deficit after government credits ran out in late 1919. Officially, they encouraged the Italian government to contract new loans privately on the New York and London markets, but domestic conditions in both countries undermined Italian initiatives. In America investors preferred the tax-exempt US government securities that the Treasury was issuing in considerable volume to refund its floating debt to foreign government securities, on which taxes were levied. The post-war boom at home, and the related demand for credit, further lessened the attractiveness of foreign issues. Americans who invested capital abroad in the period 1919–21 preferred Canadian issues for security, and Latin American issues for higher yields at greater risk. Continental Europe would become attractive to American investors only after monetary, financial, and political stabilization.[5] Some American banks, including J. P. Morgan & Co., were prepared to make new loans to the ex-Allies in late 1919 if the US Treasury would guarantee them, but the government was non-cooperative.[6] The Italian government issued 5-year Treasury securities in New York in February 1920, but raised only the disappointingly modest sum of $11.3m. at the relatively onerous net interest rate of 6.8%.

The Nitti government was no more successful in its efforts to borrow in London. The British Treasury officially encouraged the Italian government to contract a loan with private banks in August 1919, after a final agreement terminating British government financial assistance to Italy was signed; but informally the Bank of England, at the behest of the Treasury, enforced a ban on new foreign issues until 1924.

Foreign, and particularly American investors were also inhibited from making investments in Italy because of doubts about the country's economic and political future. In 1919 and early 1920, there was concern that Nitti could be replaced by a right-wing government that would pursue a bellicose foreign policy, delay demobilization and the reduction of war-

[5] Thomas Lamont, "America's Financial Attitude Toward Europe," *Journal of Commerce*, 2 January 1920; Cleona Lewis, *America's Stake in International Investments* (Washington DC: Brookings Institution, 1938), pp. 367–75.

[6] Carl Parrini, *Heir to Empire: United States Economic Diplomacy, 1916–1923* (Pittsburgh: University of Pittsburgh Press, 1969), pp. 54–55, 78–79.

related state expenditure, and possibly even embroil Italy in a new war with Yugoslavia or Turkey. Foreign investors were also concerned that left-liberal, reformist governments, seeking support from the moderate wing of the Socialist Party and the Partito Populare Italiano, the Catholic party, which was organized in 1919, would not have the resolve to eliminate the bread subsidy and other welfare-related expenditures in order to balance the budget. Although foreign investors pressed for tax reform, they were alarmed by the confiscatory tax proposals presented by the Nitti government in the fall of 1919, particularly where their interests were directly threatened. Nitti's policy of continuing or reinstating state economic controls also elicited disapproval. For example, in December 1918 as Minister of the Treasury Nitti became the target of American oilmen's wrath after he promulgated a decree establishing a state monopoly on the distribution of petroleum products. US companies, particularly Standard Oil, mobilized the support of the US embassy in Rome and the US Treasury, arguing that the law threatened substantial American investments; the Orlando ministry withdrew the legislation after Nitti's resignation.[7]

The termination of US and British government credits in the last quarter of 1919 and the reluctance of private investors to make additional loans forced Italy, and the liberal political establishment, to bear the brunt of the readjustment crisis and post-war recession with its own resources. Lack of means of payment was undoubtedly a factor in keeping Italy's imports of essential raw materials at levels considerably below those of pre-war years, and only slightly higher than during the shipping crisis in 1917–18. Italy imported 1,790m. quintals of raw cotton in 1919 and 1,789m. in 1920, compared with 1,794m. in 1917, 1,303m. in 1918, and 2,019m. in the pre-war recession year 1913. Italy's coal imports totaled 6.2m. tons in 1919 and 5.6m. tons in 1920, compared with 5.0m. in 1917, 5.8m. in 1918, and 10.8m. tons in 1913 (see Tables 18 and 19, Appendix, pp. 323–4). The dearth of raw materials prevented Italy from fully participating in the post-war boom that characterized the US and British economies from 1919 to early 1920.[8] Notwithstanding the relative depression of imports, Italy ran a substantial balance of payments deficit, estimated by McGuire at 1,897m. gold lire in 1920.[9] In the absence of long

---

[7] Crosby to Glass, 27 December 1918; Nelson Page to L. B. White and Swanson (War Trade Board), 28 December 1918; Polk to Nelson Page, 10 January 1919; War Trade Board to Vance McCormick (US Treasury), 27 January 1919, NA, Treasury, RG39/143.

[8] Derek H. Aldcroft, *From Versailles to Wall Street, 1919–1929* (Berkeley: University of California Press, 1977), pp. 64–65; Alessandra Staderini, "L'economia italiana dal 1918 al 1922," in Giovanni Sabbatucci, ed., *La crisi italiana del primo dopoguerra* (Bari: Laterza, 1976), pp. 109–30.

[9] Constantine McGuire, *Italy's International Economic Position* (New York: Macmillan, 1926), pp. 296–301.

or medium-term loans, the balance of payments deficit was financed by short-term commercial credits and purchases by Italian importers in lire. Speculative holdings of lira balances in creditor nations, particularly the United States, must have assumed significant proportions. Such lira balances contributed to the instability of exchange rates, as is evident in the erratic fluctuation of the lira, and especially in its vulnerability to unfavorable political news, such as D'Annunzio's occupation of Fiume in September 1919, and the announcement of Nitti's tax proposals one month later (see Figure 3, Appendix, p. 330).[10]

Meanwhile, the drying up of war contracts, and the return to a market economy meant that taxes no longer could be passed back to the state, and the issue of tax reform returned to the top of the political agenda. The first important step toward tax reform was taken in the fall of 1919, when Nitti appointed Pasquale D'Aroma Director General of Direct Taxes. Under D'Aroma's energetic leadership, the process of bringing up to date the direct tax rolls went forward quickly, further increasing the real burden of taxation, and the inequities of graduated taxes on single income-producing activities, rather than total personal income. However, Nitti was unable to mobilize support in parliament for reforming tax laws. The left wing of his coalition rejected the Meda Project, which had been drawn up by a parliamentary commission during the war, as too moderate; but business interests and the right wing of his coalition successfully mobilized against his draconian proposals for a forced loan based on wealth in the fall of 1919. Instead, Nitti issued a sixth war loan for Lit. 20bn. in early 1920, which proved even more inflationary, and even less effective in absorbing private purchasing power, than his fifth war loan in early 1918.

Although Nitti managed to cut military spending appreciably during his tenure in office, despite the unresolved Fiume crisis, the state continued to run huge budget deficits, and monetary expansion in 1919 was almost as great as in 1918. Food subsidies were a key factor in the budget deficits, particularly after the termination of Allied credits threw the entire burden of overseas cereals purchases and transport on the Italian government's own resources. The persistence of food and basic raw materials shortages, combined with Nitti's penchant for *dirigismo*, induced the Prime Minister to maintain rationing and economic controls despite the growing opposition of manufacturers, merchants, farmers, and middle income and wealthy consumers.

Finally, the feverish business expansion which had begun during the war reached its height in 1919 and early 1920. In the spring of 1920, the Perrone brothers and the Banca Italiana di Sconto mounted a second

[10] Ibid.

hostile take-over attempt on the Banca Commerciale. Nitti's partisanship for the Perrones was widely suspected, and the largest financial group in the country emerged from the fray determined to oust him from power.

Stringher's unsuccessful mission to Paris and London, November–December 1918

Stringher left Rome at the beginning of November 1918 with the intention of negotiating a modest increase in British and American credits earmarked for expenditure in neutral countries. He first conferred with Crosby in Paris on 4 November, the day the Italo-Austrian ceasefire took effect. After some hesitation, Crosby agreed to transfer $20m., rather than $10m., to London, to pay for purchases made in neutral countries by British government departments on Italy's behalf. However, the US Undersecretary of the Treasury also made it clear to Stringher that American credits to the Allies would have to be based on radically different principles after the termination of hostilities, and indeed would be wound up as quickly as possible. Stringher was therefore confronted with an altogether different situation than had obtained when he left Rome. He had not prepared himself to document and negotiate Italy's post-armistice financial needs. While officials in Rome were set to work on this task, Stringher insisted to Crosby that the armistice had left an additional 4 million civilians and 500,000 Austrian prisoners of war under Italian jurisdiction, and therefore, Allied financial and material assistance should be stepped up, rather than diminished.[11]

American officials were as unprepared to deal with the post-armistice situation as the Italians. Crosby had ordered a study of post-war Allied financial needs and US options only a few days before Stringher's arrival, when Allied victory already appeared imminent. A group of US experts in the various Allied capitals were to draw up recommendations on post-armistice financial assistance. The report on Italy was to be prepared by H. Bartlett Harris, who had recently arrived in Rome as the Federal Reserves' liaison with the central office of the INC.[12] In the meantime, Crosby merely indicated his willingness to continue financing Italy's purchases in the United States, and in neutral countries as before through the

[11] Crosby to Lansing, 4 November 1918; Crosby to J. P. Cotton (US Food Administration), 4 November 1918; Crosby to McAdoo, 7 November 1918, NA, Treasury, RG39/143; Stringher's diary, entries for 4–6 November 1918, Archivio Storico, Banca d'Italia (hereafter ASBI), fondo 3, "Rapporti con l'estero," bobina 108, pratica 313.

[12] Crosby to Rathbone, 26 October 1918, NA, Treasury, RG39/143; Crosby to Bonar Law, 3 December 1918, PRO, T-files, T1/12234/46337/18. The report on Italy's financial needs originally was to have been prepared by a certain Stewart, representative of the War Trade Board in Rome.

end of December 1918. Despite Crosby's non-committal stance, Stringher evidently impressed upon him the difficulties that the Allies would have in restoring equilibrium in their foreign trade and payments balances; shortly after their meeting the US Treasury, at Crosby's urging, rushed a bill before Congress authorizing the administration to make an additional $1.5bn. in loans available to the Allies.[13]

In London, Stringher found that British Treasury officials were determined to cease lending to Italy as quickly as possible. Keynes set the tone for the talks in a memo written to prepare Bonar Law, the Chancellor of the Exchequer, for negotiations with Stringher. Keynes conceded that lending to Italy could not be suspended immediately: British government departments would press additional claims for purchases already effected, and for commitments already entered into prior to the armistice:

> Further it will be impossible to resist the claim of the Italians to be given at least some breathing space and to be assured of a measure of financial assistance for new supplies during the transitional period.[14]

However, Keynes went on:

> I ask ... for instructions as to whether the policy of the Chancellor of the Exchequer is (1) to treat Italy with the same measure of liberality as during the war, peace needs now being substituted for war needs, or (2) to restrict further advances to Italy to the barest minimum which is compatible with clearing off existing commitments and avoiding a rupture of friendly relations between the two countries.
>
> If the former policy is to be adopted the United Kingdom will be left with a proportionately smaller margin of resources for her own recuperation during the transitional period. I ask in short whether the interests of the United Kingdom are to come pre-eminently and unreservedly in front of those of Italy or whether the United Kingdom is to be asked to make further substantial sacrifices in Italian interests.
>
> If a decision is taken in favor of a policy of greatly diminished liberality towards Italy, it will be necessary for this to be announced by someone of greater authority than myself; and in the absence of such an indication the negotiations on points of detail will be on a false basis.[15]

Bonar Law seems to have been undecided as to what policy Britain should pursue *vis-à-vis* Italy; in any case, he refused to accommodate Keynes by bearing his bad tidings to Stringher, and made himself unavailable until the end of November, forcing Keynes to confront the Italian central banker himself. Despite the lack of unreserved backing by the

[13] Harris informed Stringher of this in a subsequent meeting on 11 December 1918. Minutes of a meeting between Stringher and Harris in Rome, ASBI, fondo 3, bob. 108, pr. 313.
[14] Keynes to Bradbury, memo, 14 November 1918, PRO, T- files, T1/12234/46337/18.
[15] Ibid.

Chancellor, Keynes initiated his talks with Stringher by handing him a statement reading:

> England is not now self-supporting and has no surplus. Therefore, any financial assistance given to the Allies results directly or indirectly in further loans that she must ask to somebody else and especially to the U.S.A. Everybody in financial circles thinks that England has reached her lending capacity.[16]

Stringher had made the mistake of travelling on to the British capital without taking time to adequately document Italy's post-war financial needs. To Keynes's surprise, he did not present a detailed financial proposal. Keynes therefore handed Stringher his own proposal, which has the air of having been drawn up on the spur of the moment. Keynes simply proposed that Britain would give Italy additional credits totaling £st. 50m.; £st. 9.5m. for November, £st. 8.5m. for December, with future monthly advances being reduced by stages until credits were extinguished at the end of July 1919. The existing distinction between the "general credit," for expenditure within the British Empire, and the "free credit," for expenditure in neutral markets, would be eliminated.[17]

Although Stringher now apparently was reconciled to the relatively abrupt curtailment of British financial assistance, he strenuously objected to Keynes's proposal. He pointed out that it was actually far less favorable to Italy than it appeared, because interest payments on past British government loans, and payments due to British departments were to count as a first charge against the new credits. Stringher calculated that about half of the new credits would be needed simply to renew Italian treasury bills falling due in London, while charges by British government departments for past expenditures would take up most of the rest. Keynes, he argued, was offering almost nothing in fresh credits. Keynes countered by suggesting that charges by British government departments would be more modest than Stringher supposed, but he offered no documentation to this effect, and refused to accept a clause in the agreement that would have fixed a minimum amount of fresh credits.[18] It is difficult to escape the conclusion that Keynes was aware that his proposal amounted to the virtual elimination of new British lending to Italy, and that he tried to deceive the Italians into signing the agreement by suggesting that it offered them more than it actually did.

---

[16] Keynes to Stringher, 14 November 1918, ASBI, fondo 3, bob. 107, pr. 311.
[17] Keynes, memo, undated (but handed to Stringher on 14 November 1918), PRO, T-files, T1/12234/46337/18.
[18] Stringher to Keynes, 19 November 1918; Nixon to Stringher, 22 November 1918, ASBI, fondo 3, bob. 107, pr. 311.

Stringher finally saw Bonar Law in a meeting attended by Keynes on 28 November 1918. Stringher insisted with the Chancellor of the Exchequer that Italy's economic and financial situation had actually deteriorated with the signing of the armistice, and that advances at least equal to former levels would be needed for some time yet, especially given Italy's increased population and its responsibility for Austrian prisoners of war. He urged Bonar Law to maintain British advances at £st. 9.5m. monthly at least through January 1919, and to raise the total figure of the loan proposed by Keynes from £st. 50m. to £st. 79m., in order to give Italy some margin for new purchases. The Bank of Italy's minute of this meeting suggests that Bonar Law was confused by the dispute between Stringher and Keynes as to how much fresh money Keynes's proposal would provide; it further suggests that the Chancellor was on the verge of acceding to Stringher's requests, but backed down because of Keynes's vigorous objections. Stringher, in any event, declined to sign the Keynes proposal, and for the first time since Italy intervened in the war an Anglo-Italian financial conference ended in disagreement.[19]

Before leaving London, Stringher managed to obtain the concession that British monthly advances would be rearranged in such a way that Italy would continue to receive £st. 9.5m. during December and January, although he received no assurances that the total amount offered would be increased. The Chancellor also held out a ray of hope to Stringher, by suggesting that if Italy obtained additional credits from the United States he might be prepared to reconsider Britain's position.[20]

Stringher left for Rome on 4 December, emotionally exhausted, it would appear. His only accomplishment was the negotiation of a relatively modest loan with C. E. Ter Meulen, the Dutch Finance Minister, which was part of a larger economic and financial agreement between the Netherlands and the Allies.[21]

Financial uncertainty and Allied pressure

Between early December and mid-February 1919 the British and American governments refused to make new long or medium-term financial commitments to Italy. Supply programs were curtailed, and the authorities contemplated the possibility of being thrown back entirely on their own resources to finance the burgeoning trade deficit. The situation was as dramatic for Stringher and his associates as any since the outbreak of war. Only cereal supplies seemed assured, when the United States offered to

---

[19] Minutes of a meeting between Bonar Law, Keynes, and Stringher at Whitehall, 28 November 1918, ASBI, fondo 3, bob. 107, pr. 311.   [20] Ibid.

[21] Financial accord between Italy and the Netherlands, 3 December 1918, ASBI, fondo 3, bob. 1, pr. 1.

lend Britain, France, and Italy $1bn. to finance the 1919 American winter wheat harvest.[22] Coal deliveries in January totaled just over 340,000 tons, less than in any single month since the outbreak of war, save one (see Table 18, Appendix, p. 323). In England, the miners' union threatened to strike, and the virtual collapse of coal shipments, after months of inadequate supplies, seemed likely.[23] In monetary affairs the situation was no brighter: by the end of December Gidoni was forced to sell foreign exchange again to support the lira, and US authorities were insisting that the system of pegged exchange rates be dismantled.[24] In Italy, Nitti was becoming increasingly critical of the government, and his resignation seemed a foregone conclusion. As the Minister of the Treasury distanced himself from his job, the weight of dealing with the difficult international situation increasingly rested upon Stringher. Indeed, after Nitti finally resigned on 15 January 1919 Stringher would reluctantly agree to leave the Bank of Italy and take his place.[25]

---

[22] Parrini, *Heir to Empire*, p. 48.

[23] Giuseppe De Nava (Minister of Transportation) to Lloyd George, 28 January 1919; Lee (Coal Mines Dept., Board of Trade), memo on British coal deliveries to Italy, 15 February 1919, PRO, T-files, T1/12343/26960/19; Orlando to Silvio Crespi (Minister of Provisioning), 19 February 1919; Orlando to Stringher, 19 February 1919, *I documenti diplomatici italiani* (hereafter *DDI*), 6th ser., vol. 2 (Rome: Ministero degli Affari Esteri, 1980), nos. 401, 402.

[24] Stringher to Gidoni, 24 December 1918, ASBI, fondo 3, bob. 108, pr. 313; Gidoni to Kent, 7 January 1919; Rathbone to Crosby, 10 January 1919, NA, Treasury, RG39/143. In late 1918 and early 1919, Bank of Italy officials repeatedly criticized Nitti for having insisted the previous summer that the lira–dollar rate be brought up to 6.35. Stringher made the following comment to Sonnino, while in London in November 1918: "It was an error on our part to bring down the exchange rate so low, as leading financiers have told me repeatedly, but now we have to try even harder not to reverse the situation." Stringher to Sonnino (transmitted by Imperiali), 20 November 1918, *DDI*, 6th ser., vol. 1, no. 255. Arrigo Rossi, director of the INC, was even more explicit in his criticism of Nitti in a conversation with Edward Capel Cure, the British Commercial Attaché in Rome, in February 1919. According to Capel Cure, Rossi responded to his observation that the rapid revaluation of the lira in the summer may have been ill-advised by exclaiming: "Do not put it in such diplomatic terms . . . it was madness! (una pazzia). I can only tell you . . . that we [i.e. Bank of Italy officials] were against it, but what is one to do? Nitti is no doubt a man of genius, but in these matters he is an amateur. He is not a banker and we have allowed our business to be managed by amateurs. To be perfectly fair, however . . . it is right that I should tell you that the fault was not entirely his. The Americans egged him on (*lo spinsero al passo*), and here I do not want to be uncharitable, but the fact remains the same, and the fact was foreseen by us bankers. A considerable amount (*una quantità considerevole*) of our war loan had been taken in America and directly the exchange fell in so precipitate a manner, the American bankers began selling and are still continuing to do so. Of course they are realizing very heavy profits, since they had bought when the exchange was practically at its highest, but we, on the other hand, even putting aside the damage done to commerce, are losing in reality what we seem to have gained on paper!" Rodd (transmitting a dispatch of Capel Cure) to Lord Curzon, 6 February 1919, PRO, T-files, T1/12343/26969/19. It might be added, however, that Gidoni, the INC's representative in New York, also favored revaluation in the summer of 1918.

[25] On Nitti's resignation see, Alberto Monticone, *Nitti e la grande guerra (1914–1918)* (Milan: Giuffré, 1961), pp. 324–38; Francesco Barbagallo, *Nitti* (Turin: UTET, 1984), pp. 280–89.

Stringher resumed negotiations with the United States Treasury for
new credits after returning to Rome from London in early December. He
held two inconclusive meetings with Harris, the uncompromising banker
who was writing a report for Crosby on Italy's financial situation. The
Americans agreed in the middle of December to continue financing Italian
purchases in the United States for the time being, but refused to make
long-term commitments for commodities other than wheat. They also
categorically refused to approve new credits for expenditure in neutral
countries after 1 January 1919.[26] The problem of financing frozen beef
purchases in the Plata became acute once more.

American officials were divided regarding post-war financial assistance
for Italy. Norman Davis, of the US Treasury, warned from Paris that Italy
would have a more difficult time readjusting its economy and balance of
payments than the other Allies. He predicted that Italy would need two to
three years' grace before it could begin repaying war loans, and favored
additional bridging credits over the next several months. Davis also argued
that cutting financial assistance prior to or during the Peace Conference
would prove politically counterproductive. Significantly, Davis, like other
US officials, assumed that private US bankers would be willing and able to
meet Italy's requirements for additional loans by the second half of 1919.[27]
Paul Cravath sided with Davis, insisting that considerable further credits
would be necessary to help Italy through economic readjustment.[28]

Crosby and Harris, in contrast, advocated taking a harder line. In the
report on Italian finances, which Harris presented to Crosby on 11 January, he approved the financing for a brief period of additional food supplies, but felt that Italy could manage without credits for most other
commodities. Italy was mismanaging its public finances, he suggested, and
hardly merited further American support. He discounted the need to
finance further Italian purchases in neutral countries and recommended
the immediate unpegging of the lira.[29] Harris was certainly a poor choice
as Treasury informant on Italian affairs. He had not been in Italy long
enough to develop a clear understanding of the economic situation, and
his report contained serious inaccuracies. He argued, for instance, that
Italy could become agriculturally self-sufficient without great difficulty
after the war, notwithstanding the traditional Italian reliance on imported
cereals. Strangely, Crosby, who should have known better, sent on the
report to Washington with his full endorsement.[30] The Undersecretary of

[26] Minutes of a meeting between Stringher and Harris in Rome, 11 December 1918; Crosby
to Nitti, 18 December 1918, ASBI, fondo 3, bob. 108, pr. 313.
[27] Davis to Rathbone, 5 December 1918, NA, Treasury, RG39/143.
[28] Crosby to Rathbone, 7 December 1918, NA, Treasury, RG39/143.
[29] Harris, memo, 11 January 1919, NA, Treasury, RG39/143.
[30] Crosby to Glass, 13 January 1919, NA, Treasury, RG39/143.

the Treasury was exasperated with his job and with Italy. Shortly afterwards he resigned. Privately Crosby told an Italian friend that the Italian government was spending irresponsibly and approaching bankruptcy, "at breakneck speed."[31] The attitude of Crosby and Harris was colored by political considerations: both suggested that generous credits to Italy would enable political leaders there to delay demobilization, and sustain Italy's expansionist aims in the Adriatic. Crosby cabled Washington on 3 January that Serbia was asking for new credits to maintain its army in the field for defense against Italy, underscoring the absurdity of the US position.[32] Such political considerations did not go unnoticed abroad. In late December Keynes concluded:

> From the American point of view the position is probably mixed up with high politics. I think it possible that the United States Treasury may give increased assistance if Italy's territorial aims are moderated. In the present case, i.e. the supply of meat, it is believed that one ground of the pressing character of Italy's claims for large quantities of meat is that she may be in a position to use the supplies so obtained for the advertisement of her power in Jugo Slavia [sic].[33]

General Mario Di Robilant, Italy's representative to the Allied Supreme Military Council in Versailles, also voiced his apprehensions that the Allies would use loans as an instrument of pressure at the Peace Conference.[34]

Meanwhile, in Britain the permanent civil servants in the Treasury continued to take a hard line. Keynes wrote to Attolico in late December that Britain could not possibly continue to finance Italy's purchases in neutral markets if the United States refused:

> But we cannot get away from the fundamental fact of the situation that you appeal to us not because the responsibility really [lies?] with us but because the United States Treasury is [?] to you and you have found it impossible to make [further?] progress with them. For some months past the United States and we have shared the burden in making a [dvances?] to Italy in neutral countries. We are prepared, [at?] least for the present, to continue our share. [But?] they refuse to carry their's and you and they trust to our greater soft-heartedness in the matter and the greater likelihood of our doing what we can to help Italy. But you doubtless realize how impossible a position this is from our point of view. If the United States Treasury think we will carry the burden there is no prospect of their doing so and I do not see how we can answer you otherwise than that, however naturally and excusable in all the circumstances, you are addressing your entreaties to the

---

[31] Imperiali to Orlando, 7 January 1919, *DDI*, 6th ser., vol. 1 (1955), no. 802.

[32] Crosby to Glass, 3 January 1919, NA, Treasury, RG39/143.

[33] Keynes to Bradbury, 21 December 1918, PRO, T-files, T1/12296/11550/19.

[34] Di Robilant to Sonnino and Vittorio Zupelli (Minister of War), 22 November 1918, *DDI*, 6th ser., vol. 1, no. 292.

wrong quarter and that the responsibility in the matter really lies with the United States Treasury and not with us.[35]

Italy's financial situation, particularly in Britain and in neutral markets, became increasingly dramatic. On 31 December Alessandro Ceresa, the Treasury's representative in London, calculated that Italy had already used £st. 17m. of the credit of £st. 50m. offered by Keynes. Of the remainder, £st. 8.5m. would be need to renew Italian sterling treasury bills falling due, and £st. 25m. to reimburse British government departments, leaving only £st. 4.5m. in fresh credits available through May. Other Italian debts to Britain would probably wipe out even this meager sum.[36] At the beginning of January the British Treasury again suspended purchases of frozen meat in Argentina on Italy's behalf. Orlando calculated that Italy would be bereft of meat for military and civilian consumption within ten days.[37]

Because of the hard line taken by Keynes and the career civil servants in the Treasury, Italian representatives appealed over their heads to British political leaders. Attolico wrote a *calda lettera particolare* to Bonar Law in mid-December, and urged Sonnino to confront Wilson and Lloyd George directly in Paris.[38] Ceresa and Imperiali met with Lord Reading.[39] De Nava, the Minister of Transportation, appealed to Lloyd George to step up coal deliveries.[40] On 3 January, Imperiali announced hopefully to Orlando that Bonar Law would soon be replaced as Chancellor by Austen Chamberlain; unfortunately, he added, Keynes, the real architect of Treasury policy, would stay on.[41] Meanwhile, the Italian appeals to British political leaders seem to have had a positive effect. The difficulties of post-war financial readjustment in Italy and elsewhere were becoming more apparent, and British political leaders must had reached similar conclusions to those of Norman Davis and Paul Cravath, namely that abrupt termination of lending would throw the country into economic chaos and prove politically counterproductive during the Peace Conference. The British Treasury was induced to extend provisional credits to allow Italy to buy meat in Argentina, until the Italian government could negotiate a loan there directly, and the parameters of Keynes's financial proposal were overstepped, allowing Italy at least to pay for some coal and freights for January and February.[42] At the same time, the British insisted that any

[35] Keynes to Attolico, 20 December 1918, PRO, T-files, T1/12296/11550/19.
[36] Ceresa to Nitti, 31 December 1918, ASBI, fondo 3, bob. 108, pr. 313.
[37] Orlando to Imperiali, 2 January 1919, *DDI*, 6th ser., vol. 1, no. 735.
[38] Imperiali to Sonnino, 18 December 1918, *DDI*, 6th ser., vol. 1, no. 589.
[39] Imperiali to Orlando, 7 January 1919, *DDI*, 6th ser., vol. 1, no. 802.
[40] De Nava to Lloyd George, 28 January 1919, PRO, T-files, T1/12343/26960/19.
[41] Imperiali to Orlando, 3 January 1919, *DDI*, 6th ser., vol. 1, no. 743.
[42] Nixon, internal Treasury memo, 29 January 1919, PRO, T- files, T1/12343/26960/19; Attolico to Stringher, 3 February 1919, ASBI, fondo 3, bob. 108, pr. 313.

formal increase in financial assistance would be contingent on the US Treasury providing matching funds.

Stringher's second mission to Paris and London: new agreements with Britain (18 February 1919) and the United States (19 February 1919)

In the first half of February, the United States became more conciliatory *vis-à-vis* Italy with regard to financial questions. This was probably due in part, as was the case in Britain, to a growing recognition in government circles that economic readjustment on the continent would prove more difficult than the optimists had earlier predicted. Personality also played a role: Crosby had resigned, and Harris was no longer concerned with Italian affairs, while Norman Davis was now serving as personal adviser to Wilson on economic problems at the Peace Conference. British political leaders evidently indicated their willingness to take a more lenient position *vis-à-vis* Italy if the United States would do likewise. Stringher, now Minister of the Treasury, therefore journeyed in mid-February to Paris and London a second time, to conclude more satisfactory agreements with British and American officials.

In Paris Stringher hoped to meet directly with Wilson to present Italy's desperate supply situation to him. The President declined to see him, however, and he was left to negotiate with the US economic experts, Davis and William Strauss. The latter were, in any case, sympathetically disposed.

The Americans nevertheless insisted that Italy make political concessions, at least on minor points, as a precondition for new loans. Captain T.T.C. Gregory, representative of Herbert Hoover's American Relief Administration (ARA) in Trieste, had recently complained that the Italian government had requisitioned Austrian railway equipment, compromising his efforts to supply Vienna. Worse, the Italians had closed all railway lines leading into Yugoslav-held territory, including the main line to Vienna through Lubliana, after an alleged attack by Yugoslavs on Italian soldiers.[43] With Wilson's approval, Davis informed Stringher that further US credits would be contingent on the reopening of rail lines to Yugoslavia, and full Italian cooperation with the ARA in Trieste.[44] Stringher evidently gave satisfactory assurances on these points. In return, the Italian Minister of the Treasury was given to understand that the US Treasury would make further loans for expenditure in neutral countries,

---

[43] T. T. C. Gregory to Hoover, 11 February 1919, NA, Treasury, RG39/143.
[44] Davis to Wilson, 12 February 1919; Davis and Strauss to Rathbone, 14 February 1919, NA, Treasury, RG39/143.

notably for Argentinian beef, in an amount equal to future credits offered by Britain. In addition, the US Treasury agreed to the immediate transfer to London of an additional $10m. of the credit earmarked for neutral purchases remaining from 1918 to pay for Argentinian beef.[45]

With these assurances, Stringher continued to London, where he met with Chamberlain. His arrival had been preceded by dispatches from the British Embassy in Rome warmly supporting the Italian request for new credits.[46] The Italian Treasury Minister was fortunate that Keynes was in Spa at the time, conferring with German delegates on the termination of the Allied blockade and payment for foodstuffs. Even from Belgium, Keynes tried to undermine the negotiations, cabling the department that he doubted the United States would make new credits in neutral countries available to Italy in the absence of substantial political concessions at the Peace Conference.[47] Chamberlain, however, received contrary assurances from Washington.[48] Stringher quickly reached agreement with Chamberlain on a proposal that represented a considerable improvement over Keynes's offer in November. It was recognized that, "the outstanding claims of the British Government Departments are larger than had been formerly anticipated," and the Chancellor now agreed to make an additional £st. 43.5m. available to Italy, beyond the £st. 21.5m. remaining from the November proposal, for a total of £st. 65m. Monthly advances would total £st. 14m. in February, £st. 13m. in March, £st. 12m. in April, £st. 11m. in May, and £st. 10m. in June, leaving a balance of £st. 5m., which together with unexpended sums left over from earlier months, would be available during July, August, and September. Stringher received some assurances that approximately £st. 30m. of the total credit would be available for new purchases. It was estimated that the renewal of Italian sterling Treasury bills and payments to British departments would take up the other £st. 35m. through June:

[45] Ibid.
[46] Rodd to Curzon, 6 February 1919, PRO, T-files, T1/12343/26960/19. Rodd also forwarded a dispatch from Capel Cure. The British Commercial Attaché also supported generous new credits, while noting his dissatisfaction that Italy would once again be represented in financial negotiations by Stringher: "I have been present with Commendatore Stringher in financial transactions between England and Italy and I cannot consider him a good negotiator, or indeed capable of putting his case before others in a clear or tempered manner, though he is an able financier. He has little command of his voice and unless his hearer knows him well and respects his good qualities, he does not prepossess him in his favour." Capel Cure's negative assessment of Stringher's negotiating ability may well have been influenced by the inconclusive outcome of his trip to London in November 1918, and can hardly be accepted as an accurate judgment of Stringher's record as a financial diplomat as a whole.
[47] Keynes to Chamberlain, 16 February 1919, PRO, T-files, T1/12343/26960/19.
[48] Graham (Foreign Office) to Bradbury, 18 February 1919, PRO, T-files, T1/12343/26960/19.

In the event of the above estimate proving to be seriously below the actual figure, the British Treasury will be prepared to consider a further loan to Italy of the difference or of such part of it as cannot be met out of the present credits as may be shown to be necessary.[49]

Fresh credits of £st. 5m. were usable for purchases outside the British Empire, at a rate of £st. 1m. monthly. It was expected that the United States would match this credit. Another article stipulated that the agreement represented the termination of British government financial obligations to Italy arising out of the war. Finally, Stringher was forced to accept a clause stating:

The first receipts accruing to the Italian Government in respect of compensation or indemnity from the Enemy Governments shall be applied to the liquidation of £st. 30m. [i.e. the estimated amount of fresh credits provided by the agreement] of the above Treasury Bills, subject always to such general principles as may be laid down by the Peace Conference as to the disposal of the assets made available by the Enemy Powers.[50]

In order to head off eventual American objections that the agreement violated the principle of Anglo-American reciprocity in extending loans to Italy, a final paragraph was added:

The Italian Treasury may nevertheless, provided that the consent of the British Treasury be first obtained, undertake to liquidate advances received after the 1st February from any other of the Associated Governments *pari passu* with the liquidation of the £st. 30m. Treasury Bills mentioned above.[51]

Even in this form, the agreement was bound to offend the US government: the United States was confronted with the dilemma of either demanding a similar lien on Italian reparations receipts, which would violate the American principle of disassociating reparations from inter-Allied debts, or allowing Britain to claim additional guarantees on loans extended to Italy, beyond those given to the US Treasury. Very likely, Chamberlain insisted on the lien on Italian reparations payments precisely in order to entice the United States into making an agreement linking reparations to war debts.

Stringher sensed that the lien clause, which he was unable to persuade Chamberlain to leave out of what was otherwise a very satisfactory agreement, would cause trouble with the Americans. Consequently, he informed Davis in Paris that Britain had agreed to make new advances, including £st. 5m. in credits expendable in neutral markets, but stated that

---

[49] "British Advances to Italy: Agreement of 18th February 1919," PRO, T-files, T1/12343/26960/19. Also in, Bank of England, archive, C40/215 1586/4.
[50] Ibid.
[51] Ibid.

he was not at liberty to reveal the details of the accord.[52] In the meantime, President Wilson instructed the US Treasury to approve a matching US credit of $25m. for Italian purchases in neutral countries, under the condition that none of it be transferred to London, and that Italy give assurances regarding railway lines leading to Yugoslavia and the provisioning of Vienna. The new credit was made available on 28 February.[53]

It was only a matter of time, however, before US officials learned the details of the Anglo-Italian agreement. They did so at the beginning of March, and Albert Rathbone, Assistant Secretary of the Treasury, immediately fired off harsh notes to both the Italian and British governments. In his note to Lord Reading, British special envoy in Washington, Rathbone suggested that:

> both the British and American Treasuries are so vitally interested in questions of this character that it would be most advisable, in the interest of common and concerted action, if there were a full discussion of these matters between the two Treasuries.[54]

In his note to Enrico Alliata, the Italian Treasury's representative in Washington, Rathbone was far harsher, announcing the US Treasury's unwillingness to make further loans until the matter was clarified.[55]

At almost the same time, Italo-American financial relations were shaken by another confrontation, this time due to positions taken by Silvio Crespi at a meeting of the Allied Supreme Economic Council in Paris. Crespi and the French delegates to the SEC had countered an American proposal that the blockade of Germany be lifted by insisting that adequate provisioning for France and Italy first be secured. After a violent confrontation, the French and Italian delegates had insisted that a general reallocation of Allied war debts be considered.[56] Thus, within days, Italian representatives had challenged the sanctity of the twin American doctrines of full recognition of Allied war debts and the separateness of reparations and war debts on two separate occasions. The confrontation came at a bad time for Italy: a coal strike appeared imminent in Britain, and coal shipments to Italy had been curtailed. Italian experts at the Peace Conference were actually discussing with their American counterparts the possibility of coal deliveries from the United States. Italian grain stocks were also low, and the arrival of the American winter wheat harvest was being awaited

[52] Rathbone to Enrico Alliata (Italian Treasury representative in Washington), 4 March 1919, NA, Treasury, RG39/143.
[53] Wilson to Glass, 19 February 1919; Glass to Wilson, 28 February 1919, NA, Treasury, RG39/143.
[54] Rathbone to Reading, 4 March 1919, PRO, T-files, T1/12343/26960/19.
[55] Rathbone to Alliata, 4 March 1919, NA, Treasury, RG39/142.
[56] Crespi to Orlando, 18 February 1919; Pietro Arone di Valentarso (Italian Chargé d'Affaires, Washington) to Sonnino, 12 March 1919, *DDI*, 6th ser., vol. 2, nos. 379, 779.

eagerly.[57] The Italians were fortunate that Norman Davis was holding the reins of US economic policy. Davis proposed to Wilson that advances to Italy be resumed after the United States had received satisfactory reassurances that the Italian government recognized its debt to the United States, and guarantees similar to those recently demanded by Britain were extended for fresh US credits. The matter was patched up at a meeting in Paris on 15 March, between Davis and Strauss on the American side, and Crespi, Cellere, and even Sonnino on the Italian side. The reserved and forbidding Italian Foreign Minister, who normally refrained from direct intervention in economic and financial matters, was apparently so unnerved by the crisis that he felt obliged to give the Americans personal assurances. Crespi recanted his earlier statements and reconfirmed Italy's full recognition of its debts to the United States. Sonnino pledged that new American loans would be repaid *pari passu* with the British loan from reparations payments. The crisis in Italo-American financial relations was over.[58] Under Norman Davis' guidance, the US Treasury had adopted the policy that economic and financial pressure could be exerted on the Allies to force them to comply with American positions on economic and financial matters, while refraining from using such pressures to influence high politics and territorial issues. This was the line that would be followed during the Fiume crisis.

The unpegging of the lira and final arrangements with the US Treasury

American support for the fixed lira exchange rate varied inversely with the amount of US financial assistance required for its maintenance. Thus Crosby and Kent were willing to accommodate Nitti in the summer of 1918, when the stabilization of the lira stimulated remittances by Italian emigrants, allowing the INC to actually accumulate foreign exchange reserves by selling lire on the New York market. The US Treasury demonstrated its unwillingness to make substantial financial sacrifices to maintain the lira exchange rate of 6.35 in late September and early October, by refusing to allow the INC to transfer dollar balances accumulated in New York to buy lire in Paris and London. The pegged lira rate was only saved at that time by a wave of speculation in favor of Italy's currency beginning in mid-October, with the approach of Allied

---

[57] Orlando to Lloyd George, 2 March 1919; Attolico to Orlando, 7 March 1919, *DDI*, 6th ser., vol. 2, nos. 608, 699; [?Davis] to Cellere, 24 March 1919, NA, Treasury, RG39/142.
[58] Sonnino to Stringher, 15 March 1919 (18.00); Sonnino to Stringher, 15 March 1919 (19.20), *DDI*, 6th ser., vol. 2, nos. 815, 816; Strauss and Davis to Rathbone, 15 March 1919, NA, Treasury, RG39/142.

victory. By late December uncertainty with regard to Italy's economic future had replaced the optimism generated by victory, and the lira was besieged on the exchange markets once more. Gidoni proposed that to support the exchange the US Treasury make available to Italy $38m., an amount equal to INC dollar earnings that had earlier been employed to finance Italian purchases in the United States.[59] US Treasury officials insisted that the United States had never assumed any obligation to support the exchange rate of the lira on European currency markets, and that any advances for such purposes should come out of the $10m. monthly credit earmarked for Italian purchases in neutral markets.[60] In his report on Italian finances on 11 January, H. Bartlett Harris went further, recommending that US support for the lira should be terminated altogether.[61] Harris's proposal had clear political implications, as US support for sterling and the French franc would have continued. In the event, the United States continued to support the lira until 22 March 1919, when sterling and the French franc were also unpegged. This policy reflected the attitude of officials like Norman Davis, who believed that direct use of financial and economic pressure to gain political concessions from Allied governments at the Peace Conference would prove counterproductive. Davis was also influenced by Stringher's insistence in February that the unpegging of exchange rates be delayed until he could bring out a domestic victory loan in Italy.[62] Stringher delayed the loan issue several times in February and early March, due to a depression in state security prices. In the second half of March Stringher was still hoping to bring out his loan, but the US Treasury was unwilling to delay the unpegging of exchange rates any longer.[63] All three Allied currencies declined sharply following the unpegging, but the lira was consistently weaker than the franc, not to say sterling.

One month after the unpegging of exchange rates, on 21 April 1919, the US Treasury handed notes to the Italian and French governments announcing the termination of US financial assistance.[64] In the case of Italy, fresh credits were limited to $5m. monthly through May: however, arrangements already had been made to finance most of Italy's cereal and cotton needs through the fall. The note of 21 April represented a slight change from earlier US policy, in that Treasury officials had suggested

[59] Gidoni to Kent, 7 January 1919, NA, Treasury, RG39/143.
[60] Stringher to Gidoni, 24 December 1918, ASBI, fondo 3, bob. 108, pr. 313.
[61] Harris, memo, 11 January 1918, NA, Treasury, RG39/143.
[62] Davis to Wilson, 12 February 1919, NA, Treasury, RG39/143.
[63] Leffingwell to Davis, 20 March 1919; Davis to Leffingwell, 21 March 1919; Davis to Federico Brofferio (Italian Treasury representative in Paris) 21 March 1919; Leffingwell to Davis, 21 March 1919, NA, Treasury, RG39/142.
[64] Rathbone to Alliata, 21 April 1919; Rathbone to French Treasury, 21 April 1919, NA, Treasury, RG39/142.

previously that American credits would cease with the signing of a peace treaty, but the special provisions for cotton and cereals ensured that the most fundamental needs of Italy and France would continue to be met for a few more months.

The note was delivered during the heated discussion of the Adriatic question in the Council of Four. Just two days later, Wilson's appeal to the Italian people provoked a crisis in US–Italian relations. However, all the evidence suggests that high politics had no overriding influence on financial decision-making. The tone and content of the US notes to France and Italy were almost identical. Moreover, it is clear that the US Treasury had planned to take this action at least since the beginning of April.[65] The evidence also suggests that Wilson took only mildly retaliatory action against Italy in financial affairs in the days after Sonnino and Orlando left the Peace Conference. On 6 May, Wilson instructed Davis to write to Carter Glass, who had taken McAdoo's place as Secretary of the Treasury, expressing his concern about recent newspaper reports that the US Treasury had extended new credits to Italy. Glass wrote back, explaining that the new credit appropriations were routine, and were merely meant to meet previous commitments: Wilson made no further objections.[66] On 22 May Davis recommended that an Italian request for a relatively modest sum to finance the expenditures of Italian expeditionary forces in Macedonia and Corfu out of the US credit for neutral countries be turned down, on political grounds; but at the same time he reaffirmed US commitments to provision Italy.[67] During the same period, J. H. Nixon, the acting head of the British Treasury's "A" Division, during Keynes's presence at the Peace Conference, asked the Chancellor whether the current political situation called for a change in financial policy *vis-à-vis* Italy: the answer was negative.[68]

Nevertheless, the Italian authorities remained convinced, presumably correctly, that a total rupture with the Allies and the United States would signify the end of financial and material assistance. Stringher wrote several long admonitory letters to Orlando to this effect.[69] On 2 May Stringher warned Orlando that Italy's economic dependence on the United States was so profound that a break in relations, or even action that would provoke the cessation of US lending, could not be considered:

> The United States, for a variety of reasons, has become our principal supplier of raw materials, agricultural produce, and other products; our

[65] Rathbone to Davis, 15 April 1919, NA, Treasury, RG39/142.
[66] Davis to Glass, 6 May 1919; Glass to Davis, 10 May 1919, NA, Treasury, RG39/142.
[67] Davis to Wilson, 22 May 1919, NA, Treasury, RG39/142.
[68] Nixon to Gower, 29 April 1919, PRO, T-files, T1/12367/35324/19.
[69] Stringher to Orlando, 22 April 1919; Stringher to Orlando, 2 May 1919; Stringher to Orlando, 7 June 1919, ASBI, Carte Stringher, 21/304/1/01.

economy is therefore very closely tied to that Confederation [sic]. A restriction of credit could be pregnant with consequences that would go beyond merely financial matters. But I want to hope that we will be saved from such a calamity, and that ongoing negotiations, however difficult, will come to a happy conclusion . . .[70]

Stringher and other Italian officials were in any case convinced that the dispute with Wilson impeded their efforts to negotiate new loans with private American banks. Norman Davis and other US Treasury officials had realized as early as the previous winter that continental Europe would need additional credits from the United States after the projected termination of government lending in the second half of 1919. To this end, in late April, Italy and other European governments were encouraged to make arrangements with private American bankers for fresh loans. Stringher oversaw the formation of an Italian banking consortium, consisting of the three issue banks, and the four largest commercial banks, to negotiate with American financial institutions. He was inclined to attribute the failure of these talks in mid-1919 to the Adriatic controversy, and it is not impossible that the administration discouraged American bankers from taking any action at the height of the Fiume crisis.[71] However, Stringher underestimated the extent to which American bankers declined to take up Italian government loans for economic, rather than political reasons. The American economy was booming, and remunerative investment opportunities existed at home. More importantly, the US government was issuing long-term securities at attractive rates to refund the large floating debt built up during the war years: such securities were tax-exempt, whereas heavy taxes were assessed on foreign securities.[72] The leading US banks insisted that they would be unable to provide substantial financial assistance to Europe unless the Treasury guaranteed their loans; this the Treasury consistently declined to do.[73] Other countries were scarcely more successful in raising capital in the United States in 1919 than Italy. Britain and France issued bonds to refund debts they had contracted with private American firms prior to US intervention, but net British and French repayments exceeded new borrowing from private US financial institutions in 1919–20.[74] In the final analysis, the difficult readjustment of Italy's trade and international accounts in 1919 owed little to Fiume, and much to American and British reluctance to assume new financial burdens to assist continental Europe.

---

[70] Stringher to Orlando, 2 May 1919, ASBI, Carte Stringher, 21/304/1/01.
[71] Ibid.
[72] Lamont, "America's Financial Attitude Toward Europe."
[73] Parrini, *Heir to Empire*, p. 54.
[74] Lewis, *America's Stake in International Investments*, pp. 620–21.

Nitti as Prime Minister: new efforts to negotiate loans with the Allies (July–August 1919)

In international affairs, Nitti's overriding concern on assuming office in June 1919 was to resolve the Adriatic conflict, so as to reestablish the diplomatic preconditions for new loans from the United States and Britain.[75] The new Italian Prime Minister was convinced that economic readjustment in the absence of further US and British lending was too difficult and too traumatic to be considered a valid policy option. Nitti's unspoken assumption was that readjustment without external aid was incompatible with his domestic program of social reform and political opening to the mass Socialist and Catholic Parties. In Nitti's view, the resolution of the Adriatic question required territorial sacrifice, and Italy's room for diplomatic maneuver was narrowly circumscribed. In a telegram to Tommaso Tittoni, the new Foreign Minister, and leader of the Italian delegation in Paris, Nitti argued that Italy's economic weakness meant every delay merely weakened their diplomatic position: "With our economic resources resistance is a question of a few weeks, and every delay puts us in an inferior condition. We will be able to get less tomorrow than today, and less than that the day after, because everybody knows that our state of weakness is progressive."[76] Later Nitti advised his Foreign Minister that Italy stood before two alternatives: refusing to sign a treaty acceptable to the Americans, leading to famine and internal chaos, "with all of the foreseeable Bolshevik consequences"; or signing.[77] Tittoni agreed that the alternatives were stark: "For us it is truly a case of *force majeure*, hence we have to resolve the question at any cost."[78]

However, Tittoni and Nitti soon found themselves confronted with nearly the same dilemma that had brought down Sonnino and Orlando before them: Wilson was no longer prepared to accept any resolution of the Adriatic question that gave Fiume to Italy or made the eventual cessation of Fiume to Italy likely; and no Italian government could maintain the support of parliament and the core institutions of the state – the monarchy, the military, and the foreign policy establishment – without insisting on Fiume. Buoyed by American support, the Yugoslavs also became increasingly intransigent. Yugoslavia eventually got less from Gio-

---

[75] On Nitti's foreign policy see Paolo Alatri, *Nitti, D'Annunzio e la questione adriatica (1919–1920)* (Milan: Feltrinelli, 1959), pp. 318–19, and passim.
[76] Nitti to Tittoni, 23 August 1919, quoted in Alatri, *Nitti, D'Annunzio e la questione adriatica*, p. 148.
[77] Nitti to Tittoni, 12 September 1919, quoted in Alatri, *Nitti, D'Annunzio e la questione adriatica*, p. 173.
[78] Tittoni to Nitti, 11 September 1919, quoted in Alatri, *Nitti, D'Annunzio e la questione adriatica*, p. 172.

litti and Carlo Sforza in the summer of 1920, after Italy had suffered the
brunt of the readjustment crisis, than Nitti and Tittoni were prepared to
offer in 1919.[79] Meanwhile, Nitti's strategy was fundamentally flawed in
two respects: first, he assumed that a solution to the Adriatic question
satisfactory both to the United States and the elite of liberal Italy was
possible in 1919; and second he believed that resolution of the Adriatic
question would remove the only impediment to substantial new Italian
borrowing in Britain and the United States. In reality, British and American policymakers and bankers were unwilling to make substantial new
financial resources available to continental Europe under any circumstances, prior to general political, budgetary, and economic stabilization,
both at home and on the continent.

Even in the absence of a settlement in the Adriatic, Nitti sent Carlo
Schanzer, his Treasury Minister, to Paris and London in July to test the
prospects for new loans. The pretext for Schanzer's trip was the expiration
of the Anglo-Italian financial accord of 18 February 1919. According to
that agreement, Italy was to have received approximately £st. 30m. in fresh
credits through June 1919; if payments to British government departments for previous purchases on Italy's behalf substantially reduced the
amount available for new purchases below £st. 30m., the British Treasury
had promised to consider lending new sums to make up the difference.
The Italian Treasury calculated that they could expect an additional
£st. 7m. under the terms of the agreement. In addition, Schanzer hoped to
win the British Treasury's support for an Italian government loan from
private financial institutions in London. On his way to London, he also
arranged to meet with US government officials, and Edward R. Stettinius,
of J. P. Morgan & Co., to discuss private American loans.

Schanzer arrived in Paris on 23 July, and conferred with Stettinius and
Hermann Harjes, a senior partner of Morgan, Harjes & Co., the affiliate
of J. P. Morgan & Co. in Paris. Giuglielmo Marconi and Angelo Pogliani,
President and General Director of the Banca Italiana di Sconto respectively, were also present at this meeting, underscoring the close connection
of the *banca italianissima* with the Nitti administration. Schanzer and
Pogliani emerged from these discussions full of optimism about the
possibility of arranging a substantial loan, and there is no doubt that
the Morgan bank had a strong interest in Italian business. Thomas
Lamont, a senior Morgan partner, was Treasurer and cofounder of the
Italy–America Society, which had been established during the war as
an association of American businessmen interested in developing ties to

[79] See, René Albrecht-Carrié, *Italy at the Paris Peace Conference* (New York: Columbia
University Press, 1938), pp. 288–89.

Italy.[80] Stettinius who had headed Morgan's purchasing bureau for the Allied governments prior to US intervention, was now charged with developing a scheme for financing US exports to Europe. The Morgan partners were evidently impressed with the Italian delegation's proposals, as Stettinius noted that among the ex-Allies, Italy alone had developed a clear and acceptable program for expenditure of new American loans.[81] However, Stettinius counseled against making substantial commitments in Europe for the time being, arguing that Morgans would be ill-advised to risk substantial investments without explicit US Government guarantees.[82] At the same time, in order to maintain good relations with the Italians, Stettinius convinced them that Morgans was very interested in arranging a loan, but was prevented from doing so by the US Treasury, which had issued a temporary injunction against private lending to the ex-Allies.[83] Such an injunction actually did exist: it was prompted by a British reconstruction loan to Belgium, which stipulated that the proceeds be spent within the Empire. At more or less the same time, the British Treasury was selling Treasury notes in New York, leading US Treasury officials to charge that Britain was borrowing in the United States in order to consolidate an unfair trade advantage in Europe.[84] Unaware of the background of the US Treasury's policy, the Italians immediately concluded that the injunction was directed against Italy, and was tied to the Fiume controversy. Nitti wrote to Tittoni: "I have begun to wonder if the US government's prohibition of private lending to Italy, apparently for domestic reasons, isn't really a form of economic pressure, designed especially to damage Italy."[85] Nitti instructed his Foreign Minister to raise the issue directly with Frank Polk, who now headed the US delegation in Paris. To the probable surprise of Italian officials, Polk expressed concern about Italy's supply situation and offered to support the Italian request for credits to cover necessary purchases over the next three to four months. He further recognized that a scheme would have to be developed to give Italy new long-term credits over a period of up to three years to cover its balance of payments deficit

---

[80] On Lamont's role in the Italy–America Society see, Harvard University Business School, Baker Library, Lamont Papers, Series 1, 42/14–18.

[81] Stettinius to Henry Lockhart (of Goodrich Lockhart Co.), 26 July 1919, quoted in John Douglas Forbes, *Stettinius Sr.: Portrait of a Morgan Partner* (Charlottesville: University of Virginia Press, 1974), p. 112.

[82] Stettinius and Harjes to J. P. Morgan & Co., 25 July 1919 (forwarded by Lamont to the US Treasury), NA, Treasury, RG39/142.

[83] Pogliani to Stringher, 24 July 1919, Archivio Storico, Ministero degli Affari Esteri, Affari politici, 1919–30, Italia 1270/5337; Schanzer to Nitti, 25 July 1919, Archivio Centrale dello Stato (hereafter ACS), Archivio Nitti, VI/49/162.

[84] Tittoni to Nitti, 5 August 1919, ACS, Archivio Nitti, VI/49/160/1. See also, Parrini, *Heir to Empire*, pp. 49–50.

[85] Nitti to Tittoni, 5 August 1919, ACS, Archivio Nitti, VI/49/160/1.

with the United States.[86] True, in a subsequent conversation, Polk insisted that the United States government expected Italy to resolve its territorial dispute with Yugoslavia, and substantially reduce military expenditure, in exchange for new American loans. Tittoni concluded after this meeting that further negotiations with US bankers prior to the resolution of the Adriatic dispute would be not only fruitless, but even harmful.[87] It is evident, however, that Italian officials consistently overestimated the importance of the political dispute as an impediment to new borrowing in the United States, and consistently underestimated the importance of economic factors.

Meanwhile, Schanzer travelled on to London. His reception there was rather warm, reflecting the British desire to mend relations with Italy, after the confrontation with the Orlando government, and perhaps also Lloyd George's personal esteem for Nitti (see below).[88] Schanzer signed a financial agreement with Chamberlain on 8 August 1919 that gave him most of what he had requested. Britain agreed to make available fresh credits of £st. 7m., confirming the earlier promise of a total of approximately £st. 30m. in fresh credits for the period after 1 February 1919. Italy's previous debts to Britain would continue to be rolled over, by the renewal of Italian sterling Treasury bills as they fell due, until the end of June 1920. In addition, the British Treasury agreed to make no objection to the Italian government's borrowing privately on the London market.[89]

In arranging private loans, however, Schanzer found the going tougher. Brian Cokayne, the Governor of the Bank of England, and Montagu Norman, the Deputy Governor, raised objections to foreign lending in London while the pound was weak and the domestic economy overheated.[90] Schanzer returned to the Treasury, attempting to persuade the government to overrule the Bank's veto. The Treasury reiterated its support for Italian borrowing in London, but in reality it was behind the Bank of England's embargo on foreign lending.[91] Schanzer sought out the directors of merchant banking firms with old ties to the Italian government, including Hambros. The English bankers showed little disposition to make substantial loans to Italy; however, in order to maintain their long-standing ties to the Italian Treasury, they offered to accept

[86] Tittoni to Nitti, 5 August 1919, ACS, Archivio Nitti, VI/49/160/1.
[87] Tittoni to Nitti, 14 August 1919, ACS, Archivio Nitti, VI/49/160/1.
[88] Schanzer to Nitti, 1 August 1919, ACS, Archivio Nitti, VI/49/162.
[89] Bank of England, archive, C40/215 1586/4.
[90] Schanzer to Nitti (forwarded by Imperiali), 6 August 1919, ACS, Archivio Nitti, VI/49/162; Bank of England, archive, Norman's Diary, entry for 7 August 1919. Norman wrote: "E. Hambro as to £st. 10 mil. Italian 3 yr. Treasuries to be placed privately among Banks. Alas!"
[91] See, John Atkin, "Official Regulation of British Overseas Investment, 1914–1931," *Economic History Review*, 2nd ser., 23 (1970), no. 2, pp. 324–35.

£st. 5m.–10m. in 3-year Italian Treasury bonds, denominated in sterling. The banking syndicate would receive the bonds at 0.97, interest would be 5%, with a commission of 1.5%. Thus the Italian government would pay a net interest of 6.7%, but Schanzer pointed out that British Treasury bills were at 5.5% and concluded: "everything considered, I think affair opportune."[92] Schanzer believed the matter settled, when a key bank withdrew from the English syndicate on 12 August, bringing his efforts to naught.[93] Unbeknownst to Schanzer, Eric Hambro had written to Chamberlain the day before, asking whether the Treasury looked with favor on the affair. Hambro made clear his own lack of enthusiasm for the loan, noting that, "my firm's close association with all matters connected with Italy made it impossible for me to refuse."[94] Chamberlain's reply was so cool that Hambro evidently decided to withdraw his offer. The Chancellor reproduced the relevant clause of the Anglo-Italian financial agreement signed four days before and added:

> It must of course be clearly understood that any arrangements which are concluded between the Italian Government and lenders in this country will be on ordinary commercial lines upon the sole credit of the Italian Government or Italian undertakings and that His Majesty's Government is not prepared to accept any financial responsibility either directly or indirectly.
>
> Subject to this I have much pleasure informing you that, in accordance with the Clause in the Agreement quoted above, His Majesty's Government will raise no objection to the completion of such an arrangement as you describe . . .
>
> In no case could Italy contemplate their [the proceeds of the loan] use for the purpose of giving general support to the lira exchange.[95]

Schanzer was left with no choice but to return to Rome, having secured fresh credits of only £st. 7m., in accordance with the provisions of the Anglo-Italian agreement of 18 February, and a one-year grace period for repayment of British government loans.

Soon after Schanzer's return from Paris, Italy was shaken by a series of crises that undermined not just the government, but also the foundations of the liberal state. On 12 September Gabriele D'Annunzio occupied Fiume with renegade army units. Admiral Enrico Millo, the commander of Italian armed forces in the Adriatic, assumed a mediating role between D'Annunzio and Nitti. For the first time in the history of unified Italy, a civilian government was faced with the insubordination of its armed forces. The impossibility of reaching a settlement to the Adriatic question

[92] Schanzer to Nitti, 8 August 1919, ACS, Archivio Nitti, VI/49/162.
[93] Ceresa to Nixon, 12 August 1919, PRO T-files, T1/12367/35323/19.
[94] Hambro to Chamberlain, 11 August 1919, PRO, T-files, T1/12367/35323/19.
[95] Chamberlain (drafted by Nixon) to Hambro, 12 August 1919, PRO, T-files, T1/12367/35323/19.

satisfactory both to the United States and to the core institutions of the Italian state was rendered fully apparent.

Meanwhile, Nitti called new parliamentary elections in November. They were held under the universal male franchise which Giolitti had pushed through parliament in 1911. In contrast to the elections which Giolitti "made" in 1913, Nitti refrained from using strong-arm tactics to intimidate voters in southern districts. Instead of the old system based on single member constituencies, Nitti had induced parliament to approve a new electoral law, creating larger electoral districts and proportional representation; now voters cast their ballots for a party or an electoral slate, rather than individual candidates. The result was a "Caporetto for the liberals": the socialists increased their parliamentary delegation from 52 to 156 seats; the newly founded Partito Populare captured 100 seats (29 deputies elected in 1913 described themselves as Catholics); while deputies describing themselves as liberals, democrats, radicals, reformists, republicans, etc. were reduced collectively from 427 to 252.[96] It was now impossible to form a government majority against the combined forces of the socialists and Catholics. Social and labor unrest, which had subsided somewhat after violent protests and strikes in June and July, reached a new apex in January 1920. The confidence of domestic and foreign investors was shaken, and exchange rates and state security prices plummeted.[97]

The sixth war loan

The sixth national loan of January 1920 was a response to Italy's first major post-war financial crisis. As British and American credits ran out in the final months of 1919, the full burden of grain and coal imports fell on the Italian exchange. For domestic political reasons, the Nitti government felt it could not terminate the bread subsidy, and the government role in food purchasing and distribution actually increased. Despite the demobilization of the army and the liquidation of war contracts, public spending remained extremely high. At the same time, Nitti's efforts to impose new taxes were stymied. The government felt it could not adopt the Meda tax reform project drawn up during the war, because broad

---

[96] The figures are taken from, Christopher Seton-Watson, *Italy from Liberalism to Fascism, 1870–1925* (New York: Methuen, 1967), p. 549. Roberto Vivarelli analyses the membership of the Chamber of Deputies elected in November 1919 exhaustively in, *Storia delle origini del fascismo. L'Italia dalla grande guerra alla marcia su Roma*, vol. II (Bologna: Il Mulino, 1991), pp. 160–92 and passim.

[97] Alatri, *Nitti, D'Annunzio e la questione adriatica*; Roberto Vivarelli, *Il dopoguerra in Italia e l'avvento del fascismo (1918–1922)*, vol. I, *Dalla fine della guerra all'impresa di Fiume* (Naples: Istituto Italiano per gli Studi Storici, 1967); Paolo Frascani, *Politica economica e finanza pubblica in Italia nel primo dopoguerra (1918–1922)*, (Naples: Giannini, 1975).

sectors of public opinion, outraged at the huge wealth transfers engendered by the war economy, considered it too mild. The main features of the Meda project were a mildly progressive personal income tax, a modest wealth tax, and a thorough reform of tax assessments. Instead, the government assembled a committee of financial experts including economists Luigi Einaudi and Attilio Cabiati, and the director of the Finance Ministry's bureau of direct taxes, Pasquale D'Aroma, to draw up a project that presented taxpayers with a choice between a drastic capital levy and a forced loan at only 1%. In addition, a permanent wealth tax was to be imposed. News of the proposed new taxes leaked out to the business community in late September or early October 1919, at about the same time that the exchange crisis became grave. Stock and bond prices plummeted, and business interests mounted concerted opposition to the government's proposed financial measures.[98]

In effect, the tax proposals of the Nitti administration would have imposed an intolerable burden on many industries. The government had encouraged audacious expansion during the war, and many businesses were now having difficulty adjusting to post-war market conditions. The evidence suggests the far more modest taxes ultimately approved by Nitti and Giolitti in 1919–21 created serious difficulties for many industries. Nitti faced a classic financial crisis: he could not reduce expenditure, particularly for the bread subsidy, without risking the withdrawal of political support by the left. On the other hand, he could not raise taxes to a level that would have satisfied public opinion and stabilized the budget without endangering the forced industrial expansion he had supported during the war.

Sensitive to the needs of industry, Nitti agreed to abandon the proposed capital levy for a voluntary loan at 2.5%–3%. As the industrialists and bankers regained confidence, they pressed the government to raise the interest rate on the loan to 5%. In its final version, the loan was a relatively attractive investment. It was a 5% perpetual, like the fourth and fifth loans, and the issue price was 87.5. Special advantages were offered for the conversion of medium and short-term Treasury securities. As had been the case in 1918, the National Insurance Institute offered to accept the loan at par for new life insurance policies. Nitti set a fantastic subscription goal of Lit. 20bn.

In effect, Nitti sought to avoid the difficult financial dilemmas of late 1919 by reproducing the political extravaganza of the fifth national loan on a far greater scale. Attilio Cabiati, perhaps the most progressive of his economic advisers, denounced government policy and withdrew from the advisory committee:

[98] Frascani, *Politica economica*, pp. 224–29.

After much reflection, I do not believe in the efficacy and the results of the loan, as it is being set up . . .

When I think about the measures that you want to propose, and confront them with the financial situation as it is, I cannot rid myself of the impression that it is purely and simply a political measure. Political measures are the responsibility of the ministers, who enact them with the assistance of their functionaries, but they have nothing to do with a technical adviser, who may want to retain his independence of judgment.[99]

It must have been clear to both government officials and the business community that the loan would lead to another round of private borrowing against the new security with predictable inflationary consequences. Referring to conversations with Milanese bankers, Cabiati reported as much to Schanzer in early November:

these bankers in turn will have the energy to induce their bigger clients to make large subscriptions to the loan. With my rather brutal frankness I asked them if this were the case, to which they responded affirmatively: but when I asked them if they would buy the new loan seriously or in jest, to hold on to it, or to use it as collateral for loans with the banks, they shrugged their shoulders. Probably they couldn't do otherwise.[100]

Again Nitti mobilized a massive publicity campaign to support the loan. There were the usual speaking tours, newspaper articles and advertisements, and patriotic sermons from the pulpit. Even Cabiati promised to support the loan publicly, "without reservations."[101] Central bank pressure on bankers and industrialists was pushed to new extremes. Subscriptions totaled Lit. 8,759m. in cash, Lit. 5,578m. in ordinary Treasury bills, and Lit. 3,393m. in medium-term Treasury securities. The total nominal issue of the new loan was Lit. 20,591m. Nitti had achieved his political victory, but the financial results of the loan were dubious. The commercial lending operations of the issue banks mushroomed by a factor of 2.4 between the beginning of November 1919 and June 1920. The commercial note circulation increased by 87% over the same period, and total note circulation increased by 39%. Bachi's wholesale price index climbed from 558 to 775; it had reached 856 in April.[102] Even an official publication of the Association of Joint Stock Companies and the Confindustria, Italy's largest employer organization, characterized the loan as, "grandiose, but in part fictitious."[103]

[99] Cabiati to Schanzer, 8 November 1919, ACS, Archivio Schanzer, 5/30/2.
[100] Cabiati to Schanzer, 4 November 1919, ACS, Archivio Schanzer, 5/30/2.
[101] Cabiati to Schanzer, 26 November 1919, ACS, Archivio Schanzer, 5/30/2.
[102] Bachi, *L'Italia economica 1920*, p. 143.
[103] Associazione fra le società italiane per azione, and Confederazione generale dell'industria italiana (sezione economica), *Note sulla situazione economica dell'Italia* (Rome: Athenaeum, 1921), p. 187, quoted in Frascani, *Politica economica*, p. 300.

In return for so much inflation – in addition to the burden of servicing the new debt – the government had obtained only a brief financial respite. Nitti was unable to utilize a part of the loan to retire currency notes issued on account of the state as he had hoped. The budget deficit swallowed the proceeds of the loan and the government soon was constrained to issue new 3-year and 5-year Treasury bonds. After the sixth loan, further long-term security issues prior to genuine financial stabilization were out of the question. The issue banks could no longer sustain the market value of 5% securities, which plummeted to Lit. 77.96 by the end of June.

Attolico's financial mission to the United States

Even though D'Annunzio's *coup de main* in Fiume ended any hope for a rapid settlement of the Adriatic question, Nitti made new inquiries about raising a loan in the United States. Indeed, to the extent that Nitti still had a strategy for coming to grips with the post-war crisis, it was predicated on securing substantial new loans from Italy's former Allies. For some time Britain and France had been issuing Treasury bonds denominated in dollars on the New York market to refinance old debts, and the Italian government asked whether the US Treasury was disposed to consent to a similar Italian issue.[104] On 23 September, Rathbone replied affirmatively: evidently Schanzer's talks with the Morgan partners and Polk in Paris had convinced US officials that Italy's need for fresh credits was real, and should be supported, political differences notwithstanding. However, Rathbone also warned the Italian government of the potential disadvantages of their proposal, given the high interest rates prevailing in New York:

> I think it is important that the utmost care should be taken that a transaction of this character, which I understand does not involve a very considerable sum, should not by its terms injure the credit of Italy in this country and make it more difficult in the future for your Government, if it should decide to do so, to negotiate a larger financial transaction here except upon onerous terms.[105]

Needless to add, Rathbone's letter is further evidence of the primacy of economic as opposed to political impediments to substantial Italian borrowing in the United States.

Nitti decided to use the occasion of the International Commercial Conference in Atlantic City in October to dispatch a special economic mission to the United States. The moment seemed auspicious for negotiating new loans. A major topic of discussion at the Atlantic City meeting

---

[104] Alliata to Rathbone, 20 September 1919, NA, Treasury, RG39/142.
[105] Rathbone to Alliata, 23 September 1919, NA, Treasury, RG39/142.

was a proposal championed by Sen. Walter Edge, authorizing American banks and manufacturing firms to form joint ventures that would make long-term loans to European countries and issue debentures on the American capital market. The proposal would also authorize the War Finance Corporation, a Federal agency, to purchase up to 10% of the debentures of an Edge Corporation, giving such bonds an imprimature of government approval.[106]

Nitti chose Bernardo Attolico to head the Italian delegation. After the Commercial Conference, he was to remain in the United States as Minister Plenipotentiary to arrange the Treasury bond issue, and, if possible, more substantial loans from Edge Corporations. In addition to being a close associate of the Prime Minister, Attolico was well acquainted with leading American bankers and Treasury officials through his work on Allied supply committees during the war, and as a technical representative at the Peace Conference. He was well received in America. Paul Cravath commended him to Russell Leffingwell, Assistant Secretary of the Treasury, in glowing terms:

> Crosby and I came to look upon him as a real friend as well as an official associate. He had a better understanding of American and Americans than any Italian we met. He thinks and speaks our language, and he can accomplish more than any man I know in bringing about a satisfactory understanding between his government and ours as to economic and financial matters.[107]

However, despite the sympathy that Attolico elicited in banking and business circles, and despite the passage of the Edge Act in December, American investors held back from making substantial commitments in Europe. Although several Edge Corporations were formed in early 1920, no substantial credits to European countries were arranged.[108] Attolico was constrained to confine his activity to a relatively modest issue of Treasury bonds.

The issue was to follow subscriptions to the sixth Italian National Loan, which was also offered in New York (in lire). Nitti hoped that a spectacular success of the domestic loan would bolster the confidence of foreign investors, and create a favorable climate for Attolico's loan. However, neither the sixth national loan, nor the Treasury bond issue was particularly successful in the United States. The lira, which had been weak on the

[106] Gidoni to Stringher, 27 October 1919, ASBI, fondo 3, bob. 2, pr. 4. See also, Parrini, *Heir to Empire*, pp. 79–82; Frank Costigliola, *Awkward Dominion: American Political, Economic, and Cultural Relations with Europe, 1919–1933* (Ithaca: Cornell University Press, 1984), pp. 35–36.
[107] Cravath to Leffingwell, 15 October 1919, NA, Treasury, RG39/142.
[108] Parrini, *Heir to Empire*, pp. 79–100; Costigliola, *Awkward Dominion*, pp. 35–36.

exchange markets since March 1919, fell precipitately in late January 1920. A contributing factor was a speech by Glass, in which he excluded further US government loans to Europe, and advised American investors that the US government accepted no responsibility for new foreign issues they might purchase on the New York market.[109] The collapse of the lira discouraged subscriptions to the sixth national loan among Italian emigrants in the United States. Only 15% of the total foreign subscriptions to the loan, or about Lit. 309m., stemmed from North America, despite the presence of the largest and most affluent Italian emigrant colony there.[110]

Attolico's loan was designed to appeal both to emigrants unwilling to risk investments denominated in lire and to the broader American investing public. It consisted of 5-year Treasury bonds issued in denominations ranging from $50 to $5,000. Interest was 6.5% and the issue price was 97.5%. Bank commissions brought the effective price for the Italian government to 6.8%. Attolico had authority from the Italian parliament to issue up to $100m. in bonds, but US Treasury officials urged him to confine his offer to $25m., so as to avoid compromising the Italian government's credit in the event of a mediocre market response.[111] The bonds were issued in early February, approximately one month after subscriptions to the sixth national loan had opened. The Treasury bonds were sold by the New York agencies and affiliates of the Banco di Napoli, the Banca Commerciale, the Credito Italiano, and the Banca di Sconto. Only $11.3m. of the bonds were taken up.[112] The failure of the loan reflected the tightness of the New York credit market. Nitti had Attolico stay on in New York through the spring, in the hope that the financial situation might improve, but it proved impossible for Italy to raise more capital in New York.

Nitti at Whitehall and San Remo

While Attolico was in New York, Nitti himself took the lead in pursuing financial negotiations in London. Nitti attempted to exploit his rather warm personal relationship with Lloyd George to secure new loans for Italy in Britain. The British and Italian Prime Ministers' mutual esteem

[109] Alfred P. Dennis (US Commercial Attaché, Rome) to Bureau of Foreign and Domestic Commerce, Department of Commerce, 17 February 1920, NA, Treasury, RG39/142.

[110] Frascani, *Politica economica e finanza pubblica nel primo dopoguerra*, p. 297.

[111] Davis to Attolico, 15 January 1920, NA, Treasury, RG39/142.

[112] Attolico, circular memo announcing loan, 6 January 1920, NA, Treasury, RG39/142; Gidoni to Stringher, 11 January 1921; Stringher to Antonio Monzilli (Editor, *Economista dell'Italia moderna*), 16 February 1921, ASBI, fondo 3, bob. 2, pr. 4; Lewis, *America's Stake in International Investment*, p. 641.

dated from Nitti's visits to the British capital as Minister of the Treasury during the war. In early 1920 the two politicians were united by the common conviction that European recovery required moderating reparations claims on Germany, and reintegrating Russia into the world economy.[113] Nitti would discover, however, that his support for British diplomatic positions was insufficient to overcome the lack of enthusiasm of British investors for Italy, or overcome the Bank of England's ban on new foreign capital issues.

In mid-January Nitti paid a quick visit to London, accompanied by Dante Ferraris, his Minister of Industry, Commerce, and Labor, to talk with British Treasury officials and London bankers.[114] In mid-February Nitti returned to London, officially in order to participate in preparatory discussions among British, French, Belgian, and Italian representatives for the international monetary conference later convened in Brussels, and unofficially to press his requests for sufficient credits to at least finance Italy's requirements of British coal and tonnage for the rest of 1920. Nitti's February visit coincided with the closing phase of the Italian national loan drive, and the Prime Minister emphatically insisted that a great success on the domestic loan was necessary to bolster his negotiating position in London.[115] But, unfortunately for Nitti, his arrival in London coincided with the collapse of the lira on the exchange markets, which tended to erase any favorable impression the nominal success of the loan might have produced.

Nitti met with other Allied representatives at Whitehall on 23 February, in a session devoted to inflation. The Italian delegation took the position that the high prices pervasive in Europe were the consequence of the disequilibrium between consumption and production; consequently, it saw the primary remedy as being in the revitalization of Europe's productive apparatus; which in turn required adequate provisioning of essential raw materials, including coal. Significantly, in opposition to all of the other delegations, the Italians argued that increases in the money stock were a secondary factor in causing inflation.[116] The unorthodox monetary policy espoused by the Italian government rationalized its reluctance to alienate the mass socialist and Catholic political parties by cutting welfare expenditure, but it was unlikely to attract the sympathy of British investors.

On the same day, Nitti privately presented a proposal for a loan, by a

[113] Barbagallo, *Nitti*, p. 356, and passim.   [114] Ibid., p. 364.
[115] Nitti to Schanzer, 13 February 1920; Nitti to Schanzer, 20 February 1920, ACS, Archivio Nitti, VI/26/95/13.
[116] "High Prices," conference in Whitehall, 23 February 1920, memos of British, French and Italian delegations, ACS, Archivio Nitti, VI/25/93/13.

syndicate of British banks to a syndicate of Italian banks, to finance raw materials imports from Britain and the Empire. The Italian banks would issue 12-month bills, which would be renewable. As the object was to set Italian industries going again, "it [seemed] vital to have assurance that the financing of purchases will be maintained at least during three or four seasons."[117] Nitti found little sympathy in London for loans based on the assumption that his country would be unable to pay for basic raw materials imports for at least a year, and possibly much longer. Although British officials evidently reiterated their *nulla osta* to Italian borrowing in London, the informal ban of the Bank of England on foreign lending, which was supported, and indeed promoted by the Treasury, remained in force. British merchant bankers were even more adamant in refusing to consider lending to Italy than they had been in their discussions with Schanzer the previous summer. Lord Norman's diary bears the following entry on 26 February:

> Revelstoke [i.e. Lord Revelstoke, the former John Baring, of Baring Bros., and a Director of the Bank of England] tells us of visit from Schurter [?] yesterday pleading for advance in any form of at least £st. 20m. to *Italy* [Norman's emphasis]. Wd. R. join other Banks? Wd. he urge Treasury to assist? Wd. he persuade G. to smile on the scheme? Answer was absolute refusal – on a/c of our poverty & inflation.[118]

Nitti returned to Rome at the beginning of March with empty hands, to face an increasingly unruly parliament and country. His first government fell almost immediately thereafter. Although he was able to form a new ministry and win a vote of confidence in mid-March, his hold on parliament was clearly weakening.[119]

Despite the unfavorable prospects for foreign loans, Nitti renewed his efforts to persuade the British government to make financial concessions. The San Remo Conference in April seemed to offer a new opportunity to turn Italy's support for Britain's foreign policy to financial advantage; Lloyd George would need Italian backing to overcome French resistance to moderating Allied claims on Germany, and renewing commercial relations with Russia. In effect, Lloyd George signaled his willingness in early April to consider any proposal that Italy might make to stabilize exchange rates.[120] On 12 and 14 April, Schanzer, now Minister of Finance, and Luigi Luzzatti, the aging economist who served as Minister of the Treasury in Nitti's second cabinet, held new discussions with Edward Capel Cure, the British commercial attaché in Rome. Schanzer predicted catastrophe in

---

[117] Memo, unsigned, 23 February 1920, ACS, Archivio Nitti, VI/49/160/2.
[118] Bank of England, archive, Norman's diary, 26 February 1920.
[119] Barbagallo, *Nitti*, pp. 364–70.
[120] Nitti to Luzzatti, 3 April 1920, ACS, Archivio Nitti, VI/49/162.

the absence of further British loans. He told Capel Cure that Italy was on the verge of bankruptcy and revolution because of the high cost of coal, grain, and other basic imports. Germany and Austria were already in political chaos, and if the trouble spread to Italy, it would undoubtedly envelop France and Switzerland too. It was in Britain's interest, he suggested, that Italy's problem of coal shortages and falling exchange rates be addressed. Capel Cure forwarded this information to the Foreign Office without proffering his own opinion. He noted however, that any new credits would have to come from the British government, as the London banker who had negotiated with Schanzer in August 1919 (Eric Hambro must have been meant) had recently told him that the City would probably not entertain any proposals from Italy until the bread subsidy had been abolished, and other improvements in government finances had been achieved. Capel Cure may have given the last bit of intelligence to Schanzer as well; in any case, the Minister of Finance insisted in his first interview with Capel Cure that the government was considering the abolition of the bread subsidy.[121] Nitti was unable to obtain greater concessions from Lloyd George at San Remo. In reply to an appeal for new credits of £st. 25m. delivered personally by Nitti at the Conference, the British Prime Minister merely replied that the Italians could tell London bankers that the British government looked favorably on their efforts to raise money in London; he added, however, that the money market was very tight, and even British municipalities were paying over 6% for medium-term loans.[122]

The fall of the lira, and the "Defense of the Currency" Decree

The lira registered its most prolonged and dramatic decline on the exchange markets during the entire war and post-war period in the first four months of 1920. In January the lira stood on average at 13.99 to the dollar and 51.60 to sterling; in April the average figures were 22.94 and 90.42 respectively. Even against the French franc the lira fell from 120.51 to 142.40. The lira was vulnerable to erratic fluctuations because of the large holdings of Italian currency built up by exporters in countries with relatively stable currencies during the war and post-war years. Particularly after the termination of Allied credits in the latter half of 1919, foreign exporters accepted payment in lire for goods shipped to Italy, lira balances which they or their conationals retained in the hope of making a specula-

---

[121] Capel Cure to George Buchanan (British ambassador to Rome), 12 April 1920; Capel Cure to Buchanan, 14 April 1920, PRO, T-files, T1/12551/19122/20.

[122] Nitti to Lloyd George, 27 April 1920; Lloyd George to Nitti, 21 May 1920, ACS, Archivio Nitti, VI/49/160/2.

tive profit following the expected rise and stabilization of the Italian currency. These large foreign lira balances were now thrown on to the exchange markets, as it became clear that new credits in favor of Italy would not be forthcoming; as political and social unrest in the Italian peninsula increased; and as alarm about the inflationary consequences of Nitti's financial policies grew. Italian Treasury and central bank representatives abroad insisted on the political aspects of the crisis of confidence of foreign holders of lira balances: in New York, Gidoni noted that one considered the Italian political and economic situation to be worse than that of France; and in London Ceresa concluded that political factors were largely responsible for the lira's persistent decline.[123]

As a response to the crisis, Schanzer and Nitti prepared a decree, "in defense of the currency," in February, that would have prohibited Italian exporters from accepting the depreciated currencies of East Central Europe in payment. The decree reflected a concern shared by Bank of Italy officials that the boom in exports to countries with severely depreciated currencies, which had commenced shortly after the lifting of the Allied blockade in March 1919, was actually damaging, rather than improving Italy's balance of payments. Stringher had pointed out as early as June 1919 that Italy was unable to purchase badly needed raw materials and foodstuffs from hard currency areas with the German marks and Austrian crowns earned through exports to East Central Europe. Much like American holders of lire balances, Italian holders of balances of severely depreciated currencies kept them in the country of origin, in the hope of appreciation and stabilization, only to throw them on the exchange markets at a loss in periods of political crisis. At the same time, Stringher pointed out, Italian manufactures sold against payment in severely depreciated currencies often required raw material inputs from hard-currency areas.[124] By the beginning of 1920, Schanzer and Nitti concluded that if such transactions were allowed to continue, the lira would be dragged down inexorably with the mark and the crown.[125]

A recent study of the German inflation suggests that Stringher's reasoning was essentially correct, even if the fears of the Bank of Italy and the Treasury with regard to the impact of East-Central European hyperinflation on the stability of the lira may have been exaggerated.[126] In any event,

---

[123] Gidoni to Stringher, 6 February 1920, ASBI, fondo 3, bob. 2, pr. 4; Ceresa to Schanzer, 11 February 1920; [?Ceresa] to Schanzer, 22 February 1920, ACS, Archivio Schanzer, 4/24/2.

[124] Memo, 28 June 1919, unsigned [but evidently prepared by Stringher for Schanzer, his successor at the Treasury], ACS, Archivio Schanzer, 4/24/2.

[125] Schanzer to Nitti, 17 February 1920, ACS, Archivio Schanzer, 4/24/1; Schanzer to Nitti, undated [but from shortly after the above], ACS, Archivio Nitti, VI/26/95/13.

[126] Carl-Ludwig Holtfrerich, "Amerikanische Kapitalexport und Wiederaufbau der deutschen Wirtschaft 1919–1923 im Vergleich zu 1924–1929," *Vierteljahrsschrift für Sozial-*

the proposed legislation provoked a major confrontation between the government and business interests associated with the Banca Commerciale Italiana. The premier Italian commercial bank was aggressively expanding its presence in East Central Europe by founding subsidiaries and buying into existing banks. Manufacturing firms associated with the Commerciale, notably in the textile sector, had taken advantage of the post-war paralysis of German export industries to expand their market share in that region. The Commerciale rejected any attempt by the state to regulate its foreign business. Cabiati, who was doing consulting work for the Commerciale at the time, wrote to Schanzer:

> I don't understand how the bureaucracy thinks it can decide which currency our exporters should be paid in, and establish what a "useful currency" is: does anybody exist who wants to be paid in an "useless" currency? If a currency is useful, it is so in "any market": directly, or through arbitrage. This is not theory, Excellency, it is experience pure and simple, which I have made by watching, for example, how my friend Sig. [Leo] Goldschmidt, of the "Commerciale" maneuvers on the exchange markets.[127]

Given Nitti's relationship with the rival Banca Italiana di Sconto, the Commerciale leadership must have concluded that the decree was directed specifically against them.[128] Significantly, the Nitti government was involved at the time in intensive negotiations with the Banca di Sconto to form an Italo-Russian export bank, a project which must have appeared as an alternative scheme for developing Italy's trade with Eastern Europe.[129]

The second "Escalade" on the Banca Commerciale and Nitti's fall

While Italy was awash in liquidity due to the issue of the sixth war loan, and the government was skirmishing with the Milanese banks, the Bansconto–Ansaldo group was buying up shares of the Banca Commerciale quietly, in order to take control of the rival institution at the shareholders' meeting in late March. The Ansaldo group had emerged from the war far and away the country's largest industrial enterprise, with

---

und Wirtschaftsgeschichte, 64 (1977), pp. 497–529; Holtfrerich, *Die deutsche Inflation, 1914–1923. Ursachen und Folgen in internationaler Perspektive* (Berlin: de Gruyter, 1980), pp. 277–98.

[127] Cabiati to Schanzer, 19 February 1920, ACS, Archivio Schanzer, 5/30/2. On the Banca Commerciale's activities in East-Central Europe see, Bachi, *L'Italia economica 1920* pp. 82–83; and on its activities in Austria, Eduard März, *Austrian Banking and Financial Policy: Creditanstalt at a Turning Point* (London: Weidenfeld and Nicolson, 1984), pp. 358, 444, 462–65.

[128] Anna Maria Falchero, "Il gruppo Ansaldo–Banca Italiana di Sconto e le vicende bancarie nel primo dopoguerra," in Peter Hertner and Giorgio Mori, ed., *La transizione dall'economia di guerra all'economia di pace in Italia e in Germania dopo la prima guerra mondiale* (Bologna: Il Mulino, 1983), pp. 543–71.

[129] Barbagallo, *Nitti*, p. 374.

over 100 factories, and a workforce which exceeded 100,000 at its peak. Not surprisingly, the group experienced particular difficulty coping with the winding up of state contracts, and readjusting to a market economy. By the second half of 1919, Ansaldo had long since used up the proceeds of its massive, unprecedented share capital issue for Lit. 400m. in the spring of 1918. The Bansconto's exposure to the firm had reached alarming proportions, and the bank's director, Angelo Pogliani, felt compelled to limit new advances to his largest industrial client. As in 1918, the group sought to escape from this difficult situation by taking control of the Comit, and thereby gaining access to its considerable resources. It seems hardly coincidental that this second "escalade" on Italy's largest commercial bank was undertaken during Nitti's tenure in office; nor that it took place at a time of exceptionally liberal issue bank credit, on account of the sixth war loan.[130]

In early March an open battle for control of the Milanese bank erupted on the stock exchange, with the price of Commerciale shares rising from Lit. 1,250 on 4 March to Lit. 2,450 on 9 March. The newspapers controlled by the rival groups engaged in bitter polemics, with the old accusations of German or foreign domination of the Comit, and disloyalty to Italy's national interests being resurrected. At this juncture, the Perrone brothers announced they held over 200,000 out of a total of 520,000 Comit shares, which almost certainly would have given them control of the shareholders' meeting on 30 March.

The Comit's directors took two measures to thwart the Perrones. First, they demanded that the government suspend the so-called *diritto allo sconto*, i.e. a law which allowed a stock purchaser to demand immediate consignment upon payment for shares which had been bought on time contract. Evidently, the Perrones had bought substantial shares on time contracts, which would have fallen due after the shareholders' meeting. Nitti, however, refused to alter the law, arguing that this would amount to taking sides in the dispute between the two groups.

Secondly, the Comit's directors proposed raising the share capital of the bank. Evidently they assumed that the Perrone brothers and the Bansconto–Ansaldo group, already overextended because of Comit stock purchases, would be unable to participate in the new stock issue. This measure was approved over the objections of Nabor Soliani, Ansaldo's representative on the board of the Comit, in a meeting on 9 March.[131] However, the

---

[130] On Ansaldo see, Thomas Row, "Economic Nationalism in Italy: The Ansaldo Company, 1882–1921," Ph.D. dissertation, Johns Hopkins University (1988). On the "escalade" see, Falchero, "Il gruppo Ansaldo–Banca Italiana di Sconto"; Piero Sraffa, "The Bank Crisis in Italy," *Journal of Economic History*, 32 (1922), no. 126, pp. 178–97.

[131] Banca Commerciale Italiana, Archivio Storico (hereafter ASBCI), Consiglio d'Amministrazione, verbali, 9 March 1920.

new stock issue had to be approved by the shareholders' meeting, and thus the advantage seemed to remain with the Perrones.

Why the Perrones came to a new agreement with the directors of the Commerciale on 11 March, and why a few days later they agreed to cede 200,000 Comit shares to a newly constituted holding company, the Consorzio Mobiliare Finanziario, in which their rivals acquired a controlling interest, has remained a mystery until this day. It has been suggested that the Bansconto was heavily overextended through advances to the Perrones to purchase Comit shares, and that it could not keep such enormous sums locked up until the shareholders' meeting on 30 March.[132] Pogliani, in any event, took the leading role in patching together an agreement, evidently against the wishes of the Perrones. Nitti seems to have supported Pogliani's efforts as well, and presumably the agreements contained provisions envisaging the sort of "bank cooperation" the Prime Minister had long espoused.

In compensation for abandoning their attempt to gain control of the institution, the Perrone brothers were elected to the Comit's Board, with Pio becoming Vice-President. The Perrones made a substantial profit through the sale of their Comit shares. The "friends of the Banca Commerciale" were to be compensated for the losses they sustained in defending the institution against the Perrones by receiving part of the new stock issue at a discount. Whether or not the Perrones received additional commitments regarding financing for Ansaldo is unclear. At the shareholders' meeting on 30 March, Pio Perrone had only laudatory words for Giuseppe Toeplitz and the Banca Commerciale. The only discordant voice at the meeting was that of a Turinese lawyer named Umberto Turletti, who accused both groups of benefiting from stock market speculation at the expense of the minority shareholders.[133]

By early May, however, the two groups had fallen out again, and the newspapers resumed their attacks and counter-attacks. The Perrone brothers accused the Comit's directors of violating the agreements reached in March, a charge which the Nittian *Finanza Italiana* echoed.[134] Whatever the March agreements may have entailed, Ansaldo received no relief from its financial troubles. Indeed, after the resumption of polemics between the Commerciale and the Perrones in May, Toeplitz drew up a plan for liquidating the bank's existing credits to Ansaldo. The Perrones' positions on the board of the Commerciale were declared forfeit.[135] In the

[132] Sraffa, "The Bank Crisis in Italy," p. 183.
[133] On Turletti see, Anna Maria Falchero, *La Banca Italiana di Sconto, 1914–1921. Sette anni di guerra* (Milan: Angeli, 1990), pp. 199–200.
[134] "Gli aumenti di capitali nel 'Credito' e nella 'Commerciale,' " unsigned, *Finanze Italiana*, 22 May 1920.
[135] ASBCI, Consiglio d'Amministrazione, verbali, 28 May 1920; 2 July 1920.

absence of external support, the collapse of the Bansconto–Ansaldo trust was now a forgone conclusion.

Moreover, the leaders of Italy's most powerful bank were convinced that Nitti had aided and abetted their rivals, and they were determined to oust him from power. According to his own testimony, it was the Banca Commerciale that engineered the collapse of his third, and final ministry in early June. Nitti met with two Board members of the Commerciale, Ettore Conti and Lorenzo Allievi, on 4 June. In his memoirs, Nitti states that the two bankers insisted a dramatic measure was necessary to restore domestic and foreign confidence in Italy's public finances, and suggested that he immediately abolish the bread subsidy. In return, the two bankers supposedly promised to prevail on their industrial clients to increase workers' pay. Two days later, Nitti's final government fell on a bill submitted to the Camera which envisaged the abolition of the bread subsidy. According to Nitti's account, the Commerciale mounted every effort to gather votes against the proposal.[136]

Whatever the role of the Banca Commerciale in Nitti's fall, the decision of the PPI's parliamentary delegation to vote against him was clearly crucial. The Catholic party expressed its willingness to support the abolition of the bread subsidy, but only if Nitti approved new taxes on the well-to-do.[137] The vote underscored the Prime Minister's inability to maintain his parliamentary majority, and, at the same time, win the confidence of the domestic and international business communities. Likewise, his failure to secure new loans in the United States and Britain in early 1920 demonstrated that further foreign assistance could not be relied upon to ease the strains of readjusting foreign trade and the balance of payments.

---

[136] F. S. Nitti, *Rivelazioni. Dramatis personae* (Naples: Edizioni scientifiche italiane, 1948), pp. 49–51, 543–44. See also, Barbagallo, *Nitti*, pp. 397–98; Falchero, "Il gruppo Ansaldo–Banca Italiana di Sconto nel primo dopoguerra"; Gerardo Padulo, "Sui rapporti tra gli industriali ed il governo Nitti (23 giugno 1919 – 9 giugno 1920)," *Nuova rivista storica*, 60 (1976), no. 516, pp. 591–618.

[137] Gabriele De Rosa, *Il Partito Populare Italiano*, 2nd rev. ed. (Bari: Laterza, 1988), p. 39.

7

FROM GIOLITTI TO MUSSOLINI:
MONETARY AND FINANCIAL
STABILIZATION, AND POLITICAL COLLAPSE

The collapse of Nitti's third ministry in June 1920 sharply diminished the prospects of a liberal reformist solution to Italy's post-war crisis. Nitti saw himself as the *homo novus*, the liberal statesman most qualified to carry out Giolitti's project of a grand compromise between the Italian masses and the institutions and elites of the liberal state in an environment radically changed by the war.[1] In contrast to Giolitti, his former mentor, Nitti had not burned his bridges to Italy's old elites by embracing neutralism on the eve of Italian intervention. Although not a fervent interventionist, he justified Italy's declaration of war *ex post facto*, and played an active political role during the period of hostilities: as a member of the Italian mission to the United States in 1917, and as Minister of the Treasury 1917–18. In retrospect it is clear that Nitti's war loan of 1918 was largely ineffective, but in the public mind it associated him with the national resistance and recovery in the dark months after Caporetto. Almost alone among the leading Italian politicians, he fully appreciated the importance the United States was likely to assume in post-war European economic and political affairs. Moreover, Nitti developed a vision, however flawed, of how the prodigious economic machine created by the war could be transformed into an engine of post-war prosperity, creating the material basis for the grand compromise between Italy's masses and its elites.

In Nitti's judgment, Giolitti was a man of the past, and even historians sympathetic to the Piedmontese statesman have echoed this view about his post-war political career.[2] Giolitti was seventy-seven when he formed his fifth and final ministry in 1920. He had been associated with neutralism in 1915, and he reiterated his condemnation of the manner in which Italy had

---

[1] Brunello Vigezzi, "Introduzione," in, Olindo Malagodi, *Conversazioni della guerra, 1914–1919* (Milan/Naples: Ricciardi, 1960), vol. I, p. liii.

[2] On Nitti's opinion of Giolitti, see Malagodi's notes of a conversation with Nitti on 10 January 1918 in, *Conversazioni della guerra*, vol. II, p. 260; Francesco Barbagallo, *Nitti* (Turin: UTET, 1984), pp. 298–303. For a critical judgment of Giolitti's post-war government by admirers see, A. William Salamone, *Italy in the Giolittian Age: Italian Democracy in the Making* (Philadelphia: University of Pennsylvania Press, 1960), pp. 154–66; Nino Valeri, *Giovanni Giolitti* (Turin: UTET, 1971), pp. 309–10, and passim.

intervened in the war in his famous speech in Dronero during the electoral campaign of October 1919. Despite his status as a senior statesman, this estranged him from the monarchy, the military, and the foreign policy establishment, whose prestige was bound up closely with the war. It also rendered him ill-suited to develop a positive interpretation of the wartime sufferings, privations, and exertions of Italy's masses. Giolitti tended to see the social, economic, and political changes brought about by the war as an impediment, rather than a catalyst for reform. He doubted that America would effect an enduring change in the European balance of power, and he was altogether skeptical that financial aid from Britain and the United States would ease Italy's reconstruction. After taking office, he quickly moved to improve relations with Paris, as a counterweight to London and Washington, as a means of levering Italy out of the Fiume morass. He was also dubious about the value of wartime industrial expansion, and more inclined to see the disadvantages of large budget deficits, inflation, and foreign indebtedness. In brief, whereas Nitti saw the war as an opportunity, Giolitti saw it as a disaster. Nevertheless, Giolitti's political stature made him the only liberal reformist alternative to Nitti, and ensured that his success or failure to gain control of the post-war crisis would have fateful consequences.[3]

The major turning point in the post-war crisis, the transition from the *biennio rosso* (red years) to the *biennio nero* (black years) occurred during Giolitti's ministry. In September 1920, two months after he assumed office, the month-long occupation of metal and engineering factories began, marking at once the high point of post-war labor unrest, and the beginning of the left's decline. In the winter of 1920–21 the fascist squads undertook their first "punitive expeditions" against union headquarters, cooperatives, and socialist municipal officials in rural areas. By the time Giolitti's government fell in late June 1921, a fascist state-within-a-state was coming into being in much of north-central Italy, with the connivance of local and central government authorities, including Giolitti himself and his Minister of Defense, Ivanoe Bonomi. Giolitti's two successors as Prime Minister prior to the March on Rome, Bonomi (July 1921–February 1922), and Luigi Facta (February–October 1922), were figures of lesser political stature, they were hampered by weak parliamentary support, and the growing strength of the fascists in the provinces, and they undertook no important new political initiatives. But the story of post-war labor

---

[3] On Giolitti's preoccupation with foreign debts see, Malagodi's notes on interviews on 7 October 1918, and 23 November 1918, *Conversazioni della guerra*, vol. II, pp. 408–12, 455–58; see also Giovanni Giolitti, *Memories of My Life* (New York: Fertig, 1973), pp. 385–87; his Dronero speech is published in, *Discorsi extraparlamentari* (Turin: Einaudi, 1952), pp. 294–327. On relations with France see, Carlo Sforza, *L'Italia dal 1914 al 1944 quale io la vidi*, 2ed ed. (Rome: Mondadori, 1945), pp. 75–76, 102.

unrest, and the rise of fascism has been told elsewhere and need not concern us here.[4] What is important to stress in the context of this study are the economic problems confronting Giolitti and his successors, and the significance of their choices in this area in shaping the outcome of the political and social crisis.

On taking office in June 1920, Giolitti faced much the same dilemma in economic policy as his predecessor Nitti – how to achieve financial and monetary stabilization without alienating the mass political constituencies that were now crucial to maintaining a stable parliamentary majority; and like his predecessor, Giolitti's policies alienated and infuriated both the left and the right. But taken as a whole, Nitti on the one hand and Giolitti and his two successors on the other, tended to fall on opposite sides of the liberal reformist dilemma: Nitti had been reluctant to reduce social spending, for fear of alienating the reformist left and the Catholics, and thereby incurred the wrath of conservatives and business interests; Giolitti reduced social spending, notably by abolishing the bread subsidy, but he lost the support of the Catholics, ushering in a period of chronic parliamentary instability that persisted until Mussolini's March on Rome. To some degree, Giolitti's choices were shaped by changes in the post-war business cycle. About the time he took office, the boom in Britain and America broke, and raw material prices and shipping tariffs began to fall. This reduced the cost of imported food and made the elimination of government subsidies during the winter of 1920–21 less painful for consumers than it would have been earlier. Moreover, by late fall and early winter, Italian manufacturers began to feel the impact of the post-war recession, with its predictable dampening effects on employment and labor militancy. But the shift in policy was due as much to Giolitti's temperament and judgment as to change in the business cycle. The aging Piedmontese statesman assigned higher priority to financial and monetary stabilization than to cultivating the political support of the mass parties. Bonomi and Facta essentially followed this line, which was widely supported by liberal elites, aghast at the militancy and effrontery of the socialist unions and leagues during the *biennio rosso* and the spectacle of Don Sturzo, a Catholic priest, leading a mass political party, whose support was now crucial for liberal governments. Giolitti and his successors made substantial progress toward financial and monetary restoration, but at the cost of parliamentary paralysis, and ultimately, of institutional crisis.

[4] On the post-war unrest and the rise of fascism see, Gaetano Salvemini, *The Origins of Fascism in Italy*, ed. Roberto Vivarelli (New York: Harper and Row, 1973); Angelo Tasca, *Nascita e avvento del fascismo*, 2nd rev. ed. (Florence: La Nuova Italia, 1950); Adrian Lyttleton, *The Seizure of Power: Fascism in Italy 1919–1929*, 2nd ed. (Princeton: Princeton University Press, 1987); Paul Corner, *Fascism in Ferrara, 1915–1925* (Oxford: Oxford University Press, 1975); Anthony Cardoza, *Agrarian Elites and Italian Fascism: The Province of Bologna, 1901–1926* (Princeton: Princeton University Press, 1982).

Changes in financial policy

Giolitti's cabinet quickly demonstrated impatience with the policies of Nitti in three key areas: it dismantled Nitti's system of state fiscal monopolies and economic controls; it restrained borrowing by municipal and provincial governments, many of which were controlled by socialists and Catholics; and it terminated the government's intimacy with the Banca Italiana di Sconto–Ansaldo trust, cultivating instead better relations with the rival Banca Commerciale Italiana.

As Minister of the Treasury in 1918, Nitti had created a web of state monopolies of commodities, as a means of rationing scarce supplies and foreign exchange, and as a means of collecting turnover taxes. Because of the lack of competent state personnel, the monopolies often were administered by consortia of the firms using or importing the commodities. The monopolies proved cumbersome and inefficient both at allocating resources, and at collecting taxes, while liberals attacked the system as a prelude to the cartelization of the economy, and the mechanism by which Nitti aimed to impose state *dirigismo*.[5] Soon after taking office, Giolitti presented legislation abolishing state controls on the sale of paper, wool, cotton, textiles, and footwear.[6] A few months later, Giovanni Battista Bertone, Giolitti's Undersecretary of Finance, prepared a memo which harshly judged Nitti's system of monopolies. He noted that the most important monopoly, on petroleum, had never functioned properly, remaining a dead letter from the beginning. Other monopolies, such as that on coffee, had involved consular personnel in the coffee business, against their own will and better judgment, and had hampered coffee exports from Trieste, once a major roasting and packaging center. The creation of consortia allowed the dominant firms to enhance their position against potential competitors. Bertone recommended the immediate dismantling of what remained of the monopoly system.[7] These steps towards deregulation were applauded by the business community, and anticipated the militantly *laissez-faire* economic program produced by Massimo Rocca and Ottavio Corgini for the Fascist Party in September 1922.[8]

Giolitti and his Minister of the Treasury, Filippo Meda, also acted quickly to force municipal and provincial governments to exercise greater

[5] Umberto Ricci, *La politica economica del ministero Nitti. Gli effetti dell'intervento economico dello Stato* (Rome: La Voce, 1920).
[6] Giancarlo Falco, "La politica fiscale dell'ultimo governo Giolitti (1920–1921)," *Rivista di storia contemporanea*, 11 (1982), no. 4, pp. 560–604, esp. p. 567. Note that even Nitti reluctantly concluded that such measures were necessary after the fall of his second cabinet.
[7] Giovanni Battista Bertone, memo, 20 December 1920, ACS, Carte Giolitti, B32/F100.
[8] On the Fascist Party's liberal economic program in September 1922 see, Renzo De Felice, *Mussolini il fascista*, vol. I, *La conquista del potere, 1921–1925* (Turin: Einaudi, 1966), pp. 330–32.

fiscal restraint. On 25 June 1920, Meda noted that local government authorities had become increasingly reliant on advances from the issue banks against future tax revenues to cover budget shortfalls. He suggested that the new government indicate its opposition to such practices, a recommendation which Giolitti unhesitatingly accepted.[9] This shift in government policy would have far-reaching political consequences over the next two years. Since the fall of 1919, municipal and provincial administrations controlled by socialists and Catholics had been expanding social services and public works projects. By reducing their opportunities to borrow, the state constrained local authorities to increase taxes. Not surprisingly, socialist and Catholic administrations sought above all to raise revenue through property and consumption taxes that fell mostly on the well-to-do. By the spring of 1922, this fiscal pressure led to a full-scale taxpayers' revolt across the red and white belts of north-central Italy; a tax revolt which coincided with the final fascist offensive against socialist and Catholic local and provincial administrations.

There is considerable evidence that the Bansconto–Ansaldo trust on the one hand, and the Comit and Credit groups on the other, were backing different political horses at the time of the transition from Nitti to Giolitti. Giovanni Agnelli of Fiat, a member of the board of the Credito Italiano, telegraphed Giolitti on 11 June 1920 to express his confidence in, "the only man who can solve the grave crisis the country is undergoing."[10] Giuseppe Toeplitz of the Banca Commerciale wrote to Giolitti on 26 June placing himself and his bank at the disposal of the government and its program of reconstruction, an initiative which is all the more extraordinary given Giolitti's draconian and unworkable tax proposals and his plan to abolish bearer securities (see below).[11] No such communications on the part of the Perrone brothers appear among Giolitti's papers. In fact, a few days earlier Pio Perrone paid a visit to the French embassy in Rome, where he pleaded with Charles Roux, the chargé d'affaires, to use his influence to block the formation of a Giolitti government. Roux responded that the French government did not intervene in the internal affairs of Italy.[12] In late July, Pio Perrone felt obliged to write to the Prime Minister denying that he or his brother had initiated a press campaign against the government. Perrone also indicated that he awaited the outcome of the parliamentary commission's investigation of Ansaldo with full

[9] Meda to Giolitti, memo, 25 June 1920, ACS, Presidenza del Consiglio, 1920, 6/1.
[10] Agnelli to Giolitti, 11 June 1920, published in, Giovanni Giolitti, *Quarant'anni di politica italiana. Dalle carte di Giovanni Giolitti* (Milan: Feltrinelli, 1962), no. 301, pp. 274–75.
[11] Giuseppe Toeplitz to Giolitti, 26 June 1920, *Quarant'anni di politica italiana*, no. 303, p. 278.
[12] Barbagallo, *Nitti*, p. 400.

confidence, an affirmation which rather suggests the opposite.[13] In early August, Meda informed Giolitti that his investigations suggested the Bansconto directors had supplied misleading and negative information to English newspapers about the government's financial proposals, in order to stimulate the opposition of foreign investors.[14] Whether or not the story is true, it is indicative of the distrust of the Bansconto in government circles.

Meanwhile, the new government asked the director of the Comit's Latin American subsidiary, the Banque Italo-Française de l'Amerique du Sud, to negotiate a loan on behalf of the Italian government in Argentina.[15] Significantly, the Nitti government had assigned a pre-eminent role to the Bansconto's Brazilian office in negotiations for a similar loan in that country in the spring, against the protests of the Comit.[16]

Falchero suggests that Bonaldo Stringher and the Bank of Italy began to apply pressure on the Ansaldo–Bansconto group after Giolitti's accession to power. Stringher seems to have been preoccupied with the group's financial stability, and he may well have taken advantage of the changed political climate to apply pressure on the Perrones to dislodge them from the management of the Ansaldo, before the bankruptcy of that firm took the Bansconto down with it, endangering the entire financial system.[17]

Giolitti's financial proposals

Like Nitti before him, Giolitti began his tenure as Prime Minister by proposing a series of drastic fiscal measures, designed to assuage public discontent with the war profiteers or "sharks," and to create a political climate in which deep cuts in social spending, especially in the bread subsidy, would be possible. In addition to a series of secondary measures, including increases in inheritance and wealth taxes, and a higher surtax on wine, Giolitti's fiscal package consisted of three key proposals: the total confiscation of war profits; the creation of a parliamentary commission to investigate (and revise) war contracts; and the registration of all bearer securities, except short-term Treasury notes. The latter measure was intended to prevent tax evasion. This fiscal package had already been

[13] Pio Perrone to Giolitti, 22 July 1920, *Quarant'anni di politica italiana*, no. 304, pp. 278–79.
[14] Meda to Giolitti, 10 August 1920, ACS, Presidenza del Consiglio, 1920, 9/x.
[15] Meda to Stringher (date?) June 1920, ASBI, fondo 3, bob. 1, pr. 1.
[16] Pietro Fenoglio (Administratore delegato of the Banca Commerciale Italiana) to Stringher, 8 March 1920, ASBI, fondo 3, bob. 3, pr. 7.
[17] Anna Maria Falchero, "Il gruppo Ansaldo–Banca Italiana di Sconto e le vicende bancarie nel primo dopoguerra," in, Peter Hertner and Giorgio Mori, eds., *La transizione dall'economia di guerra all'economia di pace in Italia e in Germania dopo la prima guerra mondiale* (Bologna: Il Mulino, 1983), pp. 543–71, esp. pp. 567–69.

outlined by Giolitti in his Dronero speech in October 1919. It meant once again postponing action on the Meda commission tax proposals in favor of more dramatic and allegedly more draconian measures.[18]

Giolitti's proposals were greeted with considerable skepticism. In parliament, the socialist deputy Giulio Casalini expressed his support for tough fiscal measures, but also his doubts that the government's proposals were workable. He also suggested that massive fiscal evasion would continue regardless of the new laws. Another socialist deputy, the ill-fated Giacomo Matteotti, who would be murdered by fascist thugs less than four years later, went further, accusing Giolitti of offering the Italian people only, "two or three miserable mirrors [such as] for [catching] larks"; and Filippo Turati, the leader of the reformist wing of the party, expressed a similar judgment. Even Francesco Perrone (no relation to Pio and Mario of Ansaldo), who had served as Undersecretary in the Finance Ministry under Nitti, raised questions about the seriousness of the government's financial proposals.[19]

Such doubts were well-founded. There were the pre-war precedents, in which Giolitti had proposed progressive tax legislation in order to curry favor with the left, while being fully aware that his measures stood no chance of being approved by parliament. And the Prime Minister explicitly acknowledged the political character of his proposals. In a Senate speech on 15 July 1920 Giolitti noted:

> The previous ministry – as the Senators know well – introduced a bill to increase the price of bread, with certain features to compensate the poorer classes. I believe that this bill would not have encountered such violent hostility if it had been preceded by legislation forcing the rich to pay as much as is in their power. When one saw that the rich had not yet been asked to pay that which they owed; that one hadn't demanded that those who made fortunes during the war give back their illicit gains; that a very high tax had not been placed on the inheritance of large fortunes; in sum that one had not yet demanded anything of the rich, and one had begun by demanding sacrifices from the poor – this explains the violent opposition which the bill encountered.[20]

[18] The best account of Giolitti's fiscal proposals is, Falco, "La politica fiscale dell'ultimo governo Giolitti." See also, Luigi Einaudi, *La guerra e il sistema tributario italiano* (Bari: Laterza, 1927).
[19] Giulio Casalini's opinion: *Atti del Parlamento Italiano.* Camera dei Deputati, Sessione 1919–1920, prima della XXV legislatura. Discussioni, vol. IV (Rome: Camera dei Deputati, 1920), 20 July 1920, pp. 3667–74, quoted in, Paolo, Frascani, *Politica economica e finanza pubblica in Italia nel primo dopoguerra (1918–1922)* (Naples: Giannini, 1975), p. 239. Matteotti's statement: Giacomo Matteotti, *Discorsi parlamentari. Pubblicati per deliberazioni della Camera dei Deputati* (Rome: Camera dei Deputati, 1976), vol. I, p. 46, quoted in, Falco, "La politica fiscale dell'ultimo governo Giolitti," p. 565. Turati and Francesco Perrone are referred to by Casalini.
[20] Giovanni Giolitti, *Discorsi parlamentari. Pubblicati per deliberazione della Camera dei Deputati*

Giolitti's primary motive, therefore, was to placate the constituencies of the mass parties, rather than to raise revenue. And while the socialists called into question his determination actually to implement the proposals, business spokesmen, and economists, including Luigi Einaudi in the *Corriere della Sera*, pilloried the fiscal package as ill-conceived and likely to cause grave economic damage.[21]

The total confiscation of war profits was the least realistic of Giolitti's proposals. The existing legislation, it will be recalled, defined war profits as profits in excess of an 8% return on invested capital since 1914, except for firms which had realized higher profits prior to the outbreak of war. The government now proposed to modify the law to confiscate retroactively all profits in excess of 8% from 1914 through 30 June 1920. Investments which had been deductible from the war profits tax – for instance in new shipbuilding capacity – now would be retroactively payable. As Einaudi and others were quick to point out, the bill violated the elemental principle that new taxes be imposed on current and future, but not on past income. Of course, manufacturers who had invested wartime earnings in new plant and equipment were hardly in a position to pay the tax from liquid assets. Moreover, not long after Giolitti's accession to power, the economic recession began, and the market value of fixed investments fell, making collection of the tax even less realistic than at the time it was proposed. In fact, in the course of 1921 many of the industrial firms that would have been most effected by the "confiscation" of war profits, including Ilva and Ansaldo, experienced severe liquidity problems, and were only kept afloat by rediscounting operations of their creditors, i.e. the big commercial banks, with the Bank of Italy.

A law envisaging the total confiscation of war profits was passed during the summer of 1920, but its language was vague, and collection of the tax was delayed until the Ministry of Finance developed norms for its implementation. Significantly enough, regulations to this effect were not unveiled until late March 1921, just prior to parliamentary elections. In May 1921, leading Italian industrialists met with Facta, the Minister of

(Rome: Camera dei Deputati, 1956), vol. IV, p. 1763, quoted in, Falco, "La politica fiscale dell'ultimo governo Giolitti," p. 564.

[21] Luigi Einaudi, "Le proposte del deputato," 29 May 1920; "I propositi del presidente del consiglio," 20 June 1920; "Economie difficili ed imposte insufficienti," 25 June 1920; "Nominatività, avocazione e controllo dei prezzi," 26 June 1920; "Il problema delle spese straordinarie," 29 June 1920; "Politica timida ed illusoria," 3 August 1920; "Le ritorsioni de 'La Stampa'," 6 August 1920; "Nominatività, avocazione ed inasprimenti di imposte non risolvono il problema," 24 September 1920; "Insoluto il problema del pane," 12 November 1920; "Continua il sistema delle sciabolate tributarie," 13 November 1920; "La caccia ai grossi guadagni," 19 November 1920; "Il raddoppiamento della rata della patrimoniale," 1 December 1920, all in *Corriere della Sera*, republished in *Cronache economiche e politiche di un trentennio (1893–1925)*, vol. V, *1919–1920* (Turin: Einaudi, 1961), pp. 754–96.

Finance, to voice their opposition to the law, suggesting that collection of the tax would ruin both them and the Italian economy.[22] The matter was still pending in June, when Giolitti's government fell, whereupon his successor, Bonomi, postponed further action on the war profits tax. Like the rest of Giolitti's financial proposals, the bill was laid to rest definitively after the March on Rome.

It is interesting to note that Giolitti's proposal to abolish bearer securities raised greater public furor than the "confiscation" of war profits. Both taxpayers and the government seem to have taken this measure more seriously. There was no question that evasion of the wealth and income taxes was widespread among the holders of stocks and bonds. And the example of Great Britain, where traditionally most securities had been registered, demonstrated that the proposed measure was not necessarily incompatible with a modern economy or an efficient capital market. Moreover, the second hostile take-over attempt against the Commerciale in the spring, and the questionable defensive measures taken by the Comit and Credit directors, whereby the two banks essentially came to own themselves, made a more transparent ownership structure in banking and industry seem desirable. Nitti had already imposed a 15% surtax on dividends to bearer securities in April. In order to encourage conversion, and a harsher law, which would have forbidden paying any interest or dividends on bearer stock and bonds, was to have taken effect on 31 July. This law was now withdrawn, however, as Giolitti proposed to eliminate bearer securities altogether.

The proposed law to eliminate bearer securities met with a storm of criticism from business circles. Einaudi took a discouraging view, focussing on the law's disruptive effects, and the limited revenues it was likely to produce, in his articles in the *Corriere della Sera*.[23] The stock and bond market collapsed, with the value of 5% war bonds falling from 85.14 in mid-May to 74.70 by mid-July. Giolitti succeeded in getting his bill through parliament on 24 August 1920, but the language of this bill too was exceedingly vague, and it was not to take effect until a bicameral commission came up with a plan for its implementation. Falco has pointed out recently that a proposal for converting bearer securities had been

[22] "Promemoria circa l'udienza concessa dal ministro delle Finanze, Facta, a Torino, ai rappresentanti l'industria nazionale," 4 May 1921, *Quarant'anni di politica italiana*, no. 341, pp. 336–38.

[23] In addition to the articles cited above see, Luigi Einaudi, "Cronologia sbagliata," 27 May 1920; "Nominatività e ribasso dei titoli in borsa," 13 July 1920; "Il frutto fiscale della nominatività," 25 July 1920, all in *Corriere della Sera*, republished in *Cronache*, vol. V, pp. 737–48; "A che punto siamo con la nominatività?," 12 January 1921; "Perché si deve discorrere della nominatività," 19 January 1921; "La sospensione del regolamento sulla nominatività," 19 August 1921, all in *Corriere della Sera*, *Cronache*, vol. VI, *1921–1922*, pp. 3–9; 293–98.

drawn up in April by Pasquale D'Aroma, the Director General of Direct Taxes in the Ministry of Finance; the reasons for the postponement were political, therefore, rather than technical.[24] The fall in the market value of securities persisted through the fall, aggravating the position of industrial firms suffering the first effects of the recession, and devaluing collateral for bank loans. Bonaldo Stringher now added his authoritative voice to the opponents of the law. In a letter to Filippo Meda, the Minister of the Treasury, on 27 October, Stringher warned, "Placing obstacles in the way of industry, which is making an effort to return to normal activity, would precipitate the worst possible outcome of the crisis which we are now experiencing."[25] Two weeks later, on 8 November, Stringher wrote an even more strongly worded letter to Giulio Alessio, the Minister of Industry and Commerce. He noted that 5% consolidated government bonds had fallen to 67.70 and suggested that many provincial savings banks including the largest one, the CARIPLO in Milan, would have difficulty filing their annual reports in December. Alessio reacted by proposing to Giolitti that at least the registration of state securities be postponed for a year.[26]

In the event, a decree containing norms for the registration of securities was only promulgated on 9 June 1921, in the waning weeks of the Giolitti ministry. It was promptly suspended by Bonomi after he took office, and the project was dropped altogether shortly after Mussolini took power. The third key element in Giolitti's financial package was the creation of a parliamentary commission to investigate war expenditures. War contractors were to be held financially liable for instances of fraud or wrongdoing exposed by the commission. Nothing practical ever came of the investigation, despite the historical value of the lengthy report eventually produced by the commission.[27] By the time the report went to the press, Mussolini had come to power, and the committee's activities were suspended.

But it is still worthwhile to ask what Giolitti had in mind by creating the commission. Evidently, he intended the parliamentary investigation as a forum for exposing the folly of the productivist ideologies espoused by Nitti and elements on the extreme right, including the nationalists, during and after the war. Presumably, the commission's activities would reveal that much of the enormous industrial expansion of the war years had been

[24] Falco, "La politica fiscale dell'ultimo governo Giolitti," p. 569.
[25] Stringher to Meda, 27 October 1920, appendix to, "Memoria dei rappresentanti delle quattro grandi banche e dell'Associazione bancaria italiana," undated, but probably from November 1920, *Quarant'anni di politica italiana*, no. 322, pp. 299–309.
[26] Stringher to Alessio, 8 November 1920; Alessio to Giolitti, 16 November 1920, *Quarant'anni di politica italiana*, no. 320, pp. 297–98.
[27] Camera dei Deputati, *Relazione della Commissione parlamentare d'inchiesta per le spese di guerra*, in, *Raccolta degli atti stampati*, 26.a legislatura, sessione 1921–1923, vol. 3 (*Documenti*), nos. 21–23 (Rome: Camera dei Deputati, 1923).

based on fraud perpetrated on the state and the public. It also gave Giolitti an instrument of pressure in negotiating state support for the restructuring of the iron and steel industry, as will be discussed below.

Giolitti's tax proposals failed to achieve the desired effects. Their technical deficiencies and draconian implications created turmoil on the stock market and unease in business circles, even as the government's reluctance to actually implement the proposals caused cynicism on the left. By making the tax proposals the centerpiece of his program, and pushing them in vaguely worded form through parliament in the summer of 1920, Giolitti bound his own political future to an unworkable project. In the parliamentary elections of May 1921, Giolitti felt obliged to reiterate his support for the tax proposals; indeed, as was noted above, the authorities took some half-hearted steps toward implementing the measures in the weeks before the election. But Giolitti only succeeded in alienating the business community. Abrate has demonstrated that business leaders were convinced by the spring of 1921 that Giolitti had to go, and one of their principal objections to him was his identification with an unacceptable and unworkable financial program.[28] Even after the fall of Giolitti's government in June 1921, his financial program continued to cast a shadow over liberal politics. One of the first acts of Bonomi, his successor, was to postpone any action on Giolitti's tax proposals, but neither he nor Facta had the political will to renounce them altogether. It was left to Mussolini to rescind formally the forced registration of bearer securities, cancel the confiscation of war profits, and dissolve the parliamentary commission investigating war profits, to the relief and approbation of the business community. And it was left to Mussolini's Finance Minister, Alberto De Stefani, to return finally to the recommendations of the Meda Commission, and carry out a thorough reform of the Italian tax structure.

The abolition of the bread subsidy

Just as the socialists had suspected and feared, Giolitti proved more determined to abolish the bread subsidy than to implement his tax proposals. His opportunity came during the winter of 1920–21. The left was demoralized by the onset of the industrial recession, the inconclusive outcome of the occupation of the factories in September, and by the explosion of rural *squadrismo* beginning in the late fall. Moreover, the price of grain on international markets had begun to fall in May 1920, with the onset of the world recession. If North American grain prices in dollars are given an index value of 100 for September 1919, they declined from 137 in

[28] Mario Abrate, *La lotta sindacale nella industrializzazione in Italia 1906–1926*, 2nd ed. (Milan: Angeli, 1967), pp. 341.

May 1920 to 75 in February 1921.[29] The government issued a decree that envisaged a gradual return to market prices for the sale of wheat to bakeries spread out over several months, beginning in February 1921. By the summer of 1921 grain sales were completely deregulated, and the only remaining cost to the government stemmed from bonuses to farmers.

The impact on state finances of the decline in international cereals prices first, and the abolition of the bread subsidy later, was very substantial. The confused record keeping of the grain consortia make it difficult to ascertain exactly how much the government lost on food subsidies, and during what period. An informant of J. P. Morgan & Co. in December 1920 estimated the cost of government subsidies at Lit. 7bn. during that year.[30] Riccardo Bachi estimated state losses at Lit. 8,351m. for the period July 1919 – October 1920. By contrast, Bachi estimated total government outlays for domestic grain bonuses in fiscal 1921–22 at somewhat more than Lit. 500m.[31] These figures must be compared with Einaudi's calculations for debt creation in fiscal 1919–20 (Lit. 13,118m.), 1920–21 (Lit. 13,514m.), and 1921–22 (Lit. 6,286m.).[32] Bread subsidies may have accounted for upward of half of the Italian state deficit during the Nitti and Giolitti ministries, and their elimination coincided with the first sharp post-war reduction in the budget deficit.

The recession and the restructuring of Ilva

Even while business organizations, including the Association of Italian Bankers, and the Confindustria (the national business organization) were attacking violently the government's tax proposals in public, privately commercial and central bankers, government authorities, and the managers of the country's largest iron and steelmaking concerns were negotiating the terms of a costly public rescue of most of Italy's heavy industry.[33]

[29] Elaborated from, Riccardo Bachi, *L'Italia economica nell'anno 1920* (Città di Castello: S. Lapi, 1921), p. 396, quoted in, Falco, "La politica fiscale dell'ultimo governo Giolitti," p. 596.

[30] "Italy's Social and Economic Difficulties," memo, signed G. J. W., Milan, dated December 1920, Harvard University Business School, Baker Library, Lamont Papers, Series IV, 190/11.

[31] Bachi, *L'Italia economica nell'anno 1920*, pp. 396–97; Riccardo Bachi, *L'Italia economica nell'anno 1921* (Città di Castello: S. Lapi, 1922), p. 322, quoted in Falco, "La politica fiscale dell'ultimo governo Giolitti," pp. 596–99.

[32] Luigi Einaudi, "Dove si tenta di calcolare il disavanzo del bilancio italiano," *Corriere della Sera*, 25 April 1923, *Cronache*, vol. VII, *1923–1924*, p. 212.

[33] Little is still known about the Ilva and Ansaldo–Banca di Sconto rescues, and the new documents that I have used in this study are scattered and incomplete. Therefore, only the barest of sketches of one of the most important chapters in Italy's economic history can be reconstructed here.

The international recession began to effect various branches of Italian industry between late spring and late fall of 1920. Consumer-oriented industries weathered the slump with comparative ease, although cotton and wool manufacturing were hurt by the rapid collapse of world prices of their raw materials in the spring, the consequent devaluation of their stocks, and the postponement of consumer purchases, in anticipation of substantial price reductions. Firms producing luxury goods, including automobiles, were also hurt as economic uncertainty caused sales of unnecessary items to lag. But it was heavy industry, and particularly the sectors which had been most profitable and had expanded most during the war, notably iron and steel making and shipbuilding, which were hurt most by the slump.[34] All the old problems of Italy's iron and steel industry – overcapacity, lack of comparative advantage, dependence on imported fuel, overreliance on state contracts, subsidies and tariff protection – exacted their toll. Moreover, the two largest firms, Ilva and Ansaldo, had utilized war profits for aggressive expansion: Ilva by buying up mining, shipbuilding, and shipping firms, and of course newspapers; Ansaldo by doing all of this in addition to a pharaonic program of investments in new plant and equipment. The high cost of shipping and imported coal during 1919 and early 1920, together with irregular and insufficient coal deliveries, had prevented these two firms from fully participating in the post-war boom. Their smaller domestic competitors, which produced steel with electric-powered Siemens-Martins furnaces from scrap iron, were more successful than the two giants with their open-hearth furnaces, and their reliance on coking coal and iron ore. Beginning in the summer of 1920, Ilva and Ansaldo had to contend in addition with the industrial recession, and the collapse of the stock market in the wake of Giolitti's financial proposals. Inevitably, the financial difficulties of the big iron and steel firms compromised their creditor banks, leading to a major financial crisis.

The analysis of quantitative data on issue bank commercial credit in the second half of 1920 and the first half of 1921 provides scant indication of the stress on the financial system during those months. The total volume of issue bank credit crept upwards slowly, after much more rapid expansion during the issue of the sixth war loan (see Figure 1, Appendix, p. 328). Interest rates also remained relatively stable, with the average interest rate of central bank rediscounting operations rising only from 4.97% in 1919 to 5.69% in 1920, and 5.83% in 1921.[35] But the examination of Bank of

---

[34] The best sources of information on the post-war slump in Italy are still Bachi, *L'Italia economica nell'anno 1920*, pp. v–xii, 209–35, and passim.; and Bachi, *L'Italia economica nell'anno 1921*, pp. v–xi, 193–223, and passim.

[35] Banca d'Italia, *Adunanza generale ordinaria degli azionisti, tenuta in Roma il giorno 30 Marzo 1922* (Rome: Banca d'Italia, 1922), p. 75.

Italy and government documents reveals a far different picture. Rather than raising interest rates substantially, both the commercial banks and the issue banks sought to improve their liquidity positions by rationing credit; and, as was typical in Italy in such situations, it was not the most solvent or profitable firms which benefited from rationing, but rather firms which were so large and so indebted to the banking system that their failure would be likely to induce panic.

There is evidence of tightening on the credit markets beginning in July 1920. On 11 July, Enrico Flores, the prefect in Milan, confidentially informed Giolitti that the major commercial banks were refusing to renew loans, creating something of a panic. The immediate cause of the credit squeeze was the stock market collapse, which in turn had been caused by Giolitti's announcement that bearer securities would be abolished.[36] On 26 July Stringher informed the Consiglio Superiore of the Bank of Italy that he had issued a circular letter to the branches asking them to exercise the utmost restraint in approving new loans.[37] The financial situation of heavy industry deteriorated further in the fall, reaching crisis proportions in the wake of the metalworkers' strike, in late October and early November. On 24 October Stringher informed the Select Committee (Comitato) of his Consiglio Superiore that he had asked Bank of Italy branch managers to "severely" examine loan requests, and to reject those of unfamiliar clients; habitual clients were to be "persuaded" to reduce their indebtedness to the Bank, and to refrain from seeking new loans, "within just and equitable limits."[38] Three days later Stringher wrote the letter to Meda mentioned above, alerting him to the difficulties facing industry, and by extension the issue banks, and urging that the government keep this in mind in formulating financial policy; and on 8 November Stringher issued his warning to Alessio, the Minister of Industry and Commerce, that the collapse of securities values would create problems even for the savings banks in filing their annual reports. By the latter half of November, Stringher reported to his Comitato that the situation had improved somewhat, although he admitted that the Bank of Italy's rediscounting operations were being utilized by manufacturing firms to distribute dividends (on non-existent profits) at the end of the year.[39]

It appears that the Bank of Italy's assistance in keeping the Ilva and Ansaldo trusts afloat in the winter of 1920–21 was related to far-reaching negotiations between the government and the issue banks on one hand,

---

[36] Flores to Giolitti, 11 July 1920, memo, riservata, ACS, Presidenza del Consiglio, 1920, 6/1.
[37] ASBI, Fondo 9.2, Consiglio Superiore, verbali, 26 July 1920.
[38] ASBI, Fondo 9.2, Presidenza e Giunta del Consiglio Superiore riunite in Comitato (hereafter Comitato), verbali, 24 October 1920.
[39] ASBI, Fondo 9.2, Comitato, verbali, 21 November 1920.

and the commercial bankers and steelmen on the other, regarding the restructuring of the sector.[40] An agreement with only one of the two iron and steel giants, Ilva, issued from this first round of talks. Ilva had fallen under the control of a triumvirate of speculators, Max Bondi, Arturo Luzzatto, and Cesare Fera, during the winter of 1917–18. Bondi and his associates, all of whom had long been board members of Ilva, deposed Attilio Odero as executive director of the firm in the shareholders' meeting in March 1918. Odero enjoyed the confidence of the Banca Commerciale Italiana and the Credito Italiano, and this had been the most essential qualification for office at Ilva prior to the war. However, war profits allowed the firm to repay its bank debts, reducing the commercial banks' influence. In fact, huge cash reserves permitted Bondi and his associates to embark on a feverish campaign of corporate acquisitions beginning in 1918. On the one hand, Ilva's new leadership strove for vertical integration by buying up mining facilities "upstream"; and engineering, shipbuilding and shipping firms "downstream"; on the other hand, they bought up newspapers: to acquire insurance against adverse publicity, and to create a base for Max Bondi's political career. The steelman-turned-financier had himself elected to the Chamber of Deputies in 1919, allegedly as a independent socialist![41]

But for Bondi and his associates, the advent of the recession spelt the beginning of the end. Growing liquidity difficulties forced Ilva to turn to the commercial banks for new loans in 1920. Giuseppe Toeplitz was determined to repay the Bondi-Luzzatto-Fera triumvirate for their 1918 *coup de main* by ousting them from Ilva. The Comit, the government, and the Bank of Italy seem to have reached an agreement regarding the financial restructuring of Ilva in late February, whereupon Bondi and his associates were induced to tender their resignations. Toeplitz replaced them with Attilio Odero, and a young engineer enjoying the confidence of Odero and the bank, Arturo Bocciardo.

The agreement with the government committed the Comit, and Ilva's other creditors, including the Credito Italiano, to substantial financial

---

[40] The economist Attilio Cabiati reported the existence of such talks in an article in the socialist newspaper *Avanti!* on 5 December 1920. The "bourgeois" newspapers that Cabiati generally wrote for, *La Stampa*, and *Il Secolo*, evidently demurred from publishing news of the negotiations, which the government and the Bank of Italy were at pains to keep secret. Cabiati to Einaudi, 5 December 1920, Fondazione Einaudi, Turin (hereafter FE), Carte Luigi Einaudi, Carteggio. See also, Bachi, *L'Italia economica nell'anno 1920*, p. 210.

[41] The following account of the rescue of Ilva is based largely on, Antonia Carparelli, "I perché di una 'mezza siderurgia.' La società Ilva della ghisa e il ciclo integrale negli anni Venti," in Franco Bonelli, ed., *Acciaio per l'industrializzazione. Contributi allo studio del problema siderurgico italiano* (Turin: Einaudi, 1982), pp. 3–158. On Max Bondi's career see, Franco Bonelli, and M. Barsali, "Max Bondi," *Dizionario Biografico degli Italiani* (1969).

sacrifices. In May the new management team called an emergency stock-holders' meeting to announce that the firm had suffered losses in excess of the entire share capital of Lit. 300m. In June, a new firm called the Società Esercizi Siderurgici with a share capital of Lit. 100m. was created to manage Ilva's physical plant against payment of a nominal rent. The banks guaranteed the stock issue. Half of the new share capital was offered in option to the shareholders of Ilva, but there were evidently few takers.

The new firm also announced that its agreements with Ilva were provisional, and would become permanent only if the government enacted sufficient tariff protection, and provided sufficient contracts to make the manufacture of steel products profitable again. This, of course, represented Giolitti's side of the bargain in February, and it explains why the government had been so anxious about keeping the talks secret. It also explains why high tariffs on pig iron and scrap featured prominently in the new tariff promulgated by decree law on 9 June 1921, shortly before the fall of Giolitti's government. It now became clear that the restoration of heavy protection for integrated-cycle iron and steel manufacturing was an integral part of Giolitti's program of economic and financial restoration.

Meanwhile, the Bank of Italy had made confidential undertakings to assist in the restructuring of Ilva in February. Stringher agreed to redis-count Ilva paper held by the Comit and the Credit for Lit. 50m. The Bank of Italy credit was to be secured by Ilva stock nominally worth Lit. 180m., but the Comit and the Credit were allowed to vote these shares in the shareholders' meeting in March.[42] The Bank of Italy was hence indirectly involved in the ouster of Bondi. In March the premier issue bank redis-counted additional commercial notes of two Ilva subsidiaries, the Lloyd Mediterraneo, and the Società Generale per lo Sviluppo delle Industrie Minerari e Metallurgiche, for a total of Lit. 60m. against collateral deposits of stock. In addition, the Bank of Italy agreed to accept the Bansconto's commercial credits against the Ilva group for an undisclosed, but evidently less substantial sum.[43] Subsequent to these agreements, the Comit negotiated a partial debt renunciation with the Ilva's remaining creditors. Among them were the issue banks, which wrote off Lit. 3.5m. of credits totaling Lit. 15.5m.[44]

The restructuring of Ilva was completed in June 1922. The firm was shorn of its holdings in corporations outside the iron and steel sector. Its capital was devalued from Lit. 300m. to Lit. 15m. Then it was merged with the Società Esercizi Siderurgici, giving the new Ilva a share capital of Lit. 115m. Almost all of the fresh capital came from the Credit and the Comit.

[42] ASBI, Fondo 9.2, Comitato, verbali, 25 February 1921.
[43] Ibid., 31 March 1921.   [44] Ibid., 18 June 1922.

The parliamentary elections in May 1921, and the fall of Giolitti

By the spring of 1921, Giolitti had made considerable progress in restoring Italy's public finances, and stabilizing its economy. The restructuring of Ilva was an important first step toward resolving the financial problems of banking and industry, and it was not unreasonable to expect that a similar arrangement could be worked out with the Ansaldo–Banca di Sconto group. The money supply had remained relatively stable for almost a year, and inflation had slowed considerably. The elimination of the bread subsidy and other economies in public expenditure promised to reduce the state's deficit substantially.

Giolitti had reason to be satisfied with the international political situation as well. By mending relations with France, Giolitti and Count Carlo Sforza, his Foreign Minister, had isolated Yugoslavia diplomatically. In November 1920 the Yugoslavs finally were induced to sign a treaty in Rapallo, which fixed the border with Italy, and made Fiume a Free State. In December, Giolitti had ordered the army to remove D'Annunzio from Fiume, which was accomplished during the Christmas holidays, with the loss of only fifty-three lives. During the summer Greece and Italy had agreed to recognize Albania within its 1913 borders, and Italy withdrew its forces from that troublesome country, save the island fortress of Saseno, by the end of the year.

In domestic politics the situation was more equivocal. On the one hand, the wave of post-war labor unrest had exhausted itself largely with the occupation of the factories in September. On the other hand, the socialists and Catholics maintained much of the strength they had demonstrated during parliamentary elections a year earlier, when municipal and provincial elections were held in November 1920. The socialists captured 25 out of 69 provinces and almost 2,200 of 8,300 communes, while the PPI took 10 provinces and 1,600 communes. However, the outcome of the elections was not altogether bleak for the old liberal elites. In many districts, liberal-conservative-nationalist electoral blocs were formed, and they defeated the mass parties in important centers, including Rome, Florence, Genoa and Turin. Moreover, the explosion of fascist violence in the winter of 1920–21, which the authorities made little effort to control, put socialists and Catholics on the defensive. Giolitti had hoped that the congress of the Socialist Party in Livorno in January 1921 would result in a split between reformists and revolutionaries, and that afterwards he would be able to accomplish at last his long-term goal of bringing the reformists into a coalition government. However, the party split to the left rather than the right, with only a small group of ultra-revolutionaries seceding to form the

Communist Party, and the leadership of the PSI remained firmly in the hands of the so-called "maximalists."

At this juncture, Giolitti decided to call a parliamentary election. He hoped to use it as a referendum on his policies of political and financial restoration, and break the back of the mass political parties. The national bloc electoral formula tested in the administrative elections in November was adopted again widely. Fascist *squadristi* and Giolittian notables figured in the same slates. With the aid of his fascist allies, Giolitti applied intimidating tactics in the north and center to which voters in the South had been long accustomed. Not just socialists, but also Nittians and Catholics were the targets of electoral violence.

The PPI formed part of Giolitti's parliamentary majority, and even had representatives in his cabinet. It had dutifully supported the unpopular aspects of Giolitti's economic policy, including the abolition of the bread subsidy, although it forced Giolitti to accept several minor changes, which lessened the impact of deregulating food prices on poorer consumers. But the Catholics got little in exchange from their liberal coalition partners; the Prime Minister ignored the party's proposals for land reform, refused to negotiate with Catholic trade unions, and delayed approving a bill which would have improved the legal status of parochial schools. When Don Sturzo, the party's leader, refused to join Giolitti's national bloc, the Prime Minister responded by treating the PPI as an enemy rather than a partner. Giolitti's supporters branded PPI candidates as "white bolsheviks," and his prefects looked the other way when fascists attacked Catholic organizations and leaders.

Giolitti hoped the election would mark a decisive shift to the right, and would enable him to govern without the support of either socialists or Catholics; he was disappointed. Despite the violence, the Socialists and Communists took 123 and 9 seats respectively, only 24 less than the PSI had taken in 1919. The PPI actually increased its parliamentary representation from 100 to 108 seats. Thirty-five fascists entered the Chamber of Deputies for the first time, as members of Giolitti's own electoral coalition. The remainder of the Chamber was split among nationalists, right and left liberals, and various democratic left groups with too little cohesion to form a majority against Catholics and socialists.

Under these circumstances, Giolitti had greater, rather than less difficulty managing the new Chamber. In late June his government survived a vote of confidence with a majority of only thirty-four, and some of his supporters (right liberals and Nittians) expressed reservations about his foreign policy. Giolitti decided it was time to resign. In addition to right-wing criticism of his foreign policy, he was tired of governing with the support of the PPI. The Catholics were understandably restive allies, given Giolitti's handling of the May elections and his unwillingness to make concessions to them on important policy issues. The Prime Minister had planned to ask the new parliament for extensive powers to reform the bureaucracy (and presumably cut state payrolls), but the PPI let him know that this was out of the question.

A new cabinet was formed by Giolitti's former Defense Minister, Ivanoe Bonomi. It was ostensibly oriented further to the left, with the PPI taking three important cabinet portfolios – Justice, Public Works, and Agriculture – as well as supplying an Undersecretary in the Ministry of Education. In addition, Bonomi proposed to negotiate a "pact of pacification" between fascists and socialists. However, the Catholics had little more impact on government policy than before, and Bonomi was hardly the man to stand up to the fascists. He had been elected to his parliamentary seat in Cremona with the help of Roberto Farinacci, the local fascist boss. During the election campaign, he had praised the fascists as a force for national renewal. As Giolitti's Minister of Defense he had tolerated the pervasive complicity between fascists and the military. When the local fascist leaders refused to obey the terms of the pacification pact during the summer of 1921, Bonomi refused to disarm them. In economic policy, Bonomi's government was scarcely more progressive. As was noted above, one of his first acts as Prime Minister was to reconsign Giolitti's radical financial proposals to the pigeonhole from which they had been removed temporarily to give the Piedmontese statesman's electoral campaign a populist veneer.

The collapse of the Banca Italiana di Sconto–Ansaldo group

One of the major problems confronting Bonomi when he took office was the financial condition of the Bansconto–Ansaldo group. Public authorities had been unable to reach an agreement to restructure the Bansconto–Ansaldo group along the lines of the Ilva agreement during the winter of 1920–21. There were several reasons for this. Firstly, as was mentioned above, the Ansaldo group had close ties to Giolitti's political rivals, including Nitti, creating a climate of reciprocal suspicion and hostility. Secondly, the restructuring of Ansaldo would prove far more costly, and the Bansconto was already compromised by its large loans to the concern, and unable to make further financial sacrifices of the sort undertaken by the Comit and the Credit *vis-à-vis* Ilva. Thirdly, forcing out of office the Ansaldo directors responsible for the crisis, namely the Perrone brothers, was a more delicate proposition than forcing out Bondi and his associates. The Perrone brothers not only controlled Ansaldo, but since its founding in 1915 they had exercised considerable influence at the Bansconto as well.[45]

The financial difficulties of Ansaldo predated the post-war recession. By the spring of 1920 the firm's indebtedness to the Bansconto had already reached alarming levels. The second hostile take-over attempt against the Comit mounted by the Perrone brothers at that time was undertaken in order to secure the financial resources of a second major bank to promote the Ansaldo's program of expansion. With the failure of the take-over bid, the Bansconto's exposure to Ansaldo surpassed all reasonable levels. Italy's second largest commercial bank signed an agreement with Ansaldo on 25 August 1920 that effectively turned the Bansconto into an appendage of the industrial conglomerate.[46] The collapse of stock prices during the summer and the onset of recession further aggravated the group's problems. When news of the Ilva rescue became public in the spring of 1921, sales of Ansaldo and even Bansconto stock increased, and the group was forced to expend substantial resources repurchasing its own shares, in order to prevent the stockholders' panic from turning into a depositors' panic.

During the winter and spring of 1920–21 the Bansconto resorted to increasingly desperate stratagems to obtain cash: it opened new branches in towns of modest commercial importance to attract new savings accounts; it attracted hot money from abroad by offering high interest rates on correspondence accounts. Finally, it began paying an interest premium to customers who would deposit Treasury bills with the bank; the Treasury bills were then used to secure advances from the issue banks, naturally at a very high total cost to the Bansconto.[47]

Meanwhile, protracted negotiations between the Ansaldo–Bansconto group and the Bank of Italy took place. It appears that Stringher aimed from the beginning to resolve the group's financial difficulties by severing or greatly reducing Ansaldo's ties to the Banca Italiana di Sconto. A bank consortium led by the Bank of Italy, and including the major commercial banks – among them the Perrone brothers' archrival, the Comit – would take up most or all of the Bansconto's loans to Ansaldo. Presumably, Stringher also meant to reorganize the Ansaldo group, and force the resignation of its directors. The central banker's primary preoccupation seems to have been to avert a major banking panic, which seemed almost inevitable if the Bansconto collapsed. Moreover, Stringher feared that the

[45] The following relies heavily on Falchero, "Il Gruppo Ansaldo–Banca di Sconto e le vicende bancarie nel primo dopoguerra"; and Bachi, *L'Italia economica nell'anno 1921*, pp. 52–81. See also, Piero Sraffa, "The Bank Crisis in Italy," *Journal of Economic History*, 32 (1922), no. 126, pp. 178–97.
[46] Falchero, "Il Gruppo Ansaldo–Banca di Sconto e le vicende bancarie nel primo dopoguerra," p. 567.   [47] Bachi, *L'Italia economica nell'anno 1921*, p. 56.

failure of the Bansconto would give the Comit an almost hegemonic position in the Italian commercial banking system.

But the Perrone brothers were willing to agree to none of this until the crisis of the group had become irreversible. According to Mario Perrone's later testimony in court, Stringher insisted that the Bank of Italy be allowed to conduct an investigation of the financial situation of Ansaldo prior to the negotiation of a rescue agreement. In May 1921, when the Ilva reconstruction was already well advanced, the Perrone brothers finally allowed two Bank of Italy officials, Alfredo Baccani and Rodolfo Montelatici, to begin an investigation. By the time their report was completed in October, the group was already in desperate financial straits, and the entire banking system under pressure.[48] Stringher duly formed a banking consortium, consisting of the three issue banks, the Credit, the Comit, and the Roma. It was to take up at least Lit. 300m., and possibly as much as Lit. 600m. of the estimated Lit. 750m. in Bansconto loans to Ansaldo. In exchange, Ansaldo was to deposit all of the securities held by the group as collateral, giving the Bank of Italy control over the conglomerate. But at the last minute the Perrone brothers made counter-proposals, which would have kept majority stock interests in some of the more promising firms in the Ansaldo group, including the shipping firms Transatlantica Italiana, and Società di Navigazione Roma, the engineering firm Ansaldo San Giorgio, and the electricity company Negri, in the portfolio of the Bansconto. In addition, the Perrones demanded guarantees that they would be allowed to continue directing Ansaldo![49]

While these negotiations were under way, the semi-official press agency Stefani issued a communiqué on 20 November 1921, announcing that a banking consortium had been formed to refinance Ansaldo's debt. Whether the intention of this communiqué was to calm the securities market, as the government claimed, or to apply pressure on the Perrones, as the latter would later charge, its effect was to stimulate the long-feared depositors' run on the Bansconto.[50] The Bansconto was already under pressure from foreign correspondents, who had begun withdrawing funds in October. On 3 December the Perrones finally resigned from Ansaldo, and at about the same time the rescue consortium went into action.

However, by now it was too late to save the Bansconto. On 19 December the consortium already had made available to the Bansconto the first

[48] Falchero, "Il Gruppo Ansaldo–Banca di Sconto e le vicende bancarie nel primo dopoguerra," pp. 568–69. The report by Montelatici and Baccani is published in, Emanuele Gazzo, *I cento anni dell'Ansaldo, 1853–1953* (Genoa: Ansaldo, 1953), pp. 459–72.

[49] ASBI, Fondo 9.2, Comitato, verbali, 20 November 1921; Falchero, "Il Gruppo Ansaldo–Banca di Sconto e le vicende bancarie nel primo dopoguerra," p. 569.

[50] Falchero, "Il Gruppo Ansaldo–Banca di Sconto e le vicende bancarie nel primo dopoguerra," p. 570.

tranche of Lit. 300m., but the depositors' run, and the bank's liquidity needs showed no sign of abating. When the consortium's exposure reached Lit. 424m. a few days later, the commercial banks balked at making further sacrifices. Moreover, on or about 20 December the commercial banks had begun to refuse to cash checks drawn on the Bansconto: it was discovered that the failing bank was issuing checks, supposedly to cover its clients' financial transactions, but actually to acquire capital for twenty-four hours at a time, before the cashed checks were returned.[51] The depositors' run now reached panic proportions. On 26 December the government issued a decree prohibiting time purchases of stock. The next day talks between the government, the issue banks, and the commercial banks were held to determine how to meet the banking crisis. The Bansconto directors were unable to produce reliable information as to how much the rescue of the bank was likely to cost. In any event, it was now clear that the bank's losses would be far in excess of the Lit. 600m. raised by the consortium. A full rescue by the Treasury and the Bank of Italy was therefore discounted. The authorities decided instead to proclaim a moratorium for the Bansconto and proceed with its liquidation. However, the statute in the commercial code envisaging such action had been abolished in 1903. The Bonomi government took the legally dubious step of issuing a decree on 29 December reinstituting the legal device of a bank moratorium; the Bansconto immediately filed for protection under the new provision, which went into effect the next day.[52]

Repercussions of the Bansconto crisis

The fallout from the collapse of the Bansconto–Ansaldo group decisively influenced politics and economics in the ten months prior to the March on Rome. It diminished the prestige of the government, and set off a new round of recriminations among political groups which had been financed by the two large financial-industrial trusts. In particular, an intense struggle developed after the proclamation of the moratorium regarding the future of the failed bank and its creditors. This struggle paralyzed the government, and was a key factor in the fall of Bonomi's ministry when parliament reconvened after the Christmas recess in early February.[53]

The Bank of Italy also emerged from the Bansconto affair with its financial position weakened and its prestige diminished. As Stringher noted at a meeting of the Comitato in January, the volume of domestic rediscounting operations of the Bank had increased from Lit. 3,350m. on

---

[51] Bachi, *L'Italia economica dell'anno 1921*, p. 61.   [52] Ibid., pp. 62–63.
[53] Danilo Veneruso, *La vigilia del fascismo. Il primo ministero Facta nella crisi dello stato liberale in Italia* (Bologna: Il Mulino, 1968), p. 28.

20 December to Lit. 4,139m. on 7 January; and the volume of advances
against securities had swollen from Lit. 2,509m. to Lit. 4,024.5m. during
the same three-week period. Moreover, while the Banca Commerciale and
the Credito Italiano had weathered the storm relatively well, the Banco di
Roma was also facing a depositors' run and potential failure, and a second
major bank collapse would provoke a crisis of the whole system, and had to
be avoided at all costs.[54]

Stringher had failed in his attempt to save the Bansconto, and a commercial banking system based on four large banks. In his description of the
bank crisis to the Comitato in January 1922, he placed the responsibility
for the moratorium squarely on the Banca Commerciale and the Credito
Italiano. According to Stringher, the Milanese banks had undermined the
consortium: "The Banca Commerciale and the Credito Italiano have
always had a resistant, and less than benevolent attitude, and when help is
not rendered voluntarily and quickly it lacks efficacity."[55] A high level of
tension and mutual distrust between central and commercial bankers
would continue to characterize the Italian financial system until the collapse of the Comit and the Credit in the early 1930s.

The Bank of Italy also was stymied in its efforts to reorganize the
Bansconto in the first three months of 1922. A judicial commission was
created to investigate the situation of the bank after the proclamation of
the moratorium. Stringher recalled Domenico Gidoni from New York to
participate in the commission and preside over the liquidation of the bank.
With Stringher's support, Gidoni presented a scheme for liquidating the
Bansconto on 31 January 1922. Two new institutions would have been
created: one, with a capital of Lit. 10m. to manage and slowly sell off the
Bansconto's illiquid assets, with the proceeds being used to reimburse the
failed bank's creditors; and another, with a share capital of Lit. 50–150m.
would open its doors as a new commercial bank. Gidoni proposed to pay
55% of the creditors' claims in installments during 1922 and 1923;
another 5% would be payable in shares of the new bank; and bonds would
be issued for the remainder, the redemption of which would depend on
the earnings of the institute liquidating the Bansconto's assets.[56]

This scheme (and with it the Bonomi government) failed because of the
unbending opposition of the Bansconto's creditors, who organized themselves as a lobby. The creditors wanted the new commercial bank to
assume responsibility for the Bansconto's debts, perhaps enhancing their
own prospects of repayment, but diminishing the prospects of the new
bank as a serious competitor of the Credit and the Commerciale. Negotiations between the judicial commission and the creditors continued into

[54] ASBI, Fondo 9.2, Comitato, verbali, 15 January 1922.
[55] Ibid.   [56] Bachi, *L'Italia economica dell'anno 1921*, pp. 69–75.

March, and in the end Gidoni and the Bank of Italy were forced to make major concessions. A new proposal was formulated in early March, and amended again after further discussions with the creditors. A single new bank, to be christened the Banca Nazionale di Credito was to be formed with a capital of Lit. 250m. The capital was to come from the conversion of 7% of the debts of the Bansconto into stock. Another Lit. 150m. in share capital could be raised in 1922, with not more than Lit. 50m. being offered to foreign investors, and the remaining Lit. 100m. being offered in option to Bansconto creditors. A shareholders' committee was to be formed, to which fifteen representatives of the issue banks, and eleven representatives of the creditors would be appointed. This committee was to oversee the issue of share capital. Creditors of less than Lit. 5,000 were to receive 67% of the sums owed them, 20% within one month of the legal sanctioning of the proposal, and the remaining 47% before the end of 1922. The remaining creditors were to receive 62% of the sums owed them: 7% in Banca Nazionale stock, another 10% in cash in the first month after the agreement took effect, 10% in the second month, 15% by March 1923, 10% by September 1923, and another 10% by March 1924. Although some creditors held out for an even more favorable settlement, the government imposed this proposal by decree on 13 March 1922.[57]

The Bank of Italy's defeat went beyond its failure to obtain the creation of a new commercial bank with substantial fresh capital. The repayment schedule to the Bansconto's creditors exceeded the pace at which the failed bank's assets were likely to be liquidated. This meant that the issue banks would have to come up with the difference. Thus the Bank of Italy was required to tie up its resources in the liquidation of the Bansconto, even though this sacrifice could no longer be justified as necessary to avert a bank failure, and stabilize the financial system. A new "Autonomous Section" of the Consorzio per Sovvenzioni su Valori Industriali was established in March to liquidate the Bansconto. The Autonomous Section was really just a window of the Bank of Italy. It was authorized to accept commercial notes for an unlimited amount that could be rediscounted with the issue banks. Through the Autonomous Section the Bank of Italy repaid the Bansconto's creditors, and financed the reorganization of Ansaldo, Alfa Romeo, and the other firms which had fallen into state hands as a consequence of the failure of the Bansconto, essentially by money creation. When the situation of the Banco di Roma worsened again at the end of 1922, the Autonomous Section of the CSVI was employed to undertake a full-fledged rescue.[58]

The colossal expansion of issue bank commercial credit in the fall of

---

[57] Ibid., pp. 75–79.
[58] Ernesto Cianci, *Nascita dello stato imprenditore in Italia* (Milan: Mursia, 1977), pp. 43–58.

1921 and the spring of 1922 produced by the crisis of the Bansconto coincided with the first substantial improvement in the government's financial situation. Net debt creation in fiscal 1921–22 was only about half that of 1920–21. Moreover, the state was able to retire debts to the issue banks, through the sale of new securities. Given the condition of the banking system and the financial markets, there was, not surprisingly, little competition from private capital issues. The total volume of the note circulation remained relatively stable.

But it is important to stress that the banking crisis also foreclosed political options for the final liberal governments. There could be no talk in Italy of an extensive deficitary program of public works or physical reconstruction in 1921–22, such as those undertaken by France and Belgium. Although such a program might have broadened the political base of the final liberal cabinets, Facta was constrained to limp along in 1922, with the largest industrial conglomerate in the country bankrupt and in state hands; with a second large commercial bank lurching toward failure; and with the issue banks discredited and immobilized.

Facta's government was even weaker, and rested on an even less stable parliamentary majority than Bonomi's. In addition to the controversy surrounding the liquidation of the Bansconto, the Giolittians had voted against Bonomi in February because of the PPI's strong presence in his cabinet. The Catholic leader Don Sturzo responded by vetoing PPI support for a government headed by Giolitti. It took almost a month to build a new government, making this cabinet crisis the longest since Italy's unification. In the end, the PPI accepted Luigi Facta, a loyal supporter of Giolitti, as Prime Minister, and the Giolittians agreed to let the PPI have three portfolios – Education, Finance, and Agriculture. Vincenzo Riccio, a right-wing liberal with close ties to the nationalists and the fascists, became Minister of Public Works. Government and parliament remained deadlocked, with the main source of tension continuing to be the mutual hostility of liberals and Catholics.

International accounts and finance

Despite its domestic political problems, Italy experienced an improvement in its international accounts 1921–22 that paralleled the steady reduction in state budget deficits and the trend toward monetary stabilization. Many of the factors favoring domestic economic stabilization were also at work in the international arena: the break in raw materials prices and shipping tariffs reduced the cost of Italy's main imports, and this trend was reinforced by the slump in domestic demand due to the recession. McGuire estimated Italy's current account deficit in 1920 at Lit. 1,970m.; in 1921 at

Lit. 885m.; and in 1922 at Lit. 230m. (gold lire). According to his figures, Italy's international accounts balanced for the first time in over a decade in 1923. The major factor in the restoration of equilibrium was the decline in the merchandise trade deficit, with "invisible" earnings from emigrant remittances and tourism receipts remaining relatively stable.[59]

Not surprisingly, this trend was accompanied by a shift in Italy's international economic policy. But the change in international economic policy was not dictated solely by structural factors, any more than the simultaneous change in domestic economic policy; rather, it reflected the differences in temperament and outlook of Nitti and Giolitti. The senior Piedmontese statesman and his successors were less eager to borrow abroad than Nitti had been, and also less convinced that Italy's only path to salvation lay in close relations with Britain and America. Giolitti's conception of international relations was shaped by his experience at the beginning of the century, when Italy's essentially independent course in international affairs had been facilitated by equilibrium in its international accounts, and independence from foreign bankers. Rather than floating additional loans in the United States and Britain, Giolitti aimed to negotiate a satisfactory settlement to the war debts as quickly as possible, as a prelude to stabilizing the exchange value of the lira.

The new course was particularly evident in relations with the United States. Shortly after assuming office, Giolitti recalled Bernardo Attolico, the protégé of Nitti who had been trying to arrange loans on the American market.[60] He also appointed a new ambassador, Sen. Vittorio Rolandi Ricci: a corporate lawyer, a seasoned politician, and a trusted associate. Rolandi Ricci's main assignment was to negotiate a debt settlement with the United States government. By sending a person of Rolandi Ricci's stature to Washington, Giolitti demonstrated his keen interest in reaching a financial settlement expeditiously. Perhaps only Fiume and the territorial dispute with Yugoslavia had a higher priority in the Piedmontese statesman's foreign policy, and there is little doubt that he viewed the settlement of the financial, as well as the territorial questions left pending by the war as a precondition for the normalization of international relations.[61]

However, Giolitti was unable to reproduce his success *vis-à-vis* Yugoslavia in talks with the United States. In Washington, Rolandi Ricci's

[59] Constantine McGuire, *Italy's International Economic Position* (New York: Macmillan, 1926), pp. 39–41.
[60] Attolico, at any rate, was packing his bags just over a month after Giolitti took office. Attolico to Dwight Morrow (of J. P. Morgan & Co.), 17 July 1920, Dwight Morrow Papers, Correspondence, Amherst College Library.
[61] On Rolandi Ricci's tenure in Washington see his correspondence with Giolitti in, ACS, Carte Giolitti.

initiative foundered on the American determination to settle with Britain before initiating serious negotiations with the continental allies, and the unwillingness of Italy, similar to the other debtor nations prior to 1922, to recognize formally all of the financial obligations they had incurred during the war.

Rolandi Ricci's negotiations in the United States were inconclusive. The Italian ambassador evidently presented a proposal for a debt settlement at the beginning of April 1921. Mario Alberti, of the Credito Italiano, collaborated in the preparation of the proposal and journeyed to the United States.[62] It was premature from the American point of view. The new Republican administration of Warren G. Harding had just assumed office, and the settlement of war debts was a delicate issue in American domestic policy. The new administration wanted to work out an agreement with both houses of Congress on basic principles before sitting down with the Allied governments. Such an agreement was only reached in April 1922, and even then the Americans wanted to negotiate first with Britain, their largest and most solvent debtor. In addition to bad timing, Rolandi Ricci seems to have committed another *faux pas*, which was scarcely forgivable from the American point of view. Circumstantial evidence indicates that he declined to accept all of the financial obligations Italy had incurred during the war as valid, and as the starting point for the negotiations.[63] Although the Americans later would prove to be extremely flexible with regard to the actual repayments schedules for the war loans, they were adamant, because of domestic public opinion, that formal debt repudiation be avoided. At the same time, it was difficult for Giolitti to recognize all of Italy's debts to the United States, when he was already under attack from the right because of his conciliatory policy *vis-à-vis* Yugoslavia, and the ouster of D'Annunzio from Fiume in December 1920.

As it became clear that substantial progress toward a debt settlement would not be made in the immediate future, Rolandi Ricci began to chafe at his political exile on the far side of the Atlantic. Evidently he coveted a cabinet appointment in Rome, and asked to be replaced as early as April 1921.[64] But Giolitti insisted that the *uomo d'affari* remain at his post, even

---

[62] Rolandi Ricci to Giolitti, 30 March 1921, ACS, Carte Giolitti, B32/F100; Albertini to Einaudi, 17 May 1921, published in, Luigi Albertini, *Epistolario, 1911–1926*, ed. O. Barié, vol. III, *Il dopoguerra* (Verona: Mondadori, 1968), pp. 1476–77.

[63] This is suggested by a letter of Albertini to Einaudi, 22 October 1921, *Epistolario*, vol. III, pp. 1514–15. At Albertini's request, Einaudi had prepared a draft of a memo to be presented by the Italian government in Washington as a basis for negotiations to settle the war debt. As is noted below, Albertini advised Einaudi that: "The firm intention not to pay has to ooze from the pores of the document, without being stated baldly." Albertini goes on to note that Rolandi Ricci was compromised – perhaps because of his earlier proposal.

[64] "Excellency, how much longer does my American exile have to last?" Rolandi Ricci to Giolitti, 8 April 1920, ASC, Carte Giolitti, B32/F100.

after Bonomi, and later Facta took over as Prime Minister. Giolitti seems to have counted on his return to power in Rome, and wanted to have Rolandi Ricci at his disposal in Washington to liquidate the war debts problem as expeditiously as possible thereafter.[65]

The Washington Naval Conference in the fall of 1921 presented the Italians with another opportunity to raise the debt question. Luigi Albertini, the director of the *Corriere della Sera*, was a member of the delegation. He had been in contact with Mario Alberti at the time of the earlier initiative in the spring, and he now asked Luigi Einaudi to prepare another proposal to be presented to the Americans. Aware of the Americans' categorical rejection of an outright debt repudiation, Albertini summarized the negotiating position Italy ought to take in the following terms:

> The affirmation that one doesn't intend to pay can never be made. One has to use a lot of questions: "How can Italy ever do this?", "How can . . . ?"
>
> In sum, the firm intention of not paying has to ooze through all the pores of the document, without ever being stated baldly . . .[66]

But if talks on the debt issue did take place during the presence of Albertini with the Italian delegation to the Naval Conference in Washington, they were as inconclusive as Rolandi Ricci's earlier initiative. Bonomi's government was as unwilling as Giolitti's had been to recognize Italy's full responsibility for the war debts. In June 1922 Albertini delivered a scathing attack on the American position in the Italian Senate.[67] This proved counterproductive, but it should be pointed out that British and French attitudes in the summer of 1922 were similar or even more militant.

The Anglo-American agreement on war debts was signed in January 1923, paving the way for substantive negotiations with the continental powers. It was left to Mussolini to benefit from the earlier negative experiences of liberal Italy. In the agreement signed in December 1925, Italy was awarded the most favorable terms of all America's debtors. In exchange for formal recognition of the entire debt as determined by American officials, the fascist government effectively achieved a cancellation on the order of 75.4% through low interest rates and annuities.[68]

---

[65] Rolandi Ricci to Giolitti, 29 August 1921, ACS, Carte Giolitti, Fondo Cavour, S18/F47/SF8; Rolandi Ricci to Giolitti, 9 March 1922; Rolandi Ricci to Giolitti, 1 November 1922, S19/F48/SF12.

[66] Albertini to Einaudi, 22 October 1921, Albertini, *Epistolario*, p. 1514.

[67] Ronald Graham (British Ambassador in Rome) to Arthur James Balfour, 19 June 1922, PRO, FO 371/7658/1922.

[68] The best account of the war debt settlement between the United States and Italy is in Gian Giacomo Migone, *Gli Stati Uniti e il fascismo. Alle origini dell'egemonia americana in Italia* (Milan: Feltrinelli, 1980), pp. 99–151.

American bankers and Italy

American portfolio lending reached a post-war trough in 1920, when new loans fell short of old loans falling due by $84.5m. In the following two years there was a rapid recovery of portfolio lending abroad, with new loans exceeding maturing old loans by $379.6m. in 1921, and $559.7m. in 1922. (Compare this with $911.9m. in 1924, the year of the Dawes loan.) At first, most of this new lending went to Canada, Latin America, and to a lesser extent Britain, with American investors remaining weary of continental Europe. Indeed, substantial new lending to continental Europe would only begin after the resolution of the Franco-German crisis, the stabilization of the mark, and the Dawes Plan.[69] Mussolini, and not liberal Italy, would benefit from the major round of inter-war American lending. Indeed, after Germany, Italy would receive the second-largest share of American portfolio investment capital during the heyday of American lending, 1924–29.[70] Anti-fascists in the 1920s, and more recently historians, have excoriated the American banking community, particularly Thomas Lamont and the other senior partners of J. P. Morgan & Co. for their partisanship for the Italian dictatorship.[71] There is no question that American bankers admired Mussolini, and that their loans buoyed the regime in the mid to late twenties. Further, the American financial community was instrumental in shaping the very favorable image of the dictator in the American press, a favorable image that changed only slowly in the 1930s.

However, what needs to be emphasized in this context is that American bankers were favorably disposed toward Italy even before the March on Rome, and they cultivated liberal political leaders, including Nitti and Carlo Schanzer, just as they would later cultivate Mussolini, Dino Grandi, and Giuseppe Volpi.[72] The fascist regime's self-justificatory myth – that it

---

[69] Cleona Lewis, *America's Stake in International Investments* (Washington: Brookings Institution, 1938), pp. 367–75.

[70] Lewis, *America's Stake in International Investments*, pp. 652–55, quoted in Migone, *Gli Stati Uniti e il fascismo*, p. 174.

[71] Migone, *Gli Stati Uniti e il fascismo*; John P. Diggins, *Mussolini and Fascism: The View from America* (Princeton: Princeton University Press, 1972).

[72] The following two examples will suffice to illustrate this point. Bernardo Attolico wrote to Paul Cravath, a corporate lawyer with close ties to J. P. Morgan & Co., in early December 1920, asking him to use his influence to find an appropriate news magazine in America for which Vincenzo Giuffrida could serve as Italian correspondent. Attolico noted that Giuffrida had good ties to Nitti, having served as undersecretary in his cabinet. Cravath promptly set to work looking for a suitable forum for Giuffrida, and kept Morgans informed of his activities. Attolico to Cravath, 2 December 1920; Cravath to Irwin Smith (Italy-America Society), 20 December 1920, Morrow Papers, correspondence.

Carlo Schanzer, Nitti's Minister of the Treasury, journeyed to the United States in late 1921 as a member of the Italian delegation to the Washington Naval Conference. Alvin Krech of Equitable Trust Co. arranged to have him give a speech on Italy's (promising)

had saved Italy from Bolshevism and chaos – was widely echoed by American businessmen and journalists after October 1922, but a perusal of the *Wall Street Journal* in late 1921 and 1922 suggests that the American business community had a very favorable view of opportunities in Italy even before the advent of fascism.[73] Despite the climate of near civil war in the Po Valley, Italy seemed a model of political and social stability in American eyes, at a time when the purchasing power of the mark was disintegrating, and France and Germany were drifting toward open confrontation.

Thomas Lamont was among the co-founders of the Italy–America Society in 1917. The Morgan purchasing organization had executed large orders on behalf of the Italian military during the war, working closely with General Pasquale Tozzi and other Italian officials. There is little doubt that Morgans hoped to do a substantial underwriting business in Italian securities after the war. Moreover, as it became clear that the repegging of European currencies to gold and the dollar would require substantial lines of credit from American banks, Morgans sought to establish itself as the principal financial interlocutor of all the major European states, Italy included.

Even before the recovery of private American foreign lending in 1921, the Morgan partners were careful to cultivate ties to Italy. It will be recalled that Morgan partners met with Italian officials in Paris in the summer of 1919, and even tried to blame the US government for their inability, or better unwillingness, to lend to Italy at that time. During 1921–22 Morgans redoubled such efforts, in part because other American

economic and financial condition at the US Foreign Policy Association in New York on 14 February 1922. The New York bankers were well represented on this occasion: Cravath was among the other speakers. Later, after Schanzer had become Minister of Foreign Affairs in Facta's government, Krech asked him for permission to publish and distribute 100,000 copies of his speech in the United States, "as you are undoubtedly the best known and most talked about Italian statesman in our country." Equitable did some commercial business with the Italian government during World War I; Krech no doubt looked forward to expanding these ties in the future. Krech to Schanzer, 6 March 1922, ACS, Carte Carlo Schanzer, Secondo versamento, 13/63. Copies of the speeches of Schanzer and Cravath are also in this file.

[73] My undergraduate research assistant at MIT, Furio Ciacci, studied the *Wall Street Journal* from November 1921 to October 1922. He found the coverage of Italy by America's premier financial newspaper to be more favorable than that of any other major European country. Furio Ciacci, "The Italian and European Image in the American Financial Press: The *Wall Street Journal*, November 1921–October 1922," unpublished manuscript, MIT, 6 August 1989. Even the collapse of the Banca Italiana di Sconto did not shake the confidence of the American financial community more than momentarily. In a letter to Francesco Giannini, a financial expert attached to the Italian embassy in London, on 6 February 1922, Thomas Lamont of J. P. Morgan & Co. observed: "The moratorium pronounced with reference to the Banca di Sconto has, of course, made a painful impression over here, but it seems to me that impression is now more or less dying out." Lamont Papers, Series IV 190/12.

banks, including Equitable Trust, Kuhn, Loeb & Co., and particularly
Dillon, Read & Co. also showed an interest in Italian loans. Lamont was
the Morgan partner most closely involved with Italian business. Although
Lamont does not seem to have contemplated major loans to Italy prior to
the settlement of the Allied debts to the United States, and the stabilization of European currencies, by late 1921 he was prepared to undertake
more modest affairs in order to cement the ties between the Italian
Treasury and his firm.

As late as December 1920, an informer of Lamont's in Milan, identified
only as G. J. W., gave a rather discouraging picture of the investment
climate in Italy:

> As far as I know, Italy's effort to attract American capital only interests
> persons with speculative motives; and firms or institutions which have
> already granted credits to their Agents, or have vested interests in this
> country and feel it would work to their own detriment to sever relations or
> to adopt a conservative policy. The tendency is not to enter Italy and this is
> borne out on the Milan Bourse by the very limited demand for Italian
> securities for American account. American interests already located in Italy
> are not inclined to extend their activities or withdraw.[74]

Lamont's informant went on to discuss the financial difficulties of the
Italian government, noting that Italy had incurred a deficit of 7bn. on the
bread subsidy during the past year; and that the ongoing Fiume dispute
had prevented military demobilization.

During the spring of 1921 Lamont was in touch with the Italian government through Francesco Giannini, a financial expert attached to the
Italian embassy in London. Although he declined to visit Rome in May
during his annual trip to Europe, giving as reasons the proximity of
parliamentary elections, and the crisis in negotiations over reparations in
Paris, the investment banker promised to travel to Italy the following
year.[75] Back in America, Lamont was careful to cultivate Richard W.
Child, who had just been appointed ambassador to Italy by Harding. By
letter he extended his congratulations and added: "There are a number of
things in connection with the Italian situation that are of great interest to
me, and before you go I want to be sure to get you for luncheon and a
good talk, if agreeable to you. I know the Italian outfit quite well . . ."[76] In
early July Lamont made a speech at a banquet hosted by the Italy–America
Society for the former Foreign Minister Tommaso Tittoni. It was an
insubstantial rambling on the heroism of Italians in repelling foreign

---

[74] Lamont Papers, Series IV, 190/11.
[75] Lamont to Giannini, 3 May 1921; Lamont to Giannini, 24 May 1921, Lamont Papers,
    Series IV, 190/11.
[76] Lamont to Child, 2 June 1921, Lamont Papers, Series IV, 190/11.

invaders from Attila to the Austrians – "just the sort of thing the Italians like" – the main point of which was to underscore J. P. Morgan & Co.'s interest in Italian business.[77] In the fall of 1921 Giannini journeyed to the United States from London as a member of the Italian delegation to the Naval Disarmament Conference. In late December he presented Lamont with a proposal for a 20-year loan of $50–60m. to a consortium of the largest Italian municipal administrations. The loan was to be guaranteed by the Italian government, with the government receiving the amount in dollars, and making available to the municipalities an equivalent sum in lire.[78] Giannini's proposal was apparently not coordinated with talks on war debts held by Albertini and Rolandi Ricci with US government officials at the same time; it is not even clear whether Giannini had strong official backing for his initiative. At any event, it came at the worse possible moment, with the Bansconto moratorium only days away, and a government crisis a few weeks away. Ultimately it came to nothing, but Giannini's discussions with Lamont reveal much about the intentions of Morgans.

On 23 December Lamont noted that the proposal was purely tentative, but promised that his firm would further study it. He added:

> You realize that in proffering our good services to your Government we do so solely on the understanding conveyed by you that there are no firm existing arrangements at the present time between your Government and any other American banking house or institution. We are always scrupulous in declining to interfere with the business of our friends. We are aware that at some time in the course of the late war some financial operations were conducted between your Government and Messrs. Lee, Higginson & Co., of Boston and another one between your Government and Messrs. Kidder, Peabody & Co., of Boston. Both of these firms are friends of ours, and we should wish to discuss credit matters with you here only in the event that the arrangements of your Government with either one of these firms were only temporary and not of a permanent character. You quite understand our views on this point.[79]

All talk of consideration for competitors aside, Morgan's concern to establish a special, even a privileged relationship with the Italian government emerges fairly clearly from this letter. The Morgan partners had good reason to be solicitous of Italian officials, because other American bankers were exploring the possibility of Italian business as well in the spring of 1922. In early April Dillon, Read & Co., a smaller New York

[77] Ivy L. Lee (Italy–America Society) to Lamont, 9 September 1921, Lamont Papers, Series III, 149/35. A transcript of Lamont's speech is also preserved in this file.
[78] Giannini to Lamont, memo, 22 December 1921, Lamont Papers, Series IV, 190/11.
[79] Lamont to Giannini, 23 December 1921, Lamont Papers, Series IV, 190/11. The loan from Kidder, Peabody which Lamont refers to must have been short term.

investment banking house that would emerge as Morgan's most aggressive
competitor in the international bond market in the course of the 1920s,
informed the State Department that it was negotiating an issue of $50m.
in Italian government bonds, and inquired whether the government had
any objection. The deal never went through, but the US government
evidently gave them the green light.[80] Lamont also obtained information
that another of Morgan's principal competitors, Kuhn, Loeb and Co., was
studying Italian government business.[81]

By early March Lamont was prepared to act. He noted to Giannini that:

> our bond market here for sound foreign issues has developed further, and I
> am not at all sure but that it would be well for us to considering [sic] striking
> while the iron is hot . . . In as much as several of the foreign governments are
> waking up to the situation here, as afforded by our excellent bond market, I
> have a feeling on behalf of Italy that we ought not to lose time . . .[82]

Now, however, it was the Italian government which was cool about
foreign borrowing. Italy's international balance of payments had improved
to the point where immediate access to foreign funds was no longer
imperative. As the Morgan partners pursued Giannini's initial proposal for
a loan of $50–60m. to a consortium of Italian cities, they soon found
themselves reduced to discussing a single loan of $10–15m. to the city of
Rome, which the national government declined to guarantee. By late May
Lamont was inclined to abstain from this affair, and hold out for the more
substantial government business later.[83]

Richard Child, the new American ambassador in Rome, discovered that
government officials in the capital were less interested in American loans
than Italian diplomatic personnel abroad had given him to believe. He
alerted Washington that: "It is my conviction . . . that it would be
unfortunate if American banking interests were stimulated by Italian
diplomatic outposts to bid against each other to make loans to Italy."[84]
William Phillips, Undersecretary of the Treasury, concluded on the basis
of Child's dispatch and his exchanges with American banking firms that:
"the Italians are playing a pretty foxy game, with a view to issuing a loan

[80] Dillon, Read & Co. to Charles E. Hughes (Secretary of State), 13 April 1922; Elliott
Wordsworth (Assistant Secretary of Treasury) to Leland Harrison (Assistant Secretary of
State), 18 April 1922, NA, Treasury, RG 39. On Dillon, Read & Co. see, Vincent P.
Carosso, *Investment Banking in America: A History* (Cambridge MA: Harvard University
Press, 1970), pp. 344–46, and passim.; Harold James, *The German Slump: Politics and
Economics, 1924–1936* (New York: Oxford University Press, 1986), pp. 56–58.

[81] Lamont (in London) to J. P. Morgan & Co., 22 May 1922, Lamont Papers, Series II,
111/14.

[82] Lamont to Giannini, 7 March 1922, Lamont Papers, Series IV, 190/12.

[83] Lamont (in London) to J. P. Morgan & Co., 22 May 1922, Lamont Papers, Series II,
111/14.

[84] Child to Hughes, 1 June 1922, NA, Treasury, RG 39.

here at as small a cost as possible by stirring up competitive bidding."[85] Phillips may have been right, but American investment banking houses scarcely needed foreign encouragement to engage in competitive bidding.

The courtship of the Italian government by US bankers continued after the March on Rome: J. P. Morgan & Co. now had a small office and a permanent representative – Giovanni Fummi – in the Italian capital; Dillon, Read, & Co. also continued its negotiations with the new government. Morgan's position was enhanced by Mussolini's appointment of Guido Jung as Special Commercial and Financial Adviser to the ambassador in Washington. The Sicilian financier had become acquainted with Lamont during the Versailles Peace Conference, and he was well aware of the preeminence of Morgans on Wall Street. Shortly after Jung's arrival in the United States, Lamont communicated to him the following cable from Fummi in Rome:

> I am confidentially informed that government has had further talks with Dillon Read & Co. representative. Owing to the aggressive policy of Dillon Read & Co. and also to the desire in government circles for early attempting of financial operations, I am told that there is possibility of negotiations starting with them.

To this Lamont added:

> It is true that the firm Mr. Fummi mentions is exceedingly aggressive, and it has been trying very hard for some time to get in on Italian business. I think that you and I are agreed that it would be a pity for your government to start business here in any but the right way.[86]

The implications of this message were not lost on Jung, and presumably they were appreciated by the Duce, with his craving for international prestige. In any event, when Italy returned to the gold standard in 1925 it was aided by a $100m. stand-by credit from J. P. Morgan & Co., and the premier American investment banking firm remained the Italian government's principal financial interlocutor for the rest of the decade.[87]

While Wall Street's leading investment banking houses were courting the Italian government, other smaller firms, including Aldred & Co. of New York, and Lee, Higginson & Co. of Boston were negotiating the refinancing of the floating debt of various Italian electrical companies to the Banca Commerciale Italiana and the Credito Italiano. Thirty-year obligations were to be issued in dollars in the United States. To make the issue more attractive to American investors, the obligations would be

[85] Phillips, handwritten note, 26 June 1922, attached to Child to Hughes, 1 June 1922, NA, Treasury, RG 39.
[86] Lamont to Jung, 9 March 1923, Lamont Papers, Series IV, 190/13.
[87] On J. P. Morgan & Co.'s privileged relationship with Mussolini's government in the 1920s see Migone, *Gli Stati Uniti e il fascismo*.

issued by an American firm, the "American Italian Power Co.," which would in turn extend loans to the Italian companies. Giuseppe Toeplitz of the Commerciale told his board on 4 July 1922 that negotiations were in an advanced state.[88] Loans of this nature would prove extremely popular after 1924, but for reasons that remain unclear the affair fell through in the summer of 1922. Dispatches from US and British diplomatic personnel in late June and early July suggest that foreign investors viewed government policy as discouraging. Francis B. Keene, the US Consul General in Rome, suggested that controls on foreign investment instituted during Nitti's premiership, and the foot-dragging of government officials, had stymied proposed loans.[89] J. H. Harden, the Commercial Secretary of the British embassy in Rome, suggested that a recent decree law making foreign capital subject to the wealth tax was undermining efforts in Italy to raise capital abroad.[90] The evidence suggests, therefore, that Italian government policy or inertia, rather than the lack of interest abroad inhibited foreign investment in Italy in the spring and summer of 1922.

One affair that would later assume importance was realized by an American firm in Italy in 1922. In late March the Bank of Italy and America, as the San Francisco based Bank of America was still known at that time, acquired a controlling interest in the Banca dell'Italia Meridionale of Naples, rechristening it Banca d'America e d'Italia.[91] The latter would become an important conduit of emigrant remittances and Italo-American commercial finance, and indeed, one of the Bank of America's most profitable subsidiaries until its sale to Deutsche Bank in 1986.[92]

The March on Rome and the formation of Mussolini's first government

Although foreign bankers were showing renewed interest in Italy during the summer of 1922, the domestic political situation was deteriorating. On 12 July fascist squads attacked the headquarters of Catholic organizations in Cremona, and destroyed the house of Guido Miglioli, one of the most respected leaders of the popular wing of the Catholic party. The PPI withdrew from Facta's government, and another cabinet crisis ensued. Among the fascists there was open talk of a "march on Rome" and the

---

[88] Consiglio d'Amministrazione, verbali, 23 March 1922, Banca Commerciale Italiana, Archivio Storico (hereafter ASBCI).
[89] Keene to Hughes, 27 June 1922, NA, Treasury, RG 39.
[90] Harden to Graham, 4 July 1922, PRO, FO, 371/7656.
[91] Edward Capel Cure (British Commercial Attaché in Rome) to Dept. of Overseas Trade, undated, but after 29 March 1922, PRO, FO, 371/7656.
[92] "Confidence Factor; Bold Strike," *The Banker*, 137 (1987), no. 731, pp. 6–7.

imposition of a dictatorship. The reformist wing of the Socialist Party, led by Filippo Turati and Claudio Treves, finally decided to defy the party directorate's ban on coalitions with non-socialist formations. They announced their willingness to support externally a coalition government which would pursue a vigorous anti-fascist policy; later they even offered to assume ministerial responsibility in such a government. For a time it appeared that Bonomi might succeed in forming a new cabinet supported by Catholics, reformist socialists, and anti-fascist liberals. But few liberals were still interested in building a reformist coalition with socialists and Catholics. Giolitti discounted the participation of his group in an anti-fascist ministry in an open letter to Olindo Malagodi, the editor of the *Tribuna*. "What good," he asked, "can come of a marriage between Sturzo and Turati–Treves?" Giolitti, and many other liberal leaders, including Luigi Albertini and Salandra, preferred a government with the fascists, which would pursue a conservative economic policy; if Catholics and socialists were willing to join such a government, so much the better. After various political combinations were tried and rejected, the PPI agreed on 30 July to support a second cabinet headed by Facta, with essentially the same political composition as before; by so doing the Catholics acknowledged their own political impotence. Facta was expected to stay in power just long enough for the liberal leaders to negotiate the terms of fascist participation in a new ministry.

Mussolini now found himself in a position of strength. The leading liberal politicians were disinclined to form a government without fascist participation, giving him considerable leverage in negotiating the terms of an alliance. While Mussolini negotiated with Giolitti, Salandra, Facta, Nitti and Orlando, he proclaimed his willingness to seize power by force, and organized his squads to march on Rome. Not only did the future Duce insist on the prime ministership in a future government, he also meant in any case to marshal his paramilitary forces in Rome, to demonstrate that he held power by force, and not solely by parliamentary mandate. Although Facta seemed prepared at the last moment to call out the military and use force to defend the constitutional order, the King rescinded his emergency decree, and called Mussolini to Rome to form a new government. With prominent liberals preferring dictatorship to a reformist coalition, the PPI felt it had no choice but to join Mussolini's coalition cabinet, which presented itself to the Chamber on 31 October. Although it would take Mussolini years to eradicate political pluralism completely in Italy, normal parliamentary politics was suspended already with this act.

Monetary and financial policy under Alberto De Stefani, October 1922 – July 1925

After the March on Rome, Italy experienced over two years of economic recovery, coupled with relative price and foreign exchange stability, and moderate monetary expansion. The extraordinarily favorable circumstances during this period contributed significantly to the consolidation of the fascist dictatorship, just as the post-war recession had contributed to the weakening of the liberal state.[93] Mussolini's first Finance Minister, Alberto De Stefani, exploited the economic recovery, and the dictatorial powers which parliament promptly voted the new government, to accomplish key reforms that had eluded the last liberal governments: national and local tax reform, and the reorganization of two big state agencies with massive, chronic budget deficits, namely the railways and the postal system. In addition, De Stefani presided over the definitive liquidation of the financial crisis by rescuing the troubled Banco di Roma. This operation demanded far greater sacrifices from public institutions than the collapse of the Banca di Sconto a year earlier, but it also brought Mussolini a big political dividend: the Vatican in effect acquiesced in the destruction of the Partito Populare Italiano, and thus of democracy in Italy, in exchange for the rescue of the largest Catholic financial institution. Needless to say, this episode underscores in a particularly direct way the connection between financial and political crisis in post-war Italy.

Tax reform

As we have seen, Giolitti's immediate successors acted quickly to postpone the implementation of his "demagogic" tax proposals. However, neither Bonomi nor Facta was prepared to scrap the draconian tax proposals altogether, and return to the more moderate project developed by the Meda Commission. True, Bonomi's Minister of Finance issued a decree law on 25 November 1921 which substantially embraced the Meda project, but it was not to go into effect until 1923, and in the meantime Giolitti's confiscatory tax legislation remained on the books as well.

During the summer of 1922, an important faction of the liberal right came out in favor of an extraparliamentary solution to the fiscal crisis. As we have seen, Giolitti had been contemplating asking for full powers to reform the bureaucracy prior to his resignation in June 1921. The issue came up again when Camillo Peano, the Minister of the Treasury in Facta's first government, presented the annual budget in July 1922. Peano

---

[93] On Italy's economy, 1922–25 see, Gianni Toniolo, *L'economia dell'Italia fascista* (Bari: Laterza, 1980), pp. 31–43, and passim.

described the financial situation of the state in the darkest possible terms, so as to mobilize political support for budget cuts and new taxes. Antonio Salandra, the former Prime Minister and leading exponent of the right, responded by proposing that the government create by decree law a commission of twelve deputies, nine senators, and six state functionaries. This commission would be given extensive powers to reform the bureaucracy and change tax law. Its recommendations were to be binding, and not subject to parliamentary approval. Evidently Salandra was unruffled that his proposal struck at the heart of the European parliamentary tradition, and violated in no uncertain terms the Statuto Albertino, Italy's constitution. Presciently, the reformist socialist Claudio Treves argued that dictatorship in financial matters would be the first step toward total dictatorship.[94]

Thanks to Salandra's proposals, and the public discussion they engendered, Mussolini could count on broad consensus on the right, and even in the center, that parliament must be circumvented in instituting financial and bureaucratic reform, when he came to power three months later. In presenting his new government in mid-November, Mussolini discarded Salandra's proposal for a commission, asking instead that his government be granted full powers to reform the tax system, and the public administration. He offered no indications as to the directions, conditions or limits of the reorganization.

These unprecedented powers were wielded by Alberto De Stefani during the first years of the dictatorship. De Stefani was a respected liberal professor of economics at the University of Padua, who had rallied early to the fascist cause.[95] He was appointed Minister of Finance in Mussolini's first ministry. After the sudden illness and death of Vincenzo Tangorra, Minister of the Treasury, and one of three Populari in the cabinet, De Stefani took over that portfolio as well, consolidating Finance and Treasury into a single Ministry of the National Economy.

In the course of 1922–23 De Stefani enacted much of the contents of the Meda proposal piecemeal, in a series of decree laws. However, the Meda Commission's proposals were modified to reflect the political and class bias of the new government. The Minister of National Economy publicly justified a fiscal reform which stacked most of the benefits on the side of higher incomes, and most of the new burdens on moderate incomes, by arguing this was necessary to promote capital accumulation and investment.[96]

[94] The above is based on Veneruso, *La vigilia del fascismo*, pp. 182–88.
[95] On De Stefani see Franco Marcoaldi, *Vent'anni di economia e politica: le carte De Stefani (1922–1941)* (Milan: Angeli, 1986), pp. 9–34.
[96] For a generally positive assessment of De Stefani's tax reform see, Einaudi, *La guerra e il*

The old division of the direct tax structure into three groups – taxes on land, buildings, and other income (*ricchezza mobile*) – was preserved. De Stefani eliminated the elements of progressivity which had accrued to these taxes during the war and post-war years. At the same time, the revaluation of tax assessments went forward rapidly. Taxpayers now also were required to pay a progressive tax on their total income, i.e. the sum of their income in all three categories. The highest tax bracket was only 10%, with municipalities being permitted to levy up to an additional 10%. In other words, the first fascist government finally endowed Italy with a progressive personal income tax, a measure which liberal reformers had advocated for decades. The financial significance of this reform proved modest, however: in fiscal 1926–27, the first year in which the new tax was collected, it constituted only 3.5% of total direct tax revenues, and this figure grew only moderately thereafter.[97]

De Stefani eliminated various exemptions to the *ricchezza mobile* tax which protected primarily social groups with more modest incomes. One of the first decrees enacted under the full powers legislation eliminated the exemption of workers' wages from the *ricchezza mobile* tax. Public employees were also required to pay the tax; as were agriculturalists holding land on certain types of tenures (*coloni, coloni parziari*), and farmer-owners, the latter having paid previously only the land tax. At the same time, extraordinary taxes created during the war which struck at the well-to-do were abolished: on the income of administrators of joint-stock companies; on directors and procurers of commercial firms; on dividends, interest, and bonuses of securities issued by non-government bodies; on *ricchezza mobile* income above Lit. 10,000. The efforts of the final liberal governments to reduce fiscal evasion on income from securities by penalizing or abolishing bearer securities were abandoned. As was noted above, the new government disbanded the parliamentary investigation of war expenditure.[98]

One of De Stefani's most controversial measures was the abolition of the inheritance tax for cousins and closer family relationships. The regime justified this measure as part of its pro-family orientation, and it was undoubtedly popular. The final liberal governments had passed draconian inheritance taxes, with the consequence that collections all but collapsed.[99]

sistema tributario. For a more critical interpretation, which emphasizes the socially regressive features of De Stefani's reform see, Toniolo, *L'economia dell'Italia fascista*, pp. 45–51.

[97] Einaudi, *La guerra e il sistema tributario*, pp. 407–8, 435–40, and passim. The figures on tax revenues are from, Francesco A. Répaci, *La finanza pubblica italiana nel secolo 1861–1960* (Bologna: Zanichelli, 1962), pp. 204–6.

[98] Einaudi, *La guerra e il sistema tributario*, pp. 373–78, 408–9, 412–15, 429–37; Toniolo, *L'economia dell'Italia fascista*, pp. 46–47.

[99] Einaudi, *La guerra e il sistema tributario*, pp. 379–406.

De Stefani also took measures to encourage foreign investment. Debts contracted abroad now could be deducted from the *ricchezza mobile*; and exemptions on incomes subject to double taxation, at home and in foreign countries, could be granted upon recommendation by the Ministry of Finance. It will be recalled that foreign investors seem to have been dissuaded from making commitments in Italy in the summer of 1922 because of the tax laws.[100]

What was the overall significance of De Stefani's tax reforms? There can be no question that the direct tax structure was more elastic and equitably distributed after the reform. The old gap between draconian tax laws in theory, and more moderate, but erratic collections in reality was attenuated considerably. Total revenues increased. However, the most radical element of the Meda proposal, the progressive personal income tax, emerged from De Stefani's reform as essentially symbolic, rather than an important source of revenue. De Stefani returned to the regressive traditions of nineteenth-century Italy's fiscal system. Between 1922 and 1925 direct tax revenues declined 4% in real terms, while indirect tax revenues increased 5%. The ratio of indirect taxes to direct taxes diminished during this period from 100:94 to 100:72. Moreover, it must be taken into account that even after the reform the Italian state continued to collect many of the extraordinary war and post-war taxes, including Nitti's wealth tax. In fiscal 1934–35 8% of direct tax revenues still stemmed from extraordinary war taxes.[101]

Local government finance

De Stefani's reform of municipal and provincial taxes was an integral part of the larger fascist project of political stabilization and repression. Regrettably, given the importance of the problem during the war and post-war years, the history of local government finance in Italy has yet to be written. Little quantitative data exists, and only the crudest summary of developments is possible here.

Even before World War I, municipal taxes and indebtedness, particularly in the larger cities, had been increasing steadily. McGuire, on the basis of estimates presented by the Italian delegation to debt settlement talks with the United States in 1925, put the total revenues of Italy's communes and provinces in 1914 at about Lit. 600m., or one-third of state revenues.[102] The financial needs of local government increased rapidly

---

[100] Ibid., pp. 418–21.
[101] Figures from Toniolo, *L'economia dell'Italia fascista*, p. 48; and Répaci, *La finanza pubblica italiana*, p. 207.
[102] McGuire, *Italy's International Economic Position*, p. 440.

during the war, with the assumption of new tasks, notably food rationing and distribution. Contemporary commentators, including Riccardo Bachi, suggest that local revenue collections lagged behind those of the national government, and that the communes fell further into debt.[103] This trend seems to have accelerated after the war. Despite revenue shortfalls, and their increasing dependence on loans, usually from the Postal Savings Bank and the local savings banks, the communes embarked on ambitious public works and social welfare programs. The accession of the mass political parties to power on the local level contributed to this trend. Several important cities, including Bologna and Milan, had elected Socialist mayors already in July 1914: as we have seen, the administrative elections of November 1920 greatly expanded the number of communes and provinces under socialist and Catholic control.[104] Local governments controlled by the mass parties were not only more inclined to spend generously on social welfare: they were also more likely to grant their employees generous wage increases. In many cases they moved aggressively to shift the fiscal burden of local government from taxes on items of mass consumption to property taxes, at times in violation of national legislation regulating municipal finance.

Not surprisingly, local taxes were a key issue in the struggle between socialist and Catholic administrations, local elites, and fascist *squadristi* in north-central Italy. When socialist or *Populare* communal administrations were forced to resign after fascist attacks, and prefectural or royal commissars were appointed in their stead, tax and spending cuts could be expected to follow. Throughout the Po Valley, landowners organized tax strikes in 1922 against local administrations that remained under the control of the mass parties.[105]

As was mentioned above, Giolitti's government imposed greater financial discipline on local governments beginning in the summer of 1920 by making it harder for them to obtain loans from the Postal Savings Bank. Exponents of the center-right demanded, however, that local government be subjected to even stricter government control. The financially troubled administration of Milan was the target of particularly bitter political attacks. In February 1922, the *Corriere della Sera* published the first in a series of articles highly critical of the city's government, accusing it of financial incompetence. In late May, the Socialist mayor, G. Gentili Filippetti, traveled to Rome to enlist the support of Facta and

---

[103] See Bachi's discussions in, *L'Italia economica nell'anno 1918*, pp. 327–35; *L'Italia economica nell'anno 1919*, pp. 362–79; *L'Italia economica nell'anno 1920*, pp. 365–71; *L'Italia economica nell'anno 1921*, pp. 390–405.

[104] For the election results see, Christopher Seaton- Watson, *Italy from Liberalism to Fascism* (New York: Methuen, 1967), pp. 567–68.

[105] On the tax strikes see, Veneruso, *La vigilia del fascismo*, pp. 186, 386–92.

Peano for a new loan from the Postal Savings Bank to stave off imminent bankruptcy. Lombardy's four parliamentary deputies of the center and right protested, successfully demanding that the government withdraw any positive assurances it had given Gentili Filippetti.[106]

To summarize, "financial restoration" for local government began before the March on Rome: through fascist assaults on socialist and Catholic administrations, and the intimidation of public officials; through taxpayers strikes; and through restrictions on municipal and provincial borrowing from the Postal Savings Bank.

De Stefani completed the process through more systematic measures. He made it even harder for local governments to borrow. Further, though a series of decree laws he closely circumscribed the types and amounts of taxes which local governments could collect. As before, the most important sources of local revenue were surtaxes on the major taxes collected by the national government. According to data presented by Italian delegates to the financial talks with the United States, local government revenues averaged about Lit. 4bn., or about one-quarter of state tax collections during fiscal years 1922–23 – 1924–25 – compare this with the figure of one-third given for 1914. Finally, in 1926, the fascist government eliminated administrative elections altogether for communes with less than 3,000 inhabitants, replacing the office of mayor with an appointed *podestà*. McGuire's informants suggested that the close supervision of local government finance was one of the principal objectives of this measure.[107]

Reform of the railway, and post, telegraph, and telephone administrations

Although the size of global state budget deficits was shrinking during the last years of liberal government, at the time of the March on Rome two administrations – Railways, and Post, Telegraphs, and Telephones – continued to run substantial deficits which weighed heavily on the general budget. Moreover, the size of the deficits of these administrations was increasing, rather than diminishing, prior to the fascist takeover. The railways had reported a deficit of Lit. 1,087m. in fiscal 1919–20, which swelled to Lit. 1,431m. in 1921–22. The deficits for Post, Telegraphs, and Telephones were Lit. 301m. in 1919–20, and Lit. 506m. in 1921–22.[108] Politics and trade union pressures were mostly responsible for this state of

---

[106] Ibid., pp. 389–91.

[107] McGuire, *Italy's International Economic Position*, pp. 441–44.

[108] For the railways see ibid., pp. 438–39; for Post, Telegraphs, and Telephones see, Ragioneria generale dello stato, *Il bilancio dello stato dal 1913–14 al 1929–30 e la finanza fascista a tutto l'anno VIII* (Rome: Istituto poligrafico dello stato, 1931), p. 349.

affairs: these administrations had long been preserves for the distribution
of jobs to reward political clients; and strong union federations insured
that wages rose more quickly than tariffs and fees in the early post-war
years. The bloated and inefficient railway and postal administrations were
an obvious target for critics of the liberal state, including the fascists prior
to the March on Rome.[109]

De Stefani reorganized the railways and the postal service with his
customary brutality, and attention to the political and class interests of the
Fascist Party and its supporters. According to a report presented to Mussolini, between October 1922 and April 1924, 65,274 jobs were cut from
the public payroll: among them 46,566 in railways, and 8,621 in Post,
Telegraphs and Telephones.[110] Socialist union organizers, "subversives,"
and the political clients of non-fascist parties were singled out for dismissal; members of the fascist union federations kept their jobs or were
promoted. In addition, the new government decreed across-the-board rate
hikes in both services. Telephone networks were sold off to private
companies.[111]

For fiscal 1924–25 De Stefani reported a profit of Lit. 176m. in the
railway administration and Lit. 45m. for Post, Telegraphs, and
Telephones. Although there is no doubt that the efficiency of these public
services improved, and the costs diminished, during his three years in
office, substantial accounts juggling, not to say the postponement of essential repairs and infrastructure investment was required to achieve such
spectacular results on paper.[112]

The rescue of the Banco di Roma

In addition to reforming the local and national tax systems, De Stefani
played a key role in the rescue of the Banco di Roma in 1923. It will be

[109] In a famous speech delivered in Udine on 20 September 1922, one month before the
March on Rome, Mussolini polemicized: "The entire apparatus of the state collapses, as
the stage setting of an old operetta, when there is no longer the internalized conscious-
ness of fulfilling an obligation, or better a mission. For this reason we want to despoil the
state of all of its economic attributes. Enough of the railway-state, the postal-state, the
insurer-state. Enough of the shop-keeper-state at the expense of Italian taxpayers,
aggravating the exhausted public finances. We will keep the police, who protect honest
men from thieves and criminals; we will keep the teacher, educator of the coming
generations; we will keep the army, which guarantees the inviolability of the fatherland;
and we will keep foreign policy." Benito Mussolini, *Opera omnia*, ed. Edoardo and Duilio
Susmel, vol. XVIII (Florence: La Fenice, 1956), p. 419, quoted in, Renzo De Felice,
Mussolini il fascista, vol. I, *La conquista del potere*, p. 332. See also Sigismondo Balducci's
polemical *Elefantiasi ferroviaria* (Milan: Società Editoriale Italiana, 1920).
[110] De Felice, *Mussolini il fascista*, vol. I, pp. 397–98.
[111] Toniolo, *L'economia dell'Italia fascista*, pp. 49–50.
[112] The figures cited are from, McGuire, *Italy's International Economic Position*, pp. 438–39
(railways); and Ragioneria generale dello Stato, *Il bilancio dello Stato*, p. 349 (Post,

recalled that the Banco di Roma was close to failure in late 1915 and early 1916, due at least in part to its "political" investments in Libya and elsewhere in the Mediterranean basin. Failure during this period was only averted by generous rediscounting operations by the issue banks; agreements with the government, signed in June 1915 and April 1917, according to which the Roma received compensation for some of its losses during the Libyan War; and the general increase in liquidity produced by the war economy. The Vatican was also constrained to play a leading role in this first rescue of the Roma, because of its own exposure to the stricken institution. Not only did prominent Vatican dignitaries, the religious orders, and the Holy See itself maintain large deposits in the Banco di Roma: the Vatican also held a substantial bloc of the bank's stock, a bloc which became a majority interest in the course of 1915 and 1916, as the Holy See propped up the troubled bank by buying additional shares on the market.[113]

The Vatican extricated itself from the Banco di Roma during late 1915 and early 1916 at the expense of other Catholic financial institutions. In 1914 a Federazione bancaria italiana had been established as an umbrella organization for regional Catholic banks. The Federazione drew up plans for the foundation of a Credito Nazionale, which would function as a sort of central bank for the member institutions. By the time the Credito Nazionale opened its doors in early 1916, it had been overtaken by the crisis of the Banco di Roma. The Vatican now induced the Credito Nazionale to acquire its bloc of Banco di Roma shares and undertake the reorganization of the stricken bank. The directors responsible for the Libyan adventure and the calamitous state of the bank's affairs – notable among them Ernesto Pacelli, president of the bank, and uncle of the future Pius XII – were forced to resign. In place of the old group entered administrators with close ties to the Catholic cooperative movement and the Credito Nazionale. Giuseppe Vicentini became director general of the Roma in summer of 1915, and held a similar post at the Credito Nazionale when it opened. Carlo Santucci, another eminence in the world of Catholic finance, became president in March 1917.[114]

The new leadership team set about transforming the Roma so as to complement the Credito Nazionale. They concentrated the exchange and

Telegraphs, and Telephones). For critical views of De Stefani's administration and creative accounting see, Toniolo, *L'economia dell'Italia fascista*, p. 50; Domenicatonio Fausto, "La politica finanziaria del fascismo," *Richerche economiche*, 39 (1975), no. 2, pp. 164–91; Giacomo Matteotti, *Reliquie* (Milan: Corbaccio, 1924), pp. 93–98, and passim.

[113] Luigi De Rosa, *Storia del Banco di Roma*, vol. II, *Dal 1911 al 1928* (Rome: Banco di Roma, 1983) (privately published, restricted distribution), pp. 47–54, 69–75, 99.

[114] De Rosa, *Storia del Banco di Roma*, vol. II, pp. 76–84, 94–100, 109, 138–42. See also, Anna Caroleo, *Le banche cattoliche dalla prima guerra mondiale al fascismo* (Milan: Feltrinelli, 1976).

international business of the Catholic banks with the Roma. As the Roma's financial position improved during the latter years of the war, it also rediscounted the Catholic banks' paper, and opened credit lines in their favor. Meanwhile, Vicentini expanded the branch network of the Banco di Roma in areas where strong local Catholic institutions did not exist. The fascist liquidators of the Roma would charge later that this policy kept the Roma out of more prosperous regions of the country where Catholic organizations were strong, such as the Veneto, Emilia, and Lombardy, confining its expansion to the relatively poor center and south.[115]

Despite its brush with collapse in 1915–16, the Banco di Roma rivalled the other commercial banks in its ambitious program of expansion in the last year of war and the early post-war period. Its prior catastrophic experiences in Libya and Turkey notwithstanding, the Roma made the Middle East the focus of its international strategy. A branch office was opened in Jerusalem in March 1919, and additional branches in Beirut, Smirna, Damascus, Aleppo, Alexandretta, Haifa, and Tripoli (Lebanon) followed. The Roma re-established itself in Constantinople, the site of its largest pre-war losses, by buying the offices of a Hungarian bank. Even a Banca di Roma d'Oriente, for business in East Asia, and subsidiaries in Russia, Poland, Bulgaria, and Romania were projected. The Banco di Roma also promoted and financed domestic industrial and commercial firms, in addition to the rapidly growing Catholic cooperative movement.[116]

The Roma's bullish expansion continued at least until the spring of 1920. The first major signs of trouble came at the bank's Egyptian branches, where large losses were discovered. During the war and early post-war years, the Roma's Egyptian operation was run almost without supervision from the main office by Riccardo Interdonato, a megalomaniacal intriguer, whose business incompetence was matched only by his political ineptness. Interdonato dreamed of turning Egypt into an economic colony of the Banco di Roma, and he assembled a business empire of local banks, steamship companies, phosphate mines, and cotton export firms, which collapsed at the first signs of weakness on the international commodities markets. At the same time he rendered himself intolerable to the British by scheming against them; alternately with Arab nationalists, and with the leaders of Egypt's Jewish community. In the spring of 1920 the head office of the Roma dispatched an investigating team to Alexandria, and Interdonato's resignation ensued. However, the bank's Middle Eastern opera-

[115] De Rosa, *Storia del Banco di Roma*, vol. II, pp. 84–88, 113–15, 183–85, 203–5, 211, 394.
[116] ASMAE, Archivio politico, 1915–1918, Siria 1918, 187/11; De Rosa, *Storia del Banco di Roma*, vol. II, pp. 176–82, 192–205, 232–43.

tions continued to produce heavy losses until the fascist reorganization of the Roma in 1923.[117]

Perhaps the most remarkable aspect of the Banco di Roma's post-war history is its survival until after the collapse of the Banca Italiana di Sconto. After the onset of the economic recession in the summer and fall of 1920, the Roma's domestic operations were as troubled as its foreign concerns. The bank's industrial and commercial clientele was less select, and suffered greater losses than those of the Banca Commerciale and the Credito Italiano. Of at least equal significance, after headlong expansion during the war and immediate post-war period, the Catholic consumer, producer, and credit cooperatives showed signs of stress with the onset of recession. These difficulties were greatly augmented by fascist violence: in May 1921 the *squadristi* turned their attention from the already weakened socialists to the Catholic cooperative movement.[118]

As early as the fall of 1920 the Roma faced a depositors' run, particularly at its Middle Eastern branches, as word of the bank's losses in Egypt spread. Although the depositors' run abated in late December, heavy withdrawals began again in late January 1921, after a fall in cotton prices, and new rumors that the Roma's Egyptian branches were faced with huge additional losses on loans secured by raw cotton. During 1920 and 1921 the Roma adopted many of the same desperate stratagems as the Bansconto to obtain liquidity: it opened branches in towns of little commercial importance to obtain new deposits; it offered high interest rates to clients who deposited Treasury bills, which in turn could be rediscounted with the issue banks; and it delayed cashing checks drawn on its own branches by foreign subsidiaries.[119]

Not surprisingly, the Roma suffered particularly large depositors' withdrawals at the time of the crisis of the Bansconto in late December 1921 and early January 1922. The Roma's rediscounting operations with the issue banks increased from Lit. 275m. at the end of December 1921 to Lit. 1,105m. at the end of February, and Lit. 1,235m. at the end of March. On 9 April 1922 Stringher wrote to Vicentini, advising him that he foresaw a bad end for the Banco di Roma, and expressing his reluctance to increase the issue banks' exposure any further, without substantial guarantees.

---

[117] Ibid., vol. II, pp. 176–82, 245–54, 260–64. Interdonato returned to Egypt after his dismissal by the Banco di Roma, to the consternation of Italian consular authorities in Alexandria in the summer of 1922. ASMAE, Affari politici, 1919–1930, Egitto, 1922, 1000/2651; 100/2652. 1000/2651 also contains an undated, unsigned memo, presumably from 1920, describing the Roma's business holdings in Egypt, and Interdonato's business and social affiliations.

[118] On the fascist attacks on Catholic cooperatives see, Caroleo, *Le banche cattoliche*, p. 85.

[119] De Rosa, *Storia del Banco di Roma*, vol. II, pp. 269–70, p. 300; Bachi, *L'Italia economica 1921*, pp. 38–40.

Stringher believed that the failure of a second major commercial bank had to be avoided at all costs. He evidently meant to solve the Roma crisis in a manner similar to the restructuring of Ilva and the Ansaldo–Bansconto groups: the old administrators would have to step down, and a new management team, enjoying the confidence of the issue banks, would take their place.[120]

In the case of the Roma this presented particular difficulties, however. Vicentini and Santucci were close to the leadership of the Partito Populare: indeed, the Roma heavily subsidized the party's newspapers. Facta's government, which of course relied on the PPI for its parliamentary majority, pressured Stringher to make new credits available to the Roma, while leaving Vicentini and his associates in control of the bank. A stalemate ensued for the next seven months: the issue banks exposure to the Banco di Roma stabilized at the high level of early spring, while Vicentini made the first timid steps to reduce the Roma's expenses by dismissing personnel, and closing unprofitable branch offices. Even after Mussolini formed his first government in late October the restructuring of the Banco di Roma was delayed, because of the influence of the Partito Populare. It will be recalled that a Populare, Vincenzo Tangorra, was Mussolini's first Minister of the Treasury.[121]

However, with Tangorra's death and De Stefani's consolidation of the Ministries of Finance and Treasury under his control, the stage was set for the liquidation of Banco di Roma. De Stefani was close to the *squadristi* of his native Verona, and a bitter foe of the PPI and the Catholic cooperative movement. Stringher was quick to sense the change in political climate, and the Bank of Italy adopted a harder line *vis-à-vis* the Roma. In late December, when the Roma applied for an increase in issue bank credits, Stringher demanded that the bank's directors provide very specific information about the institution's financial situation. Stringher in turn passed this information on to Carlo Vitali, the director of a provincial bank in Cremona, whom De Stefani was grooming as Vicentini's successor. Meanwhile, Mussolini was engaged in intensive negotiations with the Vatican in which the fate of the Banco di Roma figured prominently. The exact nature of these talks remains unclear: however, the Vatican subsequently remained silent while the Partito Populare and much of the Catholic cooperative network was destroyed; in the meantime the Banco di Roma was rescued.[122]

---

[120] De Rosa, *Storia del Banco di Roma*, vol. II, pp. 308, 312–16. Referring to the Banco di Roma, Stringher told his Comitato on 15 January 1922: "it is clear it cannot fall. Its fall probably would provoke a general catastrophe, damaging the entire country." ASBI, Fondo, 9.2, Comitato, verbali.

[121] De Rosa, *Storia del Banco di Roma*, vol. II, pp. 316–27, 342–46.

[122] Ibid., pp. 360–66; De Felice, *Mussolini il fascista*, vol. I, pp. 495–98; Anna Caroleo, *Le*

On 9 February 1923 De Stefani brought about the change of guard at the Banco di Roma with the characteristic trappings of fascist political theater. Mussolini received Vicentini and Santucci at his offices in the Palazzo Viminale, the seat of the Ministry of the Interior, in the presence of De Stefani. The Duce read an ultimatum, prepared by De Stefani, attributing the Roma's difficulties to the mismanagement of its directors, and requiring them to step down immediately. Vitali was to replace Vicentini, and Francesco Boncompagni Ludovisi, Prince of Piombino, and an ex-PPI deputy who had joined the Fascist Party, became the new President.[123]

Vitali and Boncompagni Ludovisi embarked on a ruthless reorganization of the Banco di Roma. The bank's subsidies to PPI and Nittian newspapers were immediately eliminated. The Roma's branch network and personnel were cut back radically. The Catholic cooperative movement was abandoned to its fate. In August, De Stefani arranged a second meeting at the Viminale similar to the first. This time Vicentini was forced to agree to sell the majority bloc of Banco di Roma shares, which were held by the Credito Nazionale, to the state for the symbolic price of one lira. The remaining financial relationships between the Roma and the Credito Nazionale were to be studied in a spirit of "a certain comprehension": should these relationships involve substantial additional losses for the Roma, Vicentini and the other administrators of the Credito Nazionale were to resign, being replaced by persons enjoying the confidence of the government.[124]

One month later the Banco di Roma signed an agreement with the Autonomous Section of the CSVI. Illiquid loans and participations with a nominal value of Lit. 1,693m., a sum approximately equal to the issue bank's exposure to the Roma, were ceded to the CSVI. This amounted to over 12% of the issue banks' note circulation. The Roma extended a guarantee that at least Lit. 773m. would be realized by the liquidation of these loans. Any profits in excess of this amount were to accrue to the Autonomous Section of the CSVI, as would any additional losses. The majority bloc of Banco di Roma shares was deposited with the CSVI as an additional guarantee of the realization of Lit. 773m. In subsequent years, Boncompagni Ludovisi and Vitali managed the Banco di Roma according to very conservative criteria. On the eve of the Great Depression it was the

banche cattoliche, pp. 116–21 and passim; Anna Caroleo, "La crisi e il salvataggio del Banco di Roma nei primi contatti tra Mussolini e la Santa Sede," *Belfagor*, 28 (1973), no. 4, pp. 461–74; Alberto De Stefani, *Baraonda bancaria* (Milan: Edizioni del Borghese, 1960).

[123] De Rosa, *Storia del Banco di Roma*, vol. II, pp. 372–73; De Stefani, *Baraonda bancaria*, pp. 253–62.

[124] De Rosa, *Storia del Banco di Roma*, vol. II, pp. 375–77, 381–86, 407–10; De Stefani, *Baraonda bancaria*, pp. 279–83, 353–88.

most liquid of Italy's major commercial banks, if only moderately profitable.[125]

Summary: financial rigueur and political crisis

During the dictatorship, an essential element in the regime's self-justification was the claim that fascism had saved Italy not only from Bolshevism, but also from financial collapse. De Stefani himself heavily promoted this idea in a series of books and pamphlets. It was accepted, often uncritically, by American bankers and financial experts. Anti-fascists, notably Gaetano Salvemini and the ill-fated Matteotti, argued in contrast, that the significance of De Stefani's reforms was much exaggerated by juggling accounts and misrepresentation. More importantly, they pointed out that the process of financial restoration had begun long before the March on Rome, and suggested therefore that much of the merit must be ascribed to the final liberal governments.[126]

This chapter presents a different point of view. It argues that new debt creation, the surest indicator of the size of actual state budget deficits, had declined precipitously prior to the March on Rome. Clearly, therefore, the last liberal governments made substantial progress in solving Italy's fiscal crisis. However, political stalemate blocked certain important reforms prior to the fascist takeover: the reorganization of state and local taxes, the reform of public administrations, particularly the railways, and Post, Telegraphs, and Telephones; and the restructuring of the Banco di Roma. These reforms were carried out by Alberto De Stefani, with dictatorial methods, and in accordance with the class and political interests of the Fascist Party. The significance of De Stefani's reforms probably has been underestimated by anti-fascists, but no doubt exaggerated by the regime's supporters, notably De Stefani himself. However, in my estimation, the most important aspect of the problem lies elsewhere. The real problem is the connection between the weakening of the liberal reform coalition under Giolitti and his successors, and their policies of financial *rigueur*. Salvemini was correct in arguing that the process of financial restoration was underway well before the March on Rome, but he failed to appreciate how this process undermined the liberals' political base. Giolitti set out in June 1920 to mediate between right and left; between *raison d'état* and parliamentary coalition building; between promoting economic growth and social reform, much as he had before the war. The recession, and the accumulated weight of choices long since made, cut the ground from

---

[125] De Rosa, *Storia del Banco di Roma*, vol. II, pp. 411–12, and passim.
[126] Alberto De Stefani, *La restaurazione finanziaria 1922–25* (Bologna: Zanichelli, 1926); Salvemini, *The Origins of Fascism in Italy*; Matteotti, *Reliquie*.

under him. Not only was the Italian economy unable to afford draconian taxes, but key sectors, notably the strategic industrial sector which had grown so rapidly, were unable to survive without significant government subsidies, and injections of liquidity from the issue banks. Giolitti was forced to make economies in social spending without punishing war profiteers or exacting sacrifices from business. He laid the basis for financial restoration and monetary stabilization, but eroded the government's parliamentary base. His immediate successors essentially continued his policies, with well-known and tragic consequences.

CONCLUSION

The objective of this study is to rethink and reinterpret the crisis of liberal Italy through a critical analysis of monetary and financial policy from 1914 to 1922. A complete discussion of all aspects of the collapse of the liberal regime lies beyond the scope of this work. However, the evidence and arguments presented here offer a new perspective on the two major interpretive traditions of the crisis of parliamentary government and the rise of fascism in Italy, namely liberalism and Marxism.

Salvemini and the liberal tradition

As was noted at the end of chapter 7, apologists of Mussolini's regime in the 1920s and 1930s claimed that the March on Rome rescued Italy from Bolshevik revolution and economic and financial collapse; it was therefore only natural for non-fascists to rebut what fairly can be called the regime's founding myths.

The tone of liberal historiography was set by Gaetano Salvemini, an historian and anti-fascist activist in exile, who in a series of books and articles published in the 1920s and 1930s directed much of his attention to refuting the fascists' contentions that socialist revolution was imminent in post-war Italy, and that the Italian economy and Italian state finances were on the verge of collapse.[1] The pervasiveness of Salvemini's influence among non-Marxist anti-fascist historians was underscored recently by the publication of Paolo Frascani's study of post-World-War-I state finances in Italy – the only recent study on this subject – which essentially reconfirms Salvemini's positions.[2] While recognizing that the liquidation of the war caused great dislocations in the post-war Italian economy, produced a

---

[1] See in particular, Gaetano Salvemini, *The Origins of Fascism in Italy* (the Harvard lectures) (New York: Harper and Row, 1973); but also, Gaetano Salvemini, *The Fascist Dictatorship in Italy*, 2nd rev. ed. (London: Cape, 1928); Gaetano Salvemini, *Under the Axe of Fascism* (New York: Viking, 1936).

[2] Paolo Frascani, *Politica economica e finanza pubblica in Italia nel primo dopoguerra (1918–1922)* (Naples: Giannini, 1975).

crisis in state finances, and exposed the inadequacies of the fiscal system, both Salvemini and Frascani insist that the final liberal governments were well on their way to overcoming the economic and financial crisis prior to the March on Rome.

Salvemini points out that the post-war economic recession had already reached its trough, and that recovery was underway by October 1922. With regard to state finances, Salvemini and Frascani argue that the essential measures required to reduce the large post-war budget deficits – cuts in spending and tax reform – already had been implemented or proposed prior to the fascist *coup d'état*. The two major causes of wartime and post-war budget deficits, military spending and food subsidies, were brought under control long before the March on Rome. The Nitti administration was successful in reducing military expenditure radically, despite its inability to resolve the Fiume episode and sign a peace treaty with Yugoslavia. Giolitti's ministry abolished the bread subsidy in the winter of 1920–21, at a time when the post-war recession already had provoked a significant decline in international cereal prices. Liberal historians are forced to concede that it was left to Mussolini to eliminate the large deficits of the state postal and railway administrations – largely by firing employees with anti-fascist political allegiances – but they are quick to point out that the payrolls of the public administration began to swell again in the late 1920s, as pressures to accommodate fascist clienteles mounted. In any event, on the basis of official figures, Einaudi estimated that net public borrowing declined from Lit. 13,514m. in fiscal 1920–21, to Lit. 6,286m. in 1921–22, and to Lit. 1,115m. in the last six months of 1922.[3] With reason, therefore, Salvemini and other liberal historians have claimed that the budget surpluses of the early fascist years were the product of policies inaugurated by the final liberal governments.

The liberal case on tax reform is weaker: a thoroughgoing reform of the Italian tax system was only enacted by Mussolini's first Finance Minister, Alberto De Stefani, in 1922–25, but Salvemini aptly points out that De Stefani's reform followed, in its main lines, the so-called Meda project, drawn up by a parliamentary commission during the war. The process of updating tax assessments, which was as important in reforming the fiscal system as actual changes in the tax code, was begun by Pasquale D'Aroma, Director General of the Finance Ministry's Bureau of Direct Taxes, during Nitti's government in the latter half of 1919.

Meanwhile, Italy was on the way to achieving monetary stabilization

---

[3] Luigi Einaudi, "Dove si tenta di calcolare il disavanzo del bilancio italiano," *Corriere della Sera*, 25 April 1923, republished in, *Cronache di un trentennio*, vol. VII, *1923–1924* (Turin: Einaudi, 1966), p. 212.

well before the March on Rome. The state was essentially able to finance its deficit without further recourse to the printing press by the middle of 1920. The money supply contracted moderately, and wholesale and retail price indexes reached their first peak at the end of 1920. Inflation only resumed again at a more moderate rate during the boom in the early fascist years, 1923–25.

Despite the severity of the banking crisis in post-war Italy, Salvemini suggested that the wave of expansion and investment in industry during the war created opportunities for substantial growth. The restructuring of financially distressed banking and industrial firms was also well underway under the final liberal governments. Giolitti and Stringher brokered an agreement for restructuring Ilva with the Banca Commerciale and the Credito Italiano in the spring of 1921. It is true that Stringher's efforts to eject the Perrone brothers from Ansaldo, and restructure that firm and its house bank, the Banca Italiana di Sconto, without provoking undue turbulence on the financial markets, met with failure. However, Italy's banking system weathered the collapse of the Sconto in December 1921, and although the Bank of Italy had locked up substantial resources in an insolvent industrial empire, and was forced to make further commitments to the failed Sconto's creditors, the restructuring process had begun before October 1922. There remained the grave financial problems of the Banco di Roma, and the Catholic cooperative movement with which it was associated. Stringher had been unable to eject the bank's old administrators and liquidate its bad debts prior to the March on Rome, because of the PPI's influence in government. However, Stringher had begun applying pressure on the Roma's directors in the spring of 1922, and he had at least stabilized the size of issue bank advances to the ailing institution at that time.

Such considerations led Salvemini to argue that the collapse of the liberal state was the result of a political, rather than an economic crisis. Salvemini conceived the political crisis in relatively narrow terms: the inability of the parties represented in parliament after November 1919 to form stable coalitions; the lack of institutional prestige of parliament as a consequence of the corruption prevalent in the Giolittian era; sedition in the military after D'Annunzio's *coup de main* at Fiume in September 1919; and the willingness of the king to abandon constitutional process in October 1922. Among the elements of the crisis, Salvemini insisted on parliamentary deadlock as the essential factor.

There can be no doubt that parliamentary deadlock, and, in particular, the failure of the liberal deputies to form a stable governing coalition with either of the two mass parties (Catholics and Socialists) which emerged from the November 1919 parliamentary elections with a negative majority between them, was a crucial element in the crisis of the liberal state. The problem with Salvemini's argument is that it tends to [suspend the analysis of parliamentary deadlock in mid-air] without fully recognizing how the harsh economic and financial environment of the post-war era narrowed the choices and the margins of negotiation for liberal political leaders. In particular, Salvemini obscures the relationship between the process of monetary stabilization and financial restoration undertaken by the final liberal governments, and the disintegration of stable parliamentary majorities. It is difficult to see how liberal leaders could have won the allegiance of the mass political parties, while pursuing orthodox monetary and financial policies, however necessary they felt the latter to have been.

Post-war liberal governments felt that they could not adopt the relatively moderate Meda tax reform project, because broad sectors of public opinion, outraged at the huge wealth transfers engendered by the war economy, considered it too mild. Instead, Nitti proposed a capital levy in the fall of 1919, which he subsequently felt constrained to withdraw, after it had elicited a storm of protest from business interests and the middle class. The fall of Nitti's government in the spring of 1920 was in no small measure due to the growing discontent of business interests and the more conservative wing of his parliamentary majority with his inability to control social spending and budget deficits. Like the Nitti government, Giolitti's ministry was weakened by conflicts between the more conservative and the more reform-oriented wings of his parliamentary majority over taxes and government spending. In July 1920 Giolitti proposed a confiscatory tax on wealth accumulated during and after the war, and a parliamentary investigation on war profits to placate the left; at the same time he prepared to abolish the bread subsidy and cut government spending to placate the right. The unbending opposition of business groups to the tax measures led Giolitti and his successors, Bonomi and Facta, to agree to a series of compromises and postponements, until Mussolini abolished the tax on wealth accumulated during the war altogether, along with the parliamentary commission to investigate war expenditures. Beginning with Nitti's ministry, the intolerance of business and middle-class elements for democratic, reformist politics became manifest. During Giolitti's ministry, it became increasingly clear that significant parts of the business community and the middle classes were unprepared to submit to genuine tax reform and real increases in the level of taxation, without assurances that government spending would not be held hostage to the demands of socialists and Catholics.

At the same time, post-war leaders in Italy had less margin than their counterparts in France for dealing with budgetary problems. Italian investors had shallower pockets than French investors, and they were in no position to go on financing big budget deficits for many years after the armistice. In addition, the wartime practice of allowing national loan issues to fall quickly under par, and allowing large institutional investors to regain their liquidity positions by rediscounting loan paper with the issue banks alienated the small savers who had made up the state's most loyal clientele.

Italian political leaders needed to look only at Germany and Austria to convince themselves that balanced budgets were imperative to prevent monetary chaos. Giolitti abolished the bread subsidy and took other important steps toward reducing the state budget deficit; in the process, however, he alienated the Catholics who supported his government, and the reformist socialists he hoped to lure into his majority. Cuts in welfare-related government spending alienated the reformist left, even as draconian tax proposals alienated business interests and the right, leaving the final liberal governments dependent on unstable coalitions and unable to take major policy initiatives. Parliamentary deadlock was in no small measure the expression of conflict over the role of the state and the issue banks in reallocating economic resources.

In a more general sense, Salvemini's assessment of Italy's economic situation in the post-war years does not take into account fully the political consequences of a strategy of industrial development based on transferring resources from consumers and consumer-related industries to non-competitive strategic industries. The tremendous expansion of the strategic sector during the war, which was promoted by the state's productivist economic and financial policies, contributed to the severity of Italy's post-war economic difficulties. Even before the war Italy had been exceptionally vulnerable to financial crises; because of the structural vulnerabilities of its mixed banking system; and because of longstanding tensions between the authorities in Rome and commercial bankers in Milan. State-sponsored rescues of failed banks and industrial concerns between 1921 and 1923 required considerable resources, and foreclosed other policy options. Political leaders in Rome were unwilling to accept new responsibilities in social and welfare policy or risk protracted budget deficits when macroeconomic stability was threatened already by bank failures, and when the issue banks' resources were tied up in illiquid loans.

Finally, the protective cushion which emigrant remittances and tourist receipts had provided for Italy's international accounts at the beginning of the century had largely vanished. The relatively rapid termination of British and American financial aid forced Italy to weather a difficult readjustment in its international accounts, which hardly facilitated a generous social welfare policy. Post-war leaders needed to keep their eyes on the international financial markets and the exchange value of the lira when they formulated both domestic and foreign policy, and such external constraints reduced their margin for striking compromises.

In brief, the project on which Giolitti embarked at the beginning of the century of democratizing the electoral franchise, and reconciling Italy's masses with the institutions and ideology of the liberal state required that he balance the conflicting claims of great power politics, economic growth, macroeconomic stability, and social reform. He set out to do so during an era in which economic and financial conditions were exceptionally favorable. These conditions were much less favorable during the immediate post-war years, and liberal leaders were confronted with hard choices between goals which no longer appeared to be compatible. Beginning with Giolitti in 1920–21, liberal political leaders chose macroeconomic stability over democratic reform. The range of choice at this date had been narrowed significantly by the productivist policy of promoting armaments-related industries during the Great War.

Tasca and the Marxian tradition

In contrast to Salvemini and the liberal historiographical tradition, Marxians have always placed more emphasis on the relationship between economics and politics in the crisis of the liberal state. Procacci, for example, has observed that the crisis of the liberal state and the advent of fascism in Italy stood in a similar relationship to the post-war economic recession as the crisis of the Weimar Republic and the advent of Hitler to the world economic depression in the early 1930s.[4] However, beginning with Angelo Tasca's seminal study, *La Naissance du fascisme: l'Italie de 1918 à 1922* in 1938 (written and published in exile, in France), Marxian historiography has focused more on the social and political conflict that swept Italy's cities and villages in the post-war years than on the state administration and economic and financial policy.[5] Fine monographs have been produced by Marxists, or historians influenced by Tasca and the Marxian tradition, on the political and social history of individual towns, provinces, and regions, on the political parties, and on trade unions and industrial relations, but little has been written in the way of macroeconomic analysis, or studies of the functioning of the central government.[6] Marxian historians have typi-

---

[4] Giuliano Procacci, *Storia degli italiani* (Bari: Laterza, 1968).
[5] Angelo Tasca, *La Naissance du fascisme: l'Italie de 1918 à 1922* (Paris: Gallimard, 1938); Angelo Tasca, *Nascita e avvento del fascismo*, 2nd rev. ed. (Florence: La Nuova Italia, 1950).
[6] Ernesto Ragioniere, *Un comune socialista: Sesto Fiorentino* (Rome: Riuniti, 1976) (originally published in 1953); Paolo Spriano, *Torino operaia nella grande guerra (1914–1918)* (Turin: Einaudi, 1960); Paul Corner, *Fascism in Ferrara, 1915–1925* (Oxford: Oxford University Press, 1975); Anthony Cardoza, *Agrarian Elites and Italian Fascism: The Province of Bologna,*

cally located the origins of the post-war crisis on the periphery, rather than at the center. The crisis of the liberal state is often depicted as a twofold process, with the first stage being the loss of control of public order in areas of the north and center and the consolidation of fascist power locally, and the second stage being the seizure by the fascists of the now-impotent central state apparatus. For Tasca and other Marxian historians, it was the breakdown of what Max Weber regarded as the primary attribute of the modern state, i.e. its ability to enforce a monopoly on the use of violence within its territory, which defined the crisis of the state in post-World-War-I Italy.

Since Tasca, Marxists have persisted in interpreting the post-war crisis primarily in terms of a conflict between revolution and counter-revolution. It is true that Tasca followed Salvemini in discounting the claim of the fascist regime's apologists that fascism thwarted revolution. According to Tasca, by mid-1920, when fascism started to become a serious political force, the socialist movement had already missed its chance to achieve revolutionary change, and its strength was ebbing, as a consequence of strategic errors and organizational weaknesses. The fascist counter-revolution was, "posthumous and preemptive," a product of the "great fear" of the propertied classes, rather than a response to a clear and present revolutionary socialist threat. All the same, the emphasis on the revolution–counter-revolution dichotomy in Tasca and much Marxian historiography tends to shift attention from the crisis of liberal politics.

Curiously, the wealth of regional monographs on social relations and economic conditions has produced evidence which challenges important elements of Tasca's interpretation of the post-war crisis, even though no important Marxist interpretive reformulation has yet appeared. Particularly with regard to industrial Italy, recent studies cast doubt on the utility of interpreting post-war social conflict as a struggle between revolutionaries and counterrevolutionaries. The work of Abrate on the Torinese Industrial League, and Castronovo's biography of Giovanni Agnelli, the director of Fiat, for example, have demonstrated that the most influential Italian industrialists were initially hostile to fascism and loath to abandon a system of industrial relations based on the freedom of trade unions and employers' organizations.[7] Many Italian industrialists believed they had

1901–1926 (Princeton: Princeton University Press, 1982); Alice A. Kelikian, *Town and Country under Fascism: The Transformation of Brescia, 1915–1926* (New York: Oxford University Press, 1986); Paolo Spriano, *Storia del partito communista italiano*, vol. I (Turin: Einaudi, 1967); Paolo Spriano, *L'occupazione delle fabbriche, settembre 1920* (Turin: Einaudi, 1964).

[7] Mario Abrate, *La lotta sindicale nella industrializzazione in Italia, 1906–1926*, 2nd ed. (Milan: Angeli, 1967); Valerio Castronovo, *Giovanni Agnelli. La Fiat dal 1899 al 1945* (Turin: Einaudi 1977). See also, Roland Sarti, *Fascism and Industrial Leadership in Italy, 1919–1940: A Study in the Expansion of Private Power under Fascism* (Berkeley: University of California Press, 1971).

already won their struggle with revolutionary socialist workers over authority in the factories by the end of 1920, and what is more, they had done so without having recourse to fascist squads. Meanwhile, the work of Abrate, Frascani, and Vivarelli has also brought into relief the enormous hostility of business and employers' organizations to the radical tax proposals of the Nitti and Giolitti governments, and their insistence on monetary and budgetary stabilization, regardless of the political consequences.[8] In his biography of Agnelli, Castronovo noted that in the early years of Mussolini's regime *La Stampa* described the leading Turinese industrialist as an anti-fascist in Turin and a fascist in Rome.[9] This characterization epitomizes the conclusions of much recent research, which suggests that the extent of the northern Italian industrialists' disenchantment with the final liberal governments for not repressing socialist political parties and unions has been overemphasized, while their fear of runaway inflation and budget deficits has been underemphasized.

It is of course evident that the situation in certain rural areas, most notably parts of the Po Valley, was altogether different. In some rural areas a process of revolutionary social change was underway in the postwar years. The recent studies of Corner, Cardoza, and others have confirmed Tasca's argument that the agrarian unions and consumer cooperatives, coupled with socialist control of municipal government, threatened to undermine the economic and political basis of the landowning and leaseholding elites in parts of north-central Italy.[10] Such areas were the cradles of the fascist movement, and here fascism undoubtedly exercised a counterrevolutionary function. However, the fact that fascism as a serious political phenomenon originated as a counterrevolutionary movement in rural areas of north-central Italy does not in itself fully explain the crisis of the liberal state.

It is important to note that the social and political conditions which produced explosive conflict in the Po Valley after World War I – overpopulation and underemployment, the presence of a large landless rural proletariat well organized in socialist leagues – hardly had changed by the end of World War II. Social and political revolution actually occurred in the Po Valley and other parts of rural Italy in the late 1940s. However, the decline of the landowning and leaseholding classes in parts of north-central rural Italy, their replacement by red and white agricultural cooperatives, the establishment of a "red belt" of communist and socialist administered municipal and provincial governments in much of the Emilia-Romagna, Tuscany, the Marches, and Liguria, and the establish-

---

[8] Abrate, *La lotta sindicale*; Frascani, *Politica economica e finanza pubblica*; Roberto Vivarelli, *Il fallimento del liberalismo. Studi sulle origini del fascismo* (Bologna: Il Mulino, 1981).
[9] Castronovo, *Giovanni Agnelli*, p. 282.
[10] Corner, *Fascism in Ferrara*; Cardoza, *Agrarian Elites and Italian Fascism*.

ment of a similar "white belt" in Veneto and parts of Lombardy did not prove incompatible with the consolidation of a conservative, but constitutional government on the national level after World War II. In other words, social conflict in rural Italy may explain the rise of fascism, but it does not necessarily explain Mussolini's accession to power, culminating in the crisis of the liberal state.

turgid and uninteresting

The arguments presented here suggest that the crisis of liberal Italy can be understood fully only by examining both the center and the periphery; both unmediated social conflict in the factories and villages and mediated social conflict, i.e. the struggle over monetary and economic policy in parliament and between interest groups, and within the bureaucracy; and both the breakdown in the exercise of what Weber called the primary attribute of state sovereignty, i.e. the maintenance of order, and the breakdown in the exercise of what Weber referred to as secondary attributes of state power, i.e. state economic intervention and welfare policy.

Max Weber, of course, but he is not cited in the bibliography

APPENDIX

TABLES AND FIGURES

Table 1. *Italian government expenditure and revenue, 1862–1925 (in millions Lit.)*

	Ragioneria generale (contemporary)				Répaci (1962)				Ragioneria generale (1969)			
	Expenditure	Revenue	Deficit/Surplus	R/E	Expenditure	Revenue	Deficit/Surplus	R/E	Expenditure	Revenue	Deficit/Surplus	R/E
1862	927	480	−464	52	906	450	−456	50	859	518	−341	60
1863	907	524	−477	58	891	486	−405	55	869	537	−332	62
1864	944	576	−382	61	931	534	−397	57	992	740	−252	75
1865	916	646	−271	71	877	618	−259	70	1,035	804	−231	78
1866	1,339	617	−721	46	1,318	578	−740	44	1,172	878	−294	75
1867	929	714	−214	77	915	710	−205	78	979	850	−129	87
1868	1,014	749	−266	74	980	714	−266	73	1,005	927	−78	92
1869	1,020	871	−149	85	1,045	850	−195	81	1,033	1,065	32	103
1870	1,081	866	−215	80	1,085	836	−249	77	938	860	−78	92
1871	1,013	966	−47	95	1,023	944	−79	92	1,167	1,154	−13	99
1872	1,094	1,010	−84	92	1,098	981	−117	89	1,255	1,255	0	100
1873	1,136	1,047	−89	92	1,149	1,010	−139	88	1,265	1,291	26	102
1874	1,090	1,077	−13	99	1,102	1,042	−60	95	1,281	1,272	−9	99
1875	1,082	1,096	14	103	1,091	1,058	−33	97	1,251	1,311	60	105
1876	1,102	1,123	21	102	1,112	1,084	−28	97	1,288	1,323	35	103
1877	1,208	1,243	35	103	1,224	1,201	−23	98	1,359	1,397	38	103
1878	1,175	1,192	17	101	1,191	1,149	−42	96	1,326	1,380	44	104
1879	1,180	1,223	43	104	1,188	1,179	−9	99	1,288	1,401	113	109
1880	1,194	1,221	27	102	1,215	1,180	−35	97	1,301	1,385	84	106
1881	1,225	1,276	53	104	1,276	1,251	−25	98	1,403	1,448	45	103
1882	1,293	1,299	6	100	1,366	1,267	−99	93	1,536	1,533	−3	100
1883	1,330	1,333	3	100	1,386	1,295	−91	93	1,523	1,524	1	100
1884[a]	667	658	−9	99	676	614	−62	91	1,592	1,600	8	101
1884/85	1,409	1,413	5	100	1,396	1,314	−213	94	1,673	1,595	−78	95
1885/86	1,433	1,409	−24	98	1,515	1,302	−82	86	1,647	1,760	113	107
1886/87	1,461	1,454	−8	100	1,569	1,350	−219	86	1,677	1,712	35	102

[a] 1st semester.

297

Table 1. (cont.)

	Ragioneria generale (contemporary)				Répaci (1962)				Ragioneria generale (1969)			
	Expenditure	Revenue	Deficit/Surplus	R/E	Expenditure	Revenue	Deficit/Surplus	R/E	Expenditure	Revenue	Deficit/Surplus	R/E
1887/88	1,573	1,500	−73	95	1,776	1,590	−186	78	1,923	1,783	−140	93
1888/89	1,736	1,501	−235	86	1,878	1,390	−488	74	1,941	1,758	−183	91
1889/90	1,637	1,563	−74	95	1,677	1,455	−222	87	1,925	1,829	−96	95
1890/91	1,617	1,540	−77	95	1,637	1,431	−206	87	1,840	1,846	6	100
1891/92	1,571	1,528	−43	97	1,550	1,421	−129	92	1,846	1,705	−141	92
1892/93	1,569	1,550	−19	99	1,488	1,441	−48	97	1,724	1,750	16	101
1893/94	1,617	1,517	−99	94	1,581	1,406	−174	89	1,718	1,706	−12	99
1894/95	1,600	1,570	−30	98	1,554	1,459	−95	94	1,736	1,755	19	101
1895/96	1,699	1,633	−65	96	1,621	1,523	−98	94	1,785	1,747	−38	98
1896/97	1,624	1,615	−9	99	1,540	1,504	−36	98	1,729	1,723	−6	100
1897/98	1,620	1,629	9	101	1,521	1,510	−11	79	1,679	1,728	49	103
1898/99	1,626	1,659	33	102	1,531	1,544	13	101	1,734	1,758	24	101
1899/1900	1,633	1,672	39	102	1,539	1,557	18	101	1,738	1,782	44	103
1900/1	1,652	1,721	68	104	1,552	1,602	50	103	1,770	1,856	86	105
1901/2	1,680	1,743	63	104	1,573	1,619	46	103	1,760	1,862	102	106
1902/3	1,696	1,795	99	106	1,584	1,666	82	105	1,784	1,908	124	107
1903/4	1,728	1,786	59	103	1,606	1,652	46	103	1,834	1,938	104	106

1904/5	1,767	1,843	76	104	1,637	1,700	63	104	1,841	1,981	140	108
1905/6	1,861	1,946	85	105	1,724	1,796	72	104	2,265	2,071	−194	91
1906/7	1,856	1,955	98	105	1,705	1,797	92	105	2,176	2,104	−72	97
1907/8	1,885	1,945	62	103	1,707	1,759	52	103	2,110	2,094	−16	99
1908/9	2,099	2,134	35	102	1,820	1,847	27	102	2,429	2,265	−164	91
1909/10	2,205	2,237	32	101	1,952	1,942	−10	99	2,485	2,417	−68	97
1910/11	2,392	2,403	11	100	2,130	2,095	−35	98	2,698	2,690	−8	100
1911/12	2,587	2,475	−112	96	2,491	2,151	−340	86	2,906	2,814	−92	97
1912/13	2,786	2,529	−257	91	2,843	2,287	−556	80	3,138	2,769	−369	88
1913/14	2,688	2,524	−164	94	2,501	2,287	−214	91	3,080	2,921	−159	95
1914/15	5,395	2,560	−2,835	46	5,224	2,317	−2,907	44	5,586	2,717	−2,869	49
1915/16	10,625	3,734	−6,891	35	10,550	3,014	−7,536	29	10,867	3,500	−7,367	32
1916/17	17,595	5,345	−12,250	30	16,920	4,090	−12,830	24	16,441	5,077	−11,364	31
1917/18	25,299	7,533	−17,766	30	25,334	5,812	−19,522	23	22,848	7,673	−15,175	34
1918/19	32,452	9,676	−22,776	30	30,857	7,512	−23,345	24	27,428	10,781	−16,647	39
1919/20	23,093	15,207	−7,886	66	21,704	10,210	−11,494	47	20,905	12,089	−8,816	58
1920/21	36,229	18,820	−17,409	52	35,139	13,184	−20,955	38	20,716	15,388	−5,328	74
1921/22	35,461	19,701	−15,760	56	33,612	15,444	−18,168	46	25,398	18,754	−6,644	74
1922/23	21,832	18,803	−3,029	86	20,172	15,912	−4,260	79	41,272	29,889	−11,383	72
1923/24	21,000	20,582	−418	98	19,264	17,275	−1,989	90	30,571	28,079	−2,492	92
1924/25	20,023	20,440	417	102	20,202	18,641	−1,561	92	20,638	23,866	3,228	116
1925/26	20,575	21,043	468	102	20,107	20,201	94	100	19,861	24,082	4,221	121

Sources: F. A. Répaci, *La finanza pubblica italiana nel secolo 1861–1960* (Bologna: Zanichelli, 1962), pp. 15, 28–9, 125, 142 (for the first two columns); Ragioneria generale dello stato italiano, *Il bilancio dello stato italiano dal 1862 al 1967* (Rome: Istituto poligrafico dello stato, 1969), vol. I, pp. 177–8, 192–3 (for the third). See note on sources, p. 300.

A note on the sources used to construct Table 1.

This table reproduces three sets of figures for Italy's central government finances: (1) the original figures of the Ragioneria generale dello stato italiano, Italy's public accounting administration; (2) the economist F.A. Répaci's reelaboration of this date in 1962; and (3) a new historical series produced by the Ragioneria generale dello stato in 1969, which conforms with modern government accounting procedures. The differences between these three series, particularly with regard to the size of budget surpluses and deficits, are considerable. None of them can be regarded as definitive; indeed, particularly for the World War I and post-war years all three must be regarded with extreme skepticism.

There are several grave, and perhaps intractable problems associated with the reconstruction of Italy's public financial accounts for the war and early post-war years. First, beginning in the final years of the Giolittian era, administration officials deliberately underreported state expenditure. For example, they spread out authorized expenses over several fiscal years. Private firms working on state contracts were encouraged to borrow from private lenders, using their contracts as security. L. no. 511 17 July 1910 allowed the authorities to create *esercizi fuori bilancio* (administrations outside the budget). These administrations could borrow from the issue banks or other financial institutions without the corresponding sums appearing as an expenditure in the state budget. Among the administrations operating outside the budget were the numerous consortia set up during World War I to sell subsidized grain and other foodstuffs on the retail level. Theoretically, the food consortia were to be financially self-supporting; however, when they were liquidated after the war enormous losses were reported. These losses were incorporated into the annual budgets during which the consortia were liquidated, even though the relevant expenditures had been spread over the war and early post-war years. This procedure accounts for the very high government expenditure reported by Répaci and the Ragioneria generale's old series during fiscal 1920–21 and 1921–22, and by the Ragioneria generale's 1969 series in fiscal 1922–23 and 1923–24.

Another major problem was administrative disorganization, and, in particular, lengthening delays in executing and recording expenditures, and collecting and recording revenues. During the war years, the column *residui passivi*, i.e. expenditures authorized in another annual budget, grew inexorably; in 1920–21 the *residui passivi* actually exceeded expenditure authorized and executed during the current fiscal year! Still another problem is the *partita di giro*, whereby state contractors passed taxes back to the state in the form of higher prices, discussed extensively in chapter 2 of this study.

The most reliable quantitative data on the size of state budget deficits during this era are figures on net public borrowing, as reported in Table 9. It is not possible, of course, to estimate the size of annual budgets from figures on net public borrowing. It should be noted that similar problems characterize the French and German data for public finances during this period.

These issues are discussed in, Antonio Confalonieri, *Banca e industria in Italia dalla crisi del 1907 all'agosto 1914*, vol. I, pp. 66–67; Ragioneria generale dello stato, *Il bilancio dello stato italiano dal 1862 al 1967*, vol. I, passim; Francesco A. Répaci, 'Il costo finanziario della prima guerra mondiale in Italia,' *Studi in onore di G. Pietra*, 2, special ed. of *Statistica*, 14 (1954), no. 4, pp. 579–93; Répaci, *La finanza pubblica italiana*, pp. 126–40; Enrico Luzzati and Renato Portesi, 'La spesa pubblica,' in, Sabino Cassese, ed., *L'amministrazione centrale* (Turin: UTET, 1984), p. 421; Luigi Einaudi, 'Dove si tenta di calcolare il disavanzo del bilancio italiano,' *Corriere della Sera*, 25 April 1923, republished in *Cronache di un trentennio* (Turin: Einaudi, 1966), vol. VII, pp. 210–14.

Table 2. *British government expenditure and revenue 1912–1925 (in millions £st.)*

	Nominal prices					1929 prices[a]				
	Expenditure	1913=100	Revenue	1913=100	R/E	Expenditure	1913=100	Revenue	1913=100	R/E
1912	184	96	189	95	103	259	96	225	95	103
1913	192	100	198	100	103	270	100	279	100	103
1914	559	291	227	115	41	776	287	315	113	41
1915	1,559	812	337	170	22	1,772	656	383	137	22
1916	2,198	1,145	573	289	26	1,928	714	503	180	26
1917	2,696	1,404	707	357	26	1,872	675	478	171	26
1918	2,579	1,343	889	449	34	1,573	583	542	194	34
1919	1,666	868	1,340	677	80	920	341	740	265	80
1920	1,188	619	1,426	720	120	528	196	634	227	120
1921	1,070	557	1,125	568	105	743	275	781	280	105
1922	812	423	914	462	113	700	259	788	282	113
1923	749	390	837	423	112	646	239	722	258	112
1924	751	391	799	404	106	616	228	655	235	106
1925	776	404	812	410	105	663	246	694	249	105

[a] Wholesale prices.
Source: B. R. Mitchell, *European Historical Statistics 1750–1975*, 2nd rev. ed. (New York: Facts on File, 1981), pp. 738, 762, 775.

Table 3. *French government expenditure and revenue 1912–1925 (in millions FFr.)*

	Nominal prices					1929 prices[a]				
	Expenditure	1913=100	Revenue	1913=100	R/E	Expenditure	1913=100	Revenue	1913=100	R/E
1912	4,743	94	4,857	95	102	27,900	94	28,570	95	102
1913	5,067	100	5,092	100	100	29,806	100	29,953	100	100
1914	10,065	199	4,549	89	45	59,206	199	26,759	89	45
1915	20,925	413	4,131	81	20	90,978	305	17,961	60	20
1916	28,113	555	5,259	103	19	90,687	304	16,965	57	19
1917	35,320	697	6,943	136	20	82,140	276	16,147	54	20
1918	41,897	827	7,621	150	18	74,816	251	13,609	45	18
1919	39,970	782	13,282	261	33	68,914	231	22,900	76	33
1920	39,644	782	22,502	442	57	47,764	160	27,111	91	57
1921	32,845	648	23,119	454	70	57,623	193	40,560	135	70
1922	45,188	892	23,888	469	53	83,682	281	44,237	148	53
1923	38,293	756	26,224	515	68	55,497	186	38,006	127	68
1924	42,511	839	30,568	600	72	53,139	178	38,210	128	72
1925	36,275	716	33,455	657	92	40,306	135	37,172	124	92

[a] Wholesale prices.
Source: Mitchell, *European Historical Statistics*, pp. 736, 755, 774.

Table 4. *German government expenditure and revenue 1912–1925 (in millions RM)*

	Nominal prices					1929 prices[a]				
	Expenditure	1913=100	Revenue	1913=100	R/E	Expenditure	1913=100	Revenue	1913=100	R/E
1912	2,893	82	c			2,704	81	c		
1913	3,521	100	2,095	100	60	3,353	100	1,995	100	60
1914	9,651	274	2,399	115	25	13,042	389	3,242	163	25
1915	26,689	758	1,769	84	7	26,959	804	1,787	90	7
1916	28,780	817	2,045	98	7	27,151	810	1,929	97	7
1917	53,261	1,513	7,682	367	14	42,609	1,271	6,146	308	14
1918	45,514	1,293	6,830	326	15	29,943	893	4,493	225	15
1919	54,867	1,558	9,712	464	18	18,855	562	3,337	67	18
1920	145,255	4,125	53,046	2,532	37	13,967	417	5,107	256	37
1921	298,766[b]	8,485	149,570	7,139	50	22,329[b]	666	11,179	560	50
1922										
1923										
1924	5,027	143	4,650	222	93	5,845	174	5,407	271	93
1925	5,683	161	4,731	226	83	6,245	186	5,199	261	83

[a] Wholesale prices.
[b] Beginning in 1921 expenditure for public enterprises net of receipts.
[c] Revenue calculated according to different criteria.
Source: Mitchell, *European Historical Statistics*, pp. 736, 755, 774.

Table 5. *Nominal direct tax revenues 1913/14–1924/25* (millions Lit.)

	Land	Provincial, municipal surtaxes	Total land	Building	Provincial, municipal surtaxes	Total building	*Richezza mobile*	War profits	Capital gains	Extra-ordinary capital gains	Comple-mentary	Other extra-ordinary	Total[a] perm.	Total extra-ordinary	Total direct
1913/14	85	[197]	[281]	115	[155]	[270]	353						552		552
1914/15	88	[192]	[285]	123	[164]	[295]	383						599		599
1915/16	93	[210]	[309]	133	[186]	[329]	435					62	661	62	723
1916/17	100	[216]	[325]	135	[187]	[338]	461	108				255	697	363	1,060
1917/18	115	[217]	[347]	146	[192]	[364]	492	452				328	754	779	1,533
1918/19	116	[239]	[370]	157	[213]	[389]	581	806			2	405	855	1,212	2,067
1919/20	116	[290]	[420]	163	[352]	[423]	709	982	65		65	236	989	1,348	2,337
1920/21	118	[451]	[592]	169	[315]	[513]	1,023	1,459	555	482	89	235	1,311	2,820	4,131
1921/22	120	[658]	[810]	176	[360]	[579]	1,637	1,246	490	614	212	419	1,925	2,981	4,906
1922/23	119	[688]	[839]	178	[373]	[599]	2,008	778	189	520	133	508	2,306	2,129	4,435
1923/24	120	[754]	[908]	191	[425]	[653]	2,908	514	147	833	214	636	3,220	2,344	5,563
1924/25	135	[814]	[962]	246	[432]	[727]	2,981	385	104	994	285	406	3,363	2,175	5,538

[a] Includes *Contributo sui terreni bonificati e riserve di caccia* beginning in fiscal 198/19.

Source: Ministero delle Finanze, Direzione Generale delle Imposte Dirette, *La gestione delle imposte dirette dal 1914 al 1925* (Rome: Provveditorato Generale dello Stato, 1926), pp. 200–1.

Table 6. Direct tax revenues to the central government, 1914–1925 in 1929 prices (in millions of Lit.)

	Land	Building	Ricchezza mobile	War profits	Capital gains	Extra-ordinary capital gains	Comple-mentary	Other extra-ordinary	Total perm.	Total extra-ordinary	Total direct
1913/14	430	582	1,786						2,792		2,792
1914/15	335	468	1,466						2,280		2,280
1915/16	244	349	1,141					163	1,734	163	1,897
1916/17	177	239	814	191				451	1,231	641	1,873
1917/18	135	171	579	530				385	885	914	1,799
1918/19	125	169	626	868			2	436	920	1,305	2,225
1919/20	95	134	582	806	53		53	194	811	1,106	1,917
1920/21	106	151	916	1,307	497	432	80	210	1,174	2,526	3,700
1921/22	107	157	1,456	1,109	436	546	189	373	1,713	2,652	4,365
1922/23	105	157	1,770	686	167	458	117	448	2,032	1,885	3,909
1923/24	106	169	2,578	456	130	739	190	564	2,855	2,078	4,932
1924/25	107	195	2,358	304	82	786	225	321	2,660	1,720	4,380

Sources: La gestione, pp. 200–1 (as in table 5); wholesale price coefficients: ISTAT, Il valore della lira dal 1861 al 1982 (Rome: ISTAT, 1983), p. 83.

Table 7. *Subscriptions to the six war loans (millions of lire)*

	Italy		Colonies	Abroad	Total		
	Cash	Securities	Cash and securities	Cash and securities	Cash	Securities	Total
First War Loan, renewable, 4.5% at 97 (January 1915)	998.5		1.5		1,000.0		1,000.0
Second War Loan, renewable, 4.5% at 95 (July 1915)	1,122.4		1.9	21.6	1,145.9		1,145.9
Third War Loan, renewable, 5% at 97.5 (January 1916)	1,741.6	891.4	3.9	81.2	2,126.7	891.4	3,018.1
Fourth War Loan, perpetual, 5% at 90 (January 1917)	2,663.8	1,009.5	3.0	182.2	2,789.0	1,009.5	3,798.5
Fifth War Loan, perpetual, 5% at 86.5 (January 1918)	3,696.6	1,941.9	10.6	440.2	4,146.6	1,942.5	6,089.1
Sixth War Loan, perpetual, 5% at 87.5 (January 1920)				2,059.0	8,115.0	10,353.0	20,527.0

Source: Banca d'Italia, *Sulle condizioni della circolazione e del mercato monetario durante e dopo la guerra* (Rome: Casa Editrice Italiana, 1920), p. 114; Paolo Frascani, *Politica economica e finanza pubblica in Italia nel primo dopoguerra (1918–1922)* (Naples: Giannini, 1975), p. 297.

Table 8. Market quotations of consolidated government securities, 1914–1922

3½% perpetual, 1902

	1914	1915	1916	1917	1918	1919	1920	1921
mid-Jan.		84.07	81.00	80.55	78.31	80.10	79.43	70.79
end-Jan.	97.17[a]	84.19	79.87	77.72	78.53	80.21	80.26	73.25
mid-Feb.		82.79	80.77	77.82	78.05	81.23	80.20	74.08
end-Feb.	97.21[a]	80.08	80.59	76.86	77.86	81.55	79.73	73.56
mid-Mar.		79.58	81.24	77.13	78.17	82.60	79.05	72.81
end-Mar.	6.99[a]	80.51	83.04	77.15	77.38	83.76	79.31	72.19
mid-Apr.		81.52	83.31	78.86	77.99	83.90	78.88	73.36
end-Apr.	6.21[a]	81.27	85.11	79.83	78.42	85.08	79.31	73.42
mid-May		83.37	84.43	80.76	79.28	85.35	79.64	74.66
end-May	6.83[a]	82.82	83.94	81.47	79.96	85.17	79.34	73.80
mid-June		85.75	84.90	81.46	80.43	84.54	77.69	73.69
end-June	7.34[a]	83.99	85.62	81.72	81.88	85.15	75.72	72.73
mid-July		81.79	83.94	80.59	81.74	83.37	73.25	71.66
end-July	4.91[a]	81.76	84.48	80.89	82.89	85.15	71.28	69.98
mid-Aug.		82.81	85.40	81.65	82.83	86.34	70.24	70.11
end-Aug.		83.60	85.84	81.30	82.46	86.33	69.09	70.75
mid-Sept.		84.11	86.16	81.54	81.02	86.15	68.80	70.48
end-Sept.		84.03	85.85	81.76	79.85	86.38	68.66	70.74
mid-Oct.		84.42	85.37	81.84	82.99	85.20	67.38	71.41
end-Oct.		84.73	83.45	80.76	84.45	86.04	66.25	72.27
mid-Nov.		85.75	83.06	80.05	83.26	85.93	67.48	72.44
end-Nov.		85.83	81.92	81.06	82.68	83.73	75.35	71.58
mid-Dec.		85.35	82.38	81.38	82.59	82.76	74.95	72.15
end-Dec.	9.26[a]	84.59	83.18	81.12	82.19	82.29	74.04	71.95

5% perpetual, 1917

	1915	1916	1917	1918	1919	1920	1921
mid-Jan.		94.26[c]	93.28[d]	89.24	86.12		71.73
end-Jan.		94.04[c]	92.82[d]	89.37	87.01	86.32	74.66
mid-Feb.		93.92[c]	92.54[d]	89.42	87.26	86.58	75.45
end-Feb.		93.88[c]	92.48[d]	89.48	87.56	86.46	75.25
mid-Mar.		93.09[c]	92.56[d]	89.78	88.74	86.47	75.26
end-Mar.		92.80[c]	92.60[d]	89.89	89.30	86.43	75.32
mid-Apr.		93.06[c]	92.64[d]	89.75	89.69	84.83	78.27
end-Apr.		93.21[c]	92.87[d]	89.71	90.40	85.55	79.13
mid-May	95.32[b]	93.92[c]	92.06[d]	89.48	92.16	85.14	80.30
end-May	96.12[b]	93.15[c]	92.03[d]	90.16	92.91	84.48	79.60
mid-June	93.91[b]	93.14[d]	91.69[d]	86.69	92.78	82.61	79.91
end-June	93.69[b]	92.82[d]	91.02[d]	87.20	93.00	77.96	78.67
mid-July	93.06[b]	92.55[c]	90.09	84.64	90.17	74.70	76.66
end-July	93.15[b]	95.49[d]	90.63	85.21	91.70	74.44	75.10
mid-Aug.	93.07[b]	95.44[d]	91.08	86.50	94.29	74.39	75.25
end-Aug.	93.02[b]	95.39[d]	90.64	86.43	93.45	74.14	75.90
mid-Sept.	93.92[c]	95.33[d]	91.05	86.28	93.80	72.77	75.24
end-Sept.	93.72[c]	95.42[d]	91.30	86.55	93.56	71.50	75.26
mid-Oct.	93.64[c]	95.50[d]	91.34	90.82	92.10	69.90	75.97
end-Oct.	93.64[c]	93.70[d]	91.47	91.18	92.94	68.06	77.03
mid-Nov.	93.38[c]	94.74[d]	88.40	89.96	91.57	69.05	77.77
end-Nov.	93.09[c]	92.32[d]	91.11	90.28	89.79	76.83	76.64
mid-Dec.	94.44[c]	91.49[d]	91.22	88.97	89.40	76.47	77.45
end-Dec.		93.37[d]	90.93	88.97	89.44	75.94	76.94

[a] Monthly average.
[b] 4½% loan, Jan. 1915.
[c] 4½% loan, July 1915.
[d] 5% loan, Jan. 1916.

Source: Riccardo Bachi, *L'Italia economica nell'anno 1914* and years to 1921 (Città di Castello, S. Lapi, 1915–22).

Table 9. Italy's internal public debt, 1914–1922 (millions of lire)

	Pre-war Consolidated	1st, 2nd, 3rd War Loans 4½%–5%	4th, 5th, 6th War Loans 4½%–5%	Total Consolidated	'Ordinary' Treasury bills, Contractor bills	3, 5 & 7-year t-bonds	Total short, medium-term Treasury securities	State currency notes & 'Buoni di Cassa'	Statutory advances from issue banks	Extra-ordinary advances from issue banks	Total money creation	Borrowing from Cassa depositi prestiti	Total borrowing	Einaudi's figures
30 June 1914	14,839.8			14,839.8	380.0		380.0	485.8			485.8		15,705.6	15,821.2
Variation 1914–15	87.9	1,000.0		1,087.9	2.2		21.2	268.5	406.5	585.0	1,260.0		2,369.1	2,629.3
30 June 1915	14,927.7	1,000.0		15,927.7	401.2		401.2	754.3	406.5	585.0	1,745.8		18,074.7	
Variation 1915–16	−215.9	3,628.8		3,412.9	384.1	459.1	843.2	370.0	35.0	300.0	705.0		4,961.1	5,643.0
30 June 1916	14,711.8	4,628.8		19,340.6	785.3	459.1	1,244.4	1,124.3	441.5	885.0	2,450.8		23,035.8	
Variation 1916–17	−571.5	−3,116.6	7,102.1	3,414.0	3,334.6	1,412.0	4,746.2	327.5	−5.0	400.0	722.5		8,882.7	9,555.2
30 June 1917	14,140.3	1,512.2	7,102.1	22,754.6	4,119.9	1,871.0	5,990.6	1,451.8	436.5	1,258.0	3,173.3		31,918.5	
Variation 1917–18	−448.4	−13.2	6,121.3	5,659.7	2,883.6	682.6	3,566.2	654.5	−8.3	3,250.0	3,896.2	200.0	13,322.1	14,012.5
30 June 1918	13,691.9	1,499.0	13,223.4	28,414.3	7,003.5	2,553.0	9,556.8	2,106.3	428.2	4,535.0	7,069.5	200.0	45,240.6	
Variation 1918–19	−158.8	—	137.0	−21.8	8,042.8	3,168.0	11,210.5	412.1		1,112.0	1,524.1	250.0	12,962.8	11,961.0
30 June 1919	13,537.1	1,499.0	13,360.4	28,396.5	15,046.3	5,721.0	20,767.3	2,518.4	428.2	5,647.0	8,593.6	450.0	58,207.4	
Variation 1919–20	−70.2	−0.2	19,992.4	19,922.0	−5,830.4	−1,476.0	−7,306.8	17.2	−70.8	1,390.0	1,336.4	59.0	14,010.6	13,117.5
30 June 1920	13,466.9	1,498.8	33,352.8	48,378.5	7,215.9	4,245.0	13,460.5	2,536.6	357.4	7,037.0	9,930.0	509.0	72,218.0	
Variation 1920–21	−72.3		1,109.4	1,035.1	10,278.9	1,374.0	11,653.1	8.8		102.1	110.9	113.5	12,912.6	13,513.5
30 June 1921	13,394.6	1,498.8	34,460.2	49,353.6	19,494.8	5,619.0	25,113.6	2,544.4	357.4	7,139.1	10,041.0	622.5	85,130.6	
Variation 1921–22	−45.7		65.0	19.3	5,451.9	1,629.0	7,080.8	3.6		—	3.6	−202.5	6,901.2	6,286.1
30 June 1922	13,348.9	1,498.8	34,525.2	49,372.9	24,946.3	7,232.0	32,178.5	2,548.0	357.4	7,139.1	10,045.0	420.0	92,015.9	92,539.3

Sources: Riccardo Bachi, L'Italia economica nell' anno 1921 (Città di Castello, S. Lapi, 1922), pp. 260–1; Luigi Einaudi, "Dove si tenta di calcolare il disavanzo del bilancio italiano," Corriere della Sera, 25 April 1923, in Cronache di un trentennio (Turin: Einaudi, 1966), vol. VII, p. 212.

Table 10. *Money supply and prices (billions of lire)*

	Note issue	1913=100	Note issue plus bank deposits	1913=100	Price indexes Wholesale	Retail
31 Dec. 1913	3.53	100	12.08	100	100	100
1914	4.34	123	12.98	107	107	100
1915	5.69	161	14.97	124	124	107
1916	7.25	205	18.76	155	155	134
1917	11.48	325	25.36	210	210	189
1918	15.90	450	35.08	290	290	264
1919	21.73	604	48.78	404	404	268
1920	25.00	708	59.56	493	493	352
1921	23.99	680	58.07	481	481	417
1922	22.17	628	58.83	487	487	414
1923	20.51	581	67.13	556	556	412
1924	21.76	616	75.69	627	627	426

Source: Paolo Ercolani, "Documentazione statistica di base," in Giorgio Fuà, ed., *Lo sviluppo economico in Itàlia*, 3rd ed., vol. III (Milan: Angeli, 1978), p. 470. Note however that the figures for 1918 are incorrect. For the correct data for 1918, see Renato De Mattia, *I bilanci degli Istituti di emissione italiani*, 2 vols. (Rome: Banca d'Italia, 1967), Tables 2, 22, and 23. For Price coefficients see Instituto Centrale di Statistica, *Il valore della lira dal 1861 al 1982* (Rome: ISTAT, 1983).

Table 11a. *Total assets of banks by sector (thousands of lire)*

	Issue Banks	%	Commercial Banks	%	Savings Banks	%	Popular Banks	%	Cassa Depositi e Prestiti (Postal Savings Banks)	%	Monti di Pegno	%
1898	2,079,995	31.1	974,854	14.6	1,728,873	25.9	606,128	9.1	347,072	5.2	148,552[b]	
1908	2,946,179	26.8	2,405,895	21.9	2,709,757	24.7	1,356,224	12.3	506,496	4.6	221,937	2.0
1913	3,313,700	23.9	3,473,633	25.0	3,403,931	24.5	1,574,317	11.3	804,833	5.8	312,276	2.2
1914	4,506,138	29.9	3,302,087	21.9	3,433,651	22.8	1,589,720	10.6	878,157	5.8	321,534	2.1
1915	5,932,739	34.9	3,576,237	21.0	3,537,913	29.8	1,631,760	9.6	946,378	5.6	342,095	2.0
1916	7,114,181	34.8	5,251,411	25.7	3,932,570	19.3	1,914,697	9.4	1,004,703	4.9	366,161	1.8
1917	14,364,568	48.8	6,307,289[a]	21.4	4,556,382	15.5	2,019,646	6.9	1,049,138	3.6	414,344	1.4
1918	15,838,231	46.1	9,531,760[a]	27.8	5,690,648	16.6	983,520	2.9	1,075,525	3.1	489,960	1.4
1919	21,281,888	45.7	15,753,250[a]	33.9	7,110,567	15.3			1,126,190	2.4	580,002	1.2
1920	24,926,714	43.4	20,983,849[a]	36.6	8,426,390	14.7			1,707,287	3.0	656,385	1.1
1921	25,612,549	43.9	16,739,175	29.0	10,386,102	17.8	1,302,738	2.2	2,307,190	4.0	791,031	1.4
1922	24,032,116	41.4	15,899,114	27.4	11,804,164	20.3	1,519,980	2.6	3,022,136	5.2	978,787	1.7
1923	25,634,840	34.4	28,748,259	38.6	12,781,093	17.2	1,850,137	2.5	3,481,502	4.7	1,104,761	1.5
1929	22,275,345	18.7	45,218,016	37.9	21,271,692	17.8	9,906,700	8.3	5,080,659	4.3	1,477,096	1.2

[a] Figures only for four largest commercial banks.
[b] 1899.

Table 11a (*cont.*)

	Istituti di Credito Fondario	%	Casse Rurali	%	Istituti di Diritto Pubblico	%	Ditte Bancarie	%	Total
1898	792,692	11.9	14,948	0.2					6,683,113
1908	836,772	7.6	72,838[a]						10,983,260
1913	997,057	7.2							13,879,747
1914	1,028,645	6.8							15,059,932
1915	1,045,164	6.1							17,012,286
1916	752,205	3.7							20,430,093
1917	739,073	2.5							29,450,440
1918	712,947	2.1							34,322,591
1919	705,587	1.5							46,586,474
1920	693,079	1.2							57,393,704
1921	727,830	1.2	443,000	0.8					58,309,615
1922	829,622	1.4							58,085,921
1923	906,059	1.2							74,506,651
1929	3,780,117	3.1	506,800	0.4	5,597,563	4.7	2,244,900	1.9	119,332,716

[a] 1910.

Source: Renato DeMattia, ed., *I bilanci degli istituti di emissioni italiani* (Rome: Banca d'Italia, 1967), Tables 2, 22, and 23.

Table 11b. *Total assets of banks by sector (thousands of 1913 lire)*

	Issue Banks	Commercial Banks	Savings Banks	Popular Banks	Cassa Depositi e Prestiti (Postal Savings Banks)	Monti di Pegno
1898	2,642,842	1,238,649	2,196,706	770,146	440,990	
1908	3,371,102	2,752,825	3,100,504	1,551,792	579,533	253,940
1913	3,313,700	3,473,633	3,403,931	1,574,317	804,833	312,276
1914	4,703,507	3,446,718	3,584,045	1,659,350	916,620	335,617
1915	4,660,166	2,809,134	2,779,031	1,281,747	743,380	268,716
1916	5,312,870	2,842,951	2,129,093	1,036,617	543,946	198,240
1917	7,584,492	2,299,638[a]	1,661,257	736,363	382,516	151,070
1918	3,836,020	2,308,592[a]	1,378,275	238,209	260,492	118,668
1919	4,728,836	3,507,038[a]	1,579,966		250,017	128,876
1920	4,220,093	3,552,566[a]	1,426,588		289,044	111,126
1921	4,733,199	3,093,400	1,919,352	240,746	426,369	146,183
1922	4,412,296	2,919,077	2,167,245	279,069	554,864	179,705
1923	4,662,977	5,229,308	2,324,881	336,540	633,285	200,956
1929	4,597,631	9,332,999	4,390,477	2,044,743	1,048,648	304,873

Table 11b. *(cont.)*

	Istituti di Credito Fondario	Casse Rurali	Istituti di Diritto Pubblico	Ditte Bancarie	Total
1898	1,007,194	18,993			8,491,156
1908	957,435				12,567,046
1913	997,057				13,879,747
1914	1,073,700				15,719,557
1915	820,976				13,363,150
1916	407,244				11,060,852
1917	269,466				10,737,630
1918	172,676				8,312,932
1919	156,781				10,351,514
1920	117,338				9,716,745
1921	134,503	81,866			10,775,616
1922	152,319				10,664,575
1923	164,812				13,552,759
1929	780,216	338,729	1,155,337	4,463,347	24,630,273

1913 lire.
Source: Price coefficients: ISTAT, *Il valore della lira dal 1861 at 1982 (wholesale prices).*

Table 12a. *Total deposits of banks by sector (thousands of lire)*

	Issue Banks	%	Commercial Banks	%	Savings Banks	%	Cassa Depositi e Prestiti (Postal Savings Banks)	%	Popular Banks	%	Monti di Pegno	%
1898	176,947	5.9	407,668	13.5	1,436,036	47.6	585,979	19.4	401,737	13.3	61,217[b]	
1908	107,315	1.7	1,374,642	21.3	2,249,571	34.9	1,524,263	23.6	1,015,404	15.7	125,000	1.9
1913	96,176	1.1	2,149,277	25.1	2,754,841	32.2	2,108,303	24.7	1,151,868	13.5	185,104	2.2
1914	319,801	3.7	2,024,394	23.7	2,751,185	32.2	2,021,117	23.6	1,147,951	13.4	183,393	2.1
1915	570,566	6.2	2,322,766	25.0	2,904,102	31.3	1,989,573	21.5	1,180,169	12.7	206,171	2.2
1916	444,150	3.9	3,792,811	32.9	3,301,450	28.7	2,193,036	19.0	1,421,200	12.3	227,417	2.0
1917	700,989	5.0	4,694,787[a]	33.8	3,822,146	27.5	2,707,791	19.5	1,535,673	11.1	270,037	1.9
1918	844,192	4.4	7,579,191[a]	39.5	4,885,607	25.5	3,478,235	18.1	1,854,711	9.7	340,723	1.8
1919	782,940	2.9	12,101,841[a]	44.1	6,019,113	21.9	5,189,086	18.9	2,661,060	9.7	418,039	1.5
1920	997,992	2.9	15,811,525[a]	45.8	6,942,386	20.1	6,979,838	20.2	3,004,675	8.7	464,050	1.3
1921	1,089,550	3.2	12,475,766[a]	36.6	8,541,989	25.1	8,147,652	23.9	2,804,557	8.2	576,669	1.7
1922	1,307,595	3.6	12,274,766	33.5	9,890,128	27.0	8,719,640	23.8	3,244,115	8.8	709,437	1.9
1923	1,247,731	2.7	20,079,759	43.1	10,706,961	23.0	9,078,295	19.5	3,907,097	8.4	709,567	1.7
1929	1,123,733	1.5	30,033,713	39.6	17,461,293	23.0	11,747,123	15.5	8,500,700	11.2	1,473,818	1.4

[a] Figures for four largest commercial banks only.
[b] 1899.

313

Table 12a. (cont.)

	Casse Fondarie	%	Casse Rurali	%	Credito Agricolo	%	Istituti di Diritto Pubblico	%	Ditte Bancarie	%	Total
1898	11,075	0.4									3,019,442
1908	937		57,084	0.9							6,454,716
1913	2,726		100,578	1.2							8,548,873
1914	3,036		100,611	1.2							9,276,617
1915	3,405		99,865	1.1							11,513,028
1916			132,955	1.2							13,882,297
1917			150,874	1.1							19,176,020
1918			193,361	1.0							27,454,071
1919			281,992	1.0							34,561,272
1920			380,806	1.0							34,080,729
1921			444,350	1.3							36,657,934
1922			512,253	1.4							46,646,311
1923			796,900	1.7							
1929			1,246,600	1.8	112,100	0.1	2,826,417	3.7	1,510,800	12.0	75,763,297

Source: Renato DeMattia, ed., *I bilanci degli istituti di emissione italiani* (Rome: Banca d'Italia, 1967), Tables 2, 22, and 23. For price coefficients, ISTAT, *Il valore della lira dal 1861 al 1982* (ISTAT, 1983).

Table 12b. *Total deposits of banks by sector (thousands of 1913 lire)*

	Issue Banks	Commercial Banks	Savings Banks	Cassa Depositi e Prestiti (Postal Savings Banks)	Banche populari	Monti di Pegno
1898	224,829	517,983	1,824,627	744,545	510,447	143,025
1908	122,790	1,572,865	2,573,959	1,744,062	1,161,825	185,104
1913	96,176	2,149,277	2,754,841	2,108,303	1,151,868	191,426
1914	333,808	2,113,062	2,871,687	2,109,642	1,198,231	161,947
1915	448,180	1,824,533	2,281,172	1,562,810	927,023	123,124
1916	240,463	2,053,428	1,787,405	1,187,310	769,438	98,455
1917	255,581	1,711,719[a]	1,393,554	987,261	559,906	82,523
1918	204,463	1,835,680[a]	1,183,294	842,429	449,211	92,888
1919	173,969	2,689,029[a]	1,337,447	1,153,015	591,288	78,564
1920	168,960	2,676,891[a]	1,175,346	1,181,687	508,691	106,568
1921	201,349	2,305,558[a]	1,578,560	1,505,686	518,282	130,253
1922	240,074	2,253,647	1,815,828	1,600,926	595,620	145,441
1923	226,962	3,652,508	1,947,596	1,651,342	710,701	221,636
1929	231,938	6,198,958	3,604,011	2,430,179	1,754,544	

[a] Figures only for four largest commercial banks.

Appendix

Table 12b (*cont.*)

	Credito Fondario	Casse Rurali	Credito Agricolo	Istituti di Diritto Pubblico	Ditte Bancarie	Total
1898	14,072					3,836,503
1908	1,072	62,316				7,385,486
1913	2,726	100,611				8,548,873
1914	3,169	105,018				8,926,043
1915	2,675	78,444				7,286,783
1916		71,982				6,233,153
1917		55,009				5,061,485
1918		46,832				4,644,432
1919		62,659				6,100,295
1920		61,084				5,851,223
1921		82,116				6,298,119
1922		94,050				6,730,397
1923		144,956				8,479,507
1929		277,938	23,137	583,372	311,829	15,637,544

Table 13. Assets of the largest commercial banks (millions of lire)

	Banca Commerciale Italiana	Credito Italiano	Società Bancaria Italiana	Banca di Busto Arsizio, Società di Credito Provinciale	Banco di Roma	Total	Comit and Credit as % of total assets of banking system	4 or 5 largest commercial banks as % of total assets of banking system
1895	78.7	49.8		2.6	3.7	134.8	1.9	2.0
1896	81.9	48.6		3.1	4.5	138.1	1.9	2.0
1897	141.8	59.4		3.4	5.2	209.8	3.0	3.2
1898	175.2	83.4		4.4	10.7	273.7	3.9	4.1
1899	204.8	108.6	17.6	4.7	27.0	362.7	4.5	5.5
1900	261.3	124.8	22.1	4.6	27.3	440.1	5.4	6.1
1901	315.1	150.2	22.5	7.1	34.8	529.7	6.2	7.0
1902	306.2	142.8	26.5	7.8	47.5	530.8	5.9	7.0
1903	431.3	202.7	36.6	10.5	55.6	736.7	7.7	9.0
1904	498.3	251.1	73.1	11.9	72.4	906.8	8.6	10.4
1905	599.6	267.8	122.1	24.3	133.9	1,147.7	9.1	11.9
1906	668.0	329.6	180.3	24.3	153.6	1,355.8	10.1	13.8
1907	727.9	396.0	162.4	26.7	157.1	1,470.1	10.7	14.0
1908	753.6	435.9	134.9	33.8	185.2	1,543.4	10.8	14.1
1909	776.2	470.2	157.0	44.9	266.3	1,714.6	10.7	14.7
1910	812.6	509.2	169.7	52.0	357.4	1,900.9	10.6	15.3
1911	921.9	561.9	180.9	83.4	497.7	2,245.8	11.4	17.3
1912	1,092.7	601.0	220.1	102.7	532.7	2,549.2	12.7	19.0
1913	1,186.7	667.5	221.9	151.8	535.8	2,763.7	13.4	19.9
1914	1,101.9	633.7	199.4	168.8	413.1	2,516.9	11.5	16.7
1915	1,136.5	813.8	468.5[a]		327.7	2,746.5	11.5	16.1
1916	1,672.0	1,310.9	868.9[a]		378.8	4,230.6	14.6	20.7
1917	2,515.8	1,937.2	1,469.5[a]		598.5	6,521.0	15.1	22.1
1918	3,346.0	2,682.2	2,578.8[a]		924.8	9,531.8	17.6	27.8
1919	5,030.6	4,026.5	4,315.5[a]		2,410.6	15,783.2	19.4	33.9
1920	6,847.6	5,070.6	5,842.7[a]		3,218.7	20,979.6	20.8	36.6
1921	7,383.2	5,288.7			4,067.2	16,739.1	21.7	29.0
1922	7,118.2	4,811.8			3,963.2	15,893.2	20.5	27.4
1923	7,676.5	5,082.5	643.4[b]		2,279.0	15,681.4	17.1	21.0
1924	8,650.6	6,085.1			2,586.4	17,322.1	17.1	20.2
1925	9,582.3	6,374.7	2,157.6[b]		2,444.6	20,559.2	16.9	21.5

[a] Banca Italiana di Sconto. [b] Banca Nazionale di Credito.

Source: Anna Maria Biscaini Cotula and Pierluigi Ciocca, "Le strutture finanziarie: Aspetti quantitativi di lungo periodo (1870–1970)," in Fausto Vicarelli, ed., Capitale industriale e capitale finanziario. Il caso italiano (Bologna: Il Mulino, 1979), pp. 114–16.

Table 14. Own to outside resources ratios of the major commercial banks, 1895–1925 (millions of lire)

	Banca Commerciale Italiana				Credito Italiano				Banco di Roma			
	Capital	Shareholders' Reserves	Deposits	Capital/ Reserve to Deposit Ratio	Capital	Shareholders' Reserves	Deposits	Capital/ Reserve to Deposit Ratio	Capital	Shareholders' Reserves	Deposits	Capital/ Reserve to Deposit Ratio
1895	20.0	1.3	47.1	2.21	14.0		32.2	2.30	2.5		1.2	0.48
1896	20.0	1.4	49.9	2.33	14.0	0.1	27.3	1.94	2.5		1.0	0.40
1897	30.0	1.9	89.4	2.80	14.0	0.1	35.8	2.54	2.5		2.4	0.96
1898	30.0	2.0	115.8	3.62	14.0	0.2	57.8	4.07	3.0		5.9	1.97
1899	40.0	4.5	132.8	2.98	25.0	0.9	63.8	2.46	6.0	0.3	20.6	3.27
1900	60.0	8.9	137.0	1.99	30.0	1.8	63.9	2.01	6.0	0.9	20.2	2.93
1901	60.0	9.1	178.9	2.59	35.0	2.0	57.6	1.56	6.0	1.1	23.4	3.30
1902	60.0	9.4	173.1	2.49	35.0	2.1	67.0	1.81	10.0	1.4	29.0	2.54
1903	80.0	16.3	217.2	2.26	35.0	2.2	101.2	2.72	10.0	1.8	36.8	3.12
1904	80.0	16.5	269.9	2.80	50.0	3.7	120.1	2.24	10.0	1.8	46.3	3.92
1905	82.5	33.6	384.2	3.31	50.0	3.8	157.8	2.93	30.0	4.7	67.2	1.94
1906	105.0	34.0	408.9	2.94	50.0	5.0	196.0	3.56	40.0	5.7	74.8	1.64
1907	105.0	34.4	413.0	2.96	75.0	8.5	214.1	2.56	40.0	5.8	80.0	1.75
1908	105.0	34.9	461.1	3.30	75.0	8.8	251.3	3.00	60.0	6.0	98.2	1.49
1909	105.0	35.5	482.8	3.44	75.0	9.0	288.4	3.43	70.0	6.2	141.3	1.85
1910	105.0	36.0	512.8	3.64	75.0	9.3	309.0	3.67	100.0	6.4	187.3	1.76
1911	130.0	49.9	560.8	3.12	75.0	9.5	362.0	4.28	150.0	6.7	249.0	1.59
1912	130.0	48.7	667.8	3.74	75.0	10.0	407.9	4.80	200.0	7.3	253.8	1.22
1913	130.0	47.0	749.0	4.23	75.0	10.5	423.0	4.95	200.0	8.1	252.0	1.21
1914	156.0	59.5	671.3	3.12	75.0	11.0	429.7	5.00	200.0	8.7	214.2	1.03
1915	156.0	59.5	673.7	3.13	75.0	11.5	550.4	6.36	150.0	4.0	211.1	1.37

1916	156.0	58.2	1,125.7	5.26	75.0	12.5	1,017.9	11.63	75.0		222.8	2.97
1917	156.0	59.7	1,870.7	8.67	100.0	15.0	1,557.2	13.54	75.0	0.2	397.7	5.29
1918	208.0	83.3	2,532.0	8.69	150.0	24.0	2,231.1	12.82	100.0	2.5	648.4	6.33
1919	260.0	116.0	3,628.8	9.65	200.0	32.0	3,266.8	14.08	150.0	5.1	1,871.3	12.07
1920	312.0	156.0	4,973.8	10.63	300.0	65.0	4,117.6	11.28	150.0	11.7	2,044.0	12.64
1921	348.8	176.0	5,429.8	10.35	300.0	80.0	4,419.8	11.63	150.0	20.2	3,334.6	19.59
1922	348.8	180.0	5,176.8	9.79	300.0	90.0	3,923.1	10.06	150.0	24.1	3,422.5	19.66
1923	348.8	180.0	5,517.8	10.43	300.0	100.0	4,132.0	10.33	165.0	24.1	1,821.3	9.63
1924	338.0	280.0	6,209.8	10.05	400.0	110.0	4,811.3	9.43	200.0	25.0	2,007.2	8.92
1925	605.8	460.0	6,369.9	5.98	400.0	130.0	4,820.7	9.10	200.0	30.0	1,930.2	8.39

Table 14. (*cont.*)

Società Bancaria Milanese / Società Bancaria Italiana

	Capital	Shareholders' reserves	Deposits	Own to outside resources ratio
1895				
1896				
1897				
1898				
1899	6.0		9.6	1.6
1900	9.0	0.2	9.9	1.1
1901	9.0	0.3	10.4	1.1
1902	9.0	0.3	13.4	1.4
1903	12.0	0.5	16.1	1.3
1904	20.0	1.5	43.9	2.0
1905	30.0	4.3	62.7	1.8
1906	50.0	9.6	96.3	1.6
1907	50.0	10.0	45.9	0.8
1908	40.0		58.1	1.5
1909	40.0	0.1	89.6	2.2
1910	40.0	0.2	98.4	2.4
1911	40.0	0.3	103.3	2.6
1912	50.0	0.6	135.0	2.7
1913	50.0	1.0	134.4	2.6
1914	50.0	1.2	124.1	2.4

Banca di Busto Arsizio / Società di Credito Provinciale

	Capital	Shareholders' reserves	Deposits	Own to outside resources ratio
1895	0.3		2.2	7.3
1896	0.3		2.7	9.0
1897	0.3	0.1	3.0	7.5
1898	0.3	0.1	3.9	9.6
1899	0.4	0.1	3.6	7.2
1900	0.6	0.3	3.5	3.9
1901	0.6	0.4	5.9	5.9
1902	0.6	0.5	6.5	5.9
1903	0.8	0.8	8.2	5.1
1904	1.0	1.2	8.8	4.0
1905	1.6	2.8	12.5	2.8
1906	4.0	2.5	15.9	2.4
1907	4.5	3.1	17.4	2.3
1908	4.5	3.1	23.8	3.1
1909	4.8	3.1	33.0	4.2
1910	5.0	3.3	40.1	4.8
1911	9.6	7.0	61.3	3.7
1912	10.0	7.0	77.3	4.5
1913	15.0	10.0	113.4	4.5
1914	15.0	10.0	131.8	5.3

Banca Italiana di Sconto / Banca Nazionale di Credito

	Capital	Shareholders' reserves	Deposits	Own to outside resources ratio
1915	66.5	0.4	354.7	5.3
1916	70.0	2.3	685.2	9.5
1917	115.0	5.5	1,171.7	9.7
1918	167.5	22.6	2,167.7	11.4
1919	315.0	53.8	3,446.4	9.3
1920	315.0	73.0	4,509.9	11.6
1921				
1922				
1923	250.0		599.6	2.4
1924				
1925	300.0	20.0	1,377.3	4.3

Source: Umberto Bava, *I quattro maggiori istituti italiani di credito* (Genoa: Valugani, 1926).

Table 15. *Italy's principal trading partners 1909–1913*[a] *(millions of lire)*

Country	Total volume of trade	%	Imports	%	Exports	%	E/I %
Germany	878,100	15.6	563,446	16.5	314,654	14.2	56
Great Britain	754,328	13.4	529,130	15.5	225,198	10.2	43
United States	703,950	12.5	441,302	12.9	262,648	11.9	60
France	528,084	9.4	312,638	9.1	215,446	9.7	69
Austria-Hungary	478,372	8.5	289,420	8.5	188,952	8.5	65
Switzerland	303,685	5.4	82,722	2.4	220,963	10.0	267
Argentina	295,776	5.3	128,542	3.8	167,234	7.6	130
Russia	282,726	5.0	232,332	6.8	50,394	2.3	22
India	178,878	3.2	143,066	4.2	35,812	1.6	25
Belgium	135,279	2.4	80,371	2.4	54,908	2.5	68
Ottoman Empire	129,225	2.3	52,606	1.5	76,619	3.5	146
Romania	123,264	2.2	105,769	3.1	17,495	0.8	17
12 Principal trading partners	4,791,667	85.1	2,961,344	86.6	1,830,323	82.7	62
Total trade	5,630,850	100.0	3,418,909	100.0	2,211,941	100.0	65

[a] Average figures for 1909–13.
Source: ISTAT, *Annuario statistico italiano* (1918), pp. 227–8.

Table 16. *Jannacone's estimates for emigrant remittances, 1907–1923 (in millions of lire)*

	Remittances	1913 prices
1907	729	812
1908	639	731
1909	600	681
1910	734	832
1911	774	812
1912	779	758
1913	828	828
1914	581	606
1915	497	390
1916	572	310
1917	833	304
1918	837	203
1919	2,173	483
1920	4,253	720
1921	3,372	623
1922	3,054	561
1923	3,521	640

Source: Constantine McGuire, *Italy's International Economic Position* (New York: Macmillan, 1926), p. 277; Pasquale Jannacone, "La bilancia del dare e dell'avere internazionale con particolare riguardo all'Italia," in *Prezzi e mercati*, 2nd ed. (Turin: Einaudi, 1951), p. 319.

Table 17. *Stringher's estimates for Italy's international accounts, as represented in tabular form by C. McGuire (about 1910) (millions of lire)*

	Outgo	Income	Approximate balance Outgo	Approximate balance Income
Commodities	3,070	1,920	1,100	
Specie	20	50		
Travel expenditure	25	475		450
Remittances of Italians living abroad, and their payments for transportation and the like	60	515		450
Net surplus of postal money orders		200		150
Interest on securities public and private, and other income from miscellaneous items	185	70	135	
Totals			1,235	1,100

Source: Constantine McGuire, *Italy's International Economic Position* (New York: Macmillan, 1926), p. 270.

Table 18. Italian coal imports, 1913–1925 (in 1,000s of tons)

	1913	1914	1915	1916	1917	1918	1919	1920	1921	1922	1923	1924	1925
Jan.	776.6	917.5	695.3	563.3	480.1	395.0	340.4	398.8					
Feb.	854.7	772.3	568.6	630.6	449.9	360.3	489.5	390.6					
Mar.	1,004.1	939.4	901.6	617.6	353.1	398.3	414.8	395.0					
Apr.	812.4	862.8	739.1	706.2	436.0	557.7	408.4	344.9					
May	924.9	951.0	617.4	581.4	419.1	550.3	407.6	563.6					
June	922.4	961.5	597.1	635.4	441.4	533.0	527.6	703.6					
July	1,001.8	896.4	742.4	747.1	373.2	507.3	582.0	602.8					
Aug.	797.6	688.3	660.4	970.3	375.0	634.4	450.9	447.4					
Sept.	872.0	558.0	635.5	663.5	486.3	572.7	648.3	348.4					
Oct.	877.8	693.7	783.1	798.5	459.7	446.8	622.2	567.1					
Nov.	973.3	803.7	718.6	631.0	465.8	446.8	784.1	330.6					
Dec.	1,016.3	714.3	717.9	519.7	298.0	439.3	550.9	527.8					
Annual total	10,833.9	9,758.9	8,377.0	8,064.6	5,037.6	5,841.9	6,226.7	5,620.6	7,461.5	8,834.4	9,133.7	11,170.4	10,517.2

Source: Riccardo Bachi, L'Italia economica nell' anno 1920 (Città di Castello: S. Lapi, 1921), p. 89; L'Italia economica nell' anno 1921 (1922), p. 13; Ministero per l'Industria; Commercio e il Lavoro, Annuario statistico italiano 1925 (Rome: Tipografia nazionale, 1926), p. 212.

Table 19. *Italian raw cotton imports, 1913–1925 (in 1,000s of quintals)*

	1913	1914	1915	1916	1917	1918	1919	1920	1921	1922	1923	1924	1925
Jan.	191.8	221.5	156.3	270.9			112.9	76.4					
Feb.	186.5	216.9	208.7	244.6			196.9	95.9					
Mar.	194.7	198.2	218.6	293.1			198.7	132.4					
Apr.	176.9	203.1	266.8	221.5			241.8	160.2					
May	181.8	196.7	260.1	225.5			134.1	189.0					
June	180.9	206.8	334.2	265.3			118.0	358.3					
July	145.4	208.0	255.3	101.7			54.2	79.3					
Aug.	125.1	94.4	261.6	123.7			127.7	153.5					
Sept.	102.9	67.1	210.0	193.0			136.1	142.2					
Oct.	119.7	48.7	222.3	177.2			108.1	140.7					
Nov.	197.3	89.5	205.9	172.6			131.4	97.2					
Dec.	215.3	156.1	302.8	420.2			155.2	164.3					
Annual total	2,018.3	1,907.0	2,902.6	2,709.3	1,794.42	1,303.1	1,715.1	1,789.4	1,578.9	1,777.0	1,853.4	2,014.3	2,395.6

Source: Riccardo Bachi, *L'Italia economica nell'anno 1921* (Città di Castello: S. Lapi, 1922), p. 13; *L'Italia economica nell'anno 1920* (Città di Castello: S. Lapi, 1921), p. 22; *L'Italia economica nell'anno 1916* (Città di Castello: S. Lapi, 1917), pp. 2, 26; Ministero per l'Industria, il Commercio e il Lavoro, *Annuario statistico italiano 1925* (Rome: Tipografia nazionale, 1926), p. 209.

Table 20. *Gross domestic product in Italy, 1897–1929 (in billions of 1938 Lit.)*

	GDP	% Change			GDP	% Change
1897	66.3			1914	107.0	−1.8
1898	69.9	5.4		1915	119.0	11.2
1899	71.0	1.6		1916	133.0	11.8
1900	75.9	6.9		1917	137.0	3.0
1901	79.8	5.1		1918	138.0	0.7
1902	79.1	−0.9		1919	118.0	−14.5
1903	81.3	2.8		1920	109.0	−7.6
1904	81.4	0.1		1921	107.0	−1.8
1905	84.5	3.8		1922	113.0	5.6
1906	86.6	2.5		1923	129.0	14.2
1907	94.0	8.5		1924	123.0	−4.7
1908	94.6	0.6		1925	129.0	4.9
1909	100.0	5.7		1926	130.0	0.8
1910	95.7	−4.3		1927	130.0	—
1911	102.0	6.6		1928	139.0	6.9
1912	104.0	2.0		1929	143.0	2.9
1913	109.0	4.8				

Source: Paolo Ercolani, "Documentazione statistica di base," in Girogio Fuà ed., *Lo sviluppo economico in Italia*, 3rd ed. (Milan: Angeli, 1978), vol. III, pp. 417–18.

Table 21. *Central government expenditure and revenue as a percentage of gross national product*

	Italy, Ragioneria generale (contemporary)		Italy, Répaci (1962)		Italy, Ragioneria generale (1969)		Britain		France[a]		Germany[a]	
	Ex.	Rev.	Ex.	Rev.	Ex.	Rev.	Ex.	Rev	Ex.	Rev.	Ex.	Rev.
1911/12	10.4	10.0	10.0	8.7	11.7	11.3	7.2	7.4	8.8	9.0	5.6	
1912/13	10.9	9.9	11.1	8.9	12.2	10.8	7.1	7.3	94.0 (?)	9.4	6.7	4.0
1913/14	11.2	10.5	10.4	9.5	12.8	12.1	20.4	8.3				
1914/15	19.2	9.1	18.6	8.2	19.9	9.7	47.2	10.2				
1915/16	26.2	9.2	26.1	7.4	26.8	8.6	58.0	15.1				
1916/17	31.2	9.5	30.0	7.3	29.2	9.0	57.0	14.9				
1917/18	36.7	10.9	36.8	8.4	33.2	11.1	47.6	16.4				
1918/19	39.9	11.9	38.0	9.2	33.7	13.3	29.0	23.3				
1919/20	18.6	12.3	17.5	8.2	16.9	9.8	19.1	22.9	18.2	10.3		
1920/21	31.2	16.2	30.3	11.4	17.8	13.3	20.1	21.2	23.7	16.7		
1921/22	28.6	15.9	27.1	12.4	20.5	15.1	17.1	19.2	28.4	15.0		
1922/23	16.1	13.9	14.9	11.7	30.5	22.1	16.4	18.4	17.4	11.9		
1923/24	14.7	14.4	13.5	12.1	21.4	19.6	16.3	17.3	14.4	10.3		
1924/25	11.1	11.4	11.2	10.4	11.5	13.3	15.9	16.7	10.8	10.0	8.4	7.0
1925/26	10.9	11.1	10.6	10.7	10.5	12.8	16.9	17.4	9.4	9.4	10.1	8.1

[a] Net National Product.

Sources: B. R. Mitchell, *European Historical Statistics, 1750–1975*, 2nd rev. ed. (New York: Facts on File, 1981), pp. 736, 738, 755, 774, 821, 823, 826; F. A. Répaci, *La finanza pubblica italiana nel secolo 1861–1960* (Bologna: Zanichelli, 1962), pp. 125, 142; Ministero del Tesoro. Ragioneria generale dello stato, *Il bilancio dello stato italano dal 1862 al 1967* (Roma: Istituto poligrafico dello stato, 1969), vol. I, pp. 192–93.

Table 22. *Italy's tax revenues by category 1914–1925 (millions of lire)*

	Direct taxes	%	Imposte sugli Affari	%	Consumption taxes	%	Total
1913/14	617	29	309	15	1,175	56	2,101
1914/15	659	33	315	15	1,041	52	2,015
1915/16	793	32	358	14	1,348	54	2,499
1916/17	1,141	34	486	14	1,781	52	3,408
1917/18	1,620	36	631	14	2,265	50	4,516
1918/19	2,201	38	829	14	2,779	48	5,809
1919/20	2,501	33	1,266	16	3,898	51	7,665
1920/21	4,384	37	1,889	16	5,548	47	11,821
1921/22	5,342	38	2,041	14	6,815	48	14,198
1922/23	4,920	34	2,040	14	7,442	52	14,402
1923/24	5,894	37	2,615	16	7,509	47	16,018
1924/25	5,700	33	3,175	19	8,120	48	16,995

Source: Paolo Ercolani, "Documentazione statistica di base," in Giorgio Fuà, ed., *Lo sviluppo economico in Italia* (Milan: Angeli, 1978), p. 444.

Table 23. *Italy's tax revenues by category 1914–1925, in 1929 prices (millions of lire)*

	Direct taxes	%	Imposte sugli Affari	%	Consumption taxes	%	Total
1913/14	3,121	29	1,572	15	5,975	56	10,684
1914/15	2,509	33	1,199	15	3,963	52	7,671
1915/16	2,081	32	939	14	3,537	54	6,557
1916/17	2,016	34	859	14	3,146	52	6,021
1917/18	1,901	36	741	14	2,658	50	5,300
1918/19	2,370	38	893	14	2,992	48	6,254
1919/20	2,052	33	1,039	16	3,198	51	6,288
1920/21	3,926	37	1,692	16	4,969	47	10,587
1921/22	4,753	38	1,816	14	6,063	48	12,632
1922/23	4,336	34	1,798	14	6,559	52	12,692
1923/24	5,226	37	2,318	16	6,657	47	14,202
1924/25	4,508	33	2,511	19	6,422	48	13,441

Source: Paolo Ercolani, p.444, as in Table 22; based on wholesale price coefficients in ISTAT, *Il valore della lira dal 1861 al 1982* (Rome: ISTAT, 1983).

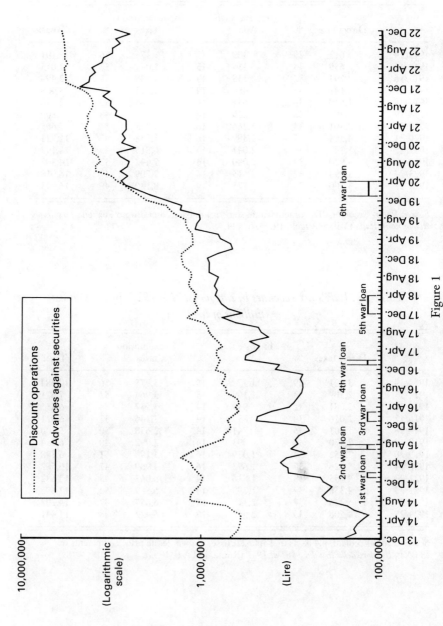

Figure 1

Commercial portfolios of the issue banks. (Total loans outstanding at the end of each month, in millions of lire.)

Source: Renato De Mattia, ed., *I bilanci degli instituti di emissione italiani,* 2 vols. (Rome: Banca d'Italia, 1967), Tables 15, 16.

328

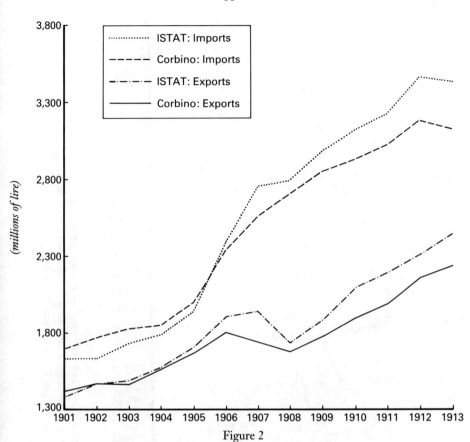

Figure 2
Italy, exports and imports, 1901–1913.
Source: Instituto Centrale di statistica, *Sommario di statistiche storiche dell'Italia, 1861–1955* (Rome: ISTAT, 1958), p. 152; Epicarmo Corbino, *Annali dell'economia italiana*, vol. V, *1901–1914*, p. 192.

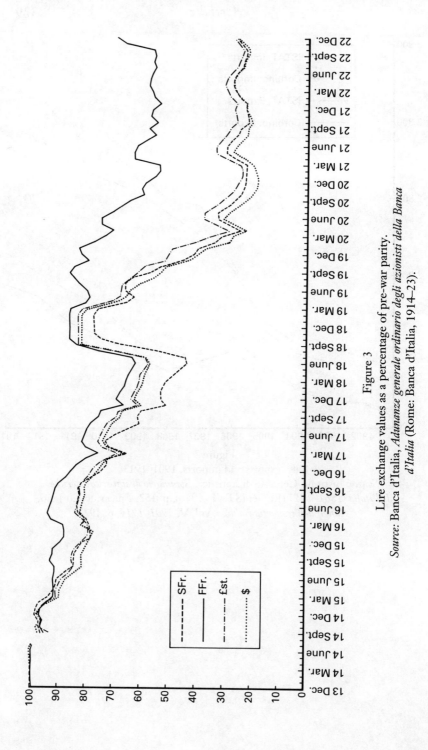

Figure 3

Lire exchange values as a percentage of pre-war parity.

Source: Banca d'Italia, *Adunanze generale ordinario degli azionisti della Banca d'Italia* (Rome: Banca d'Italia, 1914–23).

BIBLIOGRAPHY

Archival sources

Britain

Public Record Office, Kew (PRO)
Treasury Files
Foreign Office Files

Archive, Bank of England, London
ADM20 Lord Norman's Diary
C40 Chief Cashier's Policy Files
C44 Overseas Central Banks' Accounts with the Bank
G1 Governor's Files
G23 Secretary's Letter Book

France

Ministère des Affaires Etrangères, Paris
Correspondence politique, NS, 1896–1918, Italie, finances, banques, bourse

Italy

Archivio Centrale dello Stato, Rome
Carte Giovanni Giolitti
Carte F. S. Nitti
Carte Giuseppe Paratore
Carte Pio Perrone
Carte Carlo Schanzer
Ministero per le armi e munizioni
Presidenza del Consiglio

Archivio Storico, Banca d'Italia, Rome (ASBI)
Fondo 3, Rapporti con l'estero
Fondo 5, Rapporti con l'interno
Fondo 9, Segretario
Fondo 9.2, Consiglio Superiore, verbali; Presidenza e Giunta del Consiglio
    Superiore riunite in Comitato, verbali
Fondo 13, Sconti, Anticipazioni, Corrispondenti
Carte Stringher

Archivio Storico, Ministero degli Affari Esteri, Rome
Affari politici, 1919–30
Archivio politico (ordinario e di gabinetto), 1915–18
Archivio riservato di gabinetto, 1891–1923
Rappresentanze diplomatiche Londra, 1861–1950

Fondazione Luigi Einaudi, Turin
Archivio Luigi Einaudi
Archivio Francesco Saverio Nitti

Archivio Storico, Banca Commerciale Italiana, Milan
Contabilità (1895–1932)
Carte di Otto Joel (1890–1916)
Segreteria dell'Amministratore Delegato Giuseppe Toeplitz (1916–34)
Verbali del Consiglio di Amministrazione (1894–1934)
Verbali del Comitato Locale (1894–1918)

Archivio Storico, Credito Italiano, Milan
Consiglio d'Amministrazione, verbali (1914–23)
Csf. Direzione Centrale

Cassa di Risparmio per le provincie della Lombardia, Archivio Storico, Milan
Verbali delle deliberazioni della Commissione Centrale

United States

Amherst College Library, Amherst MA
Dwight W. Morrow Papers

Archive of Federal Reserve Bank of New York, New York
Benjamin Strong Papers
C261 Italy-Government of Italy, May 1917–54

Baker Library, Harvard University, Cambridge MA
Thomas W. Lamont Papers

National Archives, Washington DC
Treasury, RG 39

Mudd Library, Princeton University, Princeton NJ
Bernard Baruch Papers
Fred I. Kent Papers

Published sources

Official publications

Banca d'Italia, *Sulle condizioni della circolazione e del mercato monetario durante e dopo la guerra* (Rome: Casa Editrice Italiana, 1920).

Adunanza generale ordinaria degli azionisti della Banca d'Italia (Rome: Banca d'Italia, 1914–23) (published annually).

Camera dei Deputati, *Atti della Camera dei Deputati, Discussioni* (Rome: Camera dei Deputati, 1914–22).

Relazione della commissione parlamentare d'inchiesta per le spese di guerra, in *Raccolta degli atti stampati*, 26.a legislatura, sessione 1921–23, vol. 3 (*Documenti*), nos. 21–23 (Rome: Camera dei Deputati, 1923).

De Cecco, Marcello, ed., *L'Italia e il sistema finanziario internazionale, 1861–1914* (Bari: Laterza, 1990).

De Stefani, Alberto, *La legislazione economica della guerra* (Bari: Laterza, 1926).

Ministero degli Affari Esteri, *I documenti diplomatici italiani (DDI)* 5th ser., 1914–18 (Rome: Ministero degli Affari Esteri, 1954–).

I documenti diplomatici italiani, 6th ser., 1918–1922 (Rome: Ministero degli Affari Esteri, 1955–).

Ministero delle Finanze, "I capitali delle società stranieri in Italia dal 1912/3 al 1924/5. Dati statistici," *Bollettino di Statistica e di legislazione comparata*, 24 (1925/6), no. 11.

"Alcuni indici della entità e della orientazione del capitale italiano investito in titoli e valori esteri durante il periodo dall'esercizio 1900–1901 a tutto il 1922–1923," *Bolletino di statistica e di legislazione comparata*, 23 (1923–24), no. 5, pp. 893–997.

Ministero delle Finanze, Direzione Generale delle Imposte Dirette, *La gestione delle imposte dirette dal 1914 al 1925* (Rome: Provveditorato Generale dello Stato, 1926).

Negri, Giuglielmo, ed., *Giolitti e la nascita della Banca d'Italia nel 1893* (Bari: Laterza, 1989).

Ragioneria Generale dello stato italiano, *Il bilancio dello stato italiano dal 1862 al 1967*, 4 vols. (Rome: Istituto poligrafico della stato, 1969).

Il bilancio dello stato dal 1913–14 al 1929–30 e la finanza fascista a tutto l'anno VIII (Rome: Istituto poligrafico dello stato, 1931).

Senato del Regno, *Atti del Senato, Discussioni* (Rome: Senato del Regno, 1914–22).

Stringher, Bonaldo, *Note e cifre sulle circolazione cartacea e il mercato monetario (agosto 1914 – aprile 1918)* (Rome: Banca d'Italia, 1918).

Toniolo, Gianni, ed., *La Banca d'Italia e l'economia di guerra, 1914–1919* (Bari: Laterza, 1989).

Firms and business organizations

Associazione fra le società per azione, and, Confederazione generale dell'industria italiana (sezione economica), *Note sulla situazione economica dell'Italia* (Rome: Athenaeum, 1921).

Banca Commerciale Italiana, *Relazioni e bilanci* (1914–22).

Banca Italiana di Sconto, *Relazioni e bilanci* (1915–20).

Banco di Roma, *Relazioni e bilanci* (1914–22).

Credito Italiano, *Relazioni e bilanci* (1914–22).

Statistical sources

Barberi, Benedetto, *I consumi nel primo secolo dell'unità d'Italia (1861–1960)* (Milan: Giuffré, 1961).

De Mattia, Renato, ed., *I bilanci degli istituti di emissioni italiani*, 2 vols. (Rome: Banca d'Italia, 1967).

Ercolani, Paolo, "Documentazione statistica di base," in Fuà, Giorgio, ed., *Lo sviluppo economico in Italia*, 3rd ed., vol. III (Milan: Angeli, 1978), pp. 388–472.

Istituto Centrale di Statistica, *Il valore della lira dal 1861 al 1982* (Rome: ISTAT, 1983).

Sommario di statistiche storiche dell'Italia 1861–1965 (Rome: ISTAT, 1968).

Sommario di statistiche storiche italiane 1861–1955 (Rome: ISTAT, 1958).

Annuario statistico italiano (Rome: ISTAT, 1913–25) (published annually).

Mitchell, B. R., *European Historical Statistics 1750–1975*, 2nd rev. ed. (New York: Facts on File, 1981).

Letters, diaries, speeches

Albertini, Luigi, *Epistolario, 1911–1926*, ed. O. Barié, vols. I–III (Verona: Mondadori, 1968).

Aldrovandi Marescotti, Luigi, *Guerra diplomatica. Ricordi e frammenti di diario (1914–1919)* (Milan: Mondadori, 1936).

Conti, Ettore, *Dal taccuino di un borghese*, 3rd ed. (Bologna: Il Mulino, 1986).

Crespi, Silvio, *Alla difesa d'Italia in guerra e a Versailles Diario 1917–1919* (Milan: Mondadori, 1937).

D'Aroma, Antonio, and Martinotti Dorigo, Stefania, *Lettere di Luigi Einaudi a Pasquale D'Aroma, (1914–1927)*, *Annali della Fondazione Luigi Einaudi*, 9 (Turin: Fondazione Einaudi, 1975).

De Stefani, Alberto, *Baraonda bancaria* (Milan: Edizioni del Borghese, 1960).

Einaudi, Luigi, *Cronache economiche e politiche di un trentennio (1893–1925)* (republished articles from *Corriere della Sera*), vols. IV–VII, 1914–1924 (Turin: Einaudi, 1961–66).

Giolitti, Giovanni, *Quarant'anni di politica italiana. Dalle carte di Giovanni Giolitti*, 3 vols. (Milan: Feltrinelli, 1962).

Discorsi parlamentari. Pubblicati per deliberazione della Camera dei Deputati (Rome: Camera dei Deputati, 1956).

Discorsi extraparlamentari (Turin: Einaudi, 1952).

Johnson, Elizabeth, ed., *The Collected Writings of John Maynard Keynes*, vol. XVI, *Activities 1914–1919: The Treasury and Versailles* (London: Macmillan, 1971).

Link, Arthur S., et al., eds., *The Papers of Woodrow Wilson* (Princeton: Princeton University Press, 1966–).

Malagodi, Olindo, *Conversazioni della guerra, 1914–1919*, 2 vols., ed. Brunello Vigezzi (Milan and Naples: Ricciardi, 1960).

Marcoaldi, Franco, *Vent'anni di economia e politica: Le carte De Stefani (1922–1941)* (Milan: Angeli, 1986).

Martini, Ferdinando, *Diario 1914–1918* (Verona: Mondadori, 1966).

Matteotti, Giacomo, *Discorsi parlamentari. Pubblicati per deliberazione della Camera dei Deputati* (Rome: Camera dei Deputati, 1976).

Reliquie (Milan: Corbaccio, 1924).

Mussolini, Benito, *Opera omnia*, ed. Edoardo and Duilio Susmel, vol. XVIII (Florence: La Fenice, 1956).

Pastorelli, Pietro, ed., *Sidney Sonnino. Carteggio 1916–1922* (Bari: Laterza, 1975).

Sidney Sonnino. Carteggio 1914–1916 (Bari: Laterza, 1974).

Sidney Sonnino. Diario 1914–1916 (Bari: Laterza, 1972).

Sidney Sonnino. Diario 1916–1922 (Bari: Laterza, 1972).

Sonnino, Sidney, *Scritti e discorsi extraparlamentari, 1870–1902*, ed. Benjamin F. Brown (Bari: Laterza, 1972).

Contemporaneous newspapers, journals, and periodicals

Corriere della Sera
Finanza Italiana
Giornale degli economisti
Giornale d'Italia
Journal of Commerce
Nuova antologia
Popolo d'Italia
Riforma sociale
Rivista bancaria
Sole
Unità
Wall Street Journal

Bachi, Riccardo, *L'Italia economica nell'anno 1914* (Città di Castello: S. Lapi, 1915).

L'Italia economica nell'anno 1915 (Città di Castello: S. Lapi, 1916).

L'Italia economica nell'anno 1916 (Città di Castello: S. Lapi, 1917).

L'Italia economica nell'anno 1917 (Città di Castello: S. Lapi, 1918).

L'Italia economica nell'anno 1918 (Città di Castello: S. Lapi, 1919).

L'Italia economica nell'anno 1919 (Città di Castello: S. Lapi, 1920).

L'Italia economica nell'anno 1920 (Città di Castello: S. Lapi, 1921).

L'Italia economica nell'anno 1921 (Città di Castello: S. Lapi, 1922).

Mortara, Giorgio, *Prospettive economiche* (Città di Castello: Leonardo da Vinci, 1921).

Prospettive economiche (Città di Castello: Leonardo da Vinci, 1922).

Books and articles

Abraham, David, *The Collapse of the Weimar Republic: Political Economy and Crisis*, 2nd rev. ed. (New York: Holmes and Meier, 1986).

Abrahams, Paul P., "American Bankers and the Economic Tactics of Peace: 1919," *Journal of American History*, 56 (1969), no. 3, pp. 572–83.

Abrate, Mario, *La lotta sindacale nella industrializzazione in Italia, 1906–1926*, 2nd rev. ed. (Milan: Angeli, 1967).

Adams, R. J. Q., *Arms and the Wizard: Lloyd George and the Ministry of Munitions, 1915–1916* (College Station TX: Texas A and M University Press, 1978).

Agresti, A., "La questione dell'emigrazione italiana," *Rivista di politica economica* (1924), pp. 324–30.

Alatri, Paolo, *Nitti, D'Annunzio e la questione adriatica (1919–1920)* (Milan: Feltrinelli, 1959).

"La crisi del giolittismo," in, *Storia della società italiana*, vol. XX, *L'Italia di Giolitti* (Milan: Teti, 1981), pp. 465–84.

Albertini, Luigi, *Venti anni di vita politica*, pt. 2, *L'Italia nella guerra mondiale*, 2 vols. (Bologna: Zanichelli, 1952).

Albrecht-Carrié, René, *Italy at the Paris Peace Conference* (New York: Columbia University Press, 1938).

Aldcroft, Derek, *From Versailles to Wall Street, 1919–1929* (Berkeley: University of California Press, 1977).

Alesina, Alberto, "The End of Large Public Debts," in, Francesco Giavazzi and Luigi Spaventa, eds., *High Public Debt: The Italian Experience* (New York: Cambridge University Press, 1988), pp. 34–79.

Allen, J. E., and Hirst, F. W., *British War Budgets* (Oxford: Oxford University Press, 1926).

Ambrosoli, L., "Paolo Carcano," *Dizionario biografico italiano* (1976).

Anelli, P., Bovini, G., and Montenegro, A., *Pirelli 1914–1980. Strategia aziendale e relazioni industriali nella storia di una multinazionale*, vol. I, *Dalla prima guerra mondiale all'autunno caldo* (Milan: Angeli, 1985).

Aquarone, Alberto, *Tre capitoli sull'Italia giolittiana* (Bologna: Il Mulino, 1987).

L'Italia giolittiana (1896–1915), vol. I, *Le premesse politiche ed economiche* (Bologna: Il Mulino, 1981).

Arena, Celestino, *Italiani per il mondo. Politica nazionale dell'emigrazione* (Milan: Alpes, 1927).

Atkin, John, "Official Regulation of British Overseas Investment, 1914–1931," *Economic History Review*, 2nd ser., 23 (1970), no. 2, pp. 324–35.

Bagehot, Walter, *Lombard Street. A Description of the Money Market* (Homewood IL: R. D. Irwin, 1962).

Balderston, T., "War Finance and Inflation in Britain and Germany, 1914–1918," *Economic History Review*, 2nd ser., 42 (1989), no. 2, pp. 222–44.

Balducci, Sigismondo, *Elefantiasi ferroviaria* (Milan: Società Editoriale Italiana, 1920).

Balletta, Francesco, *Per la storia della politica finanziaria in Italia. L'opera di Marcello Soleri* (Naples: L'arte tipografica, 1983).

Il Banco di Napoli e le rimesse degli emigranti (Naples: Istitut d'histoire de la banque, 1972).

Banca Commerciale Italiana, *La Banca Commerciale Italiana, 1894–1919* (Milan: Bertieri e Vanzetti, 1920).

Banco di Roma, *Banca e industria fra le due guerre. Ricerca promossa dal Banco di Roma in occasione del suo primo centenario*, vol. II, *Le riforme instituzionali e il pensiero giuridico* (Bologna: Il Mulino, 1981).

Banca e industria fra le due guerre. Atti del convegno conclusivo della ricerca promossa dal Banco di Roma in occasione del suo primo centenario (Bologna: Il Mulino, 1981).

Barbagallo, Francesco, *Nitti* (Turin: UTET, 1984).

Barsali, M., and Bonelli, Franco, "Massimo (Max) Bondi," *Dizionario biografico italiano* (1969).

Bartolotta, Francesco, *Parlamentari e governi d'Italia dal 1848 al 1970*, 2 vols. (Rome: V. Bianco, 1971).

Bava, Umberto, *I quattro maggiori istituti italiani di credito* (Genoa: Valugani, 1926).

Bezza, Bruno, "Gli aspetti normativi nelle relazioni industriali del periodo bellico (1915–18)," in Giovanna Procacci ed., *Stato e classe operaia in Italia durante la prima guerra mondiale* (Milan: Angeli, 1983), pp. 103–20.

"Contrattazione collettiva e FIOM durante la prima guerra mondiale," *Giornale di diritto del lavoro e di relazioni industriali* (1982), no. 16, pp. 693–723.

Bigazzi, Duccio, *Il Portello. Operai, tecnici e imprenditori all'Alfa-Romeo, 1906–1926* (Milan: Angeli, 1988).

"Grandi impresi e concentrazione finanziaria, in, *Storia della società italiana*, vol. XX, *L'Italia di Giolitti* (Milan: Teti, 1981), pp. 87–143.

Biscaini Cotula, Anna Maria, and Ciocca, Pierluigi, "Le strutture finanziarie: Aspetti quantitativi di lungo periodo (1870–1970)," in Fausto Vicarelli, ed., *Capitale industriale e capitale finanziario. Il caso italiano* (Bologna: Il Mulino, 1979), pp. 61–136.

Blankart, Charles, *Devisenpolitik während des Weltkrieges (August 1914–November 1918)* (Zurich: Füssli, 1919).

Bloomfield, Arthur I., *Monetary Policy under the International Gold Standard, 1880–1914* (New York: Federal Reserve Bank of New York, 1959).

"Bold Strike," *The Banker*, 137 (1987), no. 731, pp. 6–7.

Bonaldo Stringher e i problemi del finanziamento all'industria in Italia, Atti del convegno organizzato a Udine dalla Cassa di Risparmio di Udine e Pordenone, Udine, 30 November 1984 (Udine: Cassa di Risparmio di Udine e Pordenone, 1986).

Bonelli, Franco, *Bonaldo Stringher, 1854–1930* (Udine: Casamassima, 1985).

Lo sviluppo di una grande impresa in Italia. La Terni dal 1884 al 1962 (Turin: Einaudi, 1974).

La crisi del 1907. Una tappa dello sviluppo industriale in Italia (Turin: Fondazione Luigi Einaudi, 1971).

"Riccardo Bianchi (1854–1936)," in, Alberto Mortara, ed., *Protagonisti dell'intervento pubblico* (Milan: Angeli, 1984).

"Il capitalismo italiano. Linee generale d'interpretazione," in, Ruggiero Romano and Corrado Vivanti, ed., *Storia d'Italia*. Annali I: *Dal feudalismo al capitalismo* (Turin: Einaudi, 1978), pp. 1195–255.

"Osservazioni e dati sul finanziamento dell'industria italiana all'inizio del secolo XX," *Annali della Fondazione Luigi Einaudi*, 2 (1968), pp. 264–71.

Bonelli, Franco, ed., *Acciaio per l'industrializzazione. Contributi allo studio del problema siderurgico italiano* (Turin: Fondazione Einaudi, 1982).

Bonjour, Edgar, *Geschichte der schweizerischen Neutralität. Vier Jahrhunderte eidgenössischer Aussenpolitik*, 2nd rev. ed., vol. II (Basel: Helbing and Lichtenhan, 1965).

Borgatta, Gino, *Bilancio dei pagamenti – Cambio* (Milan: Giuffré, 1933).

"Rimesse degli emigranti e turismo," *Rassegna economica*, 3 (1933), pp. 402–17.

"La gestione e liquidazione del materiale bellico," *Riforma sociale*, 29 (1922), no. 1–2, pp. 7–18.

"Crisi bellica e crisi postbellica," *Riforma sociale*, 28 (1921), nos. 3–4, pp. 65–93.

Born, Karl Erich, *Geld und Banken im 19. und 20. Jahrhundert* (Stuttgart: Kröner, 1977).

"Vom Beginn des Ersten Weltkrieges bis zum Ende der Weimarer Republik (1914–1933)," in, Ernst Klein, et al., ed., *Deutsche Bankengeschichte*, vol. III (Frankfurt a.M.: Knapp, 1983), pp. 17–146.

Bosworth, Richard J. B., *Italy and the Approach of the First World War* (London: Macmillan, 1983).

Italy, the Least of the Great Powers: Italian Foreign Policy before the First World War (New York: Cambridge University Press, 1979).

"Sir Rennell Rodd e l'Italia," *Nuova rivista storica*, 54 (1970), no. 3–4, pp. 420–36.

"The English, the Historians and the Età Giolittiana," *Historical Journal*, 12 (1969), no. 2, pp. 353–67.

Bouvier, Jean, "Monnaie et banque d'un après-guerre à l'autre: 1919–1945," in, Fernand Braudel and Ernest Labrousse, eds., *Histoire économique et sociale de la France*, vol. IV, *L'Ère industrielle et la société d'ajourd'hui (siècle 1880–1980)*, vol. II, *Le Temps des guerres mondiales et de la grande Crise (1914–vers 1950)* (Paris: PUF, 1980), pp. 687–728.

Boyle, Andrew, *Montagu Norman* (London: Cassell, 1967).

Bresciani-Turroni, Constantino, *The Economics of Inflation: A Study of Currency Depreciation in Post-War Germany* (New York: Barnes and Noble, 1937).

Brosio, Giorgio, and Marchese, Carla, *Il potere di spendere. Economia e storia della spesa pubblica dall'unificazione ad oggi* (Bologna: Il Mulino, 1986).

Brown, William Adams Jr., *The International Gold Standard Reinterpreted, 1914–1934* (Washington DC: National Bureau of Economic Research, 1940).

Burk, Kathleen, *Britain, America and the Sinews of War, 1914–1918* (Boston: George Allen and Unwin, 1985).

"J. M. Keynes and the Exchange Rate Crisis of July 1917," *Economic History Review*, 2nd ser., 32 (1979), no. 3., pp. 405–16.

Burk, Kathleen, ed., *War and the State: The Transformation of British Government, 1914–1919* (London: George Allen and Unwin, 1982).

Büsch, Otto, and Feldman, Gerald, ed., *Historische Prozesse der deutschen Inflation, 1914 bis 1924* (Berlin: Colloquium, 1978).

Cafagna, Luciano, "The Industrial Revolution in Italy, 1830–1914," in, Carlo Cipolla, ed., *The Fontana Economic History of Europe: The Emergence of Industrial Societies*, vol. I (London: Fontana, 1973).

Calandra, Piero, *Storia dell'amministrazione pubblica in Italia* (Bologna: Il Mulino, 1978).

Camarda, Alessandro, and Peli, Santo, *L'Altro esercito. La classe operaia durante la prima guerra mondiale* (Milan: Feltrinelli, 1980).

Candeloro, Giorgio, *Storia dell'Italia moderna*, vol. VIII, *La prima guerra mondiale, il dopoguerra, l'avvento del fascismo* (Milan: Feltrinelli, 1978).

Canovai, Tito, *Le banche di emissione in Italia* (Rome: Casa editrice italiana, 1912).

Canovai, Tito, interview with, in, *Report of the National Monetary Commission: Interviews on Banking in Europe* (Washington DC: National Monetary Commission, 1912), vol. I, pp. 511–42.

Caracciolo, Alberto, "La crescita e la trasformazione della grande industria durante la prima guerra mondiale," in, Giorgio, Fuà, ed., *Lo sviluppo economico in Italia*, 3rd ed., vol. III (Milan: Angeli, 1978), pp. 195–248.

"L'intervento italiano in guerra e la crisi politica del 1914–5," *Società*, 10 (1954), no. 5, pp. 809–26, no. 6, pp. 986–1012.

Cardini, Antonio, *Antonio De Viti De Marco. La democrazia incompiuta 1858–1943* (Bari: Laterza, 1985).

Cardoza, Anthony, *Agrarian Elites and Italian Fascism: The Province of Bologna, 1901–1926* (Princeton: Princeton University Press, 1982).

Carli, Guido, "Alcuni aspetti dell'evoluzione funzionale dell'istituto di emissione dalle sue origine ai nostri giorni," in *Studi in occasione del primo centenario della Corte dei Conti nell'unità d'Italia* (Milan: Giuffré, 1963).

Carocci, Giampiero, *Giolitti e l'età giolittiana* (Turin: Einaudi, 1961).

Caroleo, Anna, *Le banche cattoliche dalla prima guerra mondiale al fascismo* (Milan: Feltrinelli, 1976).

"La crisi e il salvataggio del Banco di Roma nei primi contatti tra Mussolini e la Santa Sede", *Belfagor*, 28 (1973), no. 4, pp. 461–74.

Carosso, Vincent P., *Investment Banking in America: A History* (Cambridge MA: Harvard University Press, 1970).

Carparelli, Antonia, "Ernesto Rossi (1897–1967)," in Alberto Mortara, ed., *Protagonisti dell'intervento pubblico* (Milan: Angeli, 1984), pp. 618–46.

"Uomini, idee, iniziative per una politica di riconversione industriale in Italia," in Peter Hertner and Giorgio Mori, ed., *La transizione dall'economia di guerra all'economia di pace in Italia e in Germania dopo la prima guerra mondiale* (Bologna: Il Mulino, 1983), pp. 223–47.

"I perché di una 'mezza siderurgia.' La società Ilva, l'industria della ghisa e il ciclo integrale negli anni Venti," in, Franco Bonelli, ed., *Acciaio per l'industrializzazione. Contributi allo studio del problema siderurgico italiano* (Turin: Einaudi, 1982), pp. 3–158.

Carucci, Paola, "Funzioni e caratteri del ministero per le armi e munizioni," in Giovanna Procacci, ed., *Stato e classe operaia in Italia durante la prima guerra mondiale* (Milan: Angeli, 1983), pp. 60–78.

Cassels, Alan, *Mussolini's Early Diplomacy* (Princeton: Princeton University Press, 1970).

Cassese, Sabino, *Il sistema amministrativo italiano* (Bologna: Il Mulino, 1983).

Esiste un governo in Italia? (Rome: Officina edizioni, 1970).

Castronovo, Valerio, *Storia di una banca. La Banca Nazionale del Lavoro e lo sviluppo economico italiano 1913–1983* (Turin: Einaudi, 1983).

Giovanni Agnelli. La Fiat dal 1899 al 1945 (Turin: Einaudi, 1977).

La stampa italiana dall'unità al fascismo (Bari: Laterza, 1970).

"Le relazioni tra la Fiat e il governo francese durante la guerra," in Pierre Guillen, ed., *La France et l'Italie pendant la première guerre mondiale* (Grenoble: Presses Universitaires de Grenoble, 1976), pp. 335–38.

Cavazzuti, Filippo, "Ricerca sulla dinamica della finanza locale in Italia," in *Studi sulla finanza locale* (Milan: Giuffré, 1967), pp. 1–66.

Chandler, Lester V., *Benjamin Strong, Central Banker* (Washington DC: Brookings Institution, 1958).

Cianci, Ernesto, *Nascita dello Stato imprenditore in Italia* (Milan: Mursia, 1977).

Cinquanta anni di storia d'Italia, vol. III (Milan: Hoepli, 1911).

Ciocca, Pierluigi, "Note sulla politica monetaria italiana 1900–1913," in Gianni Toniolo, ed., *Lo sviluppo economico italiano* (Bari: Laterza, 1973).

Ciocca, Pierluigi, and Toniolo, Gianni, "Industry and Finance in Italy, 1918–1940," *Journal of European Economic History*, 13 (1984), no. 2 (special issue), pp. 113–36.

Ciocca, Pierluigi, and Toniolo, Gianni, eds., *L'economia italiana nel periodo fascista* (Bologna: Il Mulino, 1976).

Cipolla, Carlo, ed., *The Fontana Economic History of Europe: The Emergence of Industrial Societies*, vol. I (London: Fontana, 1973).

Clarich, Marcello, *Le grandi banche nei paesi maggiormente industrializzati* (Bologna: Il Mulino, 1985).

Clarke, Stephen V. O., *The Reconstruction of the International Monetary System: The Attempts of 1922 and 1933*, Princeton Studies in International Finance, no. 33 (Princeton: Princeton University Press, 1973).

Central Bank Cooperation, 1924–31 (New York: Federal Reserve of New York, 1967).

Clay, Henry, *Lord Norman* (New York: St. Martin's, 1957).

Cleveland, Harold van B., and Huertas, Thomas F., *Citibank 1812–1970* (Cambridge MA: Harvard University Press, 1985).

Cohen, Jon S., *Finance and Industrialization in Italy, 1894–1914* (New York: Arno Press, 1977).

Confalonieri, Antonio, *Banca e industria in Italia dalla crisi del 1907 all'agosto 1914*, 2 vols. (Milan: Banca Commerciale Italiana, 1982).

Banca e industria in Italia (1894–1906), 3 vols. (Milan: Banca Commerciale Italiana, 1977–80).

Le due banche popolari mantovane dalle origini alla fusione, (1866–1932) (Mantova: Banca Agricola Mantovana, 1961).

Confalonieri, Antonio, and Gatti, Ettore, *La politica del debito pubblico in Italia, 1919–1943* (Bari: CARIPLO-Laterza, 1986).

"Confidence Factor," *The Banker*, 137 (1987), no. 731, pp. 6–7.

Coppa, Frank, *Planning, Protectionism and Politics in Liberal Italy: Economics and Politics in the Giolittian Age* (Washington DC: Catholic University of America Press, 1971).

Corbino, Epicarmo, *Annali dell'economia italiana*, vol. V, *1901–1914* (Città di Castello: Leonardo da Vinci, 1938).

Corner, Paul, *Fascism in Ferrara, 1915–1925* (Oxford: Oxford University Press, 1975).

Costigliola, Frank, *Awkward Dominion: American Political, Economic, and Cultural Relations with Europe, 1919–1933* (Ithaca: Cornell University Press, 1984).

"Anglo-American Financial Rivalry in the 1920s," *Journal of Economic History*, 37 (1977), no. 4, pp. 911–34.

Croce, Benedetto, *A History of Italy, 1871–1915* (New York: Russell and Russell, 1929).

De Cecco, Marcello, *Moneta e impero. Il sistema finanziario internazionale dal 1890 al 1914* (Turin: Einaudi, 1979).

De Felice, Renzo, *Mussolini il fascista*, vol. I, *La conquista del potere 1921–1925* (Turin: Einaudi, 1966).

    Mussolini il rivoluzionario 1883–1920 (Turin: Einaudi, 1965).

    "Giovanni Preziosi e le origini del fascismo (1917–1931)," *Rivista storica del socialismo*, 5 (1962), no. 17, pp. 493–555.

De Grand, Alexander, *The Italian Nationalist Association and the Rise of Fascism in Italy* (Lincoln: University of Nebraska Press, 1978).

Del Vecchio, Eduardo, *La cooperazione economica e finanziaria nella politica di guerra dell'intesa* (Naples: Liguori, 1974).

Demarco, Domenico, ed., *Studi in onore di Epicarmo Corbino* (Milan: Giuffré, 1961).

De Rosa, Gabriele, *Il Partito Populare Italiano*, 2nd rev. and enl. ed. (Bari: Laterza, 1988).

De Rosa, Luigi, *Storia del Banco di Roma*, vols. I–II (Rome: Banco di Roma, 1981–83) (privately published, restricted distribution).

De Stefani, Alberto, *La restaurazione finanziaria 1922–25* (Bologna: Zanichelli, 1926).

Diggins, John P., *Mussolini and Fascism: The View from America* (Princeton: Princeton University Press, 1972).

Dogliani, Patrizia, "Stato, imprenditori e manodopera industriale in Francia durante la prima guerra mondiale," *Rivista di storia contemporanea*, 11 (1982), no. 4, pp. 523–59.

Doria, Marco, "Dal progetto di integrazione verticale alle ristrutturazioni dell'IRI: la siderurgia Ansaldo (1900–1935)," *Annali della Fondazione Luigi Einaudi*, 18 (1984) pp. 411–53.

Einaudi, Luigi, *Il buongoverno. Saggi di economia e politica 1897–1954*, ed. Ernesto Rossi, 2 vols. (Bari: Laterza, 1973).

    La condotta economica e gli effetti sociali della guerra italiana (Bari: Laterza, 1933).

    La guerra e il sistema tributario italiano (Bari: Laterza, 1927).

    "L'industria degli armamenti," *Unità*, 22 Dec. 1916, in, Beniamino Finocchiaro, ed., *L'Unità di Gaetano Salvemini* (Venice: Neri Pozza, 1958), pp. 489–98.

Falchero, Anna Maria, *La Banca Italiana di Sconto, 1914–1921: Sette anni di guerra* (Milan: Angeli, 1990).

    "Il gruppo Ansaldo–Banca Italiana di Sconto e le vicende bancarie nel primo dopoguerra," in Peter Hertner and Giorgio Mori, eds., *La transizione dall'economia di guerra all'economia di pace in Italia e in Germania dopo la prima guerra mondiale* (Bologna: Il Mulino, 1983), pp. 543–71.

    "Banchieri e politica. Nitti e il gruppo Ansaldo–Banca di Sconto," *Italia contemporanea*, (1982), nos. 146/47, pp. 62–92.

Falco, Giancarlo, *L'Italia e la politica finanziaria degli alleati 1914–1920* (Pisa: ETS, 1983).

    "La politica fiscale dell'ultimo governo Giolitti (1920–1921)," *Rivista di storica contemporanea*, 11 (1982), no. 4, pp. 560–604.

Falco, Giancarlo, and Storace, Marina, "Fluttuazioni monetarie alla metà degli anni 20: Belgio, Francia e Italia," *Studi storici*, 16 (1975), no. 1, pp. 57–101.

Farneti, Paolo, "La crisi della democrazia italiana e l'avvento del fascismo: 1919–1922," *Rivista italiana di scienza politica*, 5 (1975), no. 1, pp. 45–82.

Fasce, Ferdinando, "L'Ansaldo in America (1915–1921)," *Studi e notizie*, Centro di studio sulla storia della tecnica del CNR presso la università di Genoa, 11 (1983).

Faucci, Riccardo, *Finanza, amministrazione e pensiero economico. Il caso della contabilità di stato da Cavour al fascismo*, Studi della Fondazione Luigi Einaudi, no. 20 (Turin: Fondazione Einaudi, 1975).

Fausto, Domenicantonio, "La politica finanziaria del fascismo," *Richerche economiche*, 39 (1975), no. 2, pp. 164–91.

Favre, J.-E., *Le Capital français au service de l'étranger. Un cas: La Banque de Paris et des Pays-Bas et son oeuvre anti-nationale* (Paris: Bibliothèque Financière, 1917).

Feis, Herbert, *The Diplomacy of the Dollar: First Era, 1919–1932* (Baltimore: Johns Hopkins Press, 1950).

Europe, the World's Banker, 1870–1914 (New Haven: Yale University Press, 1930).

Feldman, Gerald, *Iron and Steel in the German Inflation, 1916–1923* (Princeton: Princeton University Press, 1977).

Army, Industry and Labor in Germany, 1914–1918 (Princeton: Princeton University Press, 1966).

Feldman, Gerald, Holtfrerich, Carl-Ludwig, Ritter, Gerhard A., and Witt, Peter-Christian, eds., *The German Inflation Reconsidered: A Preliminary Balance* (Berlin: de Gruyter, 1982).

Fink, Carole, *The Genoa Conference: European Diplomacy, 1921–1922* (Chapel Hill: University of North Carolina Press, 1984).

Finocchiaro, Beniamino, ed., *L'Unità di Gaetano Salvemini* (Venice: Neri Pozza, 1958).

Fischer, Fritz, *Krieg der Illusionen* (Düsseldorf: Droste, 1969).

Forbes, John Douglas, *Stettinius Sr.: Portrait of a Morgan Partner* (Charlottesville: University of Virginia Press, 1974).

Forsyth, Douglas J., "The Rise and Fall of German-Inspired Mixed Banking in Italy, 1894–1936," in Harold James, Håkan Lindgren and Alice Teichova, eds., *The Role of Banks in the Interwar Economy* (New York: Cambridge University Press, 1991), pp. 179–205.

Frascani, Paolo, *Politica economica e finanza pubblica in Italia nel primo dopoguerra (1918–1922)* (Naples: Giannini, 1975).

Frenkel, J.A., and Johnson, H.G., eds., *The Monetary Approach to the Balance of Payments* (New York: George Unwin and Allen, 1976).

Fridenson, Patrick, ed., *1914–1918: L'autre front* (Paris: Éditions ouvrières, 1977).

Friedman, Milton, and Schwartz, Anna Jacobsen, *A Monetary History of the United States, 1867–1960* (Princeton: Princeton University Press, 1963).

Fritsch, Winston, "Il Brasile durante la Grande Guerra: Problemi strutturali e politiche economiche," *Rivista di storia economica*, new ser., 2 (1985), no. 1, pp. 46–88.

Fuà, Giorgio, ed., *Lo sviluppo economico in Italia*, 3rd ed., 3 vols. (Milan: Angeli, 1978).

Gaeta, Franco, *Il nazionalismo italiano*, 2nd rev. and enl. ed. (Bari: Laterza, 1981).

Gaeta, Franco, ed., *La stampa nazionalista* (Bologna: Cappelli, 1965).

Galli Della Loggia, Ernesto, "Problemi di sviluppo industriale e nuovi equilibri politici alla vigilia della prima guerra mondiale. La fondazione della Banca Italiana di Sconto," *Rivista storica italiana*, 82 (1970), no. 4, pp. 824–86.

Gangemi, Lello, "Due processi di difesa della lira nel quadro delle vicende monetarie italiane dal 1918 al 1959," in Domenico Demarco, ed., *Studi in onore di Epicarmo Corbino* (Milan: Giuffré, 1961), vol. II, pp. 384–429.

Gazzo, Emanuele, *I cento anni dell'Ansaldo, 1853–1953* (Genoa: Ansaldo, 1953).

Gerschenkron, Alexander, *Economic Backwardness in Historical Perspective: A Book of Essays* (Cambridge MA: Harvard University Press, 1962).

Gille, Bertrand, *Les Investissements français en Italie (1815–1914)* (Turin: ILTE, 1968).

Giolitti, Giovanni, *Memories of My Life* (New York: Fertig, 1973).

Giordano, Giancarlo, *Carlo Sforza: La diplomazia, 1896–1921* (Milan: Angeli, 1987).

Giuffrida, Vincenzo, and Pietra, Gaetano, *Provital. Approvvigionamenti alimentari d'Italia durante la grande guerra, 1914–1918* (Padua: CEDAM, 1936).

Giusti, Ugo, "Consumi e bilanci di una famiglia d'impiegati dall'anteguerra ad oggi," *Economia*, new ser., 10 (1932), pp. 551–68.

Godfrey, John F., *Capitalism at War: Industrial Policy and Bureaucracy in France, 1914–1918* (New York: Berg, 1987).

Grange, Daniel J., "Le convenzioni marittime in base alle Carte Stringher (1909)," *Storia contemporanea*, 11 (1980), no. 6, pp. 905–32.

Gregor, A. James, *Italian Fascism and Developmental Dictatorship* (Princeton: Princeton University Press, 1979).

Grifone, Pietro, *Il capitale finanziario in Italia* (Turin: Einaudi, 1945).

Griziotti, Benvenuto, "Finanze pubbliche e credito estero," *Rivista bancaria*, 11 (20 March 1921), no. 3, pp. 130–36.

Guillen, Pierre, ed., *La France et l'Italie pendant la première guerre mondiale* (Grenoble: Presses Universitaires de Grenoble, 1976).

Hardach, Gerd, *The First World War, 1914–1918* (Berkeley: University of California Press, 1977).

"Französische Rüstungspolitik, 1914–1918," in Heinrich August Winkler, ed., *Organisierter Kapitalismus* (Göttingen: Vandenhoeck and Ruprecht, 1974).

Harris, José, "Bureaucrats and Businessmen in British Food Control, 1916–19," in Kathleen Burk, ed., *War and the State: The Transformation of British Government, 1914–1919* (London: George, Unwin and Allen, 1982), pp. 135–56.

Hertner, Peter, *Il capitale tedesco in Italia dall'unità alla prima guerra mondiale* (Bologna: Il Mulino, 1984).

"La società 'Tubi Mannesmann' a Dalmine. Un esempio di investimento internazionale (1906–1917)," *Ricerche storiche*, 8 (1978), no. 1, pp. 105–23.

Hertner, Peter, and Mori, Giorgio, eds., *La transizione dall'economia di guerra all'economia di pace in Italia e in Germania dopo la prima guerra mondiale* (Bologna: Il Mulino, 1983).

Hirsch, Fred, and Goldthorpe, John H., *The Political Economy of Inflation* (Cambridge MA: Harvard University Press, 1978).

Hogan, Michael J., "The United States and the Problem of International Economic Control: American Attitudes Toward European Reconstruction, 1918–1920," *Pacific Historical Review*, 64 (1975), no. 1, pp. 84–103.

Holtfrerich, Carl-Ludwig, *Die deutsche Inflation, 1914–1923. Ursachen und Folgen in internationaler Perspektive* (Berlin: De Gruyter, 1980).

"Amerikanische Kapitalexport und Wiederaufbau der deutschen Wirtschaft 1919–1923 im Vergleich zu 1924–1929," *Vierteljahrsschrift für Sozial- und Wirtschaftsgeschichte*, 64 (1977), pp. 497–529.

Howson, Susan, *Domestic Monetary Management in Britain, 1919–38* (Cambridge: Cambridge University Press, 1975).

"The Origins of Dear Money, 1919–1920," *Economic History Review*, 2nd ser., 26 (1974), no. 1., pp. 88–107.

Isenghi, Mario, ed., *Operai e contadini nella grande guerra* (Bologna: Cappelli, 1982).

Le istituzioni finanziarie degli anni trenta nell'Europa continentale (Bologna: Il Mulino, 1982).

Gli italiani negli Stati Uniti. Atti del III Symposium di Studi Americani, Firenze, 27–29 Maggio 1969 (Florence: Istituto di Studi Americani, Università degli Studi di Firenze, 1972).

James, Harold, *The German Slump: Politics and Economics, 1924–1936* (New York: Oxford University Press, 1986).

James, Harold, Lindgren, Håkan, and Teichova, Alice, eds., *The Role of Banks in the Interwar Economy* (New York: Cambridge University Press, 1991).

Jannacone, Pasquale, *Prezzi e mercato*, 2nd ed. (Turin: Einaudi, 1951).

Jarach, C., *Abruzzi e Molise. Relazione della inchiesta parlamentare sulla condizioni dei contadini nelle provincie meridionali e nella Sicilia*, vol. II, tome 1 (Rome: Bertero, 1909).

Jeze, Gaston, and Truchy, Henri, *The War Finances of France* (New Haven: Yale University Press, 1927).

Justus (pseudonym), *Macchi di Cellere all'Ambasciata di Washington. Memorie e testimonianze* (Florence: Bemporad, 1920).

Katzenellenbaum, S. S., *Russian Currency and Banking, 1914–24* (London: P. S. King and Son, 1925).

Kelikian, Alice A., *Town and Country under Fascism: The Transformation of Brescia, 1915–1926* (New York: Oxford University Press, 1986).

Keynes, J. M., *Essays in Persuasion* (New York: Norton, 1963).

"A Tract on Monetary Reform," in Elizabeth Johnson, ed., *The Collected Writings of John Maynard Keynes*, vol. IV (London: Macmillan, 1971).

Kindleberger, Charles P., *A Financial History of Western Europe* (London: George Allen and Unwin, 1984).

Manias, Panics, and Crashes (New York: Basic, 1978).

Kindleberger, Charles P., and Laffargue, Jean-Pierre, eds., *Financial Crisis: Theory, history, and policy* (New York: Cambridge University Press, 1982).

Klein, Ernst, et al., eds., *Deutsche Bankengeschichte* (Frankfurt a.M.: Knapp, 1983).

Kocka, Jürgen, *Klassengesellschaft im Krieg. Deutsche Sozialgeschichte 1914–1918* (Göttingen: Vandenhoeck and Ruprecht, 1973).

Legnani, Massimo, "Espansione economica e politica estera nell'Italia del

1919–21," *Il movimento di liberazione in Italia*, 24 (1972), no. 108, pp. 3–51.

Levra, Umberto, *Il colpo di stato della borghesia: La crisi politica di fine secolo in Italia, 1896–1900* (Milan: Feltrinelli, 1975).

Lewis, Cleona, *America's Stake in International Investments* (Washington DC: Brookings Institution, 1938).

Lindert, Peter H., *Key Currencies and Gold, 1900–1913* (Princeton: Princeton University Press, 1969).

Link, Arthur S., *Wilson: Campaigns for Progressivism and Peace, 1916–1917* (Princeton: Princeton University Press, 1965).

Livi, Livio, "Un'indagine sulla dinamica dei redditi nella crisi della guerra e del dopo guerra," *Metron*, 3 (1924), nos. 3–4, pp. 556–89.

"Sperperi proletari e restrizioni borghesi," *Riforma sociale*, 28 (1921), nos. 5–6, pp. 168–75.

"Un'inchiesta sui bilanci di familigie borghesi," *Metron*, 1 (1921), no. 4, pp. 161–79.

Lowe, C. J., "Britain and Italian Intervention, 1914–1915," *Historical Journal*, 12 (1969), no. 3, pp. 533–48.

Lowe, C. J., and Marzari, F., *Italian Foreign Policy, 1870–1940* (Boston: Routledge and Kegan Paul, 1975).

Luzzati, Enrico, and Portesi, Renato, "La spesa pubblica," in Sabino Cassesse, ed., *L'amministrazione centrale* (Turin: UTET, 1984).

Lyttleton, Adrian, *The Seizure of Power: Fascism in Italy 1919–1929*, 2nd ed. (Princeton: Princeton University Press, 1987).

McCloskey, Donald N., and Zecher, Richard, "How the Gold Standard Worked, 1880–1913," in J. A. Frenkel and H. G. Johnson, eds., *The Monetary Approach to the Balance of Payments* (New York: George Unwin and Allen, 1976), pp. 357–85.

McGuire, Constantine E., *Italy's International Economic Position* (New York: Macmillan, 1926).

Mack Smith, Dennis, *Italy and its Monarchy* (New Haven: Yale University Press, 1989).

Italy: A Modern History (Ann Arbor: University of Michigan Press, 1959).

Maier, Charles S., *Recasting Bourgeois Europe: Stabilization in France, Germany, and Italy in the Decade after World War I* (Princeton: Princeton University Press, 1975).

"The Two Postwar Eras and the Conditions for Stability in Twentieth-Century Western Europe," *American Historical Review*, 86 (1981), no. 2, pp. 327–52.

Malagodi, Giovanni, "Il 'salvataggio' della Banca Commerciale nel ricordo di un testimone," in Gianni Toniolo, ed., *Industria e banca nella grande crisi 1929–1934* (Milan: Etas Libri, 1978), pp. 270–83.

Marchetti, Giuseppe, "Bonaldo Stringher," in *Il Friuli. Uomini e Tempi* (Udine, 1959), pp. 676–83.

Marconi, Mauro, *La politica monetaria del fascismo* (Bologna: Il Mulino, 1982).

Marwick, Arthur, *The Deluge: British Society and the First World War* (Boston: Little, Brown, 1965).

Mascolini, Loredana, "Il ministero per le armi e munizioni, (1915–1918)," *Storia contemporanea* (1980), no. 6, pp. 933–65.

März, Eduard, *Austrian Banking and Financial Policy: Creditanstalt at a Turning Point, 1913–1923* (London: Weidenfeld and Nicholson, 1984).

Masé-Dari, E., "La pressione tributaria sulla proprietà terriera," *Riforma sociale*, 29 (1922), nos. 1–2, pp. 45–68.

Mayer, Arno J., *Politics and Diplomacy of Peacemaking: Containment and Counterrevolution at Versailles, 1918–1919* (New York: Knopf, 1967).

    Political Origins of the New Diplomacy, 1917–1918 (New Haven: Yale University Press, 1959).

Mazzetti, Massimo, *L'industria italiana nella grande guerra* (Rome: Stato maggiore dell'Esercito, 1979).

    La prima guerra mondiale, vol. III of Renzo De Felice, ed., *Storia dell'Italia contemporanea* (Naples: Edizioni scientifiche italiane, 1978).

Meda, Filippo, *La riforma generale delle imposte dirette sui redditi* (Rome: Treves, 1920).

Melograni, Piero, *Storia politica della grande guerra, 1915–1918* (Bari: Laterza, 1977), 2 vols.

    Gli industriali e Mussolini: Rapporti tra Confindustria e fascismo dal 1919 al 1929 (Milan: Longanesi, 1972).

Menderhausen, Horst, *The Economics of War* (New York: Prentice-Hall, 1941).

Meyer, Richard Henning, *Banker's Diplomacy: Monetary Stabilization in the Twenties* (New York: Columbia University Press, 1970).

Migone, Gian Giacomo, *Gli Stati Uniti e il fascismo. Alle origini dell'egemonia americana in Italia* (Milan: Feltrinelli, 1980).

Milward, Alan S., *War, Economy and Society, 1939–1945* (Berkeley: University of California Press, 1977).

Milza, Pierre, "Les Rapports économiques franco-italiens en 1914–1915 et leurs incidences politiques," *Revue d'histoire moderne et contemporaine*, 14 (1967), pp. 31–70.

Minniti, Fortunato, "Alfredo Dallolio (1853–1952)," in Alberto Mortara, ed., *Protagonisti dell'intervento pubblico* (Milan: Angeli, 1984), pp. 186–88.

Minsky, Hyman P., *Stabilizing an Unstable Economy* (New Haven: Yale University Press, 1986).

Monticone, Alberto, *La Germania e la neutralità italiana: 1914–1915* (Bologna: Il Mulino, 1971).

    Nitti e la grande guerra (1914–1918) (Milan: Giuffré, 1961).

    "Salandra e Sonnino verso la decisione dell'intervento," *Rivista di studi politici internazionali*, 24 (1957), no. 1, pp. 64–89.

Morandi, Rodolfo, 2nd ed., *Storia della grande industria in Italia* (Turin: Einaudi, 1966).

Morgan, E. V., *Studies in British Financial Policy, 1914–25* (London: Macmillan, 1952).

Mori, Giorgio, *Il capitalismo industriale in Italia* (Rome: Riuniti, 1971).

    "Métamorphose ou réincarnation? Industrie, banque et régime fasciste en Italie 1923–1933," *Revue d'histoire moderne et contemporaine*, 25 (1978), no. 2, pp. 235–74.

Mortara, Alberto, ed., *Protagonisti dell'intervento pubblico* (Milan: Angeli, 1984).

Mortara, Giorgio, "Il bilancio degli scambi economici fra l'Italia e l'estero," *Rivista bancaria*, 5 (20 February 1924), pp. 73–93.

Muhr, Josef, *Die deutsch–italienischen Beziehungen in der Ära des Ersten Weltkrieges (1914–1922)* (Göttingen: Musterschmidt, 1977).

Nazzaro, Pellegrino, "Italy from the American Immigration Quota Act of 1921 to Mussolini's Policy of Grossraum: 1921–24," *Journal of European Economic History*, 3 (1974), no. 3, pp. 705–23.

"L'Immigration Quota Act del 1921, la crisi del sistema liberale e l'avvento del fascismo in Italia," in, *Gli Italiani negli Stati Uniti. Atti del III Symposium di Studi Americani, Firenze, 27–29 Maggio 1969* (Florence: Istituto di Studi Americani, Università degli Studi di Firenze, 1972).

Neppi Modona, Guido, *Sciopero, potere politico e magistratura, 1870–1922* (Bari: Laterza, 1969).

Nielson, Keith, *Strategy and Supply: The Anglo-Russian Alliance, 1914–17* (London: George Allen and Unwin, 1984).

Nitti, Francesco Saverio, *Rivelazioni. Dramatis personae* (Naples: Edizioni scientifiche italiane, 1948).

"Il capitale straniero in Italia," in *Scritti di economia e finanza*, Domenico Demarco, ed., vol. III, pt. 2 (Bari: Laterza, 1966), pp. 375–468.

Nitti, Vincenzo, *L'Opera di Nitti* (Turin: Gobetti, 1924).

Nouailhat, Yves-Henri, *France et Etats-Unis août 1914–avril 1917* (Paris: Sorbonne, 1979).

Ochsenbein, Heinz, *Die verlorene Wirtschaftsfreiheit, 1914–1918. Methoden ausländischer Wirtschaftskontrollen über die Schweiz* (Bern: Stämpfli, 1971).

Offe, Claus, *Strukturprobleme des kapitalistischen Staates. Aufsätze zur politischen Soziologie* (Frankfurt a.M.: Suhrkamp, 1977).

Olphe-Galliard, G., *Histoire économique et financière de la guerre (1914–1918)* (Paris: Marcel Rivière, 1925).

Padulo, Gerardo, "Sui rapporti tra gli industriali ed il governo Nitti (23 giugno 1919 – 9 giugno 1920)," *Nuova rivista storica*, 60 (1976), no. 516, pp. 591–618.

Page, Thomas Nelson, *Italy and the World War* (New York: Scribner's, 1920).

Parrini, Carl P., *Heir to Empire: United States Economic Diplomacy, 1916–1923* (Pittsburgh: University of Pittsburgh Press, 1969).

Pellegrini, Andrea, "Costruzione di serie omogenee dei valori del commercio dell'Italia con l'estero dal 1903 al 1933," *Barometro economico*, 6 (1934), pp. 296–303.

Personnettaz, Elio, "Stato e impresa: La società nazionale Cogne," *Rivista di storia contemporanea*, 5 (1976), no. 4, pp. 556–78.

Pescarolo, Alessandra, *Riconversione industriale e composizione di classe. L'inchiesta sulle industrie metalmeccaniche del 1922* (Milan: Angeli, 1979).

Petit, Lucien, *Histoire des finances éxteriéures de la France pendant la guerre (1914–1918)* (Paris: Payot, 1929).

Petricioli, Marta, "L'occupazione italiana del Caucaso: 'Un ingrato servizio' da rendere a Londra," *Il Politico*, 36 (1971), no. 4, pp. 715–45; 37 (1972), no. 1, pp. 99–141.

Phelps, Clyde William, *The Foreign Expansion of American Banks: American Branch Banking Abroad* (New York: Ronald Press, 1927).

Pieri, Piero, *L'Italia nella prima guerra mondiale, 1915–1918* (Turin: Einaudi, 1965).

Pigou, A. C., *The Political Economy of War*, rev. ed. (London: Macmillan, 1940).

Pohl, Manfred, "Die Situation der Banken in der Inflationszeit," in Otto Büsch and Gerald Feldman, eds., *Historische Prozesse der deutschen Inflation, 1914 bis 1924* (Berlin: Colloquium, 1978), pp. 83–95.

La politica estera italiana (Turin: Edizioni Radiotelevisione Italiana, 1963).

Preziosi, Giovanni, *La Germania alla conquista dell'Italia* (Florence: Liberia della Voce, 1916).

Procacci, Giovanna, ed., *Stato e classe operaia in Italia durante la prima guerra mondiale* (Milan: Angeli, 1983).

Procacci, Giuliano, *Storia degli italiani* (Bari: Laterza, 1968).

"Appunti in tema di crisi dello stato liberale e di origini del fascismo," *Studi storici*, 6 (1965), no. 2, pp. 221–37.

Ragionieri, Ernesto, *Politica e amministrazione nella storia dell'Italia unita* (Rome: Riuniti, 1979).

Un commune socialista: Sesto Fiorentino (Rome: Riuniti, 1976, 1st ed. 1953).

Raspin, Angela, *The Italian War Economy, 1940–1943, with Particular Reference to Italian Relations with Germany* (New York: Garland, 1986).

Rathbone, Albert, "Making War Loans to the Allies," *Foreign Affairs*, 3 (1925), no. 3, pp. 371–98.

Rebérioux, Madeleine, *La République radicale? 1898–1914* (Paris, Seuil, 1975).

Renzi, William A., *In the Shadow of the Sword: Italy's Neutrality and Entrance into the Great War, 1914–1915* (New York: Lang, 1987).

"Italy's Neutrality and Entrance into the Great War: A Re-examination," *American Historical Review*, 78 (1968), no. 5, pp. 1414–32.

Répaci, F. A., *La finanza pubblica italiana nel secolo 1861–1960* (Bologna: Zanichelli, 1962).

"Il costo finanziario della prima guerra mondiale in Italia," *Studi in onore di G. Pietra*, II, special ed. of *Statistica*, 14 (1954), no. 4, pp. 579–93.

"La situazione finanziaria e la pressione tributaria nei grandi communi italiani nel 1922 e nel 1923," *Riforma sociale*, 34 (1923), nos. 11–12, pp. 514–59.

Report of the National Monetary Commission: Interviews on Banking in Europe (Washington DC: National Monetary Commission, 1912).

Ricci, Umberto, *La politica annonaria italiana dell'Italia durante la grande guerra* (Bari: Laterza, 1939).

La politica economica del ministero Nitti. Gli effetti dell'intervento economico dello Stato (Rome: La Voce, 1920).

Rochat, Giorgio, *L'Italia nella prima guerra mondiale. Problemi di interpretazione e prospettive di ricerca* (Milan: Feltrinelli, 1976).

L'esercito italiano da Vittoria Veneto a Mussolini, (1919–1925) (Bari: Laterza, 1967).

"Alcuni dati sulle occupazioni militari adriatiche durante il governo Nitti," *Il Risorgimento*, 18 (1966), no. 1, pp. 29–45.

Rodd, James Rennell, *Social and Diplomatic Memories*, vol. III, *1902–1919* (London: Edward Arnold, 1925).

Romano, Roberto, *I Crespi. Origini, fortuna e tramonto di una dinastia lombarda* (Milan: Angeli, 1985).

"Silvio Benigno Crespi," *Dizionario biografico italiano* (1984).

Romano, Ruggiero, "Una tipologia economica," in, *Storia d'Italia*, vol. I, *I caratteri originali* (Turin: Einaudi, 1972), pp. 253–304.

Romano, Sergio, *Giuseppe Volpi. Industria e finanza fra Giolitti e Mussolini* (Milan: Bompiani, 1979).

Romeo, Rosario, *Breve storia della grande industria in Italia, 1861–1961* (Bologna: Cappelli, 1961).

Rosen, Edgar R., "Italiens Kriegseintritt im Jahre 1915 als innenpolitisches Problem der Giolitti-Ära. Ein Beitrag zur Vorgeschichte des Faschismus," *Historische Zeitschrift*, 187 (1959), no. 2., pp. 289–363.

Rossi, Mario G., "Il problema storico della riforma fiscale in Italia," *Italia contemporanea* (1988), no. 170, pp. 5–19.

Rugafiori, Paride, *Uomini macchine capitali. L'Ansaldo durante il fascismo, 1922–1945* (Milan: Feltrinelli, 1981).

Rumi, Giorgio, *Alle origini della politica estera fascista (1918–1923)* (Bari: Laterza, 1968).

Sabbatucci, Giovanni, ed., *La crisi italiana del primo dopoguerra* (Bari: Laterza, 1976).

Salandra, Antonio, *La neutralità italiana (1914). Ricordi e pensieri* (Milan: Mondadori, 1928).

L'intervento (1915). Ricordi e pensieri (Milan: Mondadori, 1930).

Salomone, A. William, *Italy in the Giolittian Era: Italian Democracy in the Making, 1900–1914* (Philadelphia: University of Pennsylvania Press, 1960).

Salter, J. A., *Allied Shipping Control: An Experiment in International Administration* (New York: Oxford University Press, 1921).

Salvatorelli, Luigi, "Tre colpi di stato," *Il Ponte*, 6 (1950), no. 4, pp. 340–50.

Salvemini, Gaetano, *The Origins of Fascism in Italy*, ed. Roberto Vivarelli (New York: Harper and Row, 1973).

Under the Axe of Fascism (New York: Viking, 1936).

The Fascist Dictatorship in Italy, 2nd rev. ed. (London: Cape, 1928).

"L'Italia economica dal 1919 al 1922," in, *Studi in onore di Gino Luzzatto* (Milan: Giuffré, 1950), vol. III, pp. 278–93.

Sarti, Roland, *Fascism and Industrial Leadership in Italy, 1919–1940: A Study in the Expansion of Private Power under Fascism* (Berkeley: University of California Press, 1971).

Sauvy, Alfred, *Histoire économique de la France entre les deux guerres*, ed. Anita Hirsch, rev. ed., 3 vols. (Paris: Economica, 1984).

Sayers, Richard Sidney, *The Bank of England, 1891–1944* (New York: Cambridge University Press, 1976).

Central Banking After Bagehot (Oxford: Oxford University Press, 1957).

Schmitz, David F., *The United States and Fascist Italy, 1922–1940* (Chapel Hill: University of North Carolina Press, 1988).

Schuker, Stephan A., *The End of French Predominance in Europe: The Financial Crisis of 1924 and the Adoption of the Dawes Plan* (Chapel Hill: University of North Carolina Press, 1976).

Scialoja, Antonio, "L'Istituto nazionale delle assicurazioni e il progetto giolittiano di un monopolio di stato delle assicurazioni sulla vita," *Quaderni storici*, 6 (1971), pp. 971–1027.

Segreto, Luciano, "La City e la 'dolce vita' romana. La storia della Banca Italo Britannica 1916–1930," *Passato e presente*, 13 (1987), pp. 63–95.

"Aspetti delle relazioni economiche tra Italia e Germania nel periodo della neutralità (1914–15)," *Annali della Fondazione Luigi Einaudi*, 18 (1984), pp. 455–517.

"Statalismo e antistatalismo nell'economia bellica. Gli industriali e la Mobilitazione Industriale (1915–1918)," in Peter Hertner and Giorgio Mori, ed., *La transizione dall'economia di guerra all'economia di pace in Italia e in Germania dopo la prima guerra mondiale* (Bologna: Il Mulino, 1983), pp. 301–34.

"Armi e munizioni. Lo sforzo bellico tra speculazione e progresso tecnico," *Italia contemporanea* (1982), nos. 146/7, pp. 35–66.

Serpieri, Arrigo, *La guerra e le classi rurali italiane* (Bari: Laterza, 1930).

Seton-Watson, Christopher, *Italy from Liberalism to Fascism, 1870–1925* (London: Methuen, 1967).

Sforza, Carlo, *L'Italia dal 1914 al 1944 quale io la vidi*, 2nd ed. (Rome: Mondadori, 1945).

"Italy and Fascism," *Foreign Affairs*, 3 (1925), no. 3, pp. 358–70.

Silverman, Dan P., *Reconstructing Europe after the Great War* (Cambridge MA: Harvard University Press, 1982).

Skidelsky, Robert, *John Maynard Keynes: Hopes Betrayed 1893–1920* (New York: Viking, 1986).

Sori, Ercole, *L'emigrazione italiana dall'unità alla seconda guerra mondiale* (Bologna: Il Mulino, 1979).

Spriano, Paolo, *Storia del partito communista italiano*, vol. I (Turin: Einaudi, 1967).
L'occupazione delle fabbriche, settembre 1920 (Turin: Einaudi, 1964).
Torino operaia nella grande guerra (1914–1918) (Turin: Einaudi, 1960).

Sraffa, Piero, "The Bank Crisis in Italy," *Journal of Economic History*, 32 (1922), no. 126, pp. 178–97.

Staderini, Alessandra, "L'economia italiana dal 1918 al 1922," in Giovanni Sabbatucci, ed., *La crisi italiana del primo dopoguerra* (Bari: Laterza, 1976), pp. 109–30.

Storia della società italiana, vol. XX, *L'Italia di Giolitti* (Milan: Teti, 1981).

Stringher, Bonaldo, "Gli scambi con l'estero e la politica commerciale italiana dal 1860 al 1910," in *Cinquanta anni di storia d'Italia*, vol. III (Milan: Hoepli, 1911).

Stringher, Bonaldo, and Volpi, G., *The Financial Reconstruction of Italy* (New York: Italian Historical Society Publications, 1927).

Studi in occasione del primo centenario della Corte dei Conti nell'unità d'Italia (Milan: Giuffré, 1963).

Studi in onore di Gino Luzzatto, 3 vols. (Milan: Giuffré, 1950).

Supino, Camillo, *Storia della circolazione cartacea in Italia (dal 1860 al 1928)* (Milan: Società editrice libraria, 1929).

Tasca, Angelo, *Nascita e avvento del fascismo*, 2nd rev. ed., (Florence: La Nuova Italia, 1950).

La Naissance du fascisme: l'Italie de 1918 à 1922 (Paris: Gallimard, 1938).

Tempera, Filippo, *La guerra e la pace d'Italia insidiato dalla Banca Commerciale di Joseph Toeplitz* (Rome: Società tipografica italiana, 1920).

Toeplitz, Ludovico, *Il banchiere*, 2nd ed. (Milan: Ferro, 1963).

Tomassini, Luigi, "Mobilitazione industriale e classe operaia," in Giovanna Procacci, ed., *Stato e classe operaia in Italia durante la prima guerra mondiale* (Milan: Angeli, 1983), pp. 79–102.

Toniolo, Gianni, *Storia economica dell'Italia liberale (1850–1918)* (Bologna: Il Mulino, 1988).

L'economia dell'Italia fascista (Bari: Laterza, 1980).

"Oscar Sinigaglia (1877–1955)," in, Alberto, Mortara, ed., *I protagonisti dell'intervento pubblico in Italia* (Milan: Angeli, 1984), pp. 405–30.

Toniolo, Gianni, ed., *Industria e banca nella grande crisi 1929–1934* (Milan: Etas Libri, 1978).

Lo sviluppo economico italiano (Bari: Laterza, 1973).

Toscano, Mario, *Il Patto di Londra. Storia diplomatica dell'intervento italiano, (1914–1915)* (Bologna: Zanichelli, 1934).

"Bernardo Attolico," *Dizionario biografico italiano* (1962).

Trachtenberg, Marc, "A New Economic Order: Étienne Clémentel and French Economic Diplomacy during the First World War," *French Historical Studies*, 10 (1972), no. 2, pp. 315–41.

Tranfaglia, Nicola, *Dallo stato liberale al regime fascista. Problemi e ricerche* (Milan: Feltrinelli, 1973).

Il trauma dell'invervento: 1914/1919 (Florence: Vallecchi, 1968).

Traynor, Dean E., *International Monetary and Financial Conferences in the Interwar Period* (Washington DC: Catholic University of America Press, 1949).

Truchy, Henri, "How France Met Her War Expenditure," in Gaston Jeze and Henri Truchy, *The War Finances of France* (New Haven: Yale University Press, 1927).

Valeri, Nino, *Giovanni Giolitti* (Turin: UTET, 1971).

Valiani, Leo, "Le origini della guerra del 1914 e dell'intervento italiano nelle ricerche e nelle pubblicazioni dell'ultimo ventennio," *Rivista storica italiana*, 78 (1966), no. 3, pp. 584–613.

Van Alstyne, Richard W., "Private American Loans to the Allies, 1914–1916," *Pacific Historical Review*, 2 (1933), pp. 180–93.

Veneruso, Danilio, *La vigilia del fascismo. Il primo ministero Facta nella crisi dello stato liberale in Italia* (Bologna: Il Mulino, 1968).

Ventry, Lance T., "Considerazioni sulla decisione italiana d'intervenire nel conflitto contro la Germania," *Archivio storico italiano*, 130 (1972), vol. 475, pp. 469–94.

"Prospettive delle relazioni italo-americane nell'ultimo anno della prima guerra mondiale," *Archivio storico italiano*, 129 (1971), vol. 469, pp. 103–23.

Vicarelli, Fausto, ed., *Capitale industriale e capitale finanziario. Il caso italiano* (Bologna: Il Mulino, 1979).

Vigezzi, Brunello, *Da Giolitti a Salandra* (Florence: Vallecchi, 1969).

L'Italia di fronte all prima guerra mondiale, vol. I, *L'Italia neutrale* (Milan: Ricciardi, 1966).

Vivarelli, Roberto, *Storia delle origini del fascismo. L'Italia dalla grande guerra alla marcia su Roma*, vol. II (Bologna: Il Mulino, 1991).

"Interpretations of the Origins of Fascism," *Journal of Modern History*, 63 (1991), no. 1, pp. 29–43.

Il fallimento del liberalismo. Studi sulle origini del fascismo (Bologna: Il Mulino, 1981).

Il dopoguerra in Italia e l'avvento del fascimo (1918–1922) (Naples: Istituto Italiano per gli Studi Storici, 1967).

Webster, Richard, *Industrial Imperialism in Italy, 1908–1915* (Berkeley: University of California Press, 1975).

"Una speranza rinviata. L'espansione industriale italiana e il problema del petrolio dopo la prima guerra mondiale," *Storia contemporanea*, 11 (1980), no. 2, pp. 219–81.

"La tecnocrazia italiana e i sistemi industriali verticali: il caso dell'Ansaldo," *Storia contemporanea* (1978), no. 2, pp. 205–39.

"From Insurrection to Intervention: The Italian Crisis of 1914," *Italian Quarterly*, 5 (1961), no. 20, pp. 27–50.

Wilkins, Mira, *The Maturing of Multinational Enterprise: American Business Abroad from 1914 to 1970* (Cambridge MA: Harvard University Press, 1974).

Winkler, Heinrich August, ed., *Organisertier Kapitalismus* (Göttingen: Vandenhoeck und Ruprecht, 1974).

Withers, Hartley, *Wartime Financial Problems* (New York: Dalton, 1920).

Wollemborg, Leone, "Entrate e spese effettive durante la guerra," *Nuova antologia*, 53 (16 September 1918), no. 1120, pp. 197–99.

Woytinsky, W. S., and Woytinsky, E. S., *World Commerce and Governments: Trends and Outlook* (New York: The Twentieth Century Fund, 1955).

Wrigley, Chris, "The Ministry of Munitions: An Innovatory Department," in Kathleen Burk, ed., *War and the State: The Transformation of British Government, 1914–1919* (London: George Allen and Unwin, 1982).

Zamagni, Vera, *Dalla periferia al centro. La seconda rinascita economica dell'Italia, 1861–1981* (Bologna: Il Mulino, 1990).

Zugaro, F., *Il costo della guerra italiana* (Rome: Stabilimento poligrafico per l'Amministrazione della guerra, 1921).

Unpublished theses and manuscripts

Abrahams, Paul P., "The Foreign Expansion of American Finance and its Relationship to the Foreign Economic Policies of the United States, 1907–1921," Ph.D. dissertation (University of Wisconsin, 1967).

Ciacci, Furio, "The Italian and European Image in the American Financial Press" (MIT, 1989).

Fasce, Ferdinando, "Ansaldo & Co. in the United States, 1915–1921," paper presented at the Italian–American Historical Association Annual Conference, Washington DC, October 1984.

Forsyth, Douglas J., "The Politics of Forced Accumulation: Monetary and

Financial Policy in Italy, 1914–1922," Ph.D. dissertation (Princeton University, 1987).

Gould, John Wells, "Italy and the United States, 1914–1918: Background to Confrontation," Ph.D. dissertation (Yale University, 1969).

Herzstein, Daphne Stassin, "The Diplomacy of Allied Credit Advanced to Russia in World War I," Ph.D. dissertation (New York University, 1972).

Homer, Francis Xavier J., "Foreign Trade and Foreign Policy: The British Department of Overseas Trade, 1916–1922," Ph.D. dissertation (University of Virginia, 1971).

Pfau, John M., "Economic Relations of the United States with Italy, 1919–1949," Ph.D. dissertation (University of Chicago, 1952).

Row, Thomas, "Economic Nationalism in Italy: The Ansaldo Company, 1882–1921," Ph.D. dissertation (Johns Hopkins University, 1988).

INDEX